READING INSIDE OUT

CRITICAL
VOICES

General Editor: David Jonathan Y. Bayot

CRITICAL VOICES

READING INSIDE OUT
INTERVIEWS AND CONVERSATIONS

J. HILLIS MILLER

Edited by
David Jonathan Y. Bayot

sussex
ACADEMIC
PRESS
Brighton • Portland • Toronto

Organization of this volume copyright © De La Salle University Publishing House and Sussex Academic Press, 2017; Questions in individual interviews copyright © individual interviewers, 2017; responses copyright © J. Hillis Miller, 2017.

The right of J. Hillis Miller, David Jonathan Y. Bayot, and individual interviewers to be identified as Author/Responder, Editor, and as Questionners of this work, has been asserted in accordance with the Copyright, Designs and Patents Act 1988.

2 4 6 8 10 9 7 5 3 1

Published and distributed in the Philippines under ISBN 978-971-555-651-4 *by*
De La Salle University Publishing House
2401 Taft Avenue, 0922 Manila, Philippines

This edition published and distributed under ISBN 978-1-84519-864-0 (cloth)
and ISBN 978-1-84519-865-7 (paper) *in*
Great Britain in 2017 by SUSSEX ACADEMIC PRESS
PO Box 139, Eastbourne BN24 9BP

and in North America by SUSSEX ACADEMIC PRESS
ISBS Publisher Services
920 NE 58th Ave #300, Portland, OR 97213

Cover Design: John David Roasa.

British Library Cataloguing in Publication Data
A CIP catalogue record for this book is available from the British Library.

Library of Congress Cataloging-in-Publication Data

Miller, Joseph Hillis, 1928-
Reading inside out : interviews and conversations / J. Hillis Miller ;
edited by David Jonathan Y. Bayot. Manila : De La Salle University, 2017.
320 pages ; 23 cm. — (Critical Voices)
ISBN: 978-971-555-651-4 (pbk), in the Critical Voices series
1. Criticism. 2. Literature and society. 3. Critics—Interviews.

Typeset & designed by De La Salle University Publishing House.

To all those who over the years have
interviewed me so courteously, intelligently,
and in such diversely challenging ways

Contents

Acknowledgments

My largest debt is of course to J. Hillis Miller—his close collaboration on the book's content and design enabled the book to metamorphose from possibility to reality. It has been the editor's great pleasure to collaborate with him, a scholar-critic-reader par excellence whose intellectual presence has been for years an inspiration to me. I would also like to acknowledge my debt to all the interviewers of Miller in this volume, since without their dedicated labors and consent to have their work reprinted, this book publication would definitely have been impossible. I would like to extend my special thanks to Éamonn Dunne and Julian Wolfreys who have been most generous in their offer of support for this project. And I would like to take this chance to mention to readers interested in gaining greater familiarity of the configurations of Miller's critical career and interventions to turn to Éamonn Dunne's two excellent books: *J. Hillis Miller and the Possibilities of Reading: Literature after Deconstruction* (2010) and *Reading Theory Now: An ABC of Good Reading with J. Hillis Miller* (2013). Needless to say, Julian Wolfreys' *The J. Hillis Miller Reader* (2005) is certainly indispensable. I would like to thank Frederik Van Dam for granting me the permission to use a still from his 2015 documentary featuring Miller. I owe a word of thanks to Barbara Caldwell, Senior Editor and Research Assistant to Miller at the University of California, Irvine, who helped me locate the two Miller interviews with Wolfreys for this volume.

Back here on my home ground at De La Salle University Publishing House, I would like to acknowledge Louise Jezareth "Reith" Antipala for her editorial assistance and Joanne T. Castañares for her indispensable help in preparing and designing the layout of the book.

If I am allowed to dedicate my own small part in the book's preparation, it would be to two persons:

To my mother, *Mary Bayot*, who has prompted me early on to make reading a defining act of my life and living. By allowing me to fashion a custom-made reading space of my own, she has enabled me to invent multiple senses of self and freedom that I personally find gratifying to live with.

To *Riddick Matthew P. Recoter*, a most discerning reader, my best friend, whose deep interest in the project from day one has allowed me to profit greatly from conversations and exchanges with him. He read, reread, and proofread the entire manuscript at various stages of the book's preparation, and very kindly prepared the index for the book. For all his work—whether it's for friendship or for the book or for both—I'm deeply grateful.

The interviews in this book originally appeared in the following publications and are reprinted here by permission:

"Criticism in Society: Interview with Imre Salusinszky" first appeared with an introductory note on J. Hillis Miller and his critical practice and work in *Criticism in Society* by Imre Salusinszky. New York: Methuen, 1987. 208–240.

"Rhetoric, Cultural Studies, and the Future of Critical Theory: Interview with Gary A. Olson" first appeared in *Philosophy, Rhetoric, Literary Criticism: (Inter)views*. Ed. Gary A. Olson. Carbondale and Edwardsville: Southern Illinois UP, 1994. 113–158.

"Stay! Speak, Speak, I Charge Thee, Speak: Interview with Wang Fengzhen and Shaobo Xie" first appeared in *Dialogues on Cultural Studies: Interviews with Contemporary Critics*. Ed. Shaobo Xie and Fengzhen Wang. Alberta: U of Calgary P, 2002. 115–138.

"The Degree Zero of Criticism: Interview with Julian Wolfreys" first appeared in *Thinking Difference: Critics in Conversation*. Ed. Julian Wolfreys. New York: Fordham University Press, 2004. 147–164.

"Why Literature? A Profession: Interview with Julian Wolfreys" first appeared in *The J. Hillis Miller Reader*. Ed. Julian Wolfreys. California: Stanford UP, 2005. 405–422.

"Literary Studies in Contexts" first appeared as "A Call for Literary Studies: Interview with Anfeng Sheng" in *Foreign Literature Studies* 6 (2006): 1–12.

"On Literature and Ethics: Interview with Constanza del Río Álvaro and Francisco Collado-Rodríguez" first appeared in *European English Messenger*, 15.1 (2006): 23–34.

"For the Reader to Come: Interview with Éamonn Dunne" first appeared in *J. Hillis Miller and the Possibilities of Reading: Literature After Deconstruction* by Éamonn Dunne. London: Continuum, 2010. 123–140.

"'You See You Ask an Innocent Question and You've Got a Long Answer': Interview with Éamonn Dunne, Michael O'Rourke, Martin McQuillan, Graham Allen, Dragan Kujundžić, and Nicholas Royle" first appeared in *Australian Humanities Review* 56 (2014): 1–24.

"'Isn't It a Beautiful Day?' Interview with Bradley J. Fest" first appeared in *boundary 2* 41.3 (Fall 2014): 123–58.

"A Critical Story So Far: Interview with Christopher D. Morris" first appeared as "An Interview with J. Hillis Miller" in *Derrida Today* 8.1 (2015): 77–109.

Every effort has been made to trace the copyright holders but if any have been inadvertently overlooked, the publishers will be pleased to make the necessary arrangement at the first opportunity.

                          David Jonathan Y. Bayot
                          Manila, Philippines
                          July 2017

Editor's Preface

We struggle to read from the moment we wake in the morning
until the moment we fall asleep at night, and what are our dreams
but more lessons in the pain of the impossibility of reading...

J. Hillis Miller, *The Ethics of Reading*[1]

My thinking, like everyone's, has sticking to it the shriveled husks
of my earlier dead thoughts.

Ludwig Wittgenstein, *Culture and Value*[2]

This book is, in an important sense, a personal project prompted by a desire to reckon with a memory—that of reading.

In my sophomore year, when I was studying for a degree in literature (with philosophy as my minor), I found myself enrolled in a class on "analytic philosophy." I *had to*, only because the philosophy courses of my choice were oversubscribed and I was closed out of them. I was upset that I couldn't take part in what I considered then to be "real" discussions of the "big" questions of life and its "Grenzsituationen": those of "being and nothingness," "being and time," "being and having"...

At that point of my academic journey, enthralled by the prospects of dramatic topics (cited above and which I felt were unfortunately being staged elsewhere)—of "Ubermensch," "authenticity," and "metaphysic of hope"—I found myself stuck in what I perceived then to be roundabout discussions of commonplace things muddled by what I took to be a lot of hair-splitting interjections. And I remember distinctly an encounter with a bewildering passage from an "analytic" book included in the packet of required readings for the course. The passage would circle round the subject, a word-world that I thought I knew quite well, especially since I was a literature student. The word was supposed to be *the* Word that distinguishes people like me for what we do for an education and subsequently for a living. *Reading*—that's the keyword that the philosopher "criss-crosses" in that passage.

A few lines from that philosophical reading should suffice to convey the sense of incredulity I felt then about the excessive expenditure of verbal, analytic energy on what's supposed to be a natural act, pretty much self-explanatory (or so I thought):

> ...First I need to remark that I am not counting the understanding of what is read as part of "reading" for purposes of this investigation: reading is here the activity of rendering out loud what is written or printed; and also of writing from dictation, writing out something printed, playing from a score, and so on.
>
> The use of this word in the ordinary circumstances of our life is of course extremely familiar to us. But the part the word plays in our life, and therewith the *language-game* in which we employ it, would be difficult to describe even in rough outline. A person, let us say an Englishman, has received at school or at home one of the kinds of educational usual among us, and in the course of it has learned to read his native language. Later he reads books, letters, newspapers, and other things.
>
> Now what takes place when, say, he reads a newspaper?—His eye passes—as we say—along the printed words, he says them out loud—or only to himself; in particular he reads certain words by taking in their printed shapes as wholes others when his eye has taken in the first syllables; others again he reads syllable by syllable, and an occasional one perhaps letter by letter.—We should also say that he had read a sentence if he spoke neither aloud nor to himself during the reading but was afterwards able to repeat the sentence word for word or nearly so.—He may attend to what he reads, or again—as we might put it—function as a mere reading machine: I mean, read aloud and correctly without attending to what he is reading; perhaps with his attention on something quite different (so that he is unable to say what he has been reading if he is asked about it immediately afterwards). (my emphasis)[3]

The deliberative passage quoted above is, as many would recognize, from Ludwig Wittgenstein's *Philosophical Investigations* (#156). And I must admit that for the longest time I just could not quite comprehend what the philosopher was attempting to do in that passage or in that book and even in his other writings (say, the *Tractatus* or the *Notebooks*). Happily, however, a decade or so after my uneventful first exposure to the philosopher, I encountered a refreshingly *different* reading of Wittgenstein advanced by Marjorie Perloff, which she has done so in light of avant-garde literary practice and poetics.[4] It's in fact her incisive reading of the philosopher's discussion of the word *happy* that I find especially relevant to and inspiring for the point and case I'm putting forth in this collection of interviews with J. Hillis Miller, *le philosophe lisant,* whose name is a synonym of Reading in the history of literary studies from the latter half of the twentieth century to the present.

"The world of the happy is *a happy world*"—and so Wittgenstein announces. "The *Notebook* entries on 'happy' were made over a three-month period," Perloff observes, and "in circling round and round the word *happy*, the text cannot reach conclusion."[5] Why is that so? Because *happiness*, just like *beauty* and *truth*—and I would add *reading*—is in the first place a word, a sign. As a sign, it is, for Wittgenstein, nothing more than "its use in the language" (#43). In other words, the meaning of *happiness, beauty, truth, reading*, and even of the most "basic" verb *to be*, of the adjective *false*, can only be "metaphysical" and "transcendental" or, in Perloff's annotation, "elusive" and "indefinable," no matter how self-evident their denotative meaning seems to be. And "it is only by circling round the proposition 'the world of the happy is a happy world' that we begin to understand that happiness, [one's] most persistent goal, cannot be defined or even specified"[6] outside its context(s) of actual usage or its language-game.

Thus, the task of a philosopher, a critic, or any reader who cares enough to be autocritical of the language (or the "form of life" imagined by language) that he or she inherits is, as Wittgenstein puts it, "to bring words back from their metaphysical to their everyday use" (#116); to consider a word as always a "new" word, "a fresh seed sewn on the ground of the discussion"[7]; and as such, "every morning [the task is] to break through the dead rubble afresh so as to reach the living warm seed."[8] Again, "only by beginning again and again…by reformulating a particular notion until it gradually manifests or reveals itself, can philosophy [or reading in the autocritical sense vis-à-vis its object] make any sort of progress."[9]

Reading: that's the word as well as the act that this collection of interviews seeks to bring back from its metaphysical, elusive, and all-too-familiar realm to its everyday use in the field of literary and cultural studies. And it is for this reason I've chosen to feature Miller in this *Critical Voices* series with a collection of eleven limpid, provocative, and compelling conversations he has generously offered his astute discussants and the reading community at large—on literature, literary as well as cultural studies, and, even more significantly, reading.

In the words of deconstruction scholar and critic Martin McQuillan, "Miller remains our most vital and remarkable thinker of literature…[and] without a familiarity with Miller any training in reading literature would be incomplete." While at first glance the statement may sound like an overstatement, a careful consideration, however, of Miller's big corpus of critical publications—with more than thirty books on literary/textual theory and criticism—could do no less than confirm the vital presence of Miller as "the deconstructive angel" (as M. H. Abrams critically depicted him and the reading paradigm he represents) in the history of modern and contemporary literary and cultural studies.

"To live is to read"[12]—thus writes Miller in one of his best known books, *The Ethics of Reading* (1987). What then does it mean to read or to lead a life, reading? Readers of this volume will soon have to come to terms with Miller's view that a critical factor in the ethics of reading is the readers' self-reflexive awareness of the *situations* of their readership and reading. In Wittgenstein's parlance, the word-act-event of reading "text" is none other than its use in the language-game as played out most explicitly and deliberately in the field of literary and cultural studies. In this extended set of passionate conversations, Miller foregrounds readership in contexts (in the plural), specifically those brought about by the paradigm shift in the study of literature that began in the sixties. During the evolution of this period of the so-called theory revolution in the discipline of literary and textual studies, Miller has not been a mere participant-observer; he's in fact a key player on the stage and stages of the developments in the field even "after theory."

His critical presence—marked by two keywords in his oeuvres, *repetition* and *interruption*[13]—was formally announced with the publication of *Charles Dickens: The World of His Novels* in 1958, and that presence has remained significantly palpable until his latest works: *Communities in Fiction* (2014), *An Innocent Abroad* (2015), and *Literature Matters* (2016). Miller's critical intervention, which spans almost six decades, consists of his engagement with paradigms from phenomenology to deconstruction; with philosophers from Immanuel Kant and Walter Benjamin to Jacques Derrida and Jean-Luc Nancy; with writers from "authors" of the King James Bible, the romantic poets (e.g., Wordsworth), the nineteenth-century novelists (e.g., George Eliot), to the twentieth-century icons (e.g., Stevens); with genres ranging from the conventional ones of poetry and fiction to the "other" textual forms including illustrations of novels, placemats from hotels, and paintings; and with critical thematic from rhetoric and speech acts to ethics, Auschwitz, and literary productions in the age of technology.

It's the critical presence that I have encapsulated above that the readers will get to encounter in this book. Here, they'll see Miller's vital personality in action as he circles round and round the sign and significance of "reading" with versatility and virtuosity *with-in* a broad spectrum of contexts only he can muster—contexts that are personal, professional, institutional, and more. And notably, these are contexts that have been broadened and enriched by the scholarship and shrewdness of his interlocutors.

In the discussion so far, I've told the readers how Miller, specifically in this book, denaturalizes *reading* by foregrounding the situations of the word and its attending act and event, in the contexts of theories underlain by an array of critical paradigms (e.g., feminisms, marxisms, post-structuralisms, etc.) which abound during (and even after) the "moment" of Theory or the Linguistic Revolution in literary studies.

But before the readers are allowed to *settle down* on reading and *settle with* the impression that Miller has been the champion for over five decades of the disposition that reading is theory-bound, where readers read *in accordance with* a (program of) theory and from there, *head back toward* an affirmation of the dogma of that theory—Miller promptly issues a reminder. In his version of reading as recorded in *Versions of Pygmalion* (1990), Miller writes, while "there is no reading that is not theoretical...the actual act of reading is always to some degree the disconfirmation of theory."[14] In an interview with distinguished Miller scholar Julian Wolfreys (recorded in the fourth chapter of this book), Miller says that "the greatest critics are those whose readings exceed their theoretical presuppositions." Miller adds (as readers will see in the third chapter),

> Reading encounters [the] strangeness [of literature], willy-nilly, even if efforts are made to suppress it. Theory, on the other hand, as its name suggests...has as its goal making universal generalizations...Insofar as it is the aim of literary theory to make general statements about literature, this goal is incompatible with the experience of reading. If you're a careful reader, if you're what I dare to call a "good reader," that is, a reader open to the otherness of work, reading never quite fits your theoretical presuppositions. Good readers who see not what they expected to see, but what is there to "see." Such readers don't say, "I'm going

to apply Barthes, Derrida, or whomever, and show that a given 'theory' works." Rather, they recognize through the act of reading that the presupposed theory doesn't work.

The most sensible common sense marking the "New Accents"[15] in literary studies during the paradigm shift of this academic field is that there is no reading that transpires without theory. In other words, even the most "natural" and "commonsensical" reading is always already pre-scribed by theory.[16] Thus, citizens of literary studies who have been keen on acquiring or declaring a new accent in their articulation of literature would find themselves displaying their fluency in one theoretically branded reading after another—e.g., post-structuralist, Marxist, new historicist, post-colonial—of this or that text, canonical and otherwise. While the ethos of autocritique pervading this era has undeniably and positively given rise to a great number of readings and rereadings of texts (which in the new paradigm of "literary" studies covers practically ALL signifying practices), an unfortunate aftermath of the great emphasis placed on reading (or rereading or counter-reading) has been the unwitting shift of emphasis *away from* reading or the experience of reading (as Miller calls it) to the emphasis of *the* thing that matters— the theory-qualifier that animates and distinguishes a particular reading. And in the latter context, readers would set for themselves the end of readings of texts—readings that are (or rather, expected to be) cordially in accordance with the textual or contextual presuppositions of a particular paradigm, be that from a school (e.g., psychoanalysis) or from a theorist (e.g., Emmanuel Levinas).

To readers who would impetuously conclude from what has been presented so far—or possibly from samplings of passages from this book or the critic's other work—that Miller is nostalgically and irresponsibly advocating a return to rhetorical criticism—allegedly an apolitical, ahistorical, and regressive move on the part of this deconstructionist reader—I find a citation of this short anti-note from Miller (in the third chapter) apropos:

> I just read a passage by Roland Barthes where he says a little formalism is an escape from history, while a lot of formalism is a return to history. I like that observation because it displaces the opposition against formalism in the shape of close reading because it's old fashioned, it'd be ahistorical, it's sequestered from reality, it's conservative or reactionary. These putdowns are used as a justification for not looking closely at the texts discussed.

The return to talking about characters in novels as though they were real people, based closely on the authors themselves or on historical personages, along with a summary of criticism you could possibly imagine. There's quite a bit of that in [the] cultural studies essays. It is as though the lessons of structuralism and poststructuralism, to say nothing of the New Criticism, had been forgotten almost overnight.

Whether the critic is "grounding" his reader-audience in theory or defamiliarizing them with the theme and versions of the common sense of reading, Miller speaks to a reality and an imperative of reading—that is, the joy of reading. I'll now let these words which Miller penned as president of the Modern Language Association in 1986 carry you forward to the many readings on the pages ahead—readings that, again and again, as repetition and intervention, foreground "reading inside out" as a perpetuity ensured by "the impossibility of reading." Miller writes:

> I suggest that real reading, when it occurs, which may be not all that often, is outside the institution, allergic to institutionalization, private, solitary. I suggest, finally, that real reading, when it occurs, is characterized primarily by *joy*, the joy of reading.[17]

NOTES

[1] J. Hillis Miller, *The Ethics of Reading: Kant, de Man, Eliot, Trollope, James, and Benjamin* (New York: Columbia UP, 1987) 59.
[2] Ludwig Wittgenstein, *Culture and Value*, ed. G. H. von Wright, in collaboration with Heikki Nyman; trans. Peter Winch (Oxford: Blackwell Publishers, 1998) 27.
[3] Ludwig Wittgenstein, *Philosophical Investigations*, 3rd ed., trans. G. E. M. Anscombe (New York: Macmillan, 1958) 61e.
[4] See Marjorie Perloff, *Wittgenstein's Ladder: Poetic Language and the Strangeness of the Ordinary* (Chicago: U of Chicago P, 1996).
[5] Marjorie Perloff, "Writing Philosophy as Poetry: Literary Form in Wittgenstein," *The Oxford Handbook of Wittgenstein*, ed. Oskari Kuusela and Marie McGinn (Oxford: Oxford UP, 2011) 718.
[6] Ibid.
[7] Ludwig Wittgenstein, *Culture and Value*, ed. G. H. von Wright, in collaboration with Heikki Nyman; trans. Peter Winch (Oxford: Blackwell Publishers, 1998) 4.

8 Ibid.

9 Marjorie Perloff, "Writing Philosophy as Poetry: Literary Form in Wittgenstein," *The Oxford Handbook of Wittgenstein*, ed. Oskari Kuusela and Marie McGinn (Oxford: Oxford UP, 2011) 718.

10 The statement is from Martin McQuillan's description of Éamonn Dunne's excellent book on Miller, *Reading Theory Now: An ABC of Good Reading with J. Hillis Miller* (New York: Bloomsbury, 2013).

11 See M. H. Abrams, "The Deconstructive Angel," *Critical Inquiry* 3.3 (Spring, 1977): 425–438.

12 J. Hillis Miller, *The Ethics of Reading: Kant, de Man, Eliot, Trollope, James, and Benjamin* (New York: Columbia UP, 1987) 59.

13 Paul Gordon, "J. Hillis Miller," *The Johns Hopkins Guide to Literary Theory and Criticism*, 2nd ed., ed. Martin Kreiswirth and Imre Szeman (Baltimore: Johns Hopkins UP, 2004) 655.

14 J. Hillis Miller, *Versions of Pygmalion* (Cambridge, MA: Harvard UP, 1990) 94.

15 *New Accents* is a series (first published by Methuen and later by Routledge) under the general editorship of Terence Hawkes who said in his General Editor's Preface in 1977 that "*New Accents* is intended as a positive response" to change in the field of literary studies wherein "modes and categories inherited from the past no longer seem to fit the reality experience by a new generation." According to Hawkes: "New concepts of literary forms and modes have been proposed; new notions of the nature of literature itself and of how it communicates are current; new views of literature's role in relation to society flourish. *New Accents* will aim to expound and comment upon the most notable of these." A few popular titles in the series include the following (with an indication of their respective date of first publication): *Structuralism and Semiotics* (1977) by Terence Hawkes, *Formalism and Marxism* (1979) by Tony Bennett, *Critical Practice* (1980) by Catherine Belsey, *Deconstruction* (1982) by Christopher Norris, *Fantasy: The Literature of Subversion* (1981) by Rosemary Jackson, *Sexual/ Textual Politics: Feminist Literary Theory* (1985) by Toril Moi, *The Return of the Reader: Reader-Response Criticism* (1987) by Elizabeth Freund, and *The Empire Writes Back: Theory and Practice in Post-Colonial Literatures* (1989) by Bill Ashcroft et al.

16 For a lucid discussion of the relation between theory and common sense, see Catherine Belsey, *Critical Practice*, 2nd ed. (London: Routledge, 2002), 1–12.

17 J. Hillis Miller, "President's Column: Responsibility and the Joy of Reading," *MLA Newsletter* 18 (1986): 2.

Introduction

I am deeply grateful to David Jonathan Bayot, of De La Salle University in Manila, Philippines, and to Anthony Grahame, Editorial Director at Sussex Academic Press in Brighton, England, for conceiving the project for this book. They have had confidence in the viability of this project, and have faithfully carried it out. I am also grateful to all those who have granted permission for reusing eleven of the larger collection of my interviews in *Reading Inside Out*. That larger collection is listed in the Bibliography that is included in this book. They are marked with asterisks in the Bibliography section called "Books, Reviews, Interviews, Documentaries, and Discussions of J. Hillis Miller's Work."

The many interviews I have given over the years have played a crucial role in my academic, professional, and personal life. These interviews have been given and then published in many countries around the world. This publication has often happened after a given interview has been translated into some language other than English.

I also warmly thank all those from all around the world who have interviewed me. Whether they have been young students, young professors, or older established scholars, they have all been unfailingly courteous, touchingly respectful, intelligent, learned, and clearly anxious not to score points, but to find out what I will say in answer to questions they have thoughtfully constructed.

Academic interviews have taken many diverse forms in recent times. All now depend in one way or another on recent technological developments. Interviews are these days almost always recorded, transcribed, and then published by way of digital relays. These often allow the interviewee at some stage to review and revise what he or she has said. Some of my interviews, especially the earliest ones, were transcribed directly from my speech to some form of recorder, sometimes a tiny handheld device. This can still be done today with an iPhone or some other cellphone. Sometimes we used that marvelous but now almost obsolete device for speaking at a distance: the landline telephone. These were recorded as we spoke on some device for later transcription and editing. Sometimes the interviews were my emailed answers to a set of questions sent by email. Sometimes they were recorded as videos by some form of visual/audio device, sometimes even by way of a long-distance program like Skype. In the latter case, interviewer and interviewee might be "virtually present" to one another but actually thousands of miles apart. In the new cyberworld everything is virtually everywhere at all times.

The modern academic interview is close to a number of other popular academic genres. Examples include the short essay written in invited response to some question or other, or the dialogical response, also invited, to an essay by some other scholar, or the "conversation," a word used in the subtitle of this book. A dialogue, with its echoes of Plato, sounds more formal and philosophical than a conversation. The latter suggests an informal give and take among equals. An interview, on the contrary, usually implies the subordination of the interviewer to the interviewee, however distinguished the interviewer may be. The interviewer does not in general express opinions of her or his own. The documentary film differs from all the genres I have mentioned. Two of these have been made about me: Dragan Kujundžić's *First Sail* and Frederik van Dam's *The Pleasure of that Obstinacy*. My Bibliography lists the URLs for these among the other asterisked items. Both of them contain filmed interviews, but they also follow the special laws of film-making and of documentaries, for example the use of visual images as generators of meaning. Documentaries are generally presented in a film-form that may be shown to an audience gathered somewhat like those in a movie theater, whereas interviews are generally read in solitude in some printed form.

All the forms of academic expression I have listed shade off into one another and cannot always be totally distinguished, but the academic interview has its own distinctive traits that persist throughout all the different media it may use.

The particular kind of digital technology used for a given interview is in various ways an important determinate of its nature. This is most obvious in the difference between an interview that remains fixed as what I spontaneously said in answer to some question or other and the interview that is transcribed and sent to me for review and revision. The opportunity to revise allows me to think twice and to sound smarter in what is presented as a hypothetically spontaneous response than I really am. Reading a printed interview, in any case, as opposed to hearing it spoken or seeing it performed on the screen affects its meaning in subtle ways that are difficult to specify.

The interviews included in this book, as well as interviews of me generally, reveal the national and professional interests of the interviewer. In my case, this has often meant questions that were meant to get me to explain "deconstruction" or some aspect of Western critical theory to readers of this or that newspaper or academic journal in China, Spain, Romania, etc., or even in the United States. I do not deny that I have played a role in the dissemination of what I now prefer to call "rhetorical reading" rather than "deconstruction." The media, teachers, and scholars have promulgated a distorted understanding of "deconstruction" that is difficult if not impossible to unsnarl or correct. The word "deconstruction" as meaning "taking apart" has become an indispensable part of everyday idiom. Here are three real examples: An architect says of the renovation of a building: "First we deconstructed it." A demolition company calls itself, "Deconstruction, Inc." The extreme right-winger Steve Bannon says his goal for the Trump presidency is "deconstruction of the administrative state." "Deconstruction" is a word whose time had come, but not exclusively as a name for rhetorical reading.

My own interest in critical theory has never been purely for its own sake, but for the sake of whatever use it may be in helping make me and others better readers of literary works. That does not keep many of my interviewers from being especially interested in what I have to say in response to questions about "deconstruction" and about Western literary theory generally. I have learned, however, how to make an honest answer to a question about theory but to shift gradually in my answer to talking about something else, perhaps about literature itself and why it matters to me and to social life in general.

I have always tried to answer interview questions as honestly and fully as I can. The many interviews I have given over the years, however, have served two rather different functions. When published, they have perhaps helped their readers to understand better the topics I have been asked to discuss, or at least to understand my perspective on these topics. They have also helped me to understand better what I really think and believe about these topics. As Keats says in the "Ode to a Nightingale," "the dull brain perplexes and retards." Thinking, really thinking, is hard work. One resists doing it. Interviews are a human situation in which the interviewee is more or less forced to do some hard thinking. She or he must then put the results of that thinking into words that are as clear and comprehensible as possible.

I urge readers of this book to note carefully the temporal arc of these interviews. They go from 1987 to 2014. By observing the changes in characteristic questions asked me over time and the changes in my answers, the reader will glimpse the impressive changes that have taken place in literary study and literary theory over these years. Were I to be interviewed again today (actually I have one in progress by email from a poetry journal in Buenos Aires) I would try to steer my answers away from literature and literary theory toward three issues that are beginning to seem to me more important than enthusiastically supporting literary study and literary theory, as my interviews have often done. These new issues are: 1) Disastrous political developments around the world, especially, nearest to home for me, the awful catastrophe of Donald Trump's election as President of the United States. 2) Irreversible global climate change with its concomitant threat of extinction for many species, including the human species. 3) The decline in the role print literature and literary theory play these days in United States culture and in other national cultures. This is evident, for example, in the drastic decline of enrollment in college and university literature courses in the United States. Many people these days rather than reading print literature play video games or the new board games, or watch films on Netflix, or watch Fox News. The latter activities determine to a large degree most people's ideologies, not, as in the Victorian period in England, reading novels by Anthony Trollope and George Eliot, or poems by Tennyson. It is video games as "literary works" that we should study and teach now in order to help the people who play them understand how they work their magic.

I love literature, but how can I in conscience, in the face of these three present-day happenings, go on solemnly asserting in interviews that everyone should forthwith read, according to the methods of "rhetorical reading," George Eliot's *Middlemarch*, Anthony Trollope's *Dr. Thorne*, Joseph Conrad's "Typhoon," or Alfred Lord Tennyson's "Tithonus," great literary works though they are and though I still believe rhetorical reading is the way to go? Print literature is still widely read all over the world, but, let's face it, literature read in books no longer matters as much as it used to do. If you want to understand where the action is, put down thy *Middlemarch* and open thy *World of Warcraft* or thy *Grand Theft Auto*.

J. HILLIS MILLER
Deer Isle, Maine
August 7, 2017

1

Criticism in Society

Interview with Imre Salusinszky

IMRE SALUSINSZKY: *In* The Ethics of Reading, *which has not been published yet, you talk about ethics as an effect of language and as the result of a failure to read, at the allegorical level. I find this a very difficult idea and would ask you to flesh it out.*

J. HILLIS MILLER: One way to talk about that would be to place it in the context—as all of your interviewees are invited to do—of the relation of literary study to society. My motive for turning to this topic has no doubt been a response to what's going on all around in the United States now. That is to say, a turning back to questions about the relation of literature to history and society. More specifically, it's a response to reproaches made to deconstruction, the sort of thing I do: reproaches from both the right and the left, claiming that it is elitist, that it is concerned only with language, and that it detaches language from the real world and from any questions of ethical or, especially, political responsibility.

The shift from politics to ethics is specifically motivated by a feeling I've had all along that the question of the relation of literary studies to politics is a little abstract, in a lot of senses. One sense is that it tends to assume, a little too easily, that there's a direct political intervention in the act of, let's say, writing a piece of criticism, or in the act of teaching, or in the act of reading. I have no doubt that there is a political facet to everything one does in the university; there is no question about that. But it does seem to me to be indirect and mediated: it is not as immediately political as, for example, voting. When I vote, that has an immediate political effect and has something to do with electing the candidate or not electing him. When I teach Stevens, it has a political effect all right, but it would be much more difficult to identify what that really is.

One of my feelings about all this talk about literature and politics is that it may exaggerate the political effectiveness of the study of literature. What's really making history at this moment in the United States? One would, I think, in all candor have to say that it doesn't have a heck of a lot to do with the study of Stevens in any direct way. It's likely to go, say, here at Yale, by way of indirect and uneasy-making relays, where somebody who is one of my undergraduate seminars may ten or fifteen years from now be the director of the CIA. The question of how his decisions and actions, in that situation, are affected by my teaching—it's not that it's not affected—is very hard to identify. For that reasons, I said to myself that I could be more concrete about this by focusing on what is more direct and has more to do with one person face to face with another, namely, ethics. It's obvious that it's possible then to reproach me for being, again, abstracted from my real political situation, but I think I have an answer to that now, by saying that I'm talking of that by way of the ethical situation.

The question I've asked myself is, to what degree is what we really do as students of literature—read books, write about them, teach them in the classroom—ethically effective and, therefore, politically effective? The notion about the failure to read—reading allegorically—which you correctly point to as fundamental to the argument, might be phrased in a way that would be easier to understand by saying that what fascinates me is the way in which the act of reading—and therefore these other things—does have a margin or remainder or edge, which is not accounted for by all the presuppositions I bring to it or by my institutional, political, or social situation. In that sense, it is really unpredictable, so that there is no way to know ahead of time what it's going to be, when I read or when one of my students reads. But it *is* something that, in its turn, makes something happen in the real world and may therefore be effective. Unless literature has that margin, there's not much point to it. If you can fully account for a piece of literature or for my act of reading, by social/historical determinants, then it melts into historical forces, which you might as well study by studying history. The claim that I'm making is for that margin or edge, which I think you can study best and identify best by actually looking at a text. The failure to read, and the reading allegorically, comes in as the presupposition that this act of reading, with its inaugural novelty—this tiny margin of unpredictability—does have its effects in the real world. As I began by saying, they can be exaggerated, but they are not accountable by some kind of direct causality. It's the indirection that fascinates me, and that's what I was trying to define in this notion that there is an ethical component, but not one that in any direct way follows from what the text seems to mean: "misreading" would be a name for that.

I've been teaching the short stories of Thomas Hardy recently, where there's a very good paradigmatic, textually inscribed example of this. This is the book of stories called *A Group of Noble Dames*. It's a frame-story: a men's outing club, stuck in the rain, is reading these stories, and one of Hardy's points is to show that the response of the men to the stories is always in hilarious incongruity with what the stories seem to say—it's always reductive and repressive. It seems to be one of Hardy's points not that the story doesn't produce something, but that it produces something which is incongruous with the meaning of the story. My notion is that that's probably a law. You begin by saying that literature does not make all that much happen, but it does make some things happen, and what it makes happen is something that university administrators ought not to be too reassured about. One of the ethical things a teacher can do is to choose the syllabus, but you can never know what will happen. Take Gandhi's or Yeats's reading of Thoreau: that was real history, but the relationship in each case to what Thoreau was saying was devious.

SALUSINSZKY: *And "ethics" is the name you give to this margin or edge?*

MILLER: I begin by borrowing a definition of ethics from Henry James. James defines writing a book as part of the "conduct of life"—a very Emersonian phrase that should please Harold Bloom—and then defines the conduct of life as "things done, which do other things in their turn."[1] No doubt there is ethics all right—it's the field that has to do with conduct and responsibility and choice and decision. The question is, is there an ethical component to reading? My claim is that the act of reading is a thing done which does other things in its turn.

SALUSINSZKY: *On the subject of reading, in your message to the profession in the "President's Column" of the latest* MLA Newsletter, *you say, of the act of reading,*

> *I suggest that real reading, when it occurs, which may be not all that often, is outside the institution, allergic to institutionalization, private, solitary. I suggest, finally, that real reading, when it occurs, is characterized primarily by joy, the joy of reading. (p. 2)*

That's a very Bloomian quotation, and it's interesting to hear something like that coming both from someone who styles himself as being at the very margins of the profession and then from someone who is at the very center of the profession. What does it say about the university if the main enabling act that we perform—reading—is necessarily outside it?

MILLER: That was an intentionally hyperbolic formulation of what I've just been saying about that margin. Without in any way denying the enormous multiplicity of determinants in the act of reading—reading is never solitary, in the sense that there are all sorts of things looking over my shoulder that do involve my institutional responsibilities, where I come from, family background, everything of that sort—my claim is that there is a little margin, and *that's* the solitariness I was talking about. It's that surprise, and I was trying to give it a name which corresponds to my experience of reading, which is the name *joy*. There's something joyful about that: it's an exciting moment. Whereas simply discovering that Milton means what all the other books say about it is not joyful—not for me, at any rate. One wants to read, therefore, against what other people have said.

My difference from Bloom is easy to specify. It has to do with selfhood, as opposed to language. Bloom wants to say that the thing that is performing that act of solitary reading, which is anti-institutional, is something called the "strong" self. And it looks as if he believes that that's intrinsic, essential, given to little Harold Bloom before he started reading Hart Crane: a possession that he had from the beginning, something that's inalienable and absolutely solitary. I don't believe that. What I believe is that the myth of the self is no doubt indispensable, but that the reader is a kind of locus where language takes place. It's play within language that makes it unpredictable more than anything that I can claim comes from my initial, intrinsic self. Nobody would have any trouble saying that Harold has these theories because of certain social, psychological, and historical backgrounds in himself. It's vulnerable to that, just as no doubt what I'm saying is vulnerable to somebody saying the same thing about me. Nevertheless, there's a difference between saying that this is a linguistic transaction—in which what I bring to the act of reading is a certain power of reading, which is a linguistic power that makes me a locus or a node of something that occurs within language—and saying that I, the strong self with an absolutely unique personality, make the work mean something that's caused by that.

SALUSINSZKY: *Nevertheless, Bloom's account of the "joy" of reading—tied up, as you say, with the realization and development of selfhood—is translatable in an easy, though limited, way into terms of social usefulness: he teaches others how to experience this joy and how to struggle towards their own voice or selfhood. In your account of the joy of reading as intersections occurring at a node of language, how do you make the translation to the social benefit of teaching it?*

MILLER: That's a good question. I think the danger of the Bloomian account is that it would reinforce the assumption in students that they already have whatever they are going to have and that graduating from Yale is simply going to authorize them to go on being what they already were when they came here or to impose the ideology that they had when they came here. That is, it reinforces what is already *the* ideology of Yale undergraduates—in so far as I have been able to identify it—namely, that the value of something lies in my power to give the thing value. Bloom fits that ideology. My evidence for that is a little question I ask my section in Literature 120, way back at the beginning. On the very first day, I ask them to write a one-page paper: "Tell me how you would know that you had it right with a work of literature." In so far as there is anything that pervades the answers, it is the claim that "It's right because I say it's right." I find that interesting: these are not students who've studied with Harold Bloom, but it is already Bloom's idea, and I think he's simply reinforcing that.

Now, what do I say? I was thinking about this and trying to formulate my answer. For me, the study of literature is not so much reinforcing as *apotropaic*. It's a demystifying study; it's the most concentrated area where we might be able to recognize the effects of language and learn, in a way, to protect ourselves from its enormous power in actually making us do things and making us make judgments and making history happen in these ways that are devious. It's not the only place to study that, but it's a very concentrated place to study what you might call the effects of ideology on the materiality of history. It is arming people with the power to read, which I see as an absolutely fundamental necessity in order for them to make their way in the present world: this is what I think the study of literature can really do.

SALUSINSZKY: *I guess that the reason that the students in your first-year section produce naïve Bloomian readings is because it is in line with what is truly the American religion: of self-improvement, of there being an inner power which can be realized or not realized in the world. You can see it anytime if you flick on the cable TV. And as Bloom himself points out in his seminars, it is the major strain in the Native American religions of the nineteenth century: Mormonism and Christian Science.*

MILLER: Though I would think that there is another strain in the American religious tradition, which is that side of Protestantism that is critical of graven images. This is the anti-ideological side where, by pushing just a step further, you end up somewhere like where I am. Along with that self-improving side—the Emersonian, strong-self side—there is that "I am from Missouri" side, the side that says "Prove it to me" and that tends to be suspicious of large formulations. The trouble with the strong-self side is that it's very easy for it to become Ronald Reagan saying, "The rest of you guys haven't got any guts, so I'm going to decide on my own to bomb Libya." And the response to the bombing, at the moment, is apparently largely positive.

SALUSINSZKY: *"Let's turn Libya into a parking lot!" was one comment I heard from a view on CNN yesterday (I almost said "CBN," where you'd be even* more *likely to hear it).*[2]

MILLER: Like trying to bomb Vietnam back into the Stone Age. We didn't succeed in doing that, but that was the instinctive motive: the feeling that the strong self ought to be able to go over there and subdue those people. That's the trouble with the *agonistic* model, which I was interested to see Said responding positively to in Bloom.

SALUSINSZKY: *We were talking about reading in the university: What are the consequences of deconstruction for the university, particularly in terms of curricula and the division of faculties and departments? These seem to be based on a notion of difference that would be threatened by* différance.

MILLER: The consequences would be considerable. They would be different in different universities.

One striking feature of your series of interviews in your book, *Criticism and Society*, is the way in which each of the interviewees tended to define himself as against all of the others. It's very striking in Bloom, but it's true also for the others. It's a natural move. "I am criticism, and the others are all deconstruction," says Bloom; then, Kermode says that the world is full of little Bloomians, but—the pathos of this!—"There are no Kermodians." Those statements strike me as slightly in bad faith, in the sense that Kermode knows perfectly well that he's had an enormous influence: Lots and lots of people have read his books. And Bloom says, "I have no followers, I'm all alone," as if there were not thousands of people out there reading him. On the other hand, the group of people you've taken is necessarily parochial. For example, they're all East Coast people. From other sorts of perspective, there might have been other ways of doing it. The other thing that's striking about them is their diversity. Each one of them says, "I'm not like the others," as though they were in some way at the center.

So what I think will be a salutary aspect of your book of interviews is the evidence of this diversity. It's by no means a single operation, and that's an important fact. One of the things that I have learned, and that Derrida stresses, is the heterogeneity or overdetermination of any social situation, such as a single university or, even more, higher education in the United States. So when you ask a question like the one you asked a moment ago, one would have to recognize that any single perspective is going to be very partial, that it's an enormous field, that there are people teaching at the University of Kansas, for example. Deconstruction is a good example since, like Marxism, it's diffused all around the country; it's active here, there and everywhere, in one way or another. So you can't locate it at one single place, at Yale. It's going to have different effects in different places, and they will depend on what the local university is like.

Nevertheless, one can say, I think, that one effect would be clearly to break down traditional divisions among the departments. The simplest way to define that is by way of the difference it makes to study a canonical work in juxtaposition with other works in the same national canon, as opposed to studying that same work juxtaposed to works from a different canon. It's not a matter of overturning the canon. It's the effect of teaching *Great Expectations* not in the context of other Victorian novels, but in the context of Roland Barthes' *S/Z*, Freud's "Dora," and so on. That seems to me the institutional politics of deconstruction, as much as anything. It's a different way of reading, but it's also a different assemblage of texts.

To be concrete about this, one could say that one of the really conservative things about Bloom, in his interview and in his work generally, is that it's deeply rooted in the Yale English Department. His canon *is* the Yale English Department canon. You give him a Stevens poem, and he thinks about Whitman. That's OK: "Father Whitman." He's got a sequence which is not much different from the traditional courses in the English department here. The big traditional courses in the English Department here. The big traditional courses in the English Department here are English 125, where you do Chaucer, Spenser, Shakespeare, Milton, Pope, Wordsworth—then the canon goes to pieces, no Victorians, some twentieth-century poets, and English 129—"World Literature"—which begins in Homer and Aeschylus and includes mostly works which are the traditional "background" texts for the English canon as traditionally conceived. That's still world culture for Harold Bloom. Something happens when you put Stevens side by side with Paul Celan, or Ponge, or Freud (but Bloom's Freud is primarily Freud as an English writer). I would think that one of the major things that deconstruction, as well as other importations of that sort, has done is to move in the direction of making our humanistic culture more genuinely multilingual.

SALUSINSZKY: *Well, within this broadened and more simultaneous context—in which we can read a poet next to a philosopher, a philosopher by the lights of a poet, place Barthes next to Stevens—what happens to the divisions between the departments? Would they be retained or jettisoned?*

MILLER: It depends on the university, and I wouldn't have any prescriptions. Another way to put that would be to say that there's no point in throwing out the traditional demarcations of literary history until you've got something that's pretty clearly better. An enormous number of terrible courses have been conducted in the name of some kind of thematic content: "The Beast Myth Through the Ages." I would rather both take and teach a course in "The Victorian Novel": I understand what that means and think you might get somewhere with that. On the other hand, there probably is some rearrangement going on now of the way signaled, for example, by the existence of a large number of departments which are either called departments of "Literature" or of "English and Comparative Literature" and which contain another region which is "Literary Theory": that's different from a traditional department of English, which thinks of itself primarily as teaching the canon of English literature. There would be rearrangements of that sort, as well as more team-taught courses and so on. But one would have to go very slowly in doing that.

It's a manifest fact that a great deal of the real philosophy that's been taught recently has been taught out of Philosophy departments. Philosophy departments, by insulating themselves in the very valuable but somewhat limited region of logic and analytical philosophy, have cut themselves off from doing work which then has been picked up by "amateur" philosophers outside, like Paul de Man teaching Hegel. That's a fact of humanistic studies.

SALUSINSZKY: *Early on in the history of American deconstruction, your polemics (with M. H. Abrams, for example) engaged an assault from the traditional or, if you like, "logocentric" wing of the American academy. Now, as you were saying right at the beginning of our conversation, you are much more engaged with Marxist and New Historicist criticism. I want to read you something from your response, six years ago, to an article in* Critical Inquiry *about you: "I do think the conservative aspect of deconstruction needs to be stressed. Its difference from Marxism, which is likely to become more sharply visible as time goes on, is that it views as naïve the millennial or revolutionary hopes still in one way or another present even in sophisticated Marxism. This millenarianism believes that a change in the material base or in the class structure would transform our situation in relation to language or change the human condition generally. Deconstruction, on the other hand, sees the notion of a determining material base as one element in the traditional metaphysical system it wants to put in question."*

MILLER: Did I say that?

SALUSINSZKY: *Interestingly, this seems to separate you not only from Marxism but also from the whole tradition of criticism from Matthew Arnold to Northrop Frye, which consistently—like the Marxists—imbues criticism with a millenarian, socially revelatory function. It could be said that, after placing reading outside institutional boundaries, you are there cutting deconstruction off as occurring solely inside the institution, because you want to separate it from any work for social change.*

MILLER: By no means. My target, in those remarks, was the Marxist concept of materiality. It was to say that there is something wrong with the power given to the notion of materiality as determining history and on the basis of that claiming that a change in the material base would therefore lead to social improvement. That was my target, not the notion that whatever we do ought to be socially effective. I happen to take a dim view about the millennium: if it were about to come, we probably would have it already, and things don't seem conspicuously to be getting better, from the social point of view. My belief in the millennium is, like everybody's, a belief in one that's always tomorrow, and it would be the millennium of good readers. I believe that what actually causes the materiality of history is bad reading: this goes back to that claim I was making that teaching reading might make for social improvement by making people good readers. It's so unlikely that we would have a whole nation of really good readers—good reading is so difficult and unlikely to happen—that it's a millennium I don't think is going to occur. That doesn't mean that we oughtn't to work for it, and that *is* what I'm working for: to make my teaching effective, socially, by making good reading occur.

What I mean by the way in which bad reading creates history is very straightforward. Bad reading is always, as Paul de Man says, ideological in the sense that ideology is mistaking the materiality of the sign for the materiality of the signifier. When you think you've got it in that sense—a straightforward correspondence between one and the other—you are likely to do things which result in the materiality of history. This can be very specifically defined: sure, it's the distribution of food, what's in our bodies, whether we get enough to eat, whether we're warmly clothed. More alarmingly, the *real* materiality of history is who gets killed, bombed, and so on. The places where ideology intervenes in history have, alas, tended to take the form of a lot of people getting killed. So that when de Man says that texts at a level of allegorical complexity like the *Social Contract* make history happen, to me that means all those people being guillotined in the French Revolution. And that, I think, is too bad. What one might hope to be able to lessen would be the number of people who get murdered not by being a fantastic example of that. No doubt there were all sorts of economic, social, historical causes of the Holocaust, but one of them has to be what was going on in the minds of those murderers, and that was a fantastic example of a piece of ideology: "We have to get the final solution." That's so unimaginable that it's very hard to think about it or face it, especially because we may be, ourselves in complicity, at this very moment, in doing something of the same sort. How could we know? It's easy to condemn them, but can we be sure we are exempt from similar effects of ideology? "Let's turn Libya into a parking lot." Is that so different from the Holocaust?

So I would think that the study of literature might have good social effects in eliminating that process. At the moment, the most appalling fact in our historical situation is to live under the threat of nuclear annihilation. Pushing that button that starts the bombs off cannot occur except through language. Talking about it, studying it, trying in some way to demystify it might be what the study of literature could do to prevent that from happening.

SALUSINSZKY: *This is what, nowadays, seems to be taken as the progressive social effect of Derrida's insights: the deconstruction of the rhetoric of all authority. However, your discussions with Derrida himself on this point must surely be affected by the fact that, unlike you, he has had serious engagements* *and affiliations with the hard left, in France. He wouldn't dismiss Marxism, I think, in quite the same way that you do.*

MILLER: I wanted to go back to say that, though I was quarreling and would quarrel with that specific point within Marxist doctrine, neither then nor now would I in any way dismiss Marxism. I disagree, therefore, with what Harold Bloom says, because unlike him I would see the current development of an indigenous American Marxist thinking—which is very widespread—as a fundamental feature of American university life. Just as the accommodation or appropriation of deconstruction in the United States is producing something that is specifically American—as Derrida keeps saying, he has more power and influence here than he does in France; deconstruction is really an American thing—so I would say that something is really happening in the United States to Marxist thought that is neither entirely continuous with Marx himself nor with modern French or German Marxism.

I take American Marxism very seriously now, and I would say that the field of action in humanistic and literary studies in the United States now invites or requires a kind of confrontation or dialogue or negotiation of something that may be non-negotiable in the end: between linguistically oriented studies like deconstruction on the one hand and Marxism or Foucauldianism on the other. That's one of the reasons I'm interested in going to California. I see that as a place where Foucault has always been much stronger than he is here and as a place having a slightly different kind of political-institutional area than here: it's where some of the action in this area is going to be. That's not said in a spirit of hostility—"Stupid Marxist"— but rather out of a feeling that those new sociologists of literature have to be confronted. I hope to do that: my "ethics of reading" work is generated by the beginning of that discussion in myself.

SALUSINSZKY: *In your engagements with historicisms new and old, there are two different arguments that go on in your work. The major one has to do with our inability to get outside language. I'd like to table a few quotations about this. In* The Form of Victorian Fiction, *which is a transition work for you, we hear that "human culture and the imitation of human culture in a novel have the same structure. Both have the nature of language" (p. 140). Many years later, in the* Deconstruction and Criticism *volume, you say that "language...thinks man" (p. 224). In* The Ethics of Reading, *against the New Historicism, you say that "the study of literature...remains within the study of language." Finally, and most importantly, in* Fiction and Repitition *in 1982,* *you say that "A recent skirmisher in the rarefied atmosphere of pure theory argues that criticism went wrong when it became close reading. This, if I may say so, is a major treason against our profession" (p. 21).*

Now, these quotations locate what is bound to be one of the main things that deconstruction's opponents on the left are going to say against you and deconstruction: that it is only a more sophisticated version of the old New Criticism, which you wrote your Ph.D. under the influence of.

MILLER: The dissertation was steeped in Kenneth Burke, which is not quite the same thing as Brooks and Warren. Burke was already, in his influence on me, interested in those social orientations. It was the notion of a work of literature as a strategy for encompassing a situation by means of language which attracted me in Burke and which I was applying in the dissertation (which has never been published). That would be one answer to what you've said: that the New Criticism is already diverse and heterogeneous and different people have gotten different things out of it. My New Criticism all along was much more Burke and Empson and G. Wilson Knight: a weird New Criticism, from the point of view of Yale orthodoxy. The second thing to say is that I'm not at all ashamed of that filiation or lineage. If you really understand Kenneth Burke, you don't need Derrida as much.

I was at a conference the other day at Ohio State University, where I was commenting on a paper by Shoshana Felman on some wonderful new work she's doing on testimony. It was a reading of Camus's *The Plague* as a book about the Holocaust. In my comment on it, I was trying to develop this notion that what's strange about Camus' *Plague* is that what was in fact an effect of the Nazis—that is to say, a deliberate ideological-linguistic horror—is allegorized as the plague. So what in fact was a human cause of history is allegorized as something as inhuman as the bacillus that caused the plague. Now, at a certain moment, my good friend Terry Eagleton rose up and denounced me for being an idealist, for saying that language causes history. It's exactly the question you've been asking: and that's what I'm trying to think out.

One way to think it out would be to say that, no doubt, there are all sorts of nonlinguistic things to make history happen. If there is a great earthquake in California, that's not caused by human thinking or language. Nor was the plague; nor is the AIDS virus, though the spread of the virus has a sociolinguistic component. So there are lots of things that happen without language. However, I would extend the range of language much further than Eagleton. I would say, for example, that the region of economics that has to do with the money and the valuation of things is really linguistic, if you mean by *linguistic* having to do with signs and the power that signs have. That's what Marx says. Money, economics, is in the region of the study of signs and also of the mystification we get into when we mistake the materiality of the sign for the materiality of the signifier. That's the fetishism Marx talks about. So that my response to Eagleton would be just what I was trying to say in that passage you read about materiality. *He's* being an idealist, by idealizing what are effects of language, in the broad sense, as though they were power structures that had the nature of earthquakes: they don't. Wall Street is not an earthquake; it's a whole lot of people acting in terms of something that has the structure of language.

I would then go back to say that the study of literature is not supposed to be the study of everything: it's the study of literature. It is not that the study of the historical surrounding of a work of literature is not very important, but the proof of the pudding comes when you put that work of literature within that context, and that means reading the work. My difficulty with some of the work of the New Historicists—work that I greatly admire for its life and energy and commitment—is when they come to the actual work of reading the text that they're talking about. Stephen Greenblatt, for example, has a marvelous essay about hermaphroditism in the sixteenth century, and at the end, in a rather perfunctory way, he says that this explains Shakespeare. I'm prepared to believe that it explains a lot in Shakespeare, but he doesn't really show that. Or there is another admirable book, by Catherine Gallagher, which is about my field, the Victorian novel. It is absolutely wonderful on the social background of Victorian novels. My problem comes when she talks about Mrs. Gaskell, for example, and it seems to me that she's prepared simply to summarize the plot and to talk about the people as if they were real people. That would be a concrete example of what I meant by saying that the immediate frontier of literary study is trying to bring those two things together. What would happen to Catherine Gallagher's hypotheses about the Victorian novel if she had really "read" the Elizabeth Gaskell novels that she talks about, in the sense of the close rhetorical analysis of Gaskell's figures of speech and so on? Something would happen, but something would also happen to my reading of Elizabeth Gaskell when it's put in her context. So I'm going to learn a lot from those people.

SALUSINSZKY: *You've partly answered my next question, which has to do with the second locus of your argument with historicism. In* The Ethics of Reading *you talk about the kinds of connections which the New Historicists make between literary texts and history as being shot through with fairly naïve and old-fashioned metaphors to do with mirroring and reflection. Does that* *connection* have *to be a naïve one, or could we insert a notion of* difference *into the relation between the text itself and the text of history?*

MILLER: Yes, that can be done, but I think that it's difficult and requires much methodological sophistication as well as much learning. There's no doubt that it's going to remain controversial, but that will be the life of doing it. What would really happen to Catherine Gallagher's hypothesis about Mrs. Gaskell had she done a deconstructive reading of the actual text? I've done a little bit of that with *Cranford*: Mrs. Gaskell is very interesting from that point of view. I think something would happen, but it would make immensely more complicated the models of the relationship between the text and history. That is what I was talking about: those metaphors of text and context, which are metonymic or synecdochical, or all of those images of reflection. If it isn't that, then what could it be?

It's here, I think, that the notion of heterogeneity and overdetermination might be valuable. The methodological model here might be Freud. One of the things that I've learned from Freud—take one of the great case-histories like "Dora"—is that he's doing something, in a sense, infinitely easier: all he's trying to do is account for pathological symptoms in one patient. Dora's got these problems, symptoms, and comes to see him. By the time you get through, you have this immensely complicated network of details, which he speaks of, specifically, as overdetermined. You have all those footnotes, where he's taken it back to the original thing, and then he says, "No, it wasn't that she was in love with Herr K., it was really that she was in love with Frau K.": there is an infinite regression in the identification of the causal thing. All those great images like that of the trains that come to a switching, the place of crossing, and so on. The methodological model is immensely complicated. It recognizes the heterogeneity, the multiple meanings that a given sign or symbol can have. This is just to account for one single person and her problems. If you start trying to do that with history, I think you have to be prepared for something that's even more complicated, and you have to be a little tentative about your account (avoiding the oversimplification, for example, of those institutional histories that say that all English departments are so and so).

SALUSINSZKY: *Back a further step, into your early deconstructive phase. It was concentrated, to a large degree, on the notion of unreadability or undecidability: the impossibility of reading, in the sense of determining a univocal meaning. In* Fiction and Repetition, *you say that your fundamental premise "is that the specific heterogeneity of a given text can be exactly defined,* *even though a univocal meaning cannot be justified by the text" (p. 231). This is still very much present in your latest book,* The Linguistic Moment, *where you say that "any cultural expression in our tradition, such as a literary text, is undecidable in meaning, though the choices the text offers (among which the reader cannot except arbitrarily decide) may be precisely defined" (p. 54). Here we come up against what is properly a philosophical problem and could easily slide into fruitless Platonic speculations about whether there is only, really, one thing or whether there are numerous or multiple things. By which I mean to ask, how can we determine the range of undecidability if we can't determine any single meaning within that range? Wouldn't that range, taken as a whole, constitute a univocal meaning in itself anyway? And what allows us to determine* any *of the possibilities of meaning?*

MILLER: I see the problem, but I don't see this as a pointless paradox or as regressive in the sense that I'm really saying there is only one meaning. My targets in those statements were two. One of them is, in a way, personal to me or to my situation in criticism: namely, the notion of organic meaning. In the New Criticsm that I learned, and especially in relationship to the nineteen-year dialogue with Earl Wasserman that I had at Johns Hopkins, it was the thing that he kept insisting on. So there may be something personal or parochial in my wanting to undo that idea. On the other hand, my target was all of those people who seem to have read one essay by Derrida—the one about "Structure, Sign and Play"—and who have misunderstood what's said there about play. All they know, or think they know, is that deconstruction says you can make the text mean anything you want. What I want to say is very simple, and I don't see how anybody could argue with it: complicated and heterogeneous though the field of a given text is, it nevertheless is finite. For all practical purposes, you can identify what the major components of the possible meanings are, within which any reading would fall.

The only way in which I would modify little bit, now, what I said there, would be to emphasize the feeling of a kind of virtual infinity in the experience of meaning. It's not that everything is in there, but that you can always return, even to a poem or novel that you've taught over and over again, and find something else there: another way to talk about it that you hadn't really fully talked about before. I say "virtual" because it's not infinite: *Great Expectations* has only so many words, only so many themes; it places itself in a certain way within the repertoire of possible themes in Western literature, but not all of them. It's finite, in that sense. On the other hand, it's big enough so that even the same person can go on teaching it all his or her life and go on finding new things in it. And I think that needs to be emphasized, too. My reading is controlled by the text—it's not a wanton imposition on my part—but at the same time is not easily limitable.

SALUSINSZKY: *It's interesting that you mentioned Wasserman, because what I meant to say before was, when you say that the specific heterogeneity of a given text can be exactly defined, I want to ask you what separates that from the determination of a univocal meaning, since even the most logocentric of the New Critics never said "This poem means X." They, too, would always define a field of meaning that was heterogeneous. Their point, of course, was that poetry, unlike everyday discourse, was a structure of tensional irony which could contain contradictory meanings. In other words, the argument about undecidability feeds back into the criticism of deconstruction as "just the New Criticism writ large."*

MILLER: I think I could specify the difference. Empson and Burke are closest to deconstruction, among the New Critics. I have an easier time distinguishing myself from other forms of the notion of organic unity, let's say Wasserman's: he wanted everything to fit into some kind of spatial array. But however much emphasis there is in Empson—let's say in *The Structure of Complex Words*—on diversity, and even irreconcilability, it's always within a single structure of incompatibilities, where all of these things are related to each other in some dialectical way. At least hypothetically, this would allow for a kind of synthesis, even though it would be the bringing together of lots of diversity and irony and so on. The notion in deconstruction is that the meanings between which one cannot decide are asymmetrical. That is to say, there isn't anything you can do to bring them together. They're not open to organic unification; they're not open to dialectical synthesis. The term *heterogeneity* has a different meaning, in the two regions. That's what I see in works of literature, and that, I think, is what de Man or Derrida would be saying about works of literature that differs from the New Criticism.

SALUSINSZKY: *Another difference between you and the New Critics is that their whole point was to separate this heterogeneity off, not as a language effect, but as a* poetic *effect. Language was divided into two: you had poetry, where this heterogeneity, albeit limited in its free play, was allowed to take place, and then you had the "everyday" or "normal" use of language. That's not a move made in deconstruction. Or is it? After all, you don't read the texts of the world in this way. When you receive a letter form University of California at Irvine, offering you an endowed chair and outlining the terms of the offer, you don't determine that* that *text is undecidable.*

MILLER: I look at it pretty carefully!

SALUSINSZKY: *Looking for the fissures.*

MILLER: Looking for the problems and fissures. No, on the one hand you're right: one of the controversial aspects of deconstruction that has been attacked all around is the blurring of that notion of sequestered literature. On the other hand, one of your interviewees attacks de Man because de Man wants to talk about literariness. And he does, but it's obvious that what de Man means is that there is a feature of language which you can call "literariness"—it might be given other names: rhetorical effects, places where figurative language interferes with straightforward grammatical meanings— and the effect of "literariness" is *everywhere*. It is a feature of language in general. One studies literature, as such, because that's a very concentrated place to investigate this. But what you're investigating is a universal feature of language, which would contaminate even that letter from the president of the University of California, in one way or another. I hope not in such a way that they don't pay me.

SALUSINSZKY: *The criticism that an organicist would bring to bear on your notion of the impossibility of determining univocal meaning would be that it leads to a kind of nihilism (one of the terms, I think, that Abrams used in one of your early engagements with him). What interests me about your treatment of the criticism that deconstruction is a kind of nihilism is that you're there waiting for it: nihilism is one of the most persistent themes of all your work and is by no means limited to the period after your engagement with Derrida. I'm thinking, particularly, of the first chapter of* Poets of Reality, *which is about nothing if not the question of nihilism. In the "Critic as Host" essay, which is responding to Abram's criticism on this score, you say that nihilism is not the opposite of metaphysics but is inherent in metaphysics, and vice versa. You say that deconstruction doesn't escape from this inference but moves joyfully back and forth within it (pp. 230–231). That's a fascinating description of the activity of deconstruction.*

MILLER: The context of my remarks is Nietzsche and Heidegger and their analysis of nihilism as a feature of metaphysics. One might think of passages where Heidegger says that people think that nothing isn't anything, but in fact, it's an occulted revelation of being. What I would want to say, however, is simultaneously two things. On the one hand, although it cannot really do so, deconstruction is an attempt to move as far as possible outside that oscillation within metaphysics between metaphysics and nihilism and to see it (although it's impossible) from the outside. Or to put this another way, to demystify the spookiness of those terms. I take it that that's what Derrida means when he talks about the joyful aspect of this: it's not necessary to see the experience of nothing as being apocalyptic.

On the other hand—and this "other hand" is very important—there is an aspect of what happens to me when I read Stevens or Shelley or Dickens, which is the experience of something to which I could give no name, which, in that sense, is nothing but which at the same time seems to be the encounter with something other than language which is woven into language and causes these effects. It is impossible to talk about this without mystification, without the misleading implication that you're falling back into some kind of religiosity. Nevertheless, that's the way it seems to me. You could say that what I have against the reproach of nihilism is that it's saying that deconstruction is absolutely empty, antireligious, doesn't take anything except language seriously, and so on: that is so foreign to my actual experience of literature that it makes me angry, both as a mistake about what nihilism is and as a mistaken understanding of what I try to do.

SALUSINSZKY: *I want to come back to some of those things in a moment, but not before taking another chronological step back. With Lentricchia, we were talking about the way that everyone has some particularly critical moment of self-doubt in their work, after which a complete change of direction takes place. It wouldn't take a genius to place the crisis, in your case, during the period in which you successively rewrote your important essay on Poulet, producing a final version around 1971 that contains a sort of supplement on Derrida. Over this period, you moved from being a Poulet-influenced critic of consciousness and of the presence of reality in consciousness to being a Derrida-influenced critic of language and of the absence of reality in language. Was the influence of Derrida a sudden, revelatory moment in your intellectual life?*

MILLER: No. I would say two things about that. The greatness of Poulet is to carry his own presuppositions to the point where they almost turn back on themselves. There are important essays in his work where consciousness becomes narrowed down to an infinite point and sort of dissolves. So I was prepared for that. But I was also prepared in another way. The very powerful response, on my part, to Poulet, who was tremendously exciting for me to read—there's no way to account for that, it's very personal—was a response to problems that I found apparent in Burke and Empson during that earlier stage. So I came to consciousness as a solution to problems that had to do with language. You might say that I never really solved those problems.

The reading of Derrida is a good proof of the point that you can never tell which books are going to be decisive for your life. It wasn't that anybody told me that I should read Derrida, though Eugenio Donato probably had mentioned his name. But I remember very distinctly that I just picked up the issue of *Critique* which had the early version of *Grammatologie*, started reading it, and thought it was wonderful—just as I'd thought that Poulet was wonderful. There obviously were reasons for that. It was at the moment that I was prepared to go back to where I was at the beginning. It seemed very personally motivated as a solution to problems in my own work.

The attraction of Poulet for me, in part, was that I thought that the New Critical method—even the Burkean or Empsonian one—was not all that effective as a way to deal with the works that I had been hired to teach, namely, Victorian ones. Poulet allowed me to write essays on, say, Matthew Arnold. "Dover Beach" is not all that a great poem, from the point of view of Brooks and Warren. But Matthew Arnold, *pace* Harold Bloom, strikes me as a very interesting author, especially in those late religious books. He's open both to a Pouletian and to a deconstructive reading, which is why he gets back into *The Linguistic Moment*.

SALUSINSZKY: *Let's terminate this backward movement with* Poets of Reality, *where, as I say, the big question is nihilism and where you say that "If there is to be a God in the new world it must be a presence within things and not beyond them" (p. 10): it must be an immanence, rather than a transcendence. I would use this point as a way of merging into your biography and asking you about your religious upbringing. To what extent was your attachment to the criticism-of-consciousness school, in those early years, tied up with the theological question that is so central in your early books?*

MILLER: Very little, in any explicit way, because I'd long since stopped going to church. My specific American upbringing was rural and southern. Both of my parents came from Virginia. My father was an ordained southern Baptist minister who later became a university president. I've a brother who is a Presbyterian minister. I've a grandfather who taught men's Bible class in a small country church in Virginia for forty years and knew the Bible backwards and forwards. Although I went to Sunday school until I was a senior in high school, one of my resentments about American Protestantism is that you don't get taught anything. I can find Habakkuk in the Bible, and I know how to make soap models of houses in Palestine, and that's about what I learned in twelve years of going to Sunday school. There was very little real teaching about what's going on in the Bible, and that's an interesting fact. So, in one sense I had a religious upbringing, and in another sense, I didn't. But what I *was* taught was a rigorous respect for truth, and some kind of vague assumption that the truth might be dark, ominous, not at all reassuring.

I was pretty much on my own in college and later on, but I think that some sense of a connection between the study of literature and philosophical or religious concerns has been with me all along. I remember Paul de Man saying that religious questions are the most important ones, and I'm prepared to agree with that. No matter how negative your conclusions about them might be, those are important questions, and to detach the study of literature from them seems to me a mistake.

SALUSINSZKY: *In* Poets of Reality, *nihilism is cured by rejecting transcendence and merging mind with world, where something spiritual and saving is still to be discovered. What about now? What is the theology of deconstruction? Hasn't one, in fact, moved back to a transcendence? If language thinks us, rather than us thinking language, then who made language?*

MILLER: Well, what are we, from this point of view, but language or a locus of language? The opposition that I was working on back then was between transcendence—in the sense of some kind of Platonic never-never land—and immanence, and you might say that the development since then has been in the direction of seeing that immanence as a linguistic one. This involves seeing literature not as the naming of some kind of presence in the physical world—as in the reading that I gave of Stevens or Williams in *Poets of Reality*—but rather as the exploration of some kind of otherness that is located within language itself: another kind of immanence. It's no less a rejection of any kind of transcendence. Particularly if you define language as something that is within me, when I read the poem, because I become the locus where the poem is read, interpreted and so on—rather than thinking of language as something that's out there, beyond me, somewhere else.

SALUSINSZKY: *I guess that the question that Bloom might ask here would be, then what gets meaning started in the first place? What gets language started? How do you avoid some kind of transcendental account of how meaning originates?*

MILLER: You can stay within language on that. That's the very point, I take it, of Derrida's notion of *différance* or trace: that language, from any conceivable human point of view, is something that is always already there, and that the lure of getting before it is an impossible lure. All you do is get further and further back towards a place where language is already there. That doesn't make it transcendent; it means that we are, for better or for worse, within language from the beginning and can't get outside it.

SALUSINSZKY: *We come now to Stevens. (But have we ever been outside him?) And, in fact, he has accompanied you every step of your way. In* Poets of Reality, *it's Stevens who helped you out of nihilism, by showing how the confrontation with nothing can be a supreme victory, since nothing is something: Being (pp. 278–279). And he's also there in every step of your path through deconstruction. From being the poet of grounding in reality, he accompanies you into the vertigo of language and becomes the poet of ungrounding, of groundlessness, of* mise-en-abyme *and abyss. Here, at the end of this series, I want to ask you what I asked Frye at the beginning: what is the quality in Stevens that makes him a companion of so many theoretical critics?*

MILLER: Not de Man. I remember him saying that he'd never been able to figure out Stevens. He obviously didn't like him very much.

SALUSINSZKY: *Neither does Said.*

MILLER: Neither does Said, and though Said and de Man are different kinds of non-Americans, that may be the explanation. That wouldn't explain Kermode, although I think that part of Kermode's problem with Stevens has followed from the fact that he's from the Isle of Man. He talks about Larkin, in his interview, and I think he's right to say that Larkin is hard for a non-Englishman to read. I admire Larkin, but I don't have an immediate rapport with it.

For many of us Americans, the obvious fact about Stevens is that here is a twentieth-century American poet who didn't sell out to England and become an English citizen or do the worse thing that Ezra Pound—who is clearly part of world literature—did. Stevens is very provincial. You read it, and it's terrific: it's like Paul Valéry or Goethe or something, but he worked in Hartford, Connecticut. Therefore, with an easy conscience, I can do two things at once: I can read a local poet, who writes about the thin men of Haddam—which is right up that road, across the Connecticut River—and at the same time know I'm doing something that isn't less important than reading Plato. That may be part of it.

Also, it's clear that he's especially open to academic criticism. My fascination with and admiration for William Carlos Williams is exactly the

reverse: that Williams is so resistant to intellectualizing. He is a very great poet but difficult for somebody trained in abstractions. I can deal with ideas, and the thing itself, and so on—no problem—but what do you say about "The Red Wheelbarrow" or about a poem that just describes a sycamore tree?

SALUSINSZKY: *This particular poem isn't one that you've ever given an extensive reading to, although, interestingly, in* Poets of Reality, *you use it as a kind of motto for the criticism-of-consciousness approach: "The poem is 'not ideas about the thing but the thing itself,' part of the world and not about it" (p. 9). What would you do with the poem now if, for some reason, you had to produce an essay on it?*

MILLER: Since I knew that you were going to ask me this, I've read it a little, which means that if I really gave you an answer it would take another hour and a half. I can perhaps differentiate, a little bit, the reading I would give from the reading that your other distinguished interviewees have given. It struck me as interesting, some of the things that they didn't talk about. One would be the weirdness of the title—a weirdness that I was prepared, in *Poets of Reality*, not to worry too much about: I just appropriated the phrase and did what I wanted with it.

What is it? It's not a complete sentence and just sort of hangs there: "Not Ideas about the Thing but the Thing Itself." It's the label for the poem. Does it name the poem? Is the poem not ideas about the thing but the thing itself? And what would that mean? Or does it name the experience that the poem records, which would be rather different? Or does it simply say, "I wish I could have access to, or write a poem that was, not ideas about the thing but the thing itself"? Is it a kind of wish or a hypothesis? There's obviously no way to know. The poem doesn't give you any support.

Secondly, I would say at this point that the word *thing* is a pretty pregnant word here. Again, it's a little hard to know what he means by "the thing." Does he mean, by "thing," the sun? Does he mean the scrawny cry? In what sense is a scrawny cry a thing? Either to call the sun a thing or to call the scrawny cry a thing doesn't quite seem right. The sun is not something that one normally things of as a thing. I would be inclined to move in the direction of emphasizing that word *it*, which occurs over and over again and which has a clear referent: the scrawny cry. "He knew that he heard *it*, / A bird's cry…" But then it keeps coming back: "*It* was not from the vast ventriloquism / Of sleep's faded papier-mâché…*it* was a chorister…*it* was like…" By the time you've got to the end of those "its," the "it" has detached itself from that cry and has become a kind of name for " the thing itself." I would think that, in fact, "it" could be demonstrated that he's using that word *thing* in its full etymological and historical complexity, as a name for that which is manifested by the rising of the sun.

None of the other interviewees has said that this is a poem about the appearance of something out of hiddenness, out of occultation: the sun, the cry, spring, the earliest ending of winter, and the poet waking up out of sleep, coming into consciousness. Those are all, metaphorically, said to be like one another, and I take it that they're all forms of appearance which are related to the thing itself, whatever that is: some kind of "it." A "thing," in the sense of a gathering together, as in a medieval assemblage of people, a "thing" in the sense of some substratum which is hidden and never appears.

I also found it interesting that nobody took note of another fact about the poem, which is the synesthesia: the way in which a visual thing is expressed in terms of a sound thing. The bird's cry announces the rising of the sun, so that there's a lateral metaphor which says "a chorus," a great lot of people singing a great Bach chorus, the "B Minor Mass," "is like" the appearance of the sun. This will allow me to get in a lick at Harold Bloom: that reminds me not of "our father Walt Whitman," but of Goethe and that great opening of the second part of *Faust* where the sun rises as a great racket, as a loud noise. There is precisely the same displacement from sight to sound, and it clearly has something to do with the unnameability, in literal language, of the appearance of the sun. You can't look the sun in the eye, and you can't name it as such, so instead of naming that, you name this great chorus. Said, with all his knowledge of music, missed what I take the "chorister whose c preceded the choir" to be: that little pitch-pipe noise that you hear in an a cappella choir, the muted, soft, scrawny "c" you hear before the whole noise begins. That figure here is the bird's cry, which announces the appearance of the sun, which is blinding and deafening. That mixture of sense is fundamental to the poem, because it is a lateral displacement that is an expression of the other one, the displacement from this hidden "thing" or "it" to any manifestations or metaphors of it. Hostile as Said is to Stevens, he's got hold of something with that notion of what he calls "tinkliness": so many of Stevens's poems are fragile, evanescent. This is a poem about thresholds, and it says in effect that "it"—the cry that has become all these other things—is a new knowledge of reality just at that threshold moment before the sun rises. That's when you really learn something about reality. Once the sun has risen above the horizon, and the chorus is singing full blast, you're in the ordinary world, where you have only ideas about the thing. The thing itself takes place at that point: the earliest ending of winter.

Also, nobody worried about "panache." I can tell you what a panache is, if you don't know. It's very specific: it means a tuft of feathers, as on a helmet. It's from the Italian *pennacchio*, which is from the Latin *penna*: a feather. Quote the dictionary. Only secondly does it mean flamboyant or flagrant behavior. So that when he says that "The sun is rising at six, / No longer a battered panache above snow," he must have been reading the dictionary. He must mean the sun rising as if it were that tuft of feathers on a helmet. So there is a latent personification of the sun as though it were that giant on the horizon that he talks about in "Primitive Like an Orb." The seeing of the sun as a person is another version of that displacement from sight to sound, in the sense that it's both a revelation—something we can understand—and another covering over, in the sense that prosopopoeia is an inadequate figure. The references that people made to "The Snow Man" seem to me appropriate, because if the "battered panache above snow" is a helmet with a tuft of feathers on it, it's a displacement of that famous snowman. That's all I have to say. You've made me interested in the poem: maybe I'll write about it.

SALUSINSZKY: *Your discussion was so clear that I didn't even feel the need to interrupt. Lastly, a couple of biographical questions. Where did you spend your childhood?*

MILLER: I was born in Virginia. Then, my father was a graduate student at Columbia, and I lived a whole winter on Riverside Drive. I was an academic child, in the sense that I was born while my parents were in graduate school, which put an end to my mother's graduate career. My wife was born in New Haven while her father was a graduate student here, which put an end to *her* mother's career. (As would not necessarily happen now, which is an interesting historical fact.) *Our* first child was born when I was at Harvard, so there's a tradition of that.

I lived first in Lewisburg, Pennsylvania: at Bucknell, where my father was Dean of Men. He got at Ph.D. in psychology under John Dewey. His dissertation was on "The Practice of Public Prayer": it was a pragmatic, Deweyan interpretation of prayer which said that if it works, socially, it's good—never mind whether God answers the prayer. Then I lived in upstate New York, which is where I was really in the boondocks. It was a town of fifty families, and I went to a one-room school. Then high school outside Albany, New York, on to college at Oberlin, in Ohio. Then to Harvard for graduate work, where I learned mostly from the other students. And then my real education began at Johns Hopkins, as a teacher: that was where I was really formed, by Poulet and Wasserman. For all practical purposes, I am still a Hopkins man: my idea of what you do, in our profession, is a Hopkins one, not a Yale or Harvard one.

SALUSINSZKY: *It is a good thing that an Australian is doing these interviews, because it is necessary to be quite without tact, and Australians are naturally gifted in this regard. When I first met you—which was, as it happens, in Australia—I noticed that you do not have the complete use of both arms. The reason I ask you what is the source of that is that it may well have had a determining effect upon making you more bookish as a child.*

MILLER: Unfortunately for your hypothesis, it was later. I was 21 years old, and it was polio: one of the last epidemics. I was married, at graduate school, and in Maine, staying in my wife's family's summer place there. There was a small disease going around the neighborhood, which was polio. I was the only person who got any paralysis from it. I was very lucky that it was only the one arm.

It certainly had an effect on my life. My wife was a tremendous help. She prodded me in the direction I would have gone already, which was an absolute determination to work hard and get ahead in the world. It was something I already had, but it reinforced the feeling that, whatever you do, you ought to do it with your whole heart. You should take it as far as you can go and be damned to the consequences for your ambition.

Really interesting work, in any field, involves crossing frontiers and in a way defying authority. The serious illness at that stage of my life reinforced that. The dissertation I wrote at Harvard was completely un-Harvard. My director, Douglas Bush, detested Burke, primarily because he has a bad style and uses the editorial "we" but also because he was theoretical. I was tolerated there, but writing the dissertation was in no way reinforced by the department which I found myself in. that's also been a feature of my time here at Yale. The thing that frightens me about Yale is that it has institutionalized and accommodated me so well. Everybody has been so nice to me!

SALUSINSZKY: *That brings up my last biographical question. Apart from an obvious desire to be nearer to Australia, what are the* intellectual *reasons for your decision to move to California?*

MILLER: The primary motive was intellectual or professional. It's hard to define both in ways that would be fair to Yale and how it's been to me and at the same time be not *too* nice about Yale. I wouldn't be leaving Yale if I were entirely happy here. One way to define this might be to say that, although the sort of thing I do has been very cordially received here, I have the feeling that we've gone just about as far as we can go at Yale, with deconstruction. It might, in fact, fare better here if these older people were gone. I'm 58, and what I feared about staying was that I would be in a Yale which, over the next twelve years, would be less and less intellectually stimulating for me. Whereas the risks involved in going out to California are unpredictable. I can't tell where my work is going to go, and I feared that staying here it would go on being the same. I have the feeling that if I came back to Yale in ten, twenty, or thirty years it would still be here and still be essentially the same. There's a massive intellectual inertia here that makes it a wonderful university but which also makes it hard to do anything with. Whereas Irvine—ten, or twenty, or thirty years from now—is going to be different. Twenty years ago, it was just a cow pasture; twenty years from now, it may be a cow pasture again. Let's hope that that won't happen—but you see what I'm saying. I also have the feeling that there has already been some displacement of intellectual action to the West Coast.

SALUSINSZKY: *Now that we're at the end of our critical and conversational journey, one in a series of nine which I have presented in* Criticism and Society, *maybe you'd like to offer your comments on the interview project as a whole? Where better to wash up—after a series that has been so concerned with questions of professionalism and the university—than at the feet of the president of the Modern Language Association of America? Who better to award the ribbons to the major prizewinners, to say nothing of the pen-and-ruler sets for the runners-up?*

MILLER: I would say two things about the interviews as a whole. Your enterprise is a political one or a social one, and one of the dangers of the assemblage that you have and some of the things that are said—including by you—would be to give Frye a little too much centrality, as our father. All honor to Frye, but there would be something conservative about that and about saying that everything in American criticism derives from Frye. I don't think that's the case, at least in the sense of saying that Frye's own work now—I'm agreeing with Kermode here—is broadly effective. It has diffused itself. I like Frye as a practical critic, but the grand synthetic stuff, in the *Anatomy of Criticism*, is something I've never been able to read. I like Frye, for example, on Dickens or on Wallace Stevens. But, at least for me, Frye has not had that importance.

The second thing to say, thinking of Bloom, is that, in so far as Bloom's own interview would lend reinforcement to that picture which your interviews tend to give, it is the most amazing piece of misunderstanding. The real precursor for Bloom is T. S. Eliot—anybody can see that. It's not Frye at all. Part of the strategy of his interview is to name it as Frye, because that's an easy person to be obligated to. The real person he was obsessed with at the beginning and continues to be obsessed with is the man he calls "the abominable Eliot." That's a much more interesting history. For all of us, when we were going to graduate school, the really looming figure was T. S. Eliot. If you wanted to make your way, you had to do something different from Eliot. And if you were Bloom, at Yale, how did you do this? You wrote your dissertation on Shelley. A more gentle way of putting this is to say that it's another example of heterogeneity. The actual course of the development of American, English (Kermode), and Canadian (Frye) literary criticism is, in fact, more complicated than a simple scheme that would say, "Here was Northrop Frye, who initiated something, and everybody is a tributary to him."

The final thing to say is that these interviews are already historical, in the sense that the people you've interviewed—including the younger ones, like Barbara Johnson and Frank Lentricchia—are already well established. What interests me, on the other hand, is the young trees that are growing up underneath the established ones. And that's a little less predictable. What's really interesting is the question of what's going to happen next: who those people are, where they are, and what they will use out of all this. I don't see any clear indications about that, beyond the sense that there surely is tremendous strength in that New Historicism *and* tremendous strength in deconstruction.

SALUSINSZKY: *The emphasis on Frye may be to some degree a result of my own obsession—but then, in your company there is no need to apologize for imposing one's little, marginal obsession on the world. Actually, if there's a peculiarity in your work in the 1960s, I find—from the point of view of this obsession—that you are straining not to quote from Frye. What's that all about?*

MILLER: I've given you one answer to it, which is that I didn't find the paradigmatic side of Frye attractive, so I resisted it, for better or for worse, much more than I would have resisted Eliot. I don't know why that is.

I think that the interview with Frye is a wonderful interview. Others have pointed to the wit and the irony. We were together in the abortive enterprise of trying to produce a rival to the *Norton Anthology* for a number of years, so I would see Frye fairly often. He was absolutely wonderful. I remember he looked down at his shoes at one point and said, "Yes, we'll really sell *big* in Texas!"

As for my resistance to Frye, I needed to make space for something else. One of the reasons for my reservations was in no way Frye's fault. I have been for a long time an editor of *ELH*, and there was a period during the tremendous influence of Frye when every manuscript that I opened up said, "You will notice that I am using the categories of Northrop Frye." I'm sure that Norrie was not all that happy about it either, this feeling that you got a long way just by adopting that seasonal pattern and the various generic categories. That side of Frye didn't seem to me to facilitate reading of the quality that Frye himself performs.

Until Kermode, I would say that, if somebody said "You must spend the next month reading Northrop Frye," I would be much more interested in reading the books which simply work out the implications for *actual* readings—of Shakespeare or whomever—of the presuppositions that came in the great revelation. The insights in these readings are related to Frye the systematizer, but not predictable. That has always seemed to me a good example of an important disjunction. You can read Georges Poulet and figure out what it is that you're supposed to talk about and look for, but that is not going to make it possible to write an essay anything like as good as any of Poulet's. You can read Derrida from one end to the other, but try to do what he does! What either critic sees in the works they read is not predictable from the schemas that you would work out on the basis of asking "What's archetypal criticism?" or "What's deconstruction?" That's one of the reasons that it's a mistake to try to do criticism on the basis of answers to such questions.

Notes

[1] *The Golden Bowl* (London: Macmillan, [1905] 1923), p. xxviii.
[2] CNN = Cable News Network; CBN = Christian Broadcasting Network.

2

Rhetoric, Cultural Studies, and the Future of Critical Theory

Interview with Gary A. Olson

GARY A. OLSON: *You've written about a dozen books and over one hundred articles on a multitude of literary figures and theoretical concerns. Do you consider yourself a writer?*

J. HILLIS MILLER: I never thought of myself as a writer, though, like a lot of teachers of literature, I had the idea when I was a teenager that I was going to write poetry or novels or something but soon found I had no aptitude for that at all. My writing is an adjunct to teaching. Though it's something I do seriously, I think *writer* is too big a word for what I do.

OLSON: *Would you describe your writing process?*

MILLER: The computer transformed my life. There was a period a long time ago when I wrote on a typewriter and then revised with pen, writing things up and down the margins and on the backs of the pages. Then there was a long period, essentially while I was at Yale, when I wrote longhand in notebooks. That allowed me to revise on the page and on the back of the page. (If you were to see those notebooks, you'd find them totally illegible.) Then I would read the manuscript onto a tape, it would be typed by a secretary, then I would revise it, and it would have to be typed again. With a computer, I shortcut all those procedures. I write a draft on the computer (I use a Macintosh) and revise it myself on the computer very extensively, both as I go along and later on when I come back to it. These revisions are "extensive" in that they're changes in individual sentences: cutting long sentences into two or three short sentences, rearranging phrases, moving them around, and so on. The computer has made my revision process longer and more complicated than it was because I'm not inhibited by the necessity of having it typed over again. Of course, all those stages of revision are completely lost; there's no trace of the earlier stages.

OLSON: *Clifford Geertz mentioned in JAC that Kenneth Burke was a great influence on him intellectually, and you often mention Burke, saying that he was one of the "distinguished native grandsires or at least great-uncles" of deconstruction. Was Burke an important influence on you personally? And what is your assessment of Burke's contribution?*

MILLER: Yes, Burke was an important influence on me early. When I was in graduate school, I went to Harvard, where theoretical writings were considered to be a waste of time or worse; I somehow found myself interested in theory. I read Burke, William Empson, I.A. Richards, G. Wilson Knight, and all on my own; nobody was teaching those people. I can no longer quite remember how I heard about them. Burke gave one lecture at Harvard, but I'm sure I knew about him before that. I must somehow have been steered in the direction of Burke. My dissertation, which was never published, is very Burkean; it was deeply influenced by Burke. The idea of dramatic action, the notion that a work of literature is a strategy to deal with a situation so that it makes a kind of movement and attempts to move the writer or reader from one place to another, the notion that there's a lot going on under the surface of the language that you can trace in one way or another through implications of the language that are figurative but not just figurative (that is, a tracing that goes beyond simply looking at metaphors or whatever)—all of that I learned first from Burke. I still immensely admire him, and I think he is a major theorist and critic. As I've often said, "If you have Kenneth Burke and can read him wisely, you don't need the French." For me, Burke is still the wisest and subtlest and most intelligent Freudian critic and Marxist critic of his time, certainly among the Americans. At a time when neither Freud nor Marx was being read very intelligently by American academics who claimed to be Marxists or Freudians, Burke was able to read and make use of them in ways that were very productive. And Burke's general conviction that literature ought to matter to individual human life or to society is something I believed in then and still believe in now. So, Mr. Burke is one of my heroes. I was very pleased not too many years ago (I guess he was eighty-nine at that point) to be invited to a celebration of Burke at Seton Hall University in New Jersey, and I got to meet him again, though I know him a little bit also in that we've corresponded. For me he's very important, but it's no secret that he's very important generally in many different fields. It didn't surprise me to hear that Clifford Geertz was deeply influenced by Burke because Burke's had a big influence in the social sciences.

Let me add that Burke is very difficult to appropriate or to teach. I've never really tried to teach him. For example, say someone asks, "You say Kenneth Burke is wonderful. What should I read by Burke?" It's very hard to answer that question, to say, "Here is a representative essay." That makes him different from, let's say, Derrida. You can say, "Here are representative examples of Derrida, and you can really learn something about Derrida's assumptions and procedures by reading these three or four or five essays." Burke is not so simple. You have to say, "Well, you've got to read four or five books by Burke before you begin to get the hang of it." That's curious. I'm not quite sure why that is. There are no essays by Burke that you would call landmark essays on particular authors. There are very interesting essays on Keats, let's say, or one that I immensely admire on Hawthorne's Ethan Brand, but you wouldn't call them masterpieces of literary criticism. They're very provocative, so that you say, "Well, if Burke can do this, I would like to see whether I could do it over here." That's a little different from saying, "What's William Empson about? Read *Seven Types of Ambiguity* or *The Structure of Complex Words* and you'll see." I've never quite been able to figure out why that is with Burke. His essays are all wonderfully inventive, provocative, and suggestive. And they're likely to go off in all directions, so there'd be something in there for the social scientist, something for the psychologist, something for the literary critic.

OLSON: *In "The Function of Rhetorical Study at the Present Time," you discuss the discipline of rhetoric and composition, saying it has accumulated "an impressive body of theoretical, empirical, and statistical work." You write, "People involved at the frontier of this exciting new branch of the broader discipline of English language and literature have the air of persons doing something justifiable and good, while teachers of literature sometimes seem to me to have a furtive and guilty air, as though they were doing something not altogether justifiable in the present context." What role do you see this field playing in the English department of the next decade and beyond?*

MILLER: I'm inclined to agree to some degree with Stanley Fish when he says in the *JAC* interview that the English department as we knew it is undergoing changes and that he's surprised it's still as much like it used to be as it is. These changes take a while, but I think they really have begun to occur. They certainly have in my department at Irvine. The examination given to Ph.D. candidates these days is radically different, not only because philosophy and theory overtly get into the examination but also because works by women and so-called minority writers are now a regular part of the curriculum, and people are examined on it for their Ph.D. So it's really a different department, and I think the role of composition in such a department will also be different. A lot of the changes in composition have gone along with those changes and will reinforce them in one way or another. That joke about the furtive air of the teachers of literature was meant to refer to the fact that whatever admiration we have for literature, you would have to say that it plays a smaller role in the intellectual and personal life of most Americans than it used to, even among graduate students, whereas the need to be able to write clearly and effectively for a given purpose is going to remain. There's going to be a need to teach composition well in any conceivable university. So, composition is more secure.

The other thing I meant was that among the people I know in composition there is a real excitement about the methodological and theoretical aspects of the discipline. There's something really going on there that's not unrelated to these changes in the makeup of English departments. So, I think composition in particular is going to be there. And something that will be even more important than ever before as we begin to enroll (at Duke and my university, for example) more and more people for whom English is a second language is ESL instruction. I see ESL as a frontier of composition. I know they're often thought of as separate operations; they certainly are at my university, but they seem to me really part of the same thing. One of the criticisms I would make of my own composition group, at least in the theoretical way it's set up, is that there's ESL over here and composition over there, each run by different people. It seems to me that ESL is a large part of the challenge in teaching English composition at a place like Irvine, where forty percent of the undergraduates are Asian American and very large numbers of them have English as a second language; the two problems don't seem to me separable. It's not that people who have English as a first language cannot be very bad writers—they often are—but that if you have a mixed university population like ours some very large part of the problems is ESL problems. I would see combining composition and ESL as a very interesting and challenging thing to do. Irvine is a wonderful laboratory for studying composition and ESL because there's such a mix of people in the undergraduate population. You hear five or six different languages just in crossing the campus. You hear Japanese, Chinese, Korean, Thai, Cambodian, all spoken by the students. Some of my colleagues and some of the administrators tend to say, "This problem is going to go away. We don't have to put a lot of money into ESL." It's not going to go away. It's a problem all right, but a very exciting intellectual problem, not an insuperable kind of obstacle to making people able to write.

OLSON: *You argue in many places, including "Stevens' Rock and Criticism as Cure, II," that the future of literary criticism "involves a return to the explicit study of rhetoric." You define rhetoric as "the investigation of figures of speech rather than the study of the art of persuasion, though the notion of persuasion is still present." Stanley Fish recently commented in the JAC interview you just mentioned that eventually "the English department in which we were all educated would be a thing of the past, a museum piece" and that given recent developments "it might be just as accurate to call the department 'the department of rhetoric,' with a new understanding of the old scope of the subject and province of rhetoric." Do you agree, then, that the future of both literary criticism and the English department itself lies in rhetoric?*

MILLER: I wouldn't be prepared to go quite that far because I think departments of English (or, like my department, departments of English and comparative literature) also have other obligations that could only with difficulty be put under the rubric of rhetoric obligations such as the teaching of literary history. I'm prepared to say that that's part of rhetoric, but it's obviously stretching it a little bit. And there's the obligation to teach an understanding of ethnic communities within the larger community, the teaching of women's literature, African American literature, Native American literature. To call this rhetoric might unnecessarily limit it. Nevertheless, for me all of those things—women's literature, African American literature, Native American literature, Hispanic and all ethnic literatures—are best taught by reading, not by generalizations about history or the study of sociology of those peoples (though that has to be done) but, in an English department or a department of English and comparative literature, by reading texts by those people. That's where rhetoric, a rhetorical approach, is necessary. As I've said before, there's a kind of link between "highfalutin" literary theory, which appears to have nothing to do with composition in one direction and composition theory in the other. They often come together, and so there's often a natural alliance in departments between the young people who do literary theory, who are Lacanians or Derrideans or whatever, and the people who are doing composition theory, and there ought to be a kind of bridge between them, an alliance or coalition. I see that as something a good department would want to enhance. It's one of the reasons why I would be very anxious about separating composition from literature departments in universities. I know this is an issue; it's certainly one that we discussed at length recently at Irvine. I've been on a task force committee to discuss the status of the composition program at Irvine, and one of the issues that came up (it almost always does) was the question of whether composition ought to be taken away from the English department and given to some dean, made a cross-school program that was as much the responsibility of the scientists and social scientists as of the humanists. The English department, when they were presented with this possibility—and I was interested in having people consider it—reacted very powerfully and expectedly. They said, "No, no. We can't do this," partly because they do consider teaching composition their responsibility but also, I think, because they were appalled at the thought of losing all those graduate fellowships. But I think, on principled reasons, composition ought to stay in English departments, not to help composition but to help the English departments. It's good for them to have the composition people.

OLSON: *You've made this very point in several forums, including "Composition and Decomposition" and "On Edge." You note that "independent departments or programs in composition are beginning to overshadow the adjacent departments of English literature in size, strength, and funding," and you make an urgent plea that rhetoric and composition not break away from English. Given the utter contempt that many within traditional English department power structures feel for the new discipline, as well as their reluctance to improve the material conditions under which many of us work, why should we take this plea seriously?*

MILLER: One answer would be a pragmatic one: to recognize the losses that would probably follow for composition were it separated. It might turn out to be even weaker from the point of view of having clout with the administration, getting money, and so on; it might not, but you would have to make a careful calculation about that. It's a little hard to tell. In other words, composition does gain something from having the strong budgetary support of an English department. That's certainly true at Irvine. On the other hand, we've had conversations about just how this budgetary relationship ought to work. If you had a situation in which the English department chair could move money around, taking it from composition to use, let's say, for other kinds of graduate support or even for other things, I'd be uneasy if I were in composition. We've been talking about the need to have a stated separate budget for composition within the English department to secure the support for composition.

The other thing to say is that in spite of that hostility, I think people in composition with the help of those people like me and my colleague Steve Mailloux (and various other people in my department at Irvine, to speak of that context) do patiently go on trying to explain to the people who have that hostility that they're wrong. I think much is to be gained by that. My own university is an example of how gradually that works. When I first went to Irvine, there were many more of my colleagues who were prepared to say it would be really good if we could get out of composition and who had this contempt for the research in writing that goes on in the field. That voice has gradually faded a little bit because we had a committee that evaluated the program, and the committee was composed of respectable people who strongly argued the other. I strongly argued the other, and we now have Mailloux there as a result of that. We now, believe it or not, have funding for a tenured person in composition (which has never been the case), another appointment of somebody in the department. I think the program in composition is going to be better for that, better than it would have been had it cut itself off and had that hostility allowed itself to get institutionalized. I think that might be the case in other places. It's a battle that goes on needing to be fought.

OLSON: *In "Composition and Decomposition," you insist repeatedly that "reading is itself a kind of writing, or writing is a trope for the act of reading," concluding that "we must make sure we base our rhetoric as reading on the deepest possible knowledge of what good reading would be." How do you respond to those critics who claim that while this may be true enough in the deconstructive sense, it nonetheless is used as a rationale by those in positions of power within English to appropriate the new re-emergent discipline of rhetoric and composition, to resubsume it under English as reading?*

MILLER: That's a good question. That academic/political fact doesn't really change the fact that reading and writing are closely related. The problem is to figure out an institutional way to avoid the danger you mention, and the way, it seems to me, is easy enough to see: you persuade the rest of the English department that it's their responsibility to teach reading. You can't say that composition and reading go together over here and we're doing something else over there. It's got to be an across-the-board understanding that the teaching of reading is the major responsibility of the English department as a whole, say rhetoric generally, and it then has a kind of easy transition to teaching which is primarily oriented toward composition. So the composition people have got to depend to some degree on the people in the English department and other language departments to do some, if not most, of the teaching of reading. But the theoretical point I was making (if you want to call it theoretical) is absolutely true: that students taking beginning composition who can't write are also probably unable to read well, and you could demonstrate that; you can do all the teaching of writing you want, but if they haven't somehow learned to read, it's not going to stick. So the composition people have a big stake in making sure that somebody is teaching college students how to read in its broadest sense. Insofar as that's a rhetorical skill, it goes along with Stanley's suggestion that they ought to be called departments of rhetoric.

OLSON: *In one of your president's columns in the 1986* MLA Newsletter, *you argue that "teaching is not primarily an interpersonal transaction oriented toward an interchange between teacher and students. The teacher is, rather, oriented primarily toward the text, primarily responsible to that, obligated in what he or she says to that....Students are not so much partners in an intersubjective relation as the witnesses or overhearers of an activity of reading that is the teacher's interaction with the text at hand." Many teachers interested in liberatory learning or radical pedagogy would sharply disagree with this characterization. They would argue that good teaching is first and always an intensely interpersonal, intersubjective transaction. (You may have read Jane Tompkins's "Pedagogy of the Distressed.") What are your thoughts about radical pedagogy?*

MILLER: I don't know very much about it in detail, but I know what it is. The statement you cited was meant to be deliberately provocative, but that doesn't mean I didn't mean it. I think the danger I see in libertarian pedagogy is that it will free the teacher from one of the teacher's major responsibilities: the obligation to display a way to do something. If you have a class in which the students all say what they want and the teacher just facilitates this, that display is missing, and that seems to me too bad. By the way, there's nothing new about it. I was told that Yale graduate teaching traditionally (before I went there, but in recent memory) consisted of the professor the great William Wimsatt, let's say, or whoever was sitting at the end of the table each week assigning little papers that students prepared from an assigned topic and read in class. Wimsatt didn't have to say anything, and I think that's wrong. I don't see these approaches as absolutely incompatible, but I have some sympathy with Stanley Fish's answer in *JAC* to a similar question: on the one hand, I see this as an important new direction in teaching; I understand the psychological and political reasons for it, and I'm sure it works. Nevertheless, I think there's still room for the other kind of teaching, not because the teacher is necessarily going to be showing the "right" way to do something, but because the teacher has a kind of responsibility to show how he or she does it. You don't teach a beginning carpenter how to build a building by just saying, "Let's all just get together and see if we can learn to drive nails." What you do is drive some nails, and then you let the person try it, and then you say, "Well, you haven't got the hang of it quite yet." On the one hand, the example of the master carpenter is a fundamental part of the instruction; on the other hand, the apprentice carpenter would never learn how to do it without doing it him- or herself, and I think that combination is what's needed.

OLSON: *I think what the liberatory learning person would say is that in the old model you have the master carpenter simply performing as an example and saying, "Follow my example." In the more libertarian model, the students have the opportunity to help shape their own pedagogy, and yes, the instructor may very well say, "Okay, we're learning to drive nails today. Try your hand at it. See what you can do and let's work at it from there." The objectives are the same, but the methodologies are different. It's asking students to participate in their own education and to try something right from the beginning rather than simply to mimic someone else.*

MILLER: You might do that with the driving of nails, but you might have to intervene after a while. I worked one summer years ago as a carpenter's helper, and I was taught both ways. First, they taught me how to wheel a wheelbarrow full of cement by saying, "Wheel this over there." I dumped it over, and everybody stood around and laughed. Then they gave me a few pointers, like you've got to keep it absolutely level because a wheelbarrow full of wet cement is pretty heavy and once the weight begins to shift it will turn right over. So I think it was a combination of those two. The other wisdom (I don't have any great wisdom about this) is that in my experience in visiting classes of beginning teachers I've noticed that there's a wide variety of teaching methods that work, and it is a deeply personal thing. Also, teaching has ideological and institutional determinants; that is, you teach in a way you've learned that you ought to. I think this move toward radical pedagogy is not an insignificant one, and I might also report that I've begun a little more to experiment with something like it in my own teaching just this year.

OLSON: *Long ago you renounced your allegiance to phenomenological criticism and the Geneva School with its emphasis on literature as a form of consciousness. Will there be any role for phenomenological principles in our poststructuralist criticism, or will phenomenology simply be relegated to the status of a historical curiosity?*

MILLER: The debt of poststructural criticism to phenomenology, often obscure and devious, is so great that certain aspects of phenomenology are perpetuated already in poststructuralist criticism. Therefore, anybody who is seriously interested in understanding Derrida, just to take one example, sooner or later would have to make a serious study not only of Heidegger, which is obvious enough, but also of Husserl. There are certain aspects of Derrida that remain faithful to some Husserlian assumptions. I've learned this just recently from recent work of Derrida that alludes back to Husserl in a way that's quite surprising because you'd think that Husserl was so far behind him and that the early work was so critical of Husserl that there would be no way that you could speak of Derrida as in any way consequent from phenomenology. That's not true. We have to go not by way of the superficial principles of so-called phenomenological criticism, like the "primacy of the self," and so on—those have been put in question. There are deeper, you might even say "technical," remains very much there. It's most evident in the indebtedness to Heidegger. I was interested to see Stanley Fish asserting the influence on him of Heidegger by way of Hubert Dreyfus's teaching. If you wanted to define Derrida's "field" as a philosopher, Heidegger is the author he keeps coming back to again and again, much more than Hegel, much more than Husserl. In the little essay he wrote when he was being examined for his doctorate, he makes a survey of his intellectual history in which he says, "The question of what is literature was an initial problem for me perhaps even more important than the question of philosophy." The question of what is literature was a Husserlian question. Derrida was on record to be writing a dissertation on the ideality of the literary object, and in some sense, you could say that's been his topic all along. So this question has a great deal of import and complexity.

OLSON: *In your well-publicized debate with D.A. Miller in* ADE Bulletin, *you state that perhaps the enterprise of the new historicists is threatened by* *deconstruction. Would you elaborate on what is problematic about the new historicist project and why deconstruction should be a threat to it?*

MILLER: I don't think it needs to be. There's an obvious tension between the apparent focus of the new historicism on the historical context of works of literature and the sort of intrinsic reading that one associates with deconstruction. On the other hand, it's easy to exaggerate those differences. The new historicists are or ought to be interested in the reading of literary works as much as in the context, and deconstructionists have always been interested in history and historical context. So it's a difference of emphasis. I saw a good bit of Stephen Greenblatt about a month ago at Dartmouth's School of Criticism and Theory; we had a conversation about this, and Greenblatt said something that really sticks in my mind: "For me the end point of all I do is the reading of works of literature, Shakespeare especially." There's a kind of statement of allegiance there, and I would agree with Greenblatt on that. So, I think what I meant when I said I would no longer put it quite the same way is that it may be that some of the new historicists take a little too much for granted the link between history and the literary work and that for deconstructionists that relation is extremely problematic and needs itself to be reflected on. Insofar as deconstruction would inhibit the taking for granted that once you've established the historical context you have an explanation of the work, then deconstruction would be threatening to the new historicists' project. But that would certainly not include Stephen Greenblatt or most of the other really sophisticated new historicists. Nevertheless, there's a difference, and the difference appears to me to be the genuine fascination that somebody like Greenblatt has with the historical context itself. He was teaching a seminar at the Dartmouth School of Criticism and Theory this year on witchcraft, and he is really fascinated by those "nonliterary" texts that formed the background of Shakespeare and others. Nevertheless, for him, the end point is not the historical documents and understanding them, but Shakespeare. Moreover, Greenblatt would agree with my predisposition, which would be to say that these so-called historical documents should be read just as carefully and with just as much intelligence and imagination as you would read Shakespeare, and they're going to turn out to be interesting from that point of view. So I'm now changing a little from what I said earlier, not only saying that new historicism really owes a tremendous amount to linguistically-based procedures like deconstruction but that we can now learn a lot from them and that there needn't be any insuperable crevasse between the new historicists and the so-called deconstructionists.

OLSON: *Some theorists in both rhetoric and literary criticism have argued that the sophists were the philosophical precursors to deconstructionists or that they were themselves deconstructionists. For example, Howard Felperin writes that "the search for the founder or originator of the discourse of deconstruction" leads to Gorgias and the pre-Socratics: "The first work of thoroughgoing (what I shall later term 'hard-core') deconstruction to come down to us, so striking in its wholesale anticipation of the contemporary project as to demand reconsideration of the cultural and philosophical context that could have conditioned it, is the fifth-century BC treatise* On Not-Being, *or* On Nature *by Gorgias, the argument of which was summarized by Sextus Empiricus: 'Firstly...nothing exists; secondly...even if anything exists, it is inapprehensible by man; thirdly...even if anything is apprehensible, yet of a surety it is inexpressible and incommunicable to one's neighbour.'" Do you agree that the sophists were deconstruction's forbears?*

MILLER: That's Felpie's own winning way of putting things. He was a colleague of mine at Yale and a friend. I don't think he's got it right. I don't think that passage characterizes deconstruction at all. He's accepting there, for no doubt his own purposes, a rather public notion about deconstruction that doesn't correspond very well to what it is. So, I would disagree with that way of talking about it. On the other hand, the relationship of the so-called deconstructionists to the sophists is a complicated one. There's no doubt that certain aspects of sophistic thinking do anticipate deconstruction a bit. It would take a bit more working out than Felperin does in that particular statement. I would put it a slightly different way: Plato not only gives us a good bit of what we know about the sophists in the dialogue called the *Sophist*, but Plato is a kind of lesson himself in the inextricable relationship between, let's say, foundationalist and deconstructionist thinking. In other words, Plato's dialogues are for me absolutely fascinating because they contain both of those directions in themselves, not just in the *Sophist* but in a dialogue like the *Protagoras*. I would be more willing to say that Plato is the founder of deconstruction than to say the sophists were, partly because we know relatively little about them; we only know about the sophists primarily what the people on the other side have allowed us to learn about them. Moreover, the pre-Socratics and the sophists are not at all the same. The relationship of the pre-Socratics to modern thought is very complicated. There's a brilliant young scholar at the University of Colorado, a student of mine from Yale named Paul Gordon, who has written a book about rhetoric that goes back to the sophists (he knows Greek) and all the way up to Nietzsche; this book is in a way really about that complicated continuity.

OLSON: *Does he support the lineage?*

MILLER: In the sense of a very twisted and circuitous lineage. It's not an unintelligent question to ask if there's a connection, but the answer is a complicated one, and it's not correct to say, "Deconstructionists are like the sophists because the sophists said you can't know anything and everything is based on nothing and it's all language." That bears no relation to what deconstructionists say. That's what I meant when I said I would rather say Plato is the father of deconstruction for the kind of paradoxical sound that has; nevertheless, one can learn a great deal from Plato about how to read. It's not a matter of saying that you can read Plato deconstructively but of saying that he himself read that way. It's not an accident that one of Derrida's early fundamental essays is "La Pharmacie de Platon," which is not a deconstruction of Plato but a demonstration of the complexity in Plato's dialogue. One thing that annoys me is the easy reference to Plato as though he were the foundation of Western values. Go back and read Plato and you'll see that he's not what you've been led to expect. Just as Felperin's definition of deconstruction does not correspond to deconstruction, neither does the characterization of Plato as a set of ideas about the one and the good correspond to what's really in Plato when you sit down and try to read his dialogues.

OLSON: *In* Theory Now and Then, *you talk about the "negotiations between deconstructionisms and the almost universal turn in the 1980s to forms of literary study oriented toward society, toward history, toward ethical questions and questions of institutional organization, toward questions of race, class, and gender." You go on to say, "Though some of these cultural and historical critics have been unable to recognize the fact, their work would have been impossible without 'deconstructionisms.'...These recent forms of 'cultural critique' are more the continuation of deconstruction than its cancellation." We've already discussed the tension between deconstruction and new historicism. What accounts for the tension between deconstruction and those critical approaches oriented toward culture and society? And in what way is cultural critique a "continuation" of deconstruction?*

MILLER: I think the tension is to be expected when you have a younger generation that needs to think of itself as doing something new, something that's different from what people that came before did; nevertheless, there really are differences, and they shouldn't be minimized. I think the connection lies (often these younger critics are not aware of these similarities) both in the political dimension of cultural criticism and of deconstruction (they are only apparently opposed to one another in this area) and also in assumptions about what you'd call in a broad sense "reading" or "interpretation." First, I think that cultural criticism like deconstruction assumes that quite a lot is at stake in the choice of what you study in a course, in what you write about, and in how you do it; so there is a political dimension, a social dimension. Both approaches see the need to intervene in the institution, the university, and make changes in it, not by changing the committee system and so on, but by changing what's actually taught in the classroom. They're alike in that way, and I think they've both succeeded. That is, what is actually taught now is to a considerable degree different, but they agree in seeing the teaching and writing about literature and culture as being an active intervention that goes by way of changing the university. That's why people who want things to remain the same are right to see this as threatening. As a matter of fact, I think those people who see cultural criticism as something assimilable, who say, "Well, this is really something we can make use of," are probably underestimating the degree to which it will change the university. The ease with which departments of ethnic studies and departments of African-American studies have been generated in universities suggests to me that some administrators are probably underestimating the power it will have to make things different, just as they probably see deconstruction as just another mode of literary study that won't in the long run make much difference. The other way in which they are similar and one inherits the other is an understanding that the way you make these changes is not by abstract political pronouncements but by the active work of reading or teaching something. Both deconstruction and cultural criticism would agree on that sense of how you do it, which is to say, and it sounds paradoxical, there's an antitheoretical bias in both of them: both of them see theory itself, abstract theory, as being relatively ineffective. It's like the passage in *As I Lay Dying*: language goes off like smoke and doing goes along the ground. Reading or interpretation of works and passing them on to other people as read is where the real work is effected. Using a speech act distinction, you might distinguish then between theory as being at least apparently knowledge that is constative, simply giving knowledge that's what the word sounds like it ought to mean and reading as being performative, as really making something happen. I think the two approaches are in agreement on that, but maybe part of the reason why there is some tension and hostility between them is that the directions they want to go in are not necessarily the same or they have to be adjudicated. You can't be sure that just because somebody is a deconstructionist that he or she is going to care about African-American literature, so the relationship, let's say between theory in African-American literature and deconstruction, is an uneasy one. One knows about these debates: theory is white, elitist, Eurocentric, and if we use it, we're going to be betraying cultural identity; at the same time, there's a recognition that these are the best instruments around for doing what we want to do, so we have to transform them rather than repudiate them.

One of the things that interests me is the question of the transformation of theory when it moves from one domain into another, both within the academy and also from one country to another. I've been involved with the translation of Western theory into various languages, especially Chinese. A colleague at the Chinese Academy of Social Sciences, Fengzhen Wang, and I are coeditors of a very ambitious program of translation of Western theory into Chinese for publication in the People's Republic of China. Although Tiananmen Square slowed us down a bit, the project hasn't, to my surprise, been stopped. The idea is ultimately to have as many as fifty volumes (initially about twelve or fourteen) containing ten or twelve essays each, essays by Stanley Fish, Harold Bloom, Georges Poulet, Fred Jameson, and so on translated into Chinese by good translators. Ask yourself what will happen in mainland China when they read Stanley Fish or Fred Jameson or me or Geoffrey Hartman or Harold Bloom. You can be certain that they will be transformed, that they will be assimilated and used for different purposes, that they will have an effect, but an effect that's unpredictable. In the same way, you can say that though deconstruction was not developed for the use it might be to people doing cultural criticism, it nevertheless will have a use there. Edward Said's work will be included in our series. Said has written a new essay (I don't know whether it's been published yet) which he gave as a lecture at Irvine last year, a follow-up on the traveling theory lecture. In this essay, he talks about the influence, according to him, of Lukács's *History and Class Consciousness* on Fanon, the African writer. He makes a double point. On the one hand, Lukács didn't write *History and Class Consciousness* with any idea that it would be useful to somebody in Algeria in aiding the liberation of Algeria. On the other hand, it could be used by Fanon to aid that and to aid his thinking in writing what according to Said is his most important book, *The Wretched of the Earth*. But that could only happen if Fanon did something to Lukács; Lukács is not any longer the same. I think that's the general way to think of theory as being useful, even in a personal way. What I made of Kenneth Burke was something that involved transforming Burke in order to write a dissertation about Charles Dickens. Burke had no idea of helping me do that, and it involved certain changes. This is illustrative of the usefulness of theory. That's the objection I have to teaching theory as simply a set of postulates or ideas that you learn and pass an examination on. Theory is of no use unless it's used for something, and using it means changing it.

OLSON: *In discussing how you yourself have used theory, William Cain writes, "Miller over-rates the degree of innovation that his theory introduces into literary studies, and he fails to perceive the conservative impulses that keep its subversive forces in check. He believes that he is drawing on Jacques Derrida and translating this French theorist's 'deconstructive' program for an American audience, and this is certainly true up to a point. But Miller safeguards and hedges in the 'radical' theory that he presents, so much so that to connect him with Derrida comes to feel inaccurate and misleading." What is your response to this oft-repeated charge?*

MILLER: What I've done with Derrida and other Europeans is an example of what I was talking about: it's a transformation, just as I transformed Burke. There's no doubt that that transformation has been an assimilation into my own American concerns and interests. It would be quite true to say that there are certain issues that are very important to Derrida that are not so important to me, even though I share with Derrida an interest in both Husserl and Heidegger. (Heidegger has always been very interesting to me.) It's a little difficult to answer that question because it's hard for me to get outside myself, but I'd be perfectly willing to admit that my concerns have always been somehow presupposing that literature was a good thing to study, that it could have a positive effect. Derrida, I think, would agree with me on that. A much more uneasy area for me now is to try to think of my relation to Paul de Man on this subject. I have the feeling that I differ more from de Man than from Derrida. There are many places in Derrida, particularly recently, where he, like me, wants to use deconstructive thinking as a way to imagine the possible movement toward a better form of democracy. That aspect of Derrida I find fascinating and much more positive than the normal picture of Derrida as destroying the Western tradition. And that I find much more akin to my thinking. I've only recently begun to realize that there are certain statements of de Man that influenced me greatly but that are very dark; he speaks of the impossibility of reading, of the impossibility of foreseeing what the performative effect will be of what you do, of wanting to shift the notion of responsibility away entirely and say, "What happens happens; it's all a linguistic matter." I find in myself some resistance to that. I feel a little uneasy about it because I have so much respect for the rigor of de Man's thinking, but I draw some comfort from the fact that I think that

that's Derrida's direction too. But I would make no claim to having carried all of Derrida over, to be a Derrida purist, nor would I in any way deny that my use of Derrida has been determined and limited by things like the American New Criticism. This is often said. Nevertheless, there are certain principles of the New Criticism that I think my own work is not consonant with, for example, the valuing of organic unity and the political conservatism of the New Critics, which I've always been uneasy about. I would be happy if one would say, "That's the New Criticism all right, but for Miller it was Empson and Burke rather than Brooks and Warren." Long before I'd read any Derrida at all, I had made that choice; that is, the Anglo-Americans that I was spontaneously attracted to were Empson and Richards and Burke and "wild man" G. Wilson Knight. By the way, I was emphasizing the differences among the Yale Critics; that's something I would share with Harold Bloom, for whom G. Wilson Knight and Burke were also very important, though probably not Empson so much. (I found Empson terrific and I still do; he's just wonderful.)

OLSON: *In discussing the future of deconstruction, you've said that now that poststructuralist modes of criticism have been assimilated into college and university curricula, the danger is "that deconstruction might petrify, harden into dogma, or into a rigid set of prescriptions for reading, become some kind of fixed method rather than a set of examples, very different from one another, of good reading." Some believe this is already occurring. Do you agree?*

MILLER: Since I said that, things have changed quite a lot, at least at my university, so that it would be hard to find a dyed-in-the-wool narrow deconstructionist who said, "All I do is derived directly from those people." I think the danger I saw has to a considerable degree been bypassed because now the challenges are to do things that are so different like cultural studies and so on that if you're going to do them at all, a good bit of nimbleness is required; that will keep deconstruction from being petrified in any particular person, and I think that's all to the good. It's been transformed and assimilated. I don't see it any longer as the danger (what did happen with Northrop Frye or New Criticism or F. R. Leavis in Australia and other places) of a whole set of people entrenched in departments who are teaching the dogma of deconstruction year after year. It certainly is not happening in my university. People read Derrida or de Man but in connection with a lot of other things, and I don't think there's as much danger of reducing it to a set of recipes as I once thought, certainly not in the students that I see.

OLSON: *You've said that Edward Said's* Beginnings *is "a major work of creative humanistic scholarship, a splendid demonstration of the way it might be possible, after all, to go 'beyond deconstruction,' though without wholly forgetting its insights." What do you predict will be the future of criticism beyond deconstruction?*

MILLER: Well, I think it's already happening. I think we're already seeing something that's beyond deconstruction in any kind of narrow sense of a codified dogma; it's been assimilated and transformed, "translated." I happen to feel very positive about the direction cultural studies has now taken and the move in that direction. That's obviously where we're going. The first half of my *Illustration* book is an attempt to talk about cultural studies. I have various things to say about it. Why has this happened? I think one answer would be that especially the young people teaching literature now are anxious to make what they do have some importance in our society, so they've begun to think about how that might happen. Secondly, they are the first generation of people, now taking over departments of English, who were brought up on the mass media, who've been watching television since they were small children and going to the movies and listening to popular music; it's quite natural that they should be interested in this, to try to understand it and figure out ways to talk about it. I see this not only as natural but as all to the good. I live in the city of Irvine, which is essentially an upper middle-class part of Orange County, and someone did a little questionnaire in the grade schools (I think among first graders or kindergarten kids) and found that there's something like twenty-six different languages spoken at home—not just five or six but twenty-six different languages. Well, if you live in a culture like that, it's natural that you're going to take an interest in some of these other than purely Anglo-Saxon American cultures as they are active in the United States. So I see this ethnic multiculturalism as natural and good. And as the various forms of communication around the world make it much more difficult to forget that there's an Africa, an India, the Far East, and so on, it's natural that we should begin to think in terms of global history questions, such as Francophone African literature being part of French literature generally. I have certain anxieties about this subject, but I've also got some answers. We were talking about "department of rhetoric" as a name; my feeling as a "comparative literature imperialist" is that what should happen is the disappearance of the separate study of national literatures. More and more the necessity is to study literature in more than one language, even if you're an Americanist. American studies I think is in the midst of a radical transformation. Originally, American studies meant primarily New England and was primarily Perry Miller and that kind of thing. Now a new kind of American studies that involves literature of ethnic minorities is emerging. It involves literature in several languages: you have Chicano literature, and so, you have to know Spanish, and then once you start doing that, you have to get interested in Latin American Spanish literature, and so on. Pretty soon those who began as American studies specialists, like my colleague John Rowe, have turned into comparatists. There's a natural affinity in my department between the American literature people and the comparative literature people. We tend to have the same ideas about what appointments should be made, and there's an actual overlap. For example, a colleague of mine in comparative literature, Lilian Manzor-Coates, who does Chicano literature, is also an Americanist; she's in both fields. I see this as the real direction that literary studies is taking. (And composition then will be part of that; that's why I resist calling it a department of rhetoric.) The major requirement for doing this respectably or honestly or responsibly is knowing the languages. The small anxiety I sometimes have about the cultural studies people is that they undertake very laudable projects without having had the training either in languages or in social science methodology that is necessary for doing this work well. In other words, you still have Ph.D. programs, in spite of all the changes say at Irvine, that are relatively Eurocentric, English-language centered. You now get people with a Ph.D. from an English department, and what they want to do requires training in the protocols of social science research; doing film studies requires the knowledge of several languages, sometimes very exotic, difficult languages. Nobody has really institutionalized the procedures whereby you would know you were capable of doing one of those projects. Say you want to do a great project, a big comparative study of the novel which would involve the English novel, French novel, Arabic fiction, and African works. You can't really do this well without knowing Arabic and one or two African languages. Even if the African novels were written in English, they were written by people whose first language was an African language. Those languages are very difficult. Anthropologists know how to deal with this problem. The last time I ran into Clifford Geertz, he told me how horribly difficult it was for him at the age of forty or forty-five to learn Arabic, but he had to learn Arabic. He was in Chicago then and went to an undergraduate class. It's harder to learn languages when you're older. He knew that he had to learn Arabic in order to do the research he wanted to do. I think we need to get in place procedures like those in anthropology and certain other disciplines that allow people doing cultural studies to do what they want to do in a responsible way. I notice, by the way, that Gayatri

Spivak is learning Arabic, clearly for just that reason. To do what she wants to do, she needs to know Arabic.

OLSON: *This question of intellectual border crossings is a difficult one, especially when it comes to disciplinary borders. Several scholars, such as philosopher Beverly Brown writing in* The Oxford Literary Review *and, more recently, H.P. Rickman in* Philosophy and Literature, *have criticized your "reading" of Kant in* The Ethics of Reading. *In "Making a Mess of Kant," Rickman characterizes your reading as "disastrously misunderstanding a great and frequently discussed philosopher," and he attributes this misreading to "the mistaken assumptions behind the belief that philosophy can be treated as 'just literature.'" Do you agree with the implication that academics should not cross disciplinary boundaries, deferring instead to scholars trained in a particular area, or do you believe that deconstruction allows us to dissolve such borders?*

MILLER: I don't think deconstruction particularly allows for dissolving those borders, nor would I want to dissolve them absolutely. Different disciplines have their own traditions and communities (to refer back to Stanley Fish), their own ideas about the kinds of questions it's proper to ask and the things that you can and cannot say. They have their values. There has to be a kind of community that moves forward gradually and so on, so you can't say all these borders ought always to be crossed; there ought to be these communities that develop their own ways of reading and writing. But that doesn't mean a nonphilosopher can't read philosophy. Surely, Rickman doesn't mean to say that. I haven't read the Rickman essay, and so I can only comment on your citations from him and your characterization of what he says. If he really means that, because Kant has been "frequently discussed," it is impossible to do anything more than agree with what the specialists in philosophy have already said about him, he's an idiot and certain to make a mess of Kant. If he means that it's inappropriate to pay attention to figures of speech, the choice of examples, narrative elements, and other minutiae of language in a philosophical text, he's even more certain to make a mess. Presumably he's not an idiot, so he can't mean either of those things. Certainly, literature is one thing; philosophy, another. We have different expectations of the two kinds of texts. Nevertheless, it is as true of philosophy as of literature that a given text often turns out to mean something substantially different from what the secondary authorities have led you to expect. It's the first rule in reading either kind of text or any other kind to be prepared for that. It may happen or it may not happen, but it happens pretty often. Figures of speech, choice of examples, and so on are just as important in a philosophical text as in a literary one. Good reading of any text is rhetorical reading. To say that is not to treat philosophy as "just literature." It affirms what is a primary rule in reading any sort of text, however different the protocols of philosophy are from those of literature. Philosophy is by no means "just literature," but it is, one might say, contaminated by literature in never succeeding in being no more than a set of interlocked abstract propositions. The figures of speech and choice of narrative examples tie the philosophical text to time, place, and history. They cannot be eliminated as adventitious. Kant's little story of the man who makes a promise intending not to keep it is an example of that. Since he uses it as a basic proof of one of his propositions about morals, the proposition cannot be detached from the example that is essential to making us understand it and persuading us to accept it.

One of the things we haven't talked about in the area of composition is my strong commitment to the notion that good writing differs not only for different purposes but in different professional areas. The justification for having writing across the curriculum is that assumptions about what constitutes, say, a good and effective engineering report differ from those about a good essay in art history or anthropology. Good writing goes beyond getting the grammar right. Somebody in an English department really doesn't know what the rules are about writing in the different fields; it's hard to learn these because there are built-in conventions and so on. Nevertheless, one could say that ought not to prohibit somebody trained in one discipline from, however modestly and tentatively, dealing with texts in another discipline, and often, that person will see some things that wouldn't be seen within the conventions of the primary discipline. So the answer to your question about border crossing is yes and no. I think I was a good reader of Kant, but I'm not surprised that somebody trained within the protocols of a certain way of reading Kant would have found what I said to be troubling.

OLSON: *What you're saying relates to the distinction you've made on numerous occasions between "good" and "bad" readings, good and bad readers. In another interview you said, "You can't give the same validity to every act of reading. Some people are better readers than others. Some people are better readers at some times than at others. I find the distinction between good and bad reading pragmatically valid. But the distinction is also polemical in the sense that I want to be able to say that one reading is better than another." Against what standards or criteria can we make such distinctions?*

MILLER: The easy answer (and the true answer) is to say "against the standard of the text." This is an area where I differ from Fish. For Fish, if I understand him, the text is absolutely nothing in itself without some community of readers to give it meaning. For me, the text contains so strong an inherited way of being read, which is carried from generation to generation in spite of all the changes in the community, that there are certain things that the language allows you to say and other things that you can demonstrate are very implausible. I think I would have to come back on something like that with a full awareness of the difficulties in claiming it. I see that Fish in the *JAC* interview talks about how a certain way of reading a given text can persist for a long, long time. For me, the time is even longer than it is for him. He sees a more radical possibility of changing the way of reading a text as one generational community substitutes for another than I do. I would say that there are certain readings which are (I'm thinking of how Stanley would respond to this) so unlikely to be useful that you could say that they are bad readings. Or to put this another way, I think that Fish's example of his daughter's ability to substitute one context after another in order to make a given sentence mean something entirely different is a very powerful argument for his position, but for me there are limits to that in a given piece of language. So I would be prepared to say that a good or bad reading is determined in complex ways by the oversaturated, overdetermined context for that particular act of reading but that one would nevertheless want to be able to appeal back to the text for support. And I'm aware that's a somewhat contradictory answer.

OLSON: *You've applied these same standards to deconstructive reading. You once commented that the only effective way to "attack" you or other deconstructionists would be to demonstrate that details of your readings are "false." As an example, you cite Derrida's reading of Plato and say, "The only way to refute it, I think, is not to say that deconstruction is nonsense, or it's immoral and is going to lead to the end of the western world, but to show that's not what Plato's text means. Now one might be able to do that, but nobody ever really tried." How do you respond to critics who argue that it's incongruous to appeal to what a text "means" and "true" or "false" readings as a defense of deconstructive reading?*

MILLER: I don't think it's incongruous. I see the notion of truth and falsehood as absolutely indispensable; there's no way to do without them. The same is true with good and bad readings; I wouldn't be willing to throw those away. These concepts are necessary, but I would see them not as solutions so much as in themselves problems that require a lot of definition and thoughtful consideration. I think that's true in general about so-called deconstructionists: that they would want to claim a kind of authority for their readings as being better than other people's readings, far from saying this is just a reading put forward within a certain circumstance. And I think that has to be somehow recognized and thought through in the same way that I was trying to do by way of thinking of how I differ from Fish. It's not that I feel that Fish's position leads to anarchy or chaos. I think it's very principled in his case. The position he takes is very plausible; one would want to disagree with him only in a thoughtful way. Nevertheless, I find myself feeling that the text gives more as a basis for the reading than Fish is willing to allow. That goes along for me with a sense of the recalcitrance and conservatism of language, so that when you learn a language you learn not only a way to use it or read it but, even more than that, something is carried in the signs themselves that comes down from a long, long, long time ago (I put in one more *long* than Fish).

OLSON: *You've commented that Harold Bloom is "perhaps the most dazzlingly creative and provocative of critics writing in English today." Similarly, Richard Rorty has said in* JAC *that Bloom is "strikingly original" and one of those few "people whose individual voice is so distinctive that one feels immediately attracted." What do you believe to be Bloom's important contribution?*

MILLER: I hadn't encountered Rorty's statement, but he's put his finger on a feature of Bloom's work. It's not any theoretical presuppositions in Bloom that I like; for me it's the wonderful exuberance and enthusiasm and an admiration and love for literature that's very infectious. You might even say it goes along with *taste* which is quite an old-fashioned word. I'm pertaining to that remarkable ability he has to show you, persuade you, that you ought to like something and you ought to read it, even when you disagree with what he says about a given work. I owe Bloom a lot. One of the things I owe to him is a better understanding and admiration for the Pre-Raphaelites and for people like Pater and Ruskin. Ruskin had always seemed to me a rather dull, moralistic writer until I read Bloom's preface to the Anchor edition of Ruskin's literary criticism. It's wacky Bloom, and it gives you the idea, a quite correct idea, that Ruskin himself is kind of wacky and wonderful; it makes you want to read Ruskin, and I did. The same thing goes for Meredith and Swinburne and all these out-of-fashion people that Bloom is very good on. We both share an admiration for Pater. "Ah," he says, "the divine Walter."

So that's what I would emphasize about Bloom, and it's certainly true of his teaching. He's a remarkably good dissertation director, not because the dissertations are Bloomian in the sense of using Bloomian revisionary ratios and so on, but because he somehow has a remarkable ability to bring out the best in graduate students and to allow them to be themselves. Even though he no longer officially directs dissertations in the English department at Yale, he's kind of a shadow director of a lot of dissertations, and they are among the best dissertations I've had anything to do with.

OLSON: *You argue in* The Ethics of Reading *that "there is a necessary ethical movement in that act of reading as such, a moment neither cognitive, nor political, nor social, nor interpersonal, but properly and independently ethical." Would you elaborate on your notion of the "ethical" and your attempt to shift the focus of literary study from political, historical, and social concerns to ethical considerations?*

MILLER: It was, you might say, a political move on my part to try to come to terms with the new interest in politics and society on the part of literary people. I've always been willing to admit that there's a political dimension to teaching; you don't enter a classroom exempt from political responsibility and exempt from actually making political and social changes, however small. Nevertheless, it always seemed to me rather distant and abstract to figure out how that could be, whereas the ethical dimension seemed a little more concrete and specific and a little easier to think about. For me, the political goes by way of the ethical, and it's easier for me to understand the teaching or writing situation along an ethical model, a model that is of a one-to-one reciprocity of responsibility, than it is to think of it in terms of these larger, more abstract political questions. But I think that's less true for me now than it was when I got started. For that reason, I was motivated to ask myself initially the question "Is there an ethical dimension to teaching and writing about literature?" I became interested in trying to work that out. But the ethical was for me defined as a more manageable, face-to-face, person-to-person relation, and one that seemed to me to have a little more to do with what goes on in works of literature, for example, novels. It's not that there are nonpolitical novels or that there's no political dimension in all novels but that the good political novels dramatize that in terms of ethical or even family relations. *Absalom, Absalom!* is a good example; it's a great novel about southern history, but southern history is expressed in that novel in terms of the Sutpen saga, in terms of a very personal story that involves ethical responsibility and decision; one is expressed in terms of the other.

Therefore, I asked myself what seem to me not all that transparent questions: "What ethical responsibility, if any, do I have to students when I'm teaching? What's my ethical responsibility to the text? What about the institution I teach for? The institution hired me—don't I have certain responsibilities to it?" Those questions led me to explore literature from that point of view.

OLSON: *Since elsewhere you have argued that writing is a form of reading, would you then argue that there is an ethics of writing?*

MILLER: Oh sure. I think that's a way of naming the notion that writing is always "in a situation." That's a very Kenneth Burkean idea that I would fully agree with. The key to teaching writing probably is to convince students that in some way they're in some kind of situation that they've got to write their way out of. That's ethical; it involves an ethical dimension. That's not its only dimension, but it has continuously an ethical dimension. I would define the ethical situation now as this is why I was interested in the side of Kant that appears to be not what Kant is supposed to be saying—one in which in the end you have no real help from ethical norms or preexisting codes of ethics. That is, an ethical decision is not one in which you say, "The Ten Commandments say such and such, and so I'll apply this rule and I'll know how I should act." Far from that. It's a situation in which in some way you have to innovate, and therefore it's very uncomfortable being in a real ethical situation, a situation of ethical responsibility and decision. I think that the novels I study demonstrate that. It's a theme that recurs again and again, not only in radical novels like, let's say, those of Henry James where you might expect that kind of thing, but even in what appear to be more conventional novels like those of Trollope. The lesson about ethical choice that Trollope's novels teach you is that in the end all of the advice of your family and friends and the whole community is of no help; you have to decide for yourself. I think one of the reasons students have difficulty putting pen to paper and writing is that they're confronting a situation in which all the teaching you can give them doesn't really tell them what words to put down on the page; it's a kind of paradigm of the ethical situation. I don't know if saying this, however, will help at all in teaching writing.

OLSON: *In* Victorian Subjects, *you discuss "the present state of humanistic studies in America," saying, "The concrete situation of teachers of the humanities is changing at the moment with unusual rapidity. More even than usual it seems as if we stand within the instant of a crisis, a dividing point, a 'parting hour.' Aspects of the change include the increasing emphasis on the* *teaching of writing (which may be all to the good if it does not involve the imposition of narrow notions of clarity and logic), the decline of enrollments in traditional courses in literature and other humanities, the catastrophic reduction of the number of positions open to younger humanists, and a conservative reaction in the universities." Given this "crisis," what directions do you predict the humanities, particularly English departments, will take in the next few decades?*

MILLER: A lot has changed since I wrote that essay. One thing that's changed, at least in my university, is that the enrollments are not going down anymore; they're going up. We still have the conservative reaction, and we have what appears to me to be the possibility of a major change in American higher education. It's an interesting question, but I don't know the answer: are the current cutbacks all across the country, in both private and public universities, simply part of a temporary recession, or are they part of a larger change that won't really go away? I don't know the answer to that, but it's conceivable that for various complicated reasons it might happen in the United States that there will be a change in the assumption about what percentage of the population ought to get a higher education. The United States is quite unique in the West in this; a much smaller percentage of the population goes to the university in Germany or England. Relatively speaking, you still have to be chosen, and not as many people are chosen. We've decided to make higher education almost universally accessible. We think of it as part of democracy, but England, France, and Germany are democratic countries too, and they don't give the same access to the university. It's a democratic access, but not as many people are chosen. Whether that will be the case in this country or not, I don't know. It would be a major change. I hope not. But there's no doubt at the moment that there is both a conservative attack on the universities and a reduction in funding that gives people an opportunity to begin eliminating things, especially in the humanities. It's already being used for that purpose, particularly with the so-called peripheral programs, the ones that are precisely the interdisciplinary ones. You say, "We've got to have an English department, but it's not so clear that we have to have women's studies," and so you just sort of phase women's studies out. Lack of money can always be used as an excuse for making political and ideological decisions, and one is made very uneasy about that, nor can one deny that this might happen. I hope it doesn't happen. Moreover, I think the transformation of the goals and purposes of teaching, particularly in the people who are going to be doing it, will occur especially within a few years when so many older people will have retired.

The younger professors, trained as they have been with these new interests, will for better or worse be all there is to hire, and their ideas of what you do with an English department are going to be different enough so that the changes will happen in spite of attacks from the conservative right. I think that's why the right is worried; they see this change as something that's really going to happen and is already happening. So I'm very optimistic. I think there will be a lot of interesting transformations. I'm sorry I'm not going to be around another thirty years or so because I think it's going to be very exciting to try to figure out how to deal with the possibilities of change in a responsible way. That is, in many cases you'll have an English department where within about five years forty percent of the senior faculty will retire and an entirely new set of people will be in charge, with all the power and responsibility to make changes; it's going to be both exciting and interesting but also a challenge to do that responsibly.

OLSON: *Over the years you've certainly had your share of intellectual disagreements with other scholars, and you've even complained of "a phase of irrational polemic, sometimes by distinguished older scholars who apparently feel so threatened by these new directions of literary study that they are willing to abandon all traditions of scholarly accuracy and responsibility in order blindly to attack what they appear to have made no attempt to understand." Are there any misunderstandings of your recent work that you'd like to address now?*

MILLER: Sometimes in reviews people have cited things I have said that were intended as ironic or as the miming of somebody else's position as though they were my opinions. Sometimes this is done disingenuously. You take a passage out of context. Miller says this and you quote it. However, if you look back at the context, Miller wasn't really saying this at all; he was saying something like, "People say" or "This is a position," and that ought to be clear. On the one hand, you point out that this sentence does appear in that essay or in that book; on the other hand, I thought I was making it clear that I was simply saying what my author said: it was Thomas Hardy who was saying this or George Eliot or somebody else, not me. So, I have two exhortations for my readers. First, try to notice whether I might conceivably not be speaking for myself but doing what any literary critic has to do: trying to speak for the author that I'm discussing or even for some imagined position which I'm then going to differ from.

The other exhortation would be to stress again the fact that for me and I think for my colleagues like Derrida, those theoretical formulations that can be detached and are not ironical, that are straight, nevertheless have their meaning only in the context of a reading. The relationship between theory and reading is the really fundamental one, not the detachable theory that you can make into a system. Any theoretical statement made by the theorist/critic should always be put back in the context of the reading made. Theory is never fully sponsored or generated or supported or confirmed by the reading; far from it: the reading always does something to the theoretical formulation and at the same time generates new theoretical formulations which have to be modified then in their turn. So a theory is never something that's fixed once and for all, and the thing that alters it is more reading. I think that's often forgotten, perhaps inevitably, in the attempt to reduce my work or somebody else's work to a handy set of theoretical formulations. That's certainly true with Derrida. People will say that Derrida talks about "the free play of language in the void" or something, and you go back and find he's really talking about Lévi-Strauss in that passage and the formulation is only made possible by the reading of the particular author. I think it's often forgotten in what you might call pedagogical accounts of Derrida, accounts used in teaching him, that almost all his work is the reading of some text or other. That's certainly true of my own work.

3

"Stay! Speak, Speak. I Charge Thee, Speak"

Interview with Fengzhen Wang and Shaobo Xie

"Stay! Speak, speak. I charge thee, speak." That is what Horatio says to the ghost of Hamlet's father in the opening scene of Shakespeare's *Hamlet*. Confronted with the thirty-three terrifying "interview questions" posed to me in writing by Wang Fengzhen and Shaobo Xie, I feel like the ghost of Hamlet's father charged to speak and account for myself, or I feel like George Eliot's hypothetical novelist (in *Adam Bede*) in the witness box demanded to narrate his or her experience on oath. "How would you define countries like China, since they are on the margins of modernity and postmodernity?" That's what I mean by a terrifying question. How in the world could I begin to know enough about China on the basis of a few visits there to "define" it? I have my strong "impressions," but that is far from justifying an authoritative-sounding "definition." Nevertheless, the interview questions are admirably eloquent and pertinent interrogations. They raise many essential issues that anyone working in the humanities and social sciences must confront today.

I am being interrogated in the most searching way by these penetrating and comprehensive questions. Each one would take a long essay or even a book to answer adequately. Since answering them all one by one in anything like an ample and sufficient way would be a more or less interminable process, like responses to an all-night interrogation, I shall answer in some consecutive remarks taking up as well as I can most of the various topics in the questions. The reader of these remarks should remember that I am a professor of literary study and literary theory, neither a political scientist nor a practitioner of cultural studies. My own work at the moment focuses on the question of speech acts in literature, especially in the work of Henry James and Proust, though I raise this question in the context or within the horizon of the political and cultural topics covered by the interview questions.

The topics I am charged to discuss by the latter include cultural studies, the presumed hegemony of Western capitalism, modernism and postmodernism as against modernity and postmodernity, nationalism and nationality, internationalism, the translatability of theory, ideology, globalization as the erasure of "real and objective difference," essentialism, totalization, identity politics, gender, race, and class, postcolonialism, orientalism, the neo-imperialism or neo-colonialism of Western technology and economic power, the intellectual, the university in the age of finance capital, Jamesonian "cognitive mapping," and, last of all, in a single question, almost as an afterthought, the effect of new communications technologies.

Those topics make quite a mouthful, as one says, a little too much to take in at one meal. If I may be permitted to refer to my own work, my judgements about many of these questions are recorded, from the special perspective of current changes in the Western research university and in literary study, in *Black Holes* (Asensi & Miller, 1999). I cannot repeat here for lack of space the detail of what I say in my part of the book, entitled "Black Holes," about globalization, nationalism, cultural studies, the effects of the new communications technologies, and so forth. My analysis there centers on a sense of the performative efficacy of political decision and action, that is on a claim that such decisions and actions are speech acts. I also defend there what I call a "community of dissensus" as an important feature of the democracy to come toward which all men and women of good will all over the world, I am confident, are working for.

As can easily be seen when the topics are abstracted from the questions and listed seriatim as I have just done, the subjects covered all belong to the language of a certain contemporary discourse. This discourse goes more or less under the name of "cultural studies." More specifically, the topics are the key terms in a certain style of contemporary Western Marxism. The names of theorists most often mentioned or implied in the questions (Fredric Jameson, Terry Eagleton, Edward Said, Gayatri Spivak, Ernesto Laclau and Chantal Mouffe, Gramsci, Althusser) indicate that enclosure well enough. All the experts mentioned in the interview questions with the exceptions of Gramsci and Althusser are friends or acquaintances of mine, and I greatly honor and respect the work of all of them. That work is essential today, or to put this another way, coming to terms not so much with "Marxism" as with the work of Marx himself is more than ever necessary these days. This is especially true now when, after the collapse of the Soviet Union, many in the West, for example, notoriously Francis Fukuyama, are declaring the capitalist millennium, the end of history, and the end of any need ever again to read Marx.

Nevertheless, it is worth noting that the authorities most often mentioned in the interview questions do not by any means cover the whole field of what counts today in our increasingly globalized thinking about politics, postcolonialism, the humanities, technology, the university, and so on. Derrida is not mentioned; Lyotard, barely so. No mention is made of Etienne Balibar, nor of Friedrich Kittler, nor of Walter Benjamin, nor of J. L. Austin's *How to Do Things with Words*, nor of Deleuze and Guattari, nor of Judith Butler, nor of Thomas Keenan's *Fables of Responsibility*, nor of Bill Readings' *The University in Ruins*, nor of the work of Giorgio Agamben or that of Gianni Vattimo, nor of Philippe Lacoue-Labarthe and Jean-Luc Nancy. The interviewers no doubt know the work of all these writers. Nothing obligated the interviewers to mention them, though their work, I would claim, is essential these days to thinking out the various topics mentioned in the interview questions. My point is that the questions are generated more or less completely by the terminology and conceptual apparatus of one piece of the field, not the whole expanse, in current thinking about these topics. This enclosure tends to limit to some degree the answers that might be given.

I might add that not all thinkers who are not explicitly Marxists are necessarily reactionary or "capitalist tools," though that is an ever-present danger, one that must be vigilantly guarded against. All the Western academic Marxists mentioned in the interview questions with the exception of Gramsci, it may also be worth noting, are, like me, into capitalism up to their necks, since they are paid and given the privilege of carrying on their research by universities that are increasingly supported in one way or another by transnational corporations. The latter are characteristic institutions of late capitalism in an age of globalization and in a time of the hegemony of new communications technologies. Such corporations have a strong influence on the research and teaching agendas of Western research universities these days, especially in the sciences, where support comes increasingly from multinational pharmaceutical or technology corporations. Moreover, who can deny that this shift in financial support has also had something to do with the increasing marginalization and "downsizing" of the humanities in Western research universities?

Another way to put the enclosure of the interview questions within one part of the field is to say that the questions are to some degree, in spite of the freedom they allow the interviewee to answer anything he or she wants, what in the language of the courtroom are called "leading questions," as when the lawyer asks the accused, "When did you stop beating your wife?" The questions imply and limit the parameters of the responses. An example would be the question already cited: "How would you define countries like China, since they are on the margins of modernity and postmodernity?" This question assumes the pertinence and established or accepted meanings of the terms *modernity* and *postmodernity*. If you are, as I am, dubious about those terms or suspicious of them, afraid they may beg all sorts of important questions, you have difficulty answering the question. The question programs the answer or gives the answer by already defining China as "on the margins of modernity and postmodernity." The answer could only repeat or expand the information already encoded in the question. Yet another way to put this is to say that the questions are to some degree performative utterances, not just neutral requests for constative answers. The questions performatively declare or establish the code within which they may be answered. They "charge" the respondent in a specific way. A "charge" is a species of illocutionary speech act.

Why am I suspicious of the distinction between "modernity" and "postmodernity"? Though I do not doubt the specificity of our present cultural situation nor its difference in many ways from that of the early twentieth century, I have yet to see a list of stylistic characteristics of so-called "postmodernism" or "postmodernity" that cannot one by one be shown to be already characteristics of modernism. No doubt what is called "postmodernism" exacerbates and makes more salient these features, but there is continuity rather than a clean break. An example would be the eclectic and parodic mixture of artistic, literary, or architectural styles said to characterize postmodernism. This would make Picasso, Joyce, and Frank Lloyd Wright postmodernists. Another example would be the desire to go beyond, to be "post" everything, to live beyond the end of history. This, however, is already a distinctive feature of so-called modernism, as in the work of Arthur Rimbaud. When Rimbaud said, "Il faut être absolument moderne (It is necessary to be absolutely modern)," he meant just that, a need to be "post" everything. Both modernism and postmodernism are caught in the paradox of an attempt to "make it new," to be absolutely modern, to be "post" everything, that always turns out to be a repetition, most often a parodic repetition, of something that has already occurred in the past. In an analogous way, the American Revolution of 1776 justified itself by the model of the "Glorious Revolution" in England of 1688, just as the French Revolution, in Marx's analysis, was a repetition of Republican Rome, and just as Louis Napoleon, according to Marx, repeated in the mode of farce the tragic mode of the French Revolution. These congruences between so-called modernism and so-called postmodernism are not surprising, since both belong to different stages of the new regime of telecommunications ushering in the information age. About that I shall have more to say.

I by no means deny, however, that it looks to me, on the basis of my extremely limited and amateur knowledge, that China has indeed developed quite differently from the West over the last couple of centuries. I agree that this might be defined by saying that China has not had in the same way as the West a "stage" that can, with suitable care, with many precautions and provisos, be called "modernity." I doubt, however, if this means that China should or could step back and say "Hold everything. We are not ready for postmodernity. We do not at all like its chief features. Give us time to have a good long productive period of modernity. Perhaps we'll decide to stay right there." I shall explain why I think that would be impossible and even undesirable. This will allow me at least to touch on some important aspects of the thirty-three terribly challenging questions asked, the questions that charge me to "Stay! Speak, speak."

I add, however, that though I cannot prophesy about whether China will become "modern" or "postmodern," I am confident that in the next twenty years or even less it will most likely become the largest and strongest economy in the world. The challenge will be to do that while avoiding the bad aspects of Western capitalism as it is now: radically uneven distribution of wealth and privilege, irresponsible destruction of the environment, uneven availability of healthcare because it has been turned into a business proposition, failure to honor animal rights, failures in human rights (for example, in garment-making sweatshops in Los Angeles), many remnants of racial discrimination, and so on. Western capitalist countries by no means offer ideal paradigms for that "democracy to come" for which we all work or should work. What I should like to see, utopian as it may sound, is not an arms race nor an economic race for domination, but a race to see who gets furthest soonest toward the horizon of that democracy to come. In any case, if I had my life to live over again, I would make learning Chinese a high priority, since I believe it behooves all of us in the West to learn the language and the culture of a country that will be increasingly important in the new globalized world.

The last of the thirty-three interview questions says, "The rapid development of new communications technologies has been changing the texture of our daily life. Would the development lead to new forms of constructive and powerful social organization, new kinds of communities?" I answer that new communications technologies have already decisively transformed not just daily life but political, community, and social life. My answers to all the other questions—about modernity and postmodernity, about nationalism and internationalism, about ways to resist the global hegemony of finance capitalism, about ideology, about the university, about gender, race, and class—are inflected by my conviction that the new communications technologies are decisive in all these regions. Let me try to explain why and how.

Jacques Derrida, in a striking passage written by one or another of the protagonists of *The Post Card*, says the following:

> ... an entire epoch of so-called literature, if not all of it, cannot survive a certain technological regime of telecommunications (in this respect the political regime is secondary). Neither can philosophy, or psychoanalysis. Or love letters....Refound here the American student with whom we had coffee last Saturday, the one who was looking for a thesis subject (comparative literature). I suggested to her something on the telephone in the literature of the 20th century (and beyond), starting with, for example, the telephone lady in Proust or the figure of the American operator, and then asking the question of the effects of the most advanced telematics on whatever would still remain of literature. I spoke to her about microprocessors and computer terminals, she seemed somewhat disgusted. She told me that she still loved literature (me too, I answered her, *mais si, mais si*). Curious to know what she understood by this. (Derrida, 1987: 197, 204)

"Mais si, mais si" means something like, "but still, but still," or "nevertheless," or even "perhaps…" said with a certain doubtful or interrogative intonation. "Si" is a yes in response to a negation, a doubt of that negation. English has no corresponding way of saying "yes." I have no idea how one translates either "mais si" or "perhaps" into Chinese. This small example of the difficulties of communication across languages relates to an important issue raised by question number ten, the one that begins by asking "Is theory translatable or not?" The short answer (a fully adequate one would take many pages) is that of course theory, like anything else, is translatable, but that nevertheless it is untranslatable. On the one hand, anything can be translated, perhaps especially "theory," since it deals to some degree in abstractions and universals, as its name (in Western languages at least) suggests. The word *theory* carries etymologically within it the notion of clear seeing. On the other hand, theory cannot be translated, that is, really "carried over" without loss into another language, another culture, other institutions, without being transformed into the idioms and applied within the special conditions of that other language and culture. The latter are to some degree incommensurate with those of the original language. *Translate* in this case has to be taken in a strong sense, as the name for a more or less radical transformation, not a neutral carrying over from one language to another. The problems that will no doubt arise in translating this present little essay into Chinese are an example of that. I do not see any reason to be scandalized or made anxious by this. Each culture should feel free to appropriate the theory of another culture and transform it to its own uses and purposes. A strong culture should be willing to take responsibility for doing that. I shall return later to this notion of transformative responsibility.

What Derrida or rather his protagonist in *The Post Card* says in the citation I have made is truly frightening, at least to a lover of literature like me or like the protagonist's hapless interlocutor, the American graduate student in comparative literature who was looking for a dissertation topic. What the protagonist says arouses in me the passions of anxiety, dubiety, fear, disgust, and perhaps a little secret desire to see what it would be like to live beyond the end of literature, love letters, philosophy, and psychoanalysis. It would be like living beyond the end of the world.

Derrida's words in *The Post Card* also perhaps generate in most readers the passions of disbelief and even scorn. What a ridiculous idea! We passionately and instinctively resist the statement that Derrida makes in such a casual and offhand way, as though it goes without saying. How could a change in something so superficial, mechanical, or contingent as the dominant means of preservation and dissemination of information, the change, to be precise, from a manuscript and print culture to a digital culture, actually bring to an end things that seem so universal in any civilized society as literature, philosophy, psychoanalysis, and love letters? Surely these will survive any change in the regime of telecommunications? Surely I can write love letters by email! Surely I can compose and transmit literature or philosophy or even a love letter on a computer connected to the Internet just as well as I can with handwriting or with a typewriter or through a printed book? How is psychoanalysis, based as it is on face to face interlocution (it's called the "talking cure"), tied to the regime of print and to be brought to an end by a shift to digital culture?

Derrida's curt and even insolent words arouse in me a passion of disgust like that in the graduate student to whom Derrida gave such strange advice. This advice, by the way, was taken by Avital Ronell, in her own way and no doubt not as a response to any direct solicitation from Derrida. Both Proust on the telephone and Derrida's *The Post Card* figure in Ronell's admirable *The Telephone Book* (1989), itself in its format an anticipation of the new regime of telecommunications coming into being. Laurence Rickels (1988, esp. chapters 7 and 8; 1989) has also already written brilliantly on the telephone in modern literature, psychoanalysis, and culture generally, as has Friedrich Kittler (1997: esp. 31–49).

Nevertheless, that is what Derrida is claiming: the change in "regime of telecommunications" does not simply transform but absolutely brings to an end literature, philosophy, psychoanalysis, and even love letters. It does this by a kind of death-dealing performative fiat: "Let there be no more love letters!" How in the world could this be? Insofar as Derrida's words, either those he (or one protagonist of *The Post Card*) said to the graduate student or the words you or I read now in that book, generate the passions of fear, anxiety, disgust, incredulity, and secret desire, those words are a "felicitous" performative utterance. They do what they say and help bring about the end of literature, love letters, etc., just as saying "je t'aime (I love you)," as Derrida argued in a recent seminar, not only creates love in the speaker but may generate belief and reciprocal love in the addressee, the one to whom the words are spoken. In spite of all his love for literature, Derrida's writings, for example, *Glas* or *The Post Card* itself, have certainly contributed to the end of literature as we have known it in a particular historical epoch and culture, say the last two or two and a half centuries in Europe and America. The concept of literature in the West has been inextricably tied to Cartesian notions of selfhood, to the regime of print, to Western-style democracies and notions of the nation-state, and to the right to free speech within such democracies. "Literature" in that sense began fairly recently, in the late seventeenth or early eighteenth century, and in one place: Western Europe. It could come to an end, and that would not be the end of civilization. In fact, if Derrida is right, and I believe he is, the new regime of telecommunications is bringing literature to an end by transforming all those factors that were its preconditions or its concomitants.

One of Derrida's main points in *The Post Card* is that it is a feature of the new regime of telecommunications to break down the inside/outside dichotomies that presided over the old print culture. The new regime is ironically allegorized in *The Post Card* in somewhat obsolete forms, that is, not only in the many telephone conversations the protagonist (or protagonists) have with their beloved or beloveds but also in an old-fashioned remnant of the rapidly disappearing culture of handwriting, print, and the postal system: the postcard. The postcard stands as a proleptic anticipation of the publicity and openness of the new communications regimes. A postcard is open for anyone to read, just as email today is by no means sealed or private. If an example of either happens to fall under my eye, as Derrida makes explicit for postcards and letters not only in *The Post Card* but also in the admirable essay called "Telepathy" (1988), I can make myself or am magically made into its recipient. The postcard message or the email letter that falls under my eye is meant for me, or I take it as meant for me, whatever its addressee. This certainly happens when I read the passage from *The Post Card* I have cited. The bad or even disgusting news the speaker conveyed to the graduate student, news of the end of literature, philosophy, psychoanalysis, and love letters, is also conveyed to me. I become the recipient of this bad news. The passions that what the protagonist said generated in the graduate student are also generated in me.

Perhaps the most disturbing thing Derrida says in the passage I have cited, at least from the perspective of the thirty-three interview questions, focusing as they do on politics and culture, is that in the power the new regime of telecommunications has to bring an end to literature, psychoanalysis, philosophy, and love letters, "the political regime is secondary." More exactly, Derrida says, "in this respect the political regime is secondary." "In this respect" means, I take it, that he does not deny, nor would I, the importance of political regimes, but that the power of the new regime of telecommunications is not limited or controlled, except in a "secondary" way, by the political regime of this or that nation.

I should go somewhat beyond what Derrida says here to claim that all the questions raised by Fengzhen Wang and Shaobo Xie about nationality, modernity, postmodernity, ideology, postcolonialism, globalization, gender, race, class, and so on can only be answered accurately by taking into account what is called the second industrial revolution. The second industrial revolution, as everyone knows, is the shift in the West, beginning in the mid-nineteenth century but accelerating ever since, from an economy centered on the production and distribution of commodities to an economy increasingly dominated by the creation, storage, retrieval, and distribution of information. Even money is now primarily information, exchanged and distributed all over the world at the speed of light by telecommunications networks that also transmit literature in digitized form. Several of Henry James's novels, for example, are now available on the Internet, along with innumerable other literary works, works, that is, belonging to the now rapidly fading historical epoch dominated by the printing press.

Photography, the telegraph, the typewriter, the telephone, the gramophone, cinematography, radio, tape recorders, television, and now CDs, VCRs, DVDs, cell phones, computers, communication satellites, and the World Wide Web—we all know what these new devices are and how their power and effects have accelerated over the last century and a half. The possession and consequent effect of these devices, as Masao Miyoshi and others have frequently reminded us, are unevenly distributed among various countries and peoples of the world. Only about fifty percent of United States households at this point have personal computers, and of course the percentage is immensely smaller in many other countries. Nevertheless, in one way or another and to one degree and another, almost everyone's life has already been decisively changed by these technological gadgets. The changes will accelerate as more and more people come, for example, to have access to the Internet, just as so many people already have access to television. The changes occurring include a transformation of politics, nationhood or citizenship, culture, and the individual's sense of selfhood, identity, and belonging, not to speak of literature, psychoanalysis, philosophy, and love letters—all those topics about which the interview questions ask plus some I add with Derrida's help.

In a paragraph in a recent seminar, Derrida expresses his sense of the way the new regime of telecommunications brings about the decline of the nation state (about which we hear so much these days) as well as a transformation of the individual›s sense of identity and privacy. Derrida stresses the strange combination of solitude and a new kind of being with others of the person using a computer to reach the World Wide Web, as well as the breakdown of traditional boundaries between inside and outside brought about by new communication technologies. As this epochal cultural displacement from the book age to the hypertext age has accelerated, we have, in Derrida's view, been ushered ever more rapidly into a threatening living space. This new electronic space, the space of television, cinema, telephone, videos, fax, e-mail, hypertext, and the Internet, has profoundly altered the economies of the self, the home, the workplace, the university, and the nation-state's politics. These were traditionally ordered around the firm boundaries of an inside–outside dichotomy, whether those boundaries were the walls between the home's privacy and all the world outside or the borders between the nation-state and its neighbors. The new technologies invade the home and the nation. They confound all these inside/outside divisions. On the one hand, no one is so alone as when watching television, talking on the telephone, or sitting before a computer screen reading e-mail or searching an Internet database. On the other hand, that private space has been invaded and permeated by a vast simultaneous crowd of ghostly verbal, aural, and visual images existing in cyberspace's simulacrum of presence. Those images cross national and ethnic boundaries. They come from all over the world with a spurious immediacy that makes them all seem equally close and equally distant. The global village is not out there, but in here, or a clear distinction between inside and out no longer operates. The new technologies bring the *unheimlich* "other" into the privacy of the home. They are a frightening threat to traditional ideas of the self as unified and as properly living rooted in one dear particular culture-bound place, participating in a single national culture, firmly protected from any alien otherness. They are threatening also to our assumption that political action is based in a single topographical location, a given nation-state with its firm boundaries, its ethnic and cultural unity.

Derrida calls this set of assumptions the *ontopolitopologique*. It is not surprising that since the new communications technologies challenge these assumptions there should be powerful reactions to what Derrida calls:

> une nouvelle et puissante avancée de la pro-thèse technologique qui, de mille façons, ex-proprie, dé-localise, dé-territorialise, extirpe, c'est-à-dire, au sens étymologique, donc radical de ce mot, déracine, donc désétymologise, dissocie le politique du topologique, sépare de lui-même ce qui a toujours été le concept même du politique, à savoir ce qui lie le politique au topique, à la cité, au territoire, à la frontière ethno-nationale.

> (a new and powerful advance in the technological pros-thesis that, in a thousand ways, ex-propriates, de-localizes, de-territorializes, extirpates, that is to say, in the etymological and therefore radical sense of this word, uproots, therefore de-etymologizes, dissociates the political from the topological, separates from itself what has always been the very concept of the political, that is, what links the political to the topical, to the city, to the territory, to the ethno-national frontier).["]1

The decline or weakening of the nation state's autonomy, the development of new electronic communities, communities in cyberspace, and the possible generation of a new human sensibility leading to a mutation of perceptual experience making new cyberspace persons, persons deprived of literature, psychoanalysis, philosophy, and love letters—these are three effects of the new telecommunications regime. No doubt one effect of this endangering of various privacies and enclosures by prosthetic telecommunication devices (as the telephone is an extension of the ear) is to exacerbate by reaction defensive nationalisms, often separatist nationalisms within once secure nation-states or unions, as is the case in Africa or in the Balkans today, or to inspire the horrors of genocide and "ethnic cleansing." Fear of these new technologies also generates defensive moves like attempts by the United States Congress to control the Internet, for example in the Communications Decency Act. This act is clearly unconstitutional, a breach of the right to free speech guaranteed by the United States Constitution. It has been judged so by the courts.

What is perhaps most scandalous about the radical effects of new telecommunications is the way none of these gadgets' inventors, as far as I know, intended or foresaw any such thing as the effects their inventions have had. The inventors of the telephone or of the magnetic tape recorder were doing no more than exploiting technological possibilities, playing creatively with wires, electrical currents, vibrating diaphragms, plastic tapes, etc. These scientists had no intention, so far as I know, of putting an end to literature, love letters, philosophy, or the nation-state. It is the incommensurability between cause and effect plus the accidental aspect of the huge effect, no less than a radical disruption, interruption, break, or reorientation in human history, that is so scandalous.

Some of my Chinese readers might say that these effects of new communications technologies may be salient in the West but that they are hardly important yet in China, nor are they likely to be so for the foreseeable future. That may be to some degree the case, but each time I return to China I see more and more people on the street carrying cell phones. More and more people I know there can be reached by email as well as by fax. Beijing, like Los Angeles or London, has its "cybercafés," places where people can drink coffee, talk, and have access to computer terminals. Eighty percent of Chinese citizens, I am told, now have access to television. Televisions in China, as in the United States, so I have been told, broadcast not only national programs but also local, regional programs, thereby reinforcing not only national unity but also the uniqueness and individuality of separate regions. Television is a force for what is called "glocalization."

When I was last in China, I was taken to visit the birthplace of Mao Tse-tung and to see the location of his wartime hidden headquarters, along with the museum of objects associated with his life. Among the letters, photographs, articles of clothing, weapons, and so on was an antiquated tape recorder and tape player, a huge, cumbersome, and now thoroughly outmoded affair. Nevertheless, unwieldy as it looks now, that tape machine seemed to me when I saw it a powerful emblem for the indispensable role of new telecomunications in the success of the communist revolution in China, just as World War II in Europe was fought on both sides with the radio as much as with the air bomber. The magnetic tape recorder was developed in Germany during World War II as part of the war effort, just as the Internet was the fortuitous result of an American scheme called ARPANET to connect military, government, and scientific computers so that they would survive the nuclear holocaust we all feared during the Cold War. The scientists who devised the ARPANET had no intention to make possible that seemingly irresistible force for globalization, the World Wide Web. The World Wide Web as we know it now is the result of a creative or, as I should say, "performative" appropriation of something that was devised for a quite different purpose.

A reflection on this might constitute a response to the interviewers' questions eleven and twelve, the ones about ideology. It would be a rash intellectual who would dare to affirm that we have reached an "end of ideology." Ideology does not vanish that easily, if ever or at all. Nor do I think that Marx's analysis of ideology in *The German Ideology* has by any means lost its pertinence today. For both Marx and Louis Althusser, though in somewhat different ways, ideology is a phantasmal imaginary superstructural effect of human beings, actual material conditions of existence, that is, the mode of manufacture, distribution, and circulation of goods under which those human beings live. For both Marx and Althusser, ideology is not transformed by lecturing people or by rational argument but by changes in those material conditions of existence. Nor is ideology just an innocent subjective spectral insubstantial set of mistakes. It has power, often unfortunately, to intervene in history and make things happen, as, for example in the effects in the state of California, where I live, of repressive immigration laws and of the absurd law declaring English the official language of California. Though Paul de Man was not a Marxist, he was a good reader of Marx's *The German Ideology*. Both Marx and Althusser might have agreed with the definition of ideology he gives in *The Resistance to Theory*: "This does not mean that fictional narratives are not part of the world and of reality; their impact upon the world may well be all too strong for comfort. What we call ideology is precisely the confusion of linguistic with natural reality, of reference with phenomenalism" (de Man, 1986: 11).

I would add to what de Man says that it is not so much language as such that generates the delusion of ideologies, but rather language as molded by one or another medium: voice, handwriting, print, television, or the computer connected to the Internet. All these reproductive technologies exploit the strange propensity to dwell in fictional or phantasmal spaces that each human being has. The bodies of readers, television viewers, users of the Internet—bodies in the sense of eyes, ears, nervous systems, brains, passions—are used, by way of an extravagant propensity peculiar, at least in its hyperbolic form, to human beings among living creatures, to become the theater of fictions, phantasmagoria, swarms of ghosts. We lend our bodies to the bodiless and then are prone to act in the material world on the strength of that fictitious embodiment. Cervantes's Don Quixote, Flaubert's Emma Bovary, and Conrad's Lord Jim acted in the social world on the basis of fantasies incarnated in them through reading books, in a haunting that the reader of these novels repeats in reading about it, as he or she raises in his or her turn the ghosts of Don Quixote, Emma Bovary, and Lord Jim. That is the work or working of ideology. How much more powerful even than books are these new communications technologies to do that work!

New communication technologies are making a quantum leap in the generation and imposition of ideologies. They do this by a kind of hallucinatory hypnotic conjuration. This is easy to see, though by no means easy, or perhaps even possible, to understand clearly. The means of understanding it are caught in the thing to be understood. It used to be the newspaper. Now it is television, cinema, and, increasingly, the Internet. These technologies, it might be argued, are in a sense ideologically neutral. They will transmit whatever they are told to say. Nevertheless, as Marshall McLuhan notoriously said, "the medium is the message." I take it this means, as Derrida in his own way is saying, that a change in medium will change the message. To put this another way, "the medium is the ideology." Ideology, for de Man, as for Marx and Althusser in their somewhat different ways, is not an easily correctable error existing at the level of rational consciousness. It is a powerful unconscious error. In ideology, says Althusser, "men represent their real conditions of existence to themselves in imaginary form" (1972: 163). De Man's way of putting this, in the passage I have cited, is to say that what we call ideology is a confusion between linguistic and natural reality. In ideology, something that is a purely linguistic phantasmal or spectral creation is taken to be an accurate representation of things as they are. This error is taken so much for granted as to be unconscious. Of course that is the way things are, we say to ourselves. Since an ideological aberration is so unconscious, so taken for granted, it is impossible to eradicate it simply by pointing out that it is an error, just as you cannot cure someone of being in love by pointing out the defects of the beloved.

I would add to these formulations, as I have already said, the claim that it is not just language as such that creates and enforces ideology, but language or other signs as generated, stored, retrieved, transmitted, and received by one or another technological prosthesis. This is as true of manuscript and then print culture as it is of digital culture today. Althusser lists in the essay already cited "the communications ISA (press, radio and television, etc.)" (1972: 143), as one, along with education, the political system, the juridical system, and so on, among the various ideological state apparatuses. The regime of print generated the possibility of literature, love letters, philosophy, psychoanalysis, and the modern concept of the nation-state. The new regime of telecommunications is now generating new forms replacing all these. These new media—cinema, television, the Internet—are not just passive matrices that transmit in unchanged form ideological or truth-telling content. They shape what is "sent" by their means and transform that "content," willy-nilly, into expressions of the messages the medium itself puissantly imposes. That is what Derrida means by saying "in this respect the political regime is secondary." You cannot write or send love letters or literature on the World Wide Web. When you try to do so, they turn into something else. Henry James's *The Golden Bowl* becomes a different thing when I download it from cyberspace. Nor are politics and the sense of citizenship the same to a user of the World Wide Web or to a television watcher as to an old-fashioned reader of the newspapers. The transformation of political life by television has been strikingly evident in recent presidential elections in the United States. People vote on the basis of the way the candidates come across on television, not on the basis of an objective assessment of alternative programs, nor any longer on the basis of what they read in the newspapers. Fewer people read newspapers at all.

It is easy enough to specify what are the most salient features of the new set of (no doubt ideological) presuppositions being transmitted now everywhere in the world by the new regime of telecommunications. It is easy because many authorities have already told us what they are, among them Jacques Derrida in the passages I have cited. The print age made possible the modern nation-state, the imperialist conquest of the world, colonialism, revolutions like the French and American revolutions, psychoanalysis, love letters, and philosophy from Descartes through Locke and Hume to Kant, Hegel, Nietzsche, Husserl, and Heidegger (the latter three already unwilling and anxiously part of the age of the typewriter and the gramophone).

I do not say print was the single "cause" of these features of culture from the eighteenth to early twentieth centuries. No doubt other factors contributed, other inventions like the steam engine, the postal system, the spinning jenny, gunpowder in its reinvented European form, more and more powerful and efficient guns, and so on, just as the internal combustion engine, the jet plane, the transistor, rocket engines, and so on have been necessary for the second industrial revolution. What I do claim, however, is that all these features of the now fading culture depended on print, on the newspaper, on clandestine printing presses turning out manifestos, on the printers who brought out, sometimes against censorship, the books of Descartes, Locke, Richardson, the Marquis de Sade, and so on through Dickens, Balzac, Marx, and Dostoyevsky, down to Proust and Joyce.

Print encouraged and reinforced the assumption of the separation of subject and object, the separate unity and autonomy of the self; the authority of the "author"; the difficulty or perhaps impossibility of knowing verifiably the mind and heart of the other person; the regime of representation or of a certain kind of mimesis ("There is reality," we used to say. "Here is its representation in the printed book, to be measured by its truth of correspondence to the extra-linguistic reality that is out there"); the assumption of the nation state's ethnic unity and autonomy. Reinforced by all those state apparatuses Althusser lists, including the "Communications ISA"; the enforcement of laws and regulations by printing them; the constant reinforcement of a certain national ideology through the newspaper; the development of the modern research university as the place where the ethos of a given nation-state is inculcated in future citizens and servants of that state. "Give me control of the printing presses," it used to be said, "and I shall control the whole nation." Now such a person might say, "Give me control of all the televisions stations and all the radio talk shows, and I shall control the world."

All these features of print culture, the reader will note, depend on relatively rigid boundaries, frontiers, walls: those between one person and another; one class, race, or gender and another; one medium and another (print, picture, and music); one nation-state and another; consciousness and the objects of which consciousness is conscious; extralinguistic things as they are and the representation of those things in language; one time and another (as reinforced, for example, by the tense structure of Western languages as used in printed historical narratives or in novels).

When the printing press gradually gives way to cinema, television, and the Internet, as is now happening with increasing rapidity, all that changes. All those once solid frontiers are blurred. The self dissolves into a multiplicity of selves, each generated by whatever prosthetic device I happen to be using. That is one reason why love letters will be no longer possible. I become a different self on the telephone or on the Internet, no longer the same person as the one who wrote love letters and sent them through the postal system. The subject/object dichotomy on which philosophy from Descartes to Husserl depended vanishes also, since the television or cinematic or Internet screen is neither objective nor subjective but an extension of a mobile subjectivity that is "wired" into it. That is one thing Derrida may mean by saying the new regime of telecommunications will bring an end to philosophy. The opposition between representation and reality also disappears. All that swarm of television or cinematic or Internet images, so many ghosts invoked or conjured into existence by the machines, breaks down the distinction between fiction and reality, just as it breaks down the distinction between present, past, and future. It is often difficult to distinguish between news and advertising in television "shows." A printed novel, at least in Western languages, tells the reader by the system of verb tenses whether something being described is to be thought of as taking place in an imaginary present or whether it belongs to something to be thought of as past for the present-tense narration. A television or cinematic image belongs to a strange ghostly species of nonpresent present, nor is it always easy to tell whether something is "eyewitness news," that is, something that is claimed to be happening at this moment, or whether it is a "simulation," as they say. Many people believed and perhaps still believe that the United States did not really land men on the moon but that the images of the moon landing were created in some television studio. How would you be sure, since the only testimony is those dancing images on the screen?

The new communications media are also transforming the university, for better and for worse, making it less and less a self-enclosed ivory tower serving the interests of a single nation-state, more and more penetrated by those transnational corporations that pay for its research. The new research university is also a place where new transnational communities and solidarities can be developed.

The boundaries of the nation-state are also being broken down, for example, by the Internet, since more or less instantaneous access to sites from all over the world is possible to anyone with a computer, a modem, and a service provider. The Internet is a powerful force for globalization and for the weakening of the nation-state. The frontiers between the different media, finally, are also more and more erased. Visual images, auditory sequences (such as music), and words are all indifferently transformed by digitizing into streams of zeroes and ones. Like television and cinema, the computer monitor with attached audio speakers mixes inextricably images that appeal to eye, ear, and the ability to decipher written language. The new regime of telecommunications is incorrigibly a multimedia affair. Reading as the private and exclusive activity of a man, woman, or child "curled up with a good book" gives way to "surround sight" and "surround sound." The latter inundate ear and eye with a swarm of ghosts that are neither present nor nonpresent, neither incarnated nor disincarnated, neither here nor there, neither dead nor undead. These specters have enormous power to invade the mind, feelings, and imagination of the person who raises them by pressing the button on the remote control and to bend mind and feelings to their shapes. Since many of these phantoms are figures of the utmost violence, as in so much of cinema and television today, it is as if the fears that in the old print world lurked in the depths of the unconscious are now brought out into the open, for better or for worse, where we can behold them face to face, see and hear them, not just read about them. The distinction between consciousness and unconsciousness, the basis of psychoanalysis, no longer holds. That, I suppose, is what Derrida may mean by saying the new regime of telecommunications is bringing an end to psychoanalysis.

Of course all those books on my shelves are also powerful instruments for the conjuring of ghosts when I read them. They are therefore powerful tools for reinforcing the ideologies embodied in the medium of the printed book: the ghosts of Hegel's *Geist* or Heidegger's *Sein* when I read Hegel or Heidegger; the ghosts of the unconscious or of Freud's patients, Irma, Anna, or Dora, when I read psychoanalysis; the swarming ghosts of all those characters in all those novels when I read works of fiction: Fielding's Tom Jones, Stendhal's Fabrizio, Flaubert's Emma Bovary, George Eliot's Dorothea, Henry James's Isabel, Joyce's Leopold Bloom. All books, as Friedrich Kittler says, "are books of the dead, like those from Egypt that stand at the beginning of [Western!] literature" 1997: 37. Books are so many powerful conjuring devices for raising all those phantoms, the phantoms of philosophy, psychoanalysis, and literature.

The ghosts on the television or cinema screen, however, seem much more objective, public, and shared, much less dependent on my own effort of conjuration than is the private act of reading a book. Moreover, as I have said, these new telecommunications technologies, so many new devices for raising ghosts in a new way, also generate new ideological matrices. They break down, for example, the barrier between subject and object, consciousness and the objects of consciousness, that is presupposed by Hegel's *Phenomenology*.

What should we do in this new and unprecedented situation? Most of the interview questions invite a diagnostic or constative response, that is, a description or critique of the present situation. A few of the questions, however, invite a different sort of answer, that is, an active performative engagement with the present situation or an intervention in that situation to change it for the better. An example is question three: "How to recuperate or mobilize counter-hegemonic agency or human praxis in a world so penetrated by capital? Is it possible to form an alliance of historic bloc against the dehumanizing total system?" My response so far would change the question a little to ask how it is possible to recuperate or mobilize counterhegemonic agency or human praxis in a world so penetrated by the new regime of telecommunications that is such an important a feature of the present global economic system. As I have suggested, with Derrida's help, the new telecommunications regime may have been created by capitalism, but it exceeds its creators and takes on a force and life of its own. That is what Derrida means by saying, "In this respect the political regime is secondary." This is also what gives us our chance: the openness of the new telecommunications to be appropriated for the mobilization or recuperation, the creation of the new alliances, question three invites us to imagine or project.

How can this happen? One answer is to recognize that critique or diagnosis always has a performative as well as a constative dimension. My answer to the questions has deflected the questions in an active intervention toward taking more account of new communications technologies. Though these technologies have a powerful effect on the meaning of what is encoded in the new forms, nevertheless they can be appropriated for new forms of co-operative human praxis against "the dehumanizing total system." The appropriation of new communications technology can take place in the name of new cyberspace communities of diversity. I call these, following Bill Readings (1996), "communities of dissensus." Giorgio Agamben calls this association of diversities "the coming community" (1983).

The new communications technologies can also be used to facilitate performative acts of political responsibility. Those acts respond to a demand coming from the future anterior of that "democracy to come" as a sort of possible impossibility. If it were programmed as an inevitable future, if it were "possible" in the sense of certainly foreseeable, it would not require our praxis. It is only as unforeseeable and as impossible without a break in the programmed continuity that it invites or demands or obliges our performative praxis.

A model for this might be that sentence in the United States Declaration of Independence: "We hold these truths to be self-evident, that all men are created equal, that they are endowed by their Creator with certain inalienable rights, that among these are life, liberty and the pursuit of happiness." On the one hand, this sentence asserts that these truths are self-evident. They do not require political action to be made true. On the other hand, the sentence says, "we hold these truths to be self-evident." "We hold" is a performative speech act. It creates the truths it claims are self-evident and invites whoever reads these words to endorse them, to countersign them, to work for their fulfilment, as an ancestor of mine, Samuel Hopkins of Rhode Island, signed the United States Declaration of Independence. The words invite us to work towards their fulfilment in further performative acts. The promise embodied in those words has by no means yet been entirely fulfilled in the United States. Though the words belong to the past, the past of the moment of the founding of our country, they invite from the future, as a future anterior, their more perfect fulfilment, calling to us from the horizon of that democracy to come.

References

Agamben, G. (1983). *The Coming Community*. Minneapolis: University of Minnesota Press.

Althusser, L. (1972). "Ideology and Ideological State Apparatuses (Notes Towards an Investigation)." *Lenin and Philosophy and Other Essays*. New York: Monthly Review Press.

Asensi, M., and Miller, J. H. (1999). *Black Holes (Cultural Memory in the Present)*. California: Stanford University Press.

De Man, P. (1988). *The Resistance to Theory*. Minneapolis: University of Minnesota Press.

Derrida, J. (1988). "Telepathy." *The Oxford Literary Review*, *10*, 3–41.

Derrida, J. (1987). *The Post Card*. Chicago: University of Chicago Press.

Kittler, F. (1997). *Essays: Literature, Media, Information Systems* (edited by J. Johnston). Amsterdam: G+B Arts International.

Readings, B. (1996). *The University in Ruins*. Cambridge, Massachusetts: Harvard University Press.

Rickels, L. (1988). *Aberrations of Mourning*. Detroit: Wayne State University Press.

Rickels, L. (1989). "Kafka and Freud on the Telephone." *Modern Austrian Literature: Journal of the International Arthur Schnitzler Association*, *22*(3/4), 211–225.

Ronell, A. (1989). *The Telephone Book*. Lincoln: University of Nebraska Press.

Note

[1]   From an unpublished seminar on witnessing and questions of responsibility, my translation.

4

The Degree Zero of Criticism

Interview with Julian Wolfreys

JULIAN WOLFREYS: *This interview seeks to address matters concerning what we call "theory" in relation to the practical issues of pedagogy, specifically, the matter of difference within pedagogy and a different thinking in the institution. How do we address the teaching of the quasi-concept difference and maintain the radicality of the idea of difference? How do we teach students to address difference and to work with difference?*

These questions arise as a response to certain current situations within the university, particularly in the humanities, having to do with the "collapse of difference." At one level, there is a sense that "we" have all agreed on what constitutes difference, what the epistemological identity of difference is, and "we" are all very happy about that, so that "we" can now get on with the institutional aspect of "our" work.

Now, you touch on these issues in your essay "Paul de Man as Allergen" in Material Events: Paul de Man and the Afterlife of Theory, *in which you discuss the shock or the affront to institutional convention on almost every page of Paul de Man's work, namely, his articulation of a difference within and against the situation of thinking we know what we are supposed to do conventionally when we teach and read. What you identify in de Man's writing is a resistance to common sense, to the ideological work of common sense in an institutional framework, which I read to be at work in your own essays, where you employ the phrases "good reading" or "the good teacher" to get the significance and the difficulties of "thinking difference." Though it appears to be a very general, diffuse idea, "good reading" is in fact extremely specific. By definition, it cannot be defined: it pertains in every example to the singularity of specific texts. So there is always at work a negotiation between the general and the singular that collapses. Given the attention you pay to good reading and the nonidentity of difference that acts of good reading intimate, why is the notion of difference being perceived as being so dangerous, and why is there an institutional need to define so as to control it?*

J. HILLIS MILLER: The sense of danger stems from the perception of something different about a person or a text, something threatening, more in some persons or texts than in others. We want to control that difference, to understand it, to neutralize it. We identify or prescribe a difference in order to manipulate institutionalized procedures that maintain control by methods of naming and rationalizing. This has a long history. That would be one answer.

Another answer would be a more hypothetical or aggressive one. A community, such as a department of English, operates under a tacit psychological, anthropological, or social law that orders everyone to go on doing "what we do around here," as Stanley Fish puts it. This law is spontaneously and without forethought invoked to expel outsiders or to keep out that which is different from itself so that it can go on functioning. On the one hand, that's a sinister pattern. It can lead, on a larger, national scale, to fascism, for example. On the other hand, it's a normal occurrence. We see it in everyday life. It happens all the time. The old Department of English at Johns Hopkins, of which I was a member for nineteen years (1953–72), was very small, six or seven professors, all men. I was caught up in an irresistible scapegoating. The department needed one member that was an outsider. That was the Americanist. The rest of us did European literature. This scapegoating took many forms. When this scholar won the Christian Gauss award, our response to this was to say that we couldn't understand how this could happen. It must have been a mistake. One colleague, a specialist in eighteenth-century and Romantic literature, Earl R. Wasserman, my closest friend in the department for all those years, believed until his dying day that there was no such thing as American literature. Those little things are not *poems*, he said speaking of Emily Dickinson's work. He needed American (non)literature as the other of real literature, that is, English literature. The scapegoated person in question, a distinguished Americanist named Charles Anderson, was perceived as doing something useless anyway, because he was studying a nonsubject. This attitude, I realized at a certain point, was part of a very powerful psychosocial system, of which we were the unwitting creators and victims. We needed something different from ourselves in order to complacently and with a good conscience be ourselves. What we saw as an identifiable and derisory difference was, however it may be, a haunting by the "wholly other" we were unwilling to acknowledge.

What is peculiar about this kind of social system is that people need that difference and, at the same time, despise it for being from somewhere else. No doubt in many institutions in the United States (and elsewhere), literary theory has played a role something like that played by American literature in the Johns Hopkins English Department of the 1950s and 1960s. While most literature departments recognize the need to have some theorists, or at least one, and therefore support such appointments, conservative departments, or conservative members of departments, depend on having something that at the same time they wish would go away, in this case, theory.

This is a practical, everyday, pedagogical situation. It can, however, be understood in terms of the theoretical distinction to which you were alluding. To put it in Levinasian terms, it is a question of the difference, a difference that can always be brought back to the same, and a radical difference or otherness that cannot be assimilated in a gesture of dialectical sublation. The recuperable notion of otherness is one we rely on in institutional situations. While the second notion of difference, that of the radical other, what Derrida calls "le tout autre," the wholly or completely other, is, for many people, a difficult notion to accept, or to live with, or to institutionalize, for various reasons. It's hard, for one thing, to distinguish something called "the wholly other" from some kind of quasi-religious transcendence, though Derrida has scrupulously identified that distinction. The idea of the wholly other has become most explicit fairly recently Derrida, though even his early term *différance* is a version of the wholly other. His recent discussions of the "wholly other" radicalize or make more explicit what he means by "*différance*" and the trace.

In the current scene of literary and cultural studies, or in postcolonial studies, the term *other* is appropriated for specific strategic and political moves. The term *other* is used to speak of European and American imperialist attitude toward non-European cultures and peoples. The notion of nonwhite or non-Western people as "other" is required to the hegemony of Western patriarchy. Such an idea of otherness, in Edward Said's work, for example, depends on a notion of difference in which difference remains within the order of the same. Often what is called for in politicized women's studies or postcolonial studies is a reversal of the power relation between self and other. This presupposes a necessary hierarchy between two groups. One is on the top and subordinates the other. All that can be imagined is the reversal of that, whereby the subordinate or subaltern other now becomes dominant. That kind of thinking doesn't acknowledge the radical otherness I see as present, not only in the members of other races and cultures, but also in those who are closest to us and most apparently "like us." Our closest neighbor, I claim, is just as other as the most alien person, someone from outside our culture. What we need to imagine, at the horizon of the democracy to come, are communities of dissensus. No doubt it will be difficult to get either dominant or subaltern peoples work for that.

I'm happy to have literature from non-European cultures taught. I think they should be taught. I'm all for that, especially in English department these days. English departments should be teaching world Anglophone literatures. Most departments of English in the United States don't teach Canadian literature, South African literature, literature from Australia or New Zealand. Most departments don't teach East Asian or Indian Anglophone literature. An enormous body of Anglophone literature, which, in its development, is parallel to ours in the United States, exists. It, too, has come or is coming from places that were British colonies. Their literatures in English have developed in response to British models. Their literatures seem to me important things to study, a frontier for our discipline, and we're not doing it. In my department (at the University of California, Irvine), for example, nobody, so far as I know, is teaching Australian literature.

Why is this not done? It seems an obvious move to make in an age of globalization. Part of the reason is that all these literatures are considered to be other to British literature and are therefore not part of the business of a department whose main mission is to teach Chaucer, Shakespeare, Samuel Johnson, Dickens, Woolf. Other literatures are "not necessary," and so are left out. American literature used to have that role, as in the example of Johns Hopkins I just gave. World Anglophone literature now has the place that American literature used to have. Wasserman's belief in the nonexistence of American literature is one example, from the 1950s, of the somewhat paranoid structure setting "us" against the denigrated others, but it was not an unusual attitude at that time. Even when American literature came to be more universally accepted as a necessary part of the humanistic curriculum, only a fraction of American literature got canonized, as we know. That's now rapidly changing, partly through the development of much more inclusive anthologies, including more work by women and "minorities."

Only a few years ago, the primary education in literature in U.S. colleges and universities was by English literature, that is, by teaching literature of a foreign country and, moreover, of a country that we defeated in a war of revolution more than 200 years ago. Yet we went right on acting like a colony. We didn't have to repeat what happened in India or Scotland, that is, the imposition, by imperialist occupiers, of English literature onto the school and university curriculum as a means of asserting domination or maintaining it. We did it to ourselves. As you know, English literature as a discipline was invented not for the British youth, who are still being taught almost exclusively Greek and Latin literature right through the nineteenth century and into the twentieth, but in India for the purpose of educating the Indians and in Scotland as a means of putting down the Scots' maintaining rule. This discipline of English literature has always served an imperialist function. What's amazing in the United States is that we bought this without being coerced into it.

That's not to say that Shakespeare and Chaucer are not worth reading. They are intrinsic to the rich heritage of the language that most people speak in the United States. That American universities teach English literature so universally, however, obscures the degree to which English literature is other, in the radical sense of other, to American experience. It takes a while to come to terms with that because it's hidden by the shared language. It's hard for an American to teach English literature because "we all know English." It's our native language, in the version called "American English." An English writer such as Anthony Trollope appears to share the same language and the same assumptions about human life that we Americans have. Significant differences exist, however, and these take some delicate explaining if you are trying to teach English literature.

One difference that impedes our understanding of British writers is that we don't have a class society, or rather, the U.S. class system is very different from the English one. Just what our class system is would take quite some explaining. My colleague John Rowe has made a beginning with that, in attempt to add the category of "class" in a serious way to the categories of race and gender to cultural studies. In England, in any case, class barriers were—and still are—harder to cross than in the United States. Leonard Blast, in Forster's *Howards End*, is stuck at the border between the working class and the lower middle class, in spite of the efforts he makes to raise himself by self-education. It's hard to explain that to American students. They have—or have been taught to think they have—much more social mobility, especially through education. In the United States, the boundaries between classes are to a considerable degree identified with racial differences, though there is much social mobility even for "minorities" by way of education. Leonard Bast can read John Ruskin until he's blue in the face, but it's not going to make a difference, at least according to Forster, whereas, in the United States, partly through the wider availability of higher education, you can move up, as Fitzgerald's Gatsby is shown to have done, though there are many ironies in Fitzgerald's presentation of Gatsby. I am, it happens, an example of American social mobility, though not of Gatsby's perfidy. You will remember that he got rich partly through "fixing" the World Series. I come from farming families in Virginia. My father was the first person in his family to ever go to college. He became a university president. In just one generation, in the United States, you can move up to the professional classes. I know it's easier now in Britain than it used to be, but it's still not so absolutely taken for granted as a possibility, as in this country.

I find it hard to explain to American students the differences between American and English, at least nineteenth-century English, notions of courtship and marriage. An example is the presupposition of Henry James's *The Awkward Age*, a study of upper-class London life in the late Victorian period. The heroine of that novel, Nanda Brookenham, is unmarriageable, not because she lost her virtue by having sex before marriage, but just because she knows the facts of sex. Her mother has made the mistake of allowing her too early to listen to adult conversations. It is exceedingly difficult to make that plausible to American students, to say the least.

Another form of difference is the strangeness of literary works, their absolute difference from one another, their radical heterogeneity. Much work teaching literature and writing secondary work about it is devoted, probably unconsciously, to covering up that strangeness by assimilating literary works to preconceived categories. It is extremely difficult to develop strategies of teaching or writing that honor difference in the sense of literary works' strangeness or even uncanniness. Even Anthony Trollope's novels are exceedingly peculiar in their assumptions, if you think objectively about them.

This issue is related to a distinction I would make between theory and reading. Reading encounters that strangeness, willy-nilly, even if efforts are made to suppress it. Theory, on the other hand, as its name suggests (the word *theory* implies clear seeing), has as its goal making universal generalizations. Even theoretical formulations about literature's strangeness, such as I have been making, are not much help in communicating a sense for the singular strangeness of a particular work to students or readers. Insofar as it is the aim of literary theory to make general statements about literature, this goal is incompatible with the experience of reading. If you're a careful reader, if you're what I dare to call a "good reader," that is, a reader open to the otherness of work, reading never quite fits your theoretical presuppositions.

Good readers are readers who see not what they expected to see, but what is there to "see." Such readers don't say, "I'm going to apply Barthes, Derrida, or whomever, and show that a given 'theory' works." Rather, they recognize through the act of reading that the presupposed theory doesn't work. A discrepancy between assumed theory and the actual experience of reading always exists. It is difficult to see this discrepancy, however, because the power of a particular theoretical formulation is such that it can dazzle the discriminating power of reading. The power of theoretical formulation to obliterate difference leads you to say, "Aha! It works," without recognizing that "it" always works if you set aside the singularity of the work that makes it what it is.

I've been reading recently Derrida's *Donner la mort (The Gift of Death)*. In the third chapter of that book, Derrida reads Kierkegaard's *Fear and Trembling*. That reading is one of the places where Derrida has occasion, apparently casually, to introduce the notion of "le tout autre," the wholly other. The fourth chapter then is a full-scale investigation of the phrase "Tout autre est tout autre." This phrase is more or less impossible to translate because Derrida, in a strategy he frequently employs, takes both words, *tout* and *autre*, and explores the complex and sui generis resonances they have within the confines of the French language. These resonances don't translate without loss into a different language, for example, English. Derrida must have been very happy when he came upon that phrase, "Tout autre est tout autre." He says something like "The phrase just came to me from nowhere."

The chapter about *Fear and Trembling* is fascinating because, for one thing, it's characteristically tricky and unexpected. Derrida performs an active reading. In his case, that's always interesting. Derrida is no doubt a great theorist and philosopher. Almost always, however, he does philosophy theory by way of specific acts of reading. These recognize, acknowledge, or attempt to come to terms with the singularity of something textual. In this case, it's Kierkegaard's *Fear and Trembling*. Derrida develops Kierkegaard's distinction between ethical action and speaking. Speaking is necessarily general, according to Kierkegaard. It therefore falsifies the singularity of ethical decision. The latter is incompatible with language. In the account in Genesis, God says, take your beloved son Isaac and sacrifice him. Abraham doesn't say anything to his wife or to anyone else, nor indeed does he say anything to God, the "wholly other"; within biblical tradition, after his first response to God's calling of his name, Abraham's decision to obey God is silent, mute, unworded. This is opposed to ethical discourse, which would say something like, "You should always obey God's injunctions so I shall do that." This, according to Kierkegaard, falsifies decisions that occur in response to absolute demands from the wholly other by reducing them to generalizing language. Of course, the Bible, Kierkegaard, and Derrida, all three, violate this injunction not to speak. All three attempt to speak of Abraham's decision. Both Kierkegaard and Derrida are aware of this paradox or aporia, which is irreducible. The Bible just tells a story. That story is a founding event of three great religions of the Book—Islam, Judaism, and Christianity—so it's not just a story. When Abraham does speak, Kierkegaard and Derrida aver, he speaks without speaking since what he says is deliberately evasive or misleading. Isaac asks, "My father…where is the lamb for a burnt offering?" Abraham replies, "My son, God will provide himself a lamb for a burnt offering." Abraham says this and then takes Isaac off to cut his throat. This, Kierkegaard says, ironically voices the truth in a way that obscures it from Isaac and in a way that Abraham himself does not yet understand. You still have to use some language to speak without speaking, as in Abraham's equivocating reply to Isaac. Kierkegaard says Abraham is not telling the truth, but he is not lying either.

Such speaking is a form of silence. What Derrida does with that is extremely interesting. It goes beyond Kierkegaard. It modifies or undermines Kierkegaard's distinction between the ethical and religious dimension of human experience. Derrida does this partly with the help of Husserl. He cannibalizes things he has said in earlier work about Husserl but puts that to a new use. Derrida says, following what Husserl says in the fifth meditation of the *Cartesian Meditation*, that my neighbor, the other person, the other ego, the alter ego, is unavailable to me through intuition or phenomenological experience. I have no direct access to what the other person is thinking or feeling. I have knowledge of the alter ego only through mediated signs. All we can know of the other person is by way of what Husserl, in a doubly negative phrase, calls "analogical apperception." It's *ana*logical *app*erception, something indirect and highly mediated.

Husserl was, in fact, tormented by the problem of how we can know the other, the alter ego. If the other person is unknowable, then something we know or assume exists escapes phenomenological perception. The phenomenological field would appear to be full of innumerable black holes called "other people." Husserl found this intolerable. He kept searching for a way to reinsert the other person within the phenomenological field of consciousness, to make his or her consciousness something of which I can be directly conscious, not something I know only by way of mediated uncertainties. Apparently, Husserl after his death left a huge number of papers in which he goes on and on trying to solve this problem. It's not quite so simple as to say Husserl thinks there is no direct access to the other. Admitting that is appalling to Husserl because he knows the whole phenomenological project depends on finding some way to affirm direct access to the other. Only that, he thinks, would, for example, permit the establishment of what he considers to be a viable community.

Derrida proposes to explore the consequences of assuming that Husserl's fears are well founded. There are writers, Anthony Trollope, for example, who believe each person has intuitive direct access to the other person's thinking and feeling. Certainly, Trollope's narrators know all the characters intimately, from the inside. His novels depend, for the most part, on the assumption his characters belong to so homogeneous community that they really do know what the other person is thinking and feeling on a given occasion. It might be a mistake, therefore, to universalize Derrida's assumptions since they would not apply to a writer like Trollope. What Derrida does is to say of it is the case that my neighbor remains an impenetrable secret, then what Kierkegaard applies only to Abraham's relation to Jehovah also applies to my relationships to other human beings. As a result, each of us confronts all the time the absolute demand made on us by each other person. I must take responsibility to respond to the other person's demand. Each of these demands is like the call made on Abraham by God. This demand is irrational in the sense that it can't be generalized in logical or conceptual language. It takes place in the instant and is different every time. It's a momentary experience that cannot be subject to dialectical negation or sublation. Derrida is specific about irrationality. He quotes Kierkegaard as saying, "The instant decision is a madness." It's a madness because there's no conceptual language that could be adequate to such a moment.

The ethical situation, according to Derrida, is to be forced every moment, every day, to make decisions that sacrifice our responsibilities to all the others for the sake of the one responsibility we decide to fulfill. Derrida has been criticized for one example that he gives. He says, "When I feed my cat, I am not feeding all the other thousands of cats all over the world which are starving to death." Derrida has been accused of trivializing the moment of ethical decision when he goes all the way, in a few pages, from Abraham's relation to Jehovah to the example of "my relation to my cat." I think that's just the point Derrida is making. The demand made on me by God. The multiplicity of creatures, human and animal, makes this universal responsibility, singular in each case, impossible to fulfill and yet absolutely existent.

This aporetic situation, to return to pedagogy, is related to the sense I have of absolute otherness and singularity of each and every work of literature. To choose to teach any one of them is not to teach all the others, and yet, they all demand to be read and taught. My teaching, moreover, insofar as it's theoretical—and the pedagogy that conceptualizes the results of reading is theoretical—is a falsification of my relation to that given work I have decided to teach. It falls, necessarily, into generalization. That's the double bind of teaching literature. One of the things you are tempted to say about a given literary work to your students is absurd. You want to say, "Wow! This is a wonderful book—I can't tell you, I can't explain to you what a wonderful book this is. It's absolutely unique." You want to say something more. It's your professional obligation to say more. As soon as you start conceptualizing, however, you are falsifying the uniqueness and "unspeakablity," as one might barbarously call it, of your reading experience.

This all seems clear enough. The upshot is the conclusion that true ethical decision is silent but that this causes big problems with certain activities, such as teaching literature. Matters are not quite simple, however. The notion that silence is an appropriate ethical response is directly contradicted by no less a person than Walter Benjamin in his essay on Goethe's *Elective Affinities* in *Illuminationen*, an essay omitted from the English translation book. Hannah Arendt, who supervised the English translation, told me many years ago that the *Elective Affinities* essay was left out because it would not make much sense to Americans, who do not know the German tradition of criticism on that novel. Benjamin's target is Gundolf and the other German readers of the *Elective Affinities* in the many decades since it came out. Benjamin raises the question of the ethical character of one of the main personages in Goethe's novel, Ottilie, who makes a silent vow to keep silent and then silently starves herself to death. Benjamin asks, "Does she have character?" He answers, "No, the opposite is the case." Why? Because her decision to die when she discovers that she has an irresistible passion for Eduard is silent. She never speaks it out, never articulates it. She stops speaking altogether. Benjamin says that because her decision is silent and not shared with the community around her, it's not ethical. Her decision is not a moral decision because all moral decisions have to be expressed through what he calls "Sprachgeist," the spirit of language. Benjamin's word *sittlicher* can be translated either as "ethical" or as "moral," though the nuances of the two words in English are quite different, especially these days. Today *ethical* tends to be used to name a genuine decision, "from the heart," while *moral* tends to be used to define a decision that mechanically obeys an external code of behavior. Benjamin says that not only must a proper moral decision be expressed in language but it also has to be in a language that is shared with others. Here is what Benjamin says in English: "Does she [Ottilie] have character? Is her nature, not so much thanks to openheartedness as through the power of free and decided expression, clear to the eye? She indicates the opposite of all these… No ethical decision can come to life without verbal form, and taken strictly, without having become the object of communication."[1]

This seems to be exactly the opposite of what Kierkegaard and Derrida say. For them, the proper mode of ethical decision is silence. It is silent because it is unspeakable, unspeakably singular. It's a little hard to tell what is at stake in Benjamin's assertions. One might argue or suspect that his use of the terms *moral* and *ethical* may perhaps be ironical in the sense that he might be making, in his own way, the Kierkegaardian distinction between the ethical and the religious. Benjamin elsewhere distinguishes between choice (*Wahl*), which for him is mythical, and a decision (*Entscheidung*), which is a rational, ethical decision. Benjamin's distinction would then be precisely the one that Kierkegaard makes when he says ethical decision is expressed in general terms, expressible as maxims: you should always tell the truth, you should not steal, and so on; whereas true religious decision, such as Abraham's obedience of God's terrible command, is silent. Ottilie's choice may be a religious or "mythical" rather than an ethical one.

Perhaps, then, for Benjamin, too, religious decision is the kind that cannot be expressed and has to be silent. Benjamin's covert point may be that Ottilie is religious but not ethical. Maybe. Perhaps. If so, there would be a deep irony in the passage by Benjamin in his ambiguous use of the term *sittlicher* and in his claim that the ethical does require language and does require to be shared, made overt in the community.

To return to pedagogy, is there something other than a silent answer to the question of why a given teacher decides to teach certain works and not others? Is it a "choice" or a "decision"? These sound like reasonable pedagogical questions. We might refine or make more concrete the questions by asking, in the most immediate and practical way, "Why should we, here, in Southern California, at the University of California, Irvine, teach Yeats's poetry, or the Victorian novel? Why should we ask students to read 'Leda and the Swan' or *Bleak House* or Trollope's *Can You Forgive Her?*" The "you" of the title refers not only to the question of whether Plantagenet Palliser can forgive his wife, Lady Glencora, for almost running away with the dashing and reckless Burgo Fitzgerald, whom she truly loves, nor simply to the question of whether John Gray can forgive Alice Vavasour for saying no so often to his proposals of marriage and then finally accepting his proposal. The question is also directed to the reader. Can *we* forgive these characters for behaving in the way that they do? Some readers certainly cannot. The novel makes this appeal in three ways and addresses three issues. First, do you approve of the behavior of the characters or not? This is not an unreasonable question to ask. Do they do the right thing? Second, if you had been in that situation, would you have behaved and decided in the same way? Third, to put it in Kantian terms, would you be willing to have your behavior made into a universal maxim or axiom, valid for all time? That's what Kant insists on, that you should always act in such a way that you would be willing to have your behavior made into a universal axiom or a maxim valid for all times and places.

The last question is by no means ever easy to answer. A lot hangs on it, no less than the existence of ethical universals. My inclination, with regard to works of literature, is to resist the demand that Kant makes and to say you should not make universal moral generalizations. For example, when Isabel goes back to her bad husband, Gilbert Osmund, in Henry James's *The Portrait of a Lady*, can I say that not only that she does do the right thing but also that I would have done the same thing on the same circumstances, and I think everyone should always do the same thing in similar circumstances? It's a mistake, I think, however tempting a mistake, to use literature in this way. On the other hand, what you can learn from literature about how to live your life emerges when you pay attention to the singularity of ethical situations and ethical decisions as represented in literature. Characters in great literary works, such as Isabel in *the Portrait of a Lady*, have to decide, but they don't get much help from general axioms. Their stories express the solitude of the ethical decision, the impossibility of deciding according to some kind of grand recipe telling how you should act. This means that you are in difficulties when you try to decide according to abstract calculations whether or not you are doing the right thing. James's novel ends by commenting that Isabel "had not known where to turn; but she knew now. There was a straight path."[2] She then goes back to Osmund. It evidently appears to her that this is the right thing to do. I think some or many or even most readers may approve of her decision. This is the case even though James leaves the grounds of her decision obscure, partly through giving no explicit reason at all at that ultimate moment in the novel, partly through giving multiple and contradictory, mutually canceling, possible hypothetical proleptic reasons elsewhere earlier in the novel. About her reasons for acting as she does, James, or his narrator, keeps silent. The narrator just tells the reader that now she knew where to turn, that is, away from Caspar Goodwood and back toward Gilbert Osmund.

Reading *The Portrait of a Lady* does not help you all that much in your own life, certainly not by giving you moral maxims such as "A woman should always be faithful to the husband to whom she is lawfully wedded."

The novel does, however, teach you that ethical decisions are difficult and that you don't get a lot of easily codifiable help from books, including books on moral philosophy—except to discover that you don't learn a series of infallible moral maxims from literature or from books of moral philosophy. You do not learn that, an invaluable lesson, and you do learn that ethical decision is always singular and impossible to justify in general terms. To learn that is to learn a lot from literature. Perhaps it is to learn what it is most essential to know about ethical life.

That's the end of my long answer to your question about "difference" and pedagogy! My answer has made a long zigzag trajectory, but sometimes the longest way round is the shortest way home.

WOLFREYS: *On the matter of the title of Trollope's novel* Can You Forgive Her?, *what struck me as you were speaking was that one of the ways to register the problem of difference and decision is not to follow the Kantian imperative that you were talking about, not to raise the question to the level of generality, but to say that "you" names every "you" who reads the title as a singularity. It is to understand the implications of that singular reading or response, very much in the way in which you treat the addressee in your essay on Hardy's "The Torn Letter," so that no one can at once refer to a certain aspect of generality in the process of speaking about difference and yet address the question of difference itself through singularity.*

MILLER: So you would say then that the "you" of the title could be in plural and addressed to all readers, but it could also be stressed in singular: can *you* forgive her, *you* the singular reader, in the singular act of reading? Yes, I see that.

WOLFREYS: *Which suggests that the reader becomes figured as both the intended recipient and as a kind of revenant haunting every reader and every other reader. I was also struck by your example of Kierkegaard and Derrida's question concerning what takes place "when I feed my cat"[3] from practical, pedagogical experience.*

In a seminar on literary theory, about a month ago, a student asked a question on the relevance or importance of Derrida's work. In a 50-minute seminar, I found I gave an answer lasting nearly 40 minutes, and I felt terribly guilty that, even though I had an obligation to these two singularities, to both Derrida and the student, to respond as fully possible, I also had a responsibility to answer all the other students, something I was not doing. This negotiation and the matter of singularity seem to me to signal an unresolvable, undecidable problem for any moment within teaching, with what the institution every day wants: as you put it, "to get on with things" for the most pragmatic purposes, and so to "damp down" on difference in the most violent way. So there seems to be something of a response here to Frank Kermode's remark that fashionable theory endangers the stability of the institution and interferes with its "proper, primary work."

MILLER: It's hard to know whether Sir Frank said this with any irony. His work is certainly theoretical, and he was one of the first in England to take French theory, for example, Roland Barthes, seriously.

WOLFREYS: *Of course, but there seems to be at work, despite the best of intentions in pedagogical practice, some anthropomorphic mimicry in the everyday work of institutions, so that mimicry, having to do with the politics of the self-same, involves a "making over" of difference and singularity in a fairly narcissistic way, in terms of producing a quasi-Arnoldian "best-possible image" of itself. And the way this works, if I understand you correctly, is in an act of appropriation and suppression, whereby the erasure of difference takes place through a return to "business as usual." You illustrate this through your examples of the reception of Derrida, Foucault, and others in the Anglo-American university, but I wonder whether you might also address the arrival of cultural studies and other related areas.*

MILLER: The rapid assimilation of cultural studies by the university, their acceptance by administrators who are scientists, for example, suggests that the university doesn't see cultural studies as all that threatening, however politically motivated cultural studies may sometimes be. Postcolonial and cultural studies are necessary at this time to the development of departments, and I certainly don't oppose them. Nevertheless, cultural studies sometimes involve a return to pretheoretical or precritical assumptions. A symptom of that is the tendency in essays, papers, and books in cultural studies or postcolonial studies to summarize plots or to describe characters as if they were real people and to let that stand as a reading. I just read a passage by Roland Barthes where he says a little formalism is an escape from history, while a lot of formalism is a return to history. I like that observation because it displaces the opposition against formalism in the shape of close reading because it's old fashioned, it'd be ahistorical, it's sequestered from reality, it's conservative or reactionary. These putdowns are used as a justification for not looking closely at the texts discussed. The return to talking about characters in novels as though they were real people, based closely on the authors themselves or on historical personages, along with a summary form of criticism you could possibly imagine. There's quite a bit of that in cultural studies essays. It is as though the lessons of structuralism and poststructuralism, to say nothing of the New Criticism, had been forgotten almost overnight. So we seem to be back in the 1920s and 1930s, with a not very sophisticated methodology. When what is done in cultural studies is compared to the strategies of anthropological research, the procedures of the former don't appear to be all that sophisticated in technique. I consider cultural studies to be, to a considerable degree, a form of social science. Those who practice cultural studies have much to learn from the protocols and institutional rigors of, for example, anthropology. I know many in cultural studies would say anthropology is tainted by having been to some degree an arm of Western imperialism, but anthropologists have been very much aware of that issue for decades and have debated it in sophisticated ways. I would like to see people who do cultural studies have a real training in sociology and anthropology. A whole new pedagogy and curriculum needs to be developed, quite different from traditional training in literary history and literary criticism. To some degree that is already taking place, but insofar as cultural studies are done within English departments, that will mean revolutionary changes in the curricula of those departments.

How do we come to terms with the pedagogical problems you describe? I think it's true that teaching one work rather than others, or singling out one student to help rather than others, is like feeding your own cat and not feeding the others. There's no way we can be simultaneously helpful to all the students in a given class. In a class discussion, one or two people will often dominate the conversation. Sometimes they're smart, and sometimes they're not; sometimes helpful of the others, and sometimes not. We've all had the experience of teaching a class in which a given student doesn't say anything, just sits there like a log—and then turns in a paper that's terrific. You realize that this person about whom you knew almost nothing is actually extremely intelligent. A student of mine at Yale in an undergraduate class on poetry sat and said nothing. He turned in a paper on William Carlos Williams that was wonderful. I didn't know him at all, except as a name, Roger Gilbert. Then said something condescending when I returned the paper, like "This is terrific; where did you learn this stuff?" It turned out he was Sandra Gilbert's son. So there was an answer to my query, not just that he was Sandra Gilbert's son, but that his intrinsic gifts had been added to a helpful household environment for learning how to read. I don't think he had much to learn from me. You're absolutely right about this dilemma of being forced to give uneven attention to different students, feeding one cat to the exclusion of others. I don't see any way out of this, although the possibility in American institutions for "independent reading courses" can help. These are not like universal tutorials, as in British universities, but an option that enterprising students can talk professors into doing. So there are ways around the problem you mention.

I want to say just a little more about pedagogy: in my judgment, the best way to teach good reading is not through presenting, for example, a theory of the aporia, though there might be a place for this, but by the empirical act of reading some text. The place to begin is with the (apparently) naïve act of reading, without theoretical presuppositions (impossible, of course), some literary text or other. This might lead an experience of what aporia means. In reading, you might vicariously or in imagination live with an aporia.

Dicken's *Bleak House*, for example, presents two kinds of decision as expressed in two kinds of speech acts. One is the public, institutional kind involving legal writing, documents. This is opposed to private or silent decisions, such as Esther Summerson's inward decision to accept her situation as the illegitimate daughter of Lady Dedlock. She silently resolves to do her best to be helpful to those around her and not to damage Lady Dedlock's reputation by revealing what she knows. Documents, signed affidavits, and so on, as in the law case in Chancery of Jarndyce and Jarndyce, constitute not a way to "do things with words," in J.L. Austin's phrase, but a way to use words not to do things, except to prolong an institutionalized running in place. Of course, the reader is given knowledge of Esther's silent resolve. I don't see any way you can get around the following contradiction: the novel constitutes a document, whereas the book itself shows documents to be of no use. Silence is better. How can we know that, however, unless the silence is worded, any more than we can know of Abraham's silent acceptance of God's command, except through the telling of the story in Genesis? This is an aporia, a possible impossibility. I don't think you can get beyond it. Students might perhaps better learn what an aporia is through a thoughtful reading of *Bleak House* than by having the meaning of *aporia* explained to them abstractly. Literature proves such things on the readers' pulses, as John Keats put it.

There are, by the way, documents in *Bleak House* that *are* efficacious speech acts. Sir Leicester, Lady Dedlock's husband, after he's had his stroke and can no longer speak, painfully scribbles a note to Inspector Bucket: "Full forgiveness. Find—." Bucket stops him there because he understands the rest.[4] Lady Dedlock's final note just before she dies is another such "felicitous" speech act, a request for forgiveness. It ends, "Farewell. Forgive." It is "felicitous" because it works. It puts its readers—Esther, for example—

in the situation of needing to choose whether or not to forgive. That takes us back to Trollope's title, *Can You Forgive Her?* The request for forgiveness and the granting of forgiveness are particular kinds of speech acts, with special rules. As Derrida has argued in his seminars on pardon and perjury, the only thing that requires pardon is the unpardonable, such as Lady Dedlock's guilty act. If Sir Leicester and Esther can forgive her, can we? The novel, however, ends with a return to Esther's silence: "[T]hey can very well do without much beauty in me—even supposing—."

5

Why Literature? A Profession

Interview with Julian Wolfreys

JULIAN WOLFREYS: *Why literature?*

J. HILLIS MILLER: Like all such decisions, my choice of literary study as a vocation was overdetermined. I always liked reading, but I thought of reading literature as more or less a private avocation. I wanted to be a scientist. I went to college intending to be a physics major. In the middle of my sophomore year at Oberlin College, I had a "vocational experience"—you might call it "calling." I realized that what I really wanted to do was to spend the rest of my life studying literature and teaching it. I was aided in this by my wife-to-be, Dorothy. We were what in those days called "going together" already. We used to have long conversations about poverty, about accepting poverty together so I could study literature. Dorothy said, "Yes, I'll live in a cottage with you." My father was also helpful in encouraging me.

So I turned to literature from science. That shift defined to some degree the form my interest in literature took. That interest has always been double. On the one hand, I have an immense pleasure and investment in reading literature. A literary work is for me the magic entry into an imaginary world or, as I would call it now and as other people also might, a virtual reality. Entering the imaginary, for some reason, gives me great pleasure, as it also no doubt does for others. On the other hand, I have always been fascinated by the question of how the magic is concocted, how it works, what makes it happen. I think that was as important a motive as the slightly hedonistic one of saying this is what I really want to do. I like reading Dickens. Why shouldn't I spend the rest of my life doing that, rather than doing physics experiments? But the other side was equally, important. It was a desire to account for literature and to understand it in a quasi-scientific way.

It has always seemed to me that literature is, in one way or another, differently in different cases, anomalous or strange in its use of odd language. This is a distinguishing feature of literature: the weird way in which language is used in it. I can remember still the specific example that I had in my mind. This was Tennyson. Tennyson's language seemed to me clearly contrary to fact and strange. "Tears from the depth of some divine despair." What in the world could that mean? No wonder Tennyson's speaker, or singer, says of those tears, "I know not what they mean"! My basic question was, how could somebody come to use the English language in this strange way?

Let me give you another example. I have noticed recently, in teaching *Light in August*, that the Reverend Hightower reads Tennyson. Hightower is obsessed with the Civil War and, more particularly, with the moment when his grandfather, who was in the Confederate cavalry, was killed by a shotgun blast when he and his comrades were robbing a henhouse. It's a serio-comic moment. They'd been heroically blowing up a northern supply depot. On the way back, they were very hungry, so they stopped to steal some hens or eggs from a farmer's henhouse. A woman, no doubt the farmwife who has been left behind because her husband is away fighting in the Confederate Army, shoots Hightower's grandfather. Every night, Hightower relives the sound of galloping horses and the shotgun blast. Another thing he does at one point in the novel, as an escape from painful reality, is to read Tennyson. Faulkner describes Tennyson's language as empty and gutless: "the fine galloping language, the gutless swooning full of sapless trees and dehydrated lusts." It wasn't Tennyson's emptiness that fascinated me, but what I thought of as his strange use of words. I was—and am—willing to give Tennyson the benefit of the doubt. He is supposed to be a great poet, so he must have known what he was doping. Finding out what Tennyson and the rest of the ilk are doing with words has remained a strong motivation for me.

Faulkner, by the way, uses language in strange ways too. Who but he would have thought of calling the succession mule-drawn farm wagons in which Lena Grove rides in *Light in August* "creakwheeled and limpeared avatars"? That's pure Faulknese.

So it's the linguistic peculiarity in works of literature that interests me the most. That's the quasi-scientific impulse. What scientists are supposed to do, good ones at least, is to notice anomalies, things that don't quite fit the received paradigm, and to account for them. Scientific advances are generally made in that way. I have a big resistance—and always have—to what you might call received opinions about literary works, for example, the opinions that come to be enshrined in prefaces of modern editions. I'm suspicious of such introductions though I've written some of myself. Of course, I have great admiration and respect for many of those prefaces written by other scholars, but I would read them last, in order not to have my reading of the novel, or book of poems, or whatever, distorted by them. I want to read for myself. I don't want possibly to be misled by what is always, to some degree, an expression of what everybody is supposed to know about a given work. I have found this abstinence really works if you have an eye for contradictions, inconsistencies, oddness, things that are not quite explicable by thematic descriptions of the work's features, things not highlighted by previous critics.

As you can see, I value most the idiosyncrasy of literary works, the way a given work cannot entirely be encompassed by the ideological assumptions of the period in which it was written. You can't easily fit it into history. The best works are other to their times. I no longer think of this idiosyncrasy as reflecting the idiosyncrasy of the author's mind, though those two forms of otherness may be analogous. Literature is made of language, not of bits of consciousness. That the work reflects the author's mind is an unprovable assumption. What we have is the words on the page. Though no doubt the author wrote them down, we cannot fully reconstruct the relays by which they got there on the page. Nor, for dead authors at least, do we any longer have direct access to the authors' minds. Do we even have direct access to the minds of living authors or just the people around us? I doubt it. One of the pleasures of literature is that it gives the reader the illusion of such direct access, for instance, to the minds of characters in novels or to the narrator's mind.

In Hardy's *The Return of the Native*—I've just been teaching that too—why is there so much spying on the other people? It is a bit strange. It is not evidently necessary to the story, but it happens over and over again. A grotesque embodiment of this is the way Eustacia Vye in that novel wanders around the health with her father's spyglass. So, you say, OK here's a feature that recurs. It doesn't seem to fit the story or be necessary to the story. Why is it there? It's that "why" that interests me as much as the general role that literature has played in my life and in so many people's lives—the unreflective plunge into the work in alternative world.

The same thing goes for Faulkner. *Light in August* is a spectacular and powerful novel, a double-plotted novel. One story comes out happily. Lena

Grove substitutes for Lucas Burch, who has made her pregnant and then run away, Byron Bunch, whom she accepts. She replaces Burch with Bunch! She keeps moving on through the whole novel. She keeps saying things like, "I have come from Alabama: a fur piece. All the way from Alabama a-walking. A fur piece," or "My, my,…here I ain't been on the road but four weeks, and now I am in Jefferson already. My, my. A body does get around." Eventually, at the end of the novel, she ends up in Tennessee, about to be married to Byron Bunch and presumably to live happily ever after, whereas Joe Christmas ends up committing a murder and getting lynched. The same figure of life as a journey is used for him, but for him, it is a figure of inescapable repetition. In a climactic passage, when he's being hunted after the murder of Joanna Burden, Christmas says to himself, "I have been further in these seven days than in all the thirty years…But I have never got outside the circle. I have never broken out of the ring of what I have already done and cannot ever undo." She has travelled in a circle, whereas Lena Grove has travelled in a progressing line.

The obvious question about *Light in August* is why these two stories come out so differently. There are various answers to that question. One answer is suggested by looking at one of those anomalies of the sort I've mentioned and by asking, why is there so much attention to food and to eating in the novel? It doesn't seem necessary, though I suppose you might say it serves as realistic information. There's not much eating in *The Return of the Native*, however, but it is a major topic in *Light in August*. Realism doesn't require it. Lena not only accepts rides. She also politely accepts food. When she's taken in for the night by a farmer, Armstid, his wife is very harsh on her. Here is a young woman who is clearly not married and yet is visibly pregnant. For one night, the Armstids give Lena a bed to sleep in. They offer her food. She accepts it, but she doesn't really eat as much as she wants. Later she says, "Like a lady I eat," meaning that she didn't eat as much at breakfast, only a piece of cornbread and a cup of coffee. Mrs. Armstid, by the way, though she looks at Lena with cold contempt for being so dumb as not only to have got herself pregnant but also then to believe that her seducer is actually going to marry her. In spite of her contempt, Mrs. Armstid gets out her piggybank, with her egg money in it. She breaks the piggybank because she can't shake the money out fast enough. She gives Lena all her egg money. The egg money is hers. I know this from my own grandparents in Virginia. The farm husband would work in the fields, grow the corn, take care of the cattle, milk the cows, and so on. Faulkner, I am sure, is right on the mark about this. Mrs. Armstid would have had charge of the chickens. She would have sold the eggs, and little by little, she would have gradually have collected quarters, nickels, dimes, and pennies. When her husband asks if she's going to give Lena all the money, Mrs. Armstid replies that it's her own money to do with as she pleases. She earned it, and he didn't have anything to do with it. Armstid agrees. He says, "Sho…I reckon it ain't any human in this country is going to dispute them hens with you, lessen it's the possums and the snakes." Lena accepts the money.

So Lena accepts food and money, not only from the Armstids but also from others along the way. She uses Mrs. Armstid's egg money to buy food. She goes into a country shore and orders crackers and a nickel can of what she calls "sour-deens." The storekeeper says, "we ain't got no nickel sardines." She asks how much do they cost, and he says fifteen cents. A struggle has gone on in her mind between her "providential caution" and her desire to eat for her unborn baby's sake. Faulkner says finally she wins out over caution. She buys the crackers and sardines. She says yes to the kindness of other people. "Folks have been kind," she says. "They have been right kind."

Christmas, on the contrary, always says no. In a number of scenes, he repeats the word *no*. For example, when Miss Burden wants him to get down on his knees and pray and admit that he's a terrible sinner, he says "no," "no," "no," three times in response to her repeated demand. That's one example. More interesting—and a bit more surprising—is his refusal of food from other people. He can steal food but cannot bring himself to take it as a gift. Sharing food as a kind of communion. One sign of being graceful, of being inside a community, is the ability to accept hospitality. Christmas can't do that. Several important scenes show this. When he's a child in an orphanage, he has got into the habit of stealing and eating the toothpaste that belongs to the orphanage dietician. He sneaks into her room to get some more toothpaste. The dietician comes into her room with the orphanage doctor, who is her lover. Christmas hides in the closet while they're making love on the bed outside. He eats too much toothpaste, so he throws up and is caught. He eats the toothpaste, but it's a stolen toothpaste, a transgression, not a sharing. Eating is here associated with sex.

In another scene with Mrs. McEachern, his foster mother, whose husband is trying to make him a Christian, he refuses food again. McEachern has adopted him, teaches him to work on the farm, and beats him senseless when he refuses to learn the Presbyterian catechism. Mrs. McEachern brings him food when he awakens in his room. He won't eat it. He says, "I ain't hungry." Finally, he is so hungry that he gets down on his hands and knees like an animal, eating the food that he has earlier thrown on the floor with his hands. Much later in his story, Miss Burden leaves food for him in the kitchen of her big house. It's African-American food, as he thinks to himself,

"Set out for the nigger. For the nigger." He takes each of the dishes up one by one, identifying each (e.g., "Ham," "Beans"); throws it against the wall; and smashes it. Earlier in the novel, when he first gets a job in the planning mill in Jefferson, he hasn't eaten for a good while. He won't have any money until he's paid. When Byron Bunch realizes that, he offers to share lunch food. Christmas says, "I ain't hungry. Keep your muck."

All this attention to eating or the refusal to eat is a significant, strange detail in *Light in August*. You wouldn't assume ahead of time it was going to be there, even if you knew the outlines of the story. When you begin to look at this motif and ask why is it here, it turns out to be a useful clue to what is important at the deepest level of the novel's meaning.

The interest in literature's strangeness has kept me going now for well over fifty years. I continue to read and teach literature because I expect that I am going to find something that I hadn't seen before, even with a book that I know well and have taught often before. I used to teach *Light in August* at night school at Johns Hopkins. Since this year is my last seminar at UC Irvine, I wanted to end with Faulkner and Stevens, both of whom I read when I was a graduate student, though American literature was not my "field." I don't know whether that makes me like Lena or like Joe Christmas, saying no to received opinion, or saying yes to what's there in the book. Christmas's saying no to the impossible position his surrounding society puts him in, as someone neither black nor white, is his only way of maintaining integrity and a measure of freedom, though leads him straight to his lynching. When he is tempted by the ease Joannna Burden offers him, he says to himself, "No. If I give in now, I will deny all the thirty years that I have lived to make me what I chose to be." Lena has an easier time saying yes because her situation allows that as a way to live productively within her community. No doubt there is some condescension as well as affection for Lena on the part of the narrator. Nevertheless she shows that by "an inwardlighted quality of tranquil and calm unreason," you can triumph even in such a shrewd situation she is in, whereas Christmas's more rigorous integrity and even worse situation, as neither black nor white, means that he can only triumph by saying no to every effort McEachern, Jonna Burden, and others make to get him to accept the subject position Southern racism and Southern Protestantism would determine him.

What I hadn't noticed when I used to teach *Light in August*—this is a long time ago: I left Hopkins in 1972—was the way in which Faulkner carefully and deliberately associates three ideological features as inextricably intertwined. One is the sexism that puts women on a pedestal while at the same time oppressing them and being more or less forgiving if they have sex with somebody to whom they're not married, as Lena does. That's one part of the ideology. The second part is the racial. Christmas's problem is that he is neither black nor white. He thinks he's part African American, though he is never certain. In one passage near the end, the narrator says that what really got to the people in the community is that Christmas doesn't act either like a white man or like a black man. "That was it. That was what made folks so mad." His situation is certainly worse than Lena's because he doesn't know just who or what he is, whereas Lena and the people around her know just what and who Lena is. At one point, when Christmas is still a child in that orphanage, he asks an African American working in the yard. "How come you are a nigger?...I ain't a nigger." The man answers him, "You are worse than that. You don't know what you really are. And more than that, you won't ever know." When Miss Burden asks Christmas if he knows for sure he is African-American, he admits, "I don't know it," and then he adds, "If I'm not, damned if I haven't wasted a lot of time." Lena knows who she is. She is a white woman who has borne a child out of wedlock whose father is a white man. Since Christmas doesn't know who he is and will never know, whatever "who" he becomes will be the result of his own choices and actions, as he several times says to himself.

The third feature of southern ideology is Protestant Christianity. Faulkner sees racism as inextricably linked to that form of Christianity. In a passage that I had never before seen as so important, Hightower expresses this, or as the narrator reports his thinking in it. Hightower has been thrown out of his position as minister in his Jefferson church, partly because he keeps preaching wild sermons about the Civil War. His grandfather riding his cavalry horse and getting shot in the chicken house keeps getting into his sermons. He is also evicted from his pulpit because his wife periodically runs off to Memphis, the wicked city, and sleeps with strange men. She finally kills herself by jumping out of a hotel window. Hightower's parishioners can't stand the fact that their minister's wife is living this other's life. So they drive him out of his pulpit, but he continues to live nearby. He listens especially to the organ music and to the hymn singing of Sunday night prayer services. In those southern Protestant churches, as the narrator specifies, evening prayer service differs from the Sunday morning service because there is no sermon, no fire and brimstone, simply prayer and hymns. This is much more peaceful. Hightower thinks of those small town people and country people, the families, once his congregation, coming to church. They greet one another and talk quietly to one another before the service begins. This signals their community belonging, their togetherness and peacefulness. Peace is a keyword here, not only because it's repeated here but also because it echoes through the novel. One of the things Christmas thinks to himself when he's running away after the murder and becomes aware of the quiet gray dawn and the "air, inbreathed, [that] is like spring water," is "That was all I wanted…That was all, for thirty years. That didn't seem like a whole lot to ask in thirty years." Earlier, he says to himself, "*All I wanted was peace.*" In the Hightower passage about the evening prayer service, there's modulation to a description of the hymn that the congregation sings and the organ music. These seem to Hightower a celebration of crucifixion, self-crucifixion, and worship of Christ, the crucified. Then in a further modulation, Hightower thinks to himself that these are the same people, these good people, who in the coming week will joyfully participate in Christmas's lynching. They will kill him gladly because, Hightower thinks, if they pitied him, they would have to admit that they might need to pity themselves, so they crucify somebody else: "Since to pity him would be to admit selfdoubt and to hope for and need to pity themselves. They will do it gladly, gladly." I hadn't before seen the relation between southern Protestantism and the lynching so clearly, partly perhaps because I was brought up in such a community. I was born in Virginia, but I have lived all my life in the north, unless you count Baltimore as south, which I suppose you might do. My father was a southern Baptist minister; my mother, a southern Presbyterian. My Virginia forbears were good people. They read the Bible and went to church every Sunday, and I went to church and attended Baptist Sunday school until I was twelve or thirteen. Nevertheless, I think Faulkner is right to see a deep connection between southern racism, lynch law, and Southern Protestantism. I have probably had some resistance to facing up to what Faulkner is saying. What he's saying is that you can't have this particular kind of racism without this particular kind of religion. How do you explain those thousands and thousands of lynchings, some still going on now and then in the south? The lynchings are a concomitant, Faulkner wants to demonstrate, of this particular form of Protestantism, the Christian right. All of the characters in *Light in August* are in one way or another determined in their judgment and behavior by that triple-faceted ideology.

I think I wasn't, forty years ago, as good a reader of *Light in August* as I am now, though no doubt my reading of the novel will change yet again in the future. That's one way of saying that you can teach the same book cover over and over and always see something in it that you haven't seen before.

Good reading is more or less inexplicable. It just happens or doesn't happen. Marcel Proust's dramatization of the protagonist's discovery of Charlus's homosexuality, in *A la recherché du temps perdu*, describes a closed hermeneutical circle, a circle impossible, logically, to break into. You can read signs right only because you happen to know how to read them. How do you happen to know how to read them? It's because you read the signs right. If you don't read the signs right, it's logically explicable how you can get from not reading the signs right to reading them correctly. It's not something you can explain or tell someone how to do. You must make a lucky leap, just as, for Wittgenstein, you can only learn to play a language game by playing it, not by being taught the game's rules. You learn to read by reading.

The various forms of literary criticism that I have found interesting over the years, and useful, have all been, in one way or another, valuable for me in helping me account for literature's strangeness. These critical methodologies have little to do with my preliminary immersion in a given work. They presuppose it. I don't think you learn that immersion. You either like a given work or don't like it; you get it or don't get it. But I have found other critics' procedures useful in helping me account in teaching and in writing for the results of reading. I'm not going to be so naïve or disingenuous as to say that I've never done any theory nor written any theoretical essays. Nor do I deny that I'm interested in theoretical formulations. Nevertheless, my primary interest in theory has been in the way it can come to aid of reading. In this I differ from some people, those whose interest in theory is for its own sake. Some people seem to feel that they have to know all the theoretical approaches. They feel an obligation to read all of Foucault, Lacan, Baudrillard, Lyotard, Bourdieu, and so on. I don't feel that obligation. I read the theorists that I find intrinsically interesting in themselves, and I read them as if they were literature—Levinas, de Man, Derrida, yes: Lyotard, less: Foucault, very little. I feel somewhat ashamed that I have read a good bit of Foucault, but I don't find his work very useful for my own work, except his readings of Raymond Roussel or Nietzsche, for example. Foucault was, among other things, a good reader and critic.

I'm now asking, not so much why literature, as why literary criticism? Why was I initially interested in literary criticism? Because it gave me ways of reading, models of reading, but also because I found it fun to read, though in those far off days it was never assigned in courses, not even in my graduate courses at Harvard. Maybe that is in part why I liked it. Doing so was slightly illicit. The New Critics I found most interesting, however, were the slightly odd ones, especially Burke and Empson, also G. Wilson Knight, if you can call him a New Critic. I greatly admired Empson's work, not only *Seven Types of Ambiguity* but also *Some Versions of Pastoral*, especially the latter. I thought that as a wonderful book, and still do. Of course I read the other New Critics, Brooks, Tate, Ransom, from all of whom I benefited, but I gained most from Burke and Empson. Both Burke and Empson are slightly wild and wacky. Their wildness is to some degree commensurate with the wildness of literature. Empson's chapter on *Alice's Adventures in Wonderland* is superb, as is his notion—he was on to something that I wouldn't have thought of—that Shakespeare's *As You Like It* is a dramatic working out in the different plots of the contradiction between lust and love. As Empson says, you have different versions of this in the different plots. As Empson also avers, you cannot logically reconcile lust and love. What you can do is get married and live within the contradiction. This is why, Empson argues, *As You Like It* ends with so many marriages. Marriages don't solve the contradiction. They provide a quasi-solution to the problem through life not through theory. Not that you can have both love and lust at once. You can't, but you can, in a productive way, deal with the problem if you are married or if you are living more or less permanently with a partner.

Kenneth Burke's notion that the work of literature is for the writer a strategy for encompassing a situation relates literature back to life in an unexpected way, unexpected for me at least when I was a graduate student. A literary work, Burke claims, is motivated by some kind of a problem the writer has, perhaps an Empsonian contradiction, though of course not necessarily the love/lust one. Writing the work is a way of working through the problem. I found Burke's paradigm productive. My dissertation on Dickens is strongly influenced by Burke. It tries to read Dicken's novels according to Burke's conception of literature.

Then somewhat later, when I was at the Johns Hopkins University and had George Poulet as a colleague, I quite accidentally started reading the first Poulet essays that had been translated, the introduction to *Studies in Human Time*. It had appeared in a little magazine called *The Hopkins Review*. I can still remember my excitement and intellectual elation. At that time, I really couldn't read French, though I had passed the graduate school French exam. I taught myself French in order to read Sartre, Valéry, Poulet, Levinas, Merleau-Ponty, Marcel Raymond, Gaston Bachelard, Jean-Pierre Richard, and others. A lot of Sartre, for example, was not yet translated, for example, the Genet book. What I found fascinating about Poulet's work was that he had a solution for what was for me at that point a big problem. I had many ideas and apercus about Dickens's novels. These had accumulated as notes, 200 pages of these on a given novel. I considered them, no doubt fatuously, to be brilliant insights, really great ideas, but I couldn't see how to put them together to make a chapter; I was trying to write a book on Dickens and did eventually publish my first book, *Charles Dickens: The World of His Novels*. What Poulet taught me was modes of economy. He's marvelous at this. He can put all the works of Victor Hugo in a 25-page essay, while my tendency is to go on and on. I remember Poulet telling me that essay were like *fleuve*, a great river that disperses itself in a delta at the end. Poulet achieves economy by the strategic use of a few short citations to represent a certain feature of a writer's habitual consciousness. These assumptions would seem extremely problematic to me now. Poulet also uses in his essays what you might call, to use an oversimplified term for it, a dialectical sequence. He starts with one originary motif in the author in question, often a moment of waking to self-consciousness, and then moves on to a related motif that is antithetical to the first one. The essay then moves on rapidly through such stages until it reaches its conclusion. Two strategies of criticism are marvelous modes of economy.

I learned a lot from studying how Poulet puts an essay together. It was a very practical problem that I had: how to write critical essays that would encompass the whole work of some leading Victorian and modernist poets: Arnold, Browning, Hopkins, Yeats, Stevens, Williams. I was working on what were to become my second and third books: *The Disappearance of God* and *Poets of Reality*. Poulet held that the literary works by a given author, including letters, essays, etc., represent a specific, unique consciousness, an interior space. One of Poulet's books is called *The Interior Distance, La distance intérieur*. Poulet thinks of the complete words of Victor Hugo as forming a singular space, an interior space, the space Hugo's special consciousness, and he believed the same thing was true for all writers, Rousseau or Proust or Balzac or Pascal.

When I talk these days about the way a literary work allows entry into an imaginary world or a virtual reality, I am still thinking in somewhat the same way. A critical essay then would be generated by moving around within that interior space. It would be a topographical exploration. I found that notion helpful to me as a specialist in Victorian literature. I was, for example, much interested in Mathew Arnold. He was one of the people I was supposed to teach. I found both his poetry and his prose powerful, but the New Critical approach doesn't work very well for Arnold. If you're a true New Critic and you try to read one of Arnold's poems, you find there isn't very much you can do with it. You might be likely to say, as Harold Bloom has said, that it's not good poetry. It doesn't amount to anything because it isn't like Keats or, as Bloom has said, it's a shallow pastiche of Keats. Yet Arnold's poetry seemed to me in articulating what I saw in Arnold.

Today, however, I would say that Poulet, to some degree, bypasses the specificities of language in the authors about whom he writes essays. Poulet tends to look upon the passages that he cites as transparent expressions of the author's consciousness. It's not quite so simple as that with Poulet, however, as Paul de Man long ago argued in his essay on Poulet in *Blindness and Insight*. Poulet is a very great critic. He is attentive to language almost in spite of himself. One might make a law out of that, "Miller's Law": "The greatest critics are those whose readings exceed their theoretical presuppositions." Poulet's critical procedure, nevertheless, leads him away from attention to those anomalies that are not thematic or reducible to being seen as features of consciousness. His procedure leads him away also from rhetorical or tropological aspects of literature. Those aspects for Poulet are more or less taken for granted.

When I began to read Derrida, I found someone who does pay attention to language, to put it mildly. I found articulated in his early work a presupposition opposed to the New Critical dogma that assumed a great work will be organically unified. Neither Empson nor Burke makes that assumption, but other New Critics tend to do so. Derrida liberated me to recognize that a work can be a great work and nevertheless be contradictory. It needs not to hang together, and the not-hanging-together is perhaps the most important part about it, its value, or virtue, or integrity. My reading of *De la grammatologie* and of Derrida's other early work was a turning point for me. Derrida's work combines in quite singular way the two traditions that had influenced me until then, the New Criticism and so-called phenomenological criticism. Derrida's allowed me to understand better my resistance to my closest colleague at Johns Hopkins, Earl Wasserman. He was an organic unity man through and through. If he couldn't show that a work of literature was an organic unity, it must not be a good work. Wasserman would never have written on Shelley's *The Triumph of Life* because it's not finished. He would say, "Well, who knows how it was going to come out?" Therefore, we can't write about that work, but we can write about Keats's odes and even about *Prometheus Unbound*. His goal, Wasserman assumed, was to show that given work and hangs together. What interested me instinctively, on the contrary, were those places where you can't make a work hang together, parts that seem important but that don't fit the general pattern. Both of those are useful heuristic attitudes. Wasserman had a sharp eye for details. His desire to show that they fitted was useful in his work. It led him to say, "I've got to work this in somehow." That is very different from an assumption that there may be something there that can't be fitted in, not at least in any rational scheme, but that is nevertheless important. Wasserman and I were close colleagues for nineteen years. We used to argue about these issues endlessly, often with George Poulet as a third in the discussion, and usually apropos of some work Wasserman was writing about.

Hopkins was my real formation, more than Oberlin or Harvard. It was a wonderful place at that time. Poulet was there; Leo Spitzer was there; A.O. Lovejoy and William Albright. The Humanities group was small enough so that even a nontenured member, as I was at first, knew all these people. Wasserman, Poulet, and I used to have lunch together all the time, at least once a week, with me as an assistant professor listening to these two distinguished people arguing about, say, Shelley's *Mont Blanc* and never coming to agreement. I remember one time when I thought I had a good interpretation of *Wuthering Heights*, a novel Wasserman knew very well. I went to Wasserman, and I said, "Earl, I've really got it." I then presented Wasserman with my reading. He said, "Well, what about this passage on page so and so?" I had to admit that it didn't fit with my little reading, so my reading was disqualified. He was saying, "Unless you can incorporate this passage in your reading somehow, it is not a satisfactory reading." That claim, however, was based on the assumption that you have to make everything fit into a presumed organic unity.

Derrida helped me defend my insights by not assuming a good work is necessarily unified. It was not—and still isn't—Derrida's theoretical formulations, *la différance* and so on, that have interested me most in his work. I admire Derrida most as a reader, as an absolutely spectacular literary critic and reader of philosophical texts. He is among the best literary critics in the twentieth century. I feel the same way about Paul de Man. I'm interested, for example, in de Man's theory of allegory, of course, but what I find really interesting about de Man's work and what kept me coming to his seminars at Yale is that his readings are always surprising, at least to me. I tip my hat to anyone who sees something new to me in a work that I know quite well, something I hadn't seen, but that seems right to me when is pointed out. Both Derrida and de Man can do that. With de Man, I would know that he was going to talk about some text or other, often one I had already read carefully. I would try to anticipate what he would be likely to say and I always got it wrong. He'd always seen something that I hadn't thought of. It's the same with Derrida's seminars. There are two cases, I remember, both fairly recent. In one seminar, he talked about Melville's *Bartleby the Scrivener*, on which I had written a long essay, so I knew the novel really well. Derrida talked about the very end of the story, which is a reference to Job ("He's with kings and counselors now"). His brief reading was wonderfully perceptive and original. It was certainly not something I had thought of. The other seminar was on Proust. Derrida discussed a small section of the *Recherche* on the death of Bergotte. Derrida noticed that Proust uses a whole series of words that are forms of *prendre—comprendre, apprendre,* etc. Derrida made that small detail really work to support his reading of Proust; he showed plays on strength of those French words, with their latent image of grasping, as in German *Begriff*, the word for "notion." Derrida implied that you can't really see this in the standard English translation of Proust. The translation is correct enough, but it necessarily misses the implicit play in the echoing French words. It was a splendid reading of this one episode. The reading was not overtly theoretical. It arose from a close attention to details of language, from Derrida's possession of what one might call an "ear." That's what I most value about Derrida. Think about just his work on English literature: essays on Shelley, Shakespeare, Joyce, Melville, etc. These are magnificent essays, not to speak of the ones on continental literature, on Mallarmé or Proust or Celan.

Now I take up once more your question, "Why literature?" I take the question now to refer to literature's use, its role in human life. In a sense, literature's social or psychological utility. When you read a novel or poem, you don't ordinarily say to yourself, "Am I doing something useful? Is there some further end? Is what I am doing good for something, good for me, or am I wasting my time?" The *pourquoi*, the rose doesn't have any why; it's just beautiful. Perhaps you can find the source.[1] I don't think this is aestheticism in the bad sense of that word. I think that literature has had a function *sans pourquoi*, without any why. Cinema is nowadays replacing this old function of literature. It is an end in itself. I think that would be an initial answer to the question "Why literature?"

Literature—in the sense in which we use the word in the West—is a relatively recent and historically conditioned institution. It began in the Renaissance. We tend to assume that *Beowulf* is literature, but it verges on being myth or an aid to nation building or support of a specific religion. It does not have an identifiable author, as most post-Renaissance literature in the West does. It is somewhat accidental writing down of an oral poem, whereas literature is tied to the printed word. Greek tragedy, to take another example, had a very specific ritual function, a function you wouldn't expect Tennyson to have had in his time. Modern secular literature is detached from any necessary religious function, and this change is quite recent. I think Derrida is right; literature in our culture is associated with the rise of Western-style democracies, with the spread of literacy, with the development of printing, and with freedom of speech, theoretical freedom of speech at least, the right in a democracy to write anything you want. That freedom is never complete, of course, but it is more nearly complete in modern Western democracies, than, for example, in Renaissance monarchies. So, Western literature belongs to the epoch of the Enlightenment, that is, the last three centuries. Clearly, it has had an important social function during this period, even if you say, well I'm not thinking about social utility when I am reading George Eliot's *Middlemarch*, or *Alice in Wonderland*, or *The Swiss Family Robinson*, or Shakespeare.

This new answer to the *why* is double. First, literature reinforces and to some degree creates reigning ideologies. How, for example, did people learn in nineteenth-century England how courtship and marriage ought to take place? Certainly in part through family and social conditioning, but also by reading Trollope. Trollope tells you how young marriageable women ought to behave, and how young men ought to behave, and how their parents ought to behave. No doubt Trollope's representations of courtship and marriage bear some relation to the way things really were, but their function was also performative. Trollope's novels coached people into behaving in ways similar to the behavior of Trollope's good characters. No doubt literature functions in this way. It has functioned that way from the beginning without my being aware of it. *Alice in Wonderland*, for example, had a big influence on me. I taught myself to read at age five so I could read it for myself and not be dependent on my mother to read it to me. The *Alice* books taught me all kinds of things that have to do with gender relations, with word play, and with the ways in which people are idiosyncratic. There are lots of mad hatters in the world! There are lots of rabbits with watches on their waistcoat pockets.

A second social function of literature exists, another answer to the question, "Why literature?" The *Alice* books are a good example of that. Even as a naïve, childish reader, I probably was already at least implicitly aware of this other function. Literature functions as a critique of ideology, not just as a reinforcement of it, as in the political satire in the *Alice* books. If you were to ask me what is the purest expression of Victorian middle-class ideology, I would say Trollope's novels. Nevertheless, Trollope's novels also put it into question the Victorian middle-class assumptions he dramatizes.

This side of literature is, I think, sometimes underestimated by cultural studies specialists. They may see a given work as a pure expression of, let's say, imperialist ideology. Most literary works are not that simple. Usually, questions are raised about the ideological assumptions that are dramatized in the work, if only in an ironic treatment of some of these assumptions. Faulkner's treatment of Southern post-Civil War ideology is a good example of such irony. That is one reason why Empson interested me so much. He was the first important theorist of irony I read.

I can give you another example, this one from Trollope. You might plausibly claim that Trollope's novels depend absolutely on the assumption that being in love is ontological reality. Henry James says that Trollope made the British maiden his especial subject: he wrote about her over and over again; he turned her inside out and every which way. One of Trollope's assumptions concerning these young women is that falling in love changes a person's being. If you are really in love then you will be faithful to that love even if it is against the advice of all your aunts and uncles, your parents, siblings, and friends. Often in Trollope's novels, this is the situation. Usually in Trollope, it works out that the young woman can marry the man she loves and live happily ever after. In Henry James's novels, you have the same subject, but it usually leads to disaster, for example, in the marriage of Isabel Archer to Gilbert Osmond in *The Portrait of a Lady*. In a wonderful novel by Trollope about which I have written elsewhere, *Ayala's Angel*, the reigning Victorian assumptions about falling in love are put into question. What is tricky about falling in love is that there was a time when you were not in love and then a time when you are in love. Once you really are in love, for Trollope, it's for life. If you stand back from that and think a little about it, you can see that this assumption is somewhat absurd; it is an ideologeme. The idea that being in love is an unalterable change of the person is of course still current. It is very hard to do without it. Nevertheless, it is a problematic idea, even though it is useful for keeping people married. It's good for families and family values. It makes arguments against divorce. It lies perhaps somewhere in background as part of the current hostility to same-sex marriage. Some people find it threatening to think that being in love could take place between members of the same sex. Two women, two men, cannot love one another in the way I love my wife or love my husband, such people think. Such people are clearly wrong.

Ayala's Angel is a novel in which the heroine, Ayala, a charming, intelligent young woman, thinks that the only person worth her loving would be an angel come down from heaven. She remembers the passage from the Old Testament in which the angels came down from heaven to marry the daughters of men. So she's waiting around for an angel. Nobody matches up to her ideal; in particular a red-haired, awkward young man named Jonathan Stubbs keeping on proposing to her, and she keeps turning him down. Finally, she accepts him. He asks an obvious question: "When did you begin loving me?" Ayala says, "I think I was in love with you the first time I met you." You say to yourself, or I did anyway, I must have missed something. So go back to the scene when they first meet, and look again at all the scenes of their meetings in between. In no one of these does Trollope represent a transition from harsh rejection of Stubbs to being in love with him. It must have happened without happening, so to speak, or it must not be possible to represent it, since Ayala was not aware of it happening. For Trollope, only what the characters are aware of can be represented. This suggests that there's something extremely peculiar and even dubious about the ideology of being in love. *Ayala's Angel* ends with a glorification of happy marriage, like most Trollope novels. Ayala is really in love with Stubbs, and everybody approves of her marriage choice. Nevertheless, several people ask her, Ayala's aunt for example, "When did you begin loving him? You said he was not at all to your taste." She gives the same answer: "I think I've always loved him." What this shows is that Trollope cannot show the transition from not being in love to being in love. This hints at the possibility that being in love is a subjective fantasy or an ungrounded performative commitment, not an ontological reality.

I think the function of literature as a critique ideology is just as important as its role in the reinforcement and or even creation of ideological assumptions.

Literature, I conclude, is an end in itself. It doesn't have any *why*, and yet it does have a *why*. That second *why* is in my view historically conditioned. Literature in the modern sense had a beginning in the West, and it could have an end. That would not be the end of civilization. Other cultural forms could take literature's place or even now are taking its place. I've written elsewhere about the end of literature. Literature is going to be around for a long time yet. Nevertheless, we're in the midst of a radical and fairly rapid transition to other media, as what I would call the literary or literariness is transferred into media like film but also like computer games. A lot of literary invention goes into computer games. I have no problem with that. Many new forms of "the literary" will be around, alongside printed literature. Literature in the old-fashioned sense of novels, poems, and plays, however, clearly has a smaller role in the cultural life of ordinary citizens, at least in the United States and probably in Europe too. The evidence for this is that the average American spends about five hours a day watching television. You can't watch television or play a computer game and read Shakespeare at the same time, though some students claim they can. Although a lot of books are no doubt still read, this takes place in combination with going to the movies, watching television, and using the internet. The nineteenth century didn't have those quasi-literary media. Even when I was a child, we didn't have the second two of those. That is bound to make a difference to the social function of literature. It is already doing so. That doesn't mean that literature isn't going to be around for a long time, being studied and being read. What it does mean is that literature, particularly in the United Sates the study of British literature, will have a different role, a different *why*.

It will become gradually more a matter of historical interest than of current concern.

Literature, British literature, not American literature, used to be a primary means by which American ideological assumptions were instilled in people. When I began to reflect on this some years ago, it struck me as strange—and still does—that we made the basis of the American ethos the literature of a foreign country, much more than our own literature. It was, moreover, the literature of a foreign country that we had defeated in a war of revolution. In this respect, we went right on acting like a colony. Most people still, today, especially educators, say that every American should read Shakespeare. I agree that reading Shakespeare is a good thing. Nevertheless, Shakespeare doesn't belong to us as he does to a British citizen, not to speak of the way Samuel Johnson, Chaucer, Beowulf, Mathew Arnold, Virginia Woolf, Yeats belong especially to the British. Everybody ought to read them. I understand, however, why many young Americans find knowing the whole range of British literature less obviously necessary than knowing modernist literature in a global context and why non-British literature, whether it's Anglophone or in translation, begins to have a larger and larger function among the American people, so many of whom are now not European in origin. I can see various reasons why you might say, "To assimilate them they'd better read Shakespeare," but it might be better to say, "To assimilate them they'd better read Walt Whitman or Wallace Stevens," which is not the same thing. American literature has a different tradition.

For many American readers, certainly for me, non-English literature in translation, had, even when I could not read any of them in the original languages, a special appeal, for example, Kafka, Tolstoy, Proust, or Dostoyevsky. In some ways, those writers were more important for me in my adolescence than some works in British literature. I have elsewhere told the story about how when I was a sophomore in college I read, more or less by accident, Dostoyevsky's *Notes from the Underground.* I remember saying to myself, "This is me; at last I have found somebody like me!" It begins, "I'm a sick man, I'm a spiteful man, I think my liver is diseased." As a sophomore in college, this came home to me in a way that I have never felt about, say, *Rasselas* or, to tell the truth, about Shakespeare's characters, much as I admire my delight in Shakespeare. They do not invite, for me, identification, immersion, in the same way that Dostoyevsky or that Conrad, who was after all "not English," but Polish, did. For Dickens, I have much more affinity. I think that such a selective response to British literature and an affinity for non-English literature may happen for many Americans. One has to explain why so many Americans today read with such enthusiasm Salman Rushdie or African or Indian Anglophone literatures. Their engagement is not simply political, "politically correct." Something in these works rings a bell because the stories they tell are somehow more like our own experience than is much in canonical English literature.

Well, our time is up, and I've only answered your first question.

WOLFREYS: *I had only one question: why literature?*

Irvine, CA, 27 April 2004

Note

¹   The phrase, *la rose est sans pourquoi*, first appears, as far as I have been able to ascertain, originally in German, and is from Angelus Silesius (born Johannes Scheffer b. 1624, d. 1677). *Der Cherubuusche Wandersmann* (1657) is a collection of over 1600 rhyming couplets. The phrase is a fragment of one of Silesius' epigrammatic couplets intended to render the ineffability of God somehow apprehensible. It articulates and anticipates the notion of analogical apperception proposed by Edmund Husserl in his *Cartesian Meditations: An Introduction to Phenomenology* (1950), trans. Dorion Caims (Dordrecht: Kluwer Academic Publishers, 1995). Jacques Lacan paraphrases the line in an article in *Ornicar?* No. 140 (1977) when he remarks: 'la rose en somme est la parce qu'elle est la, elle est sans pourquoi...' The idea that natural beauty is without a *why* is echoed in Kant's *Critique of Judgment* (1790), trans. James Creed Meredith (Oxford: Oxford University Press, 1952). A possible French source comes from a letter from Martin Heidegger to Luc Benoit, in a response to remarks concerning Heraclitus. Heidegger cites Silesius' aphorism as the expression of apophatic theology. Heidegger also discusses the Silestian fragment in *The Principle of Reason* (1957), trans. Reginald Lilly (Bloomington: Indiana University Press, 1996). 41.

6

Literary Studies in Contexts

Interview with Anfeng Sheng

ANFENG SHENG: *The so-called deconstruction criticism has been globally well-known for the "Yale School" scholars including Paul de Man, Geoffrey Hartman, Harold Bloom, Jacques Derrida, and you since the 80s of last century, while you identify yourself more with Derrida and de Man. So how have you found more similarities with these two than with others? And who else have ever had important influences upon your academic career?*

J. HILLIS MILLER: I have learned much from Hartman and Bloom too, but my own work has been more decisively inflected through reading works by de Man and Derrida. It would be hard to specify just why that is the case. The short answer would be, I suppose, that there is some residue of logocentrism in Hartman and Bloom. My own work veers away from that. You remember that book *Deconstruction and Criticism* (1979), with essays by all five of us, ostensibly all on Shelley's "The Triumph of Life." Hartman says in that book that he is not a deconstructionist. The personal relationships among the five of us were very friendly and close, but we were by no means all singing the same tune. Even Derrida, de Man, and I do not by any means have identical theoretical assumptions or critical procedures. Bloom and Hartman are even more different from each other and from the other three of us in the so-called "Yale School." In one place in a recent book by Derrida, *A Taste for* *the Secret* (2001), he specifies the basic difference between him and de Man, as he sees it: "…I do the best I can to mark the limits of the linguistic and the limits of the rhetorical—this was the crux of my profound debate with Paul de Man, who had a more 'rhetoricist' interpretation of deconstruction." In another late work by Derrida, "Typewriter Ribbon: Limited Ink (2)" (its English version in *Without Alibi*, 2002), Derrida turns back to Paul de Man and is delicately, gently, circumspectly critical of de Man's reading of himself in de Man's early essay, in *Blindness and Insight* (1971), on Derrida's reading of Rousseau. It's an interesting move by Derrida, because, generally speaking, Derrida says, "I completely agree with Paul de Man." And de Man characteristically says something like, "Ah, Derrida is so great. I wish I could write as he does." They were great friends and deeply respectful of one another's work. De Man used to come to all of Derrida's seminars at Yale. Not surprising, since they were intellectually exciting events.

What I most admire about all four of these theorists is that they are spectacular readers of literary texts. Hartman is a reader of genius, a wonderful reader, as is Bloom. They are both exceptional readers of literature, and they both love literature. Both de Man and Derrida, in different ways, also love literature and are spectacular readers of both philosophical and literary texts. The ability to make readings that surprise me but that seem valid is what I value most in all four, even more than their theoretical formulations.

Who else has influenced me? Kenneth Burke, William Empson, I.A. Richards, much more than the canonical New Critics, Cleanth Brooks, John Crowe Ransom, or Allen Tate. I have heard all but Empson, of these six, give lectures. The really important ones for my development were Burke and Empson. That perhaps reveals something about me, since they are both idiosyncratic, a little what we call "whacky." Empson is a marvelous—but quite atypical—British critic. These two are the same critics, it happens, that Harold Bloom also found interesting when he was a student. He and I share a great admiration for Burke, Empson, and another eccentric British critic, G. Wilson Knight. Their work, Bloom and I would agree, catches in its eccentricity something of the true untamable wildness of literature itself. Geoffrey Hartman was the first critic whose work I knew who introduced so-called phenomenology into literary criticism. His first book was on what he called *The Unmediated Vision* (1954). Reading it was for me, when I was still quite young, a revelation because I did not yet know the continental European criticism that was Hartman's inspiration. Then I discovered, when I went to teach at Johns Hopkins in 1953, the work of the Belgian phenomenological critic Georges Poulet. He was, it turned out, my colleague at Hopkins, and we became great friends. His critical procedures had a tremendous influence on my own early work, for example, my first book, the one on Dickens. I also learned much from the other critics associated with Poulet in what was called "the Geneva School": Marcel Raymond, Albert Béguin, Gaston Bachelard, and others. My doctoral dissertation, however, written of course earlier, was really Burkean. I attempted to use Burke to talk about Dickens. That dissertation has never been published and is fundamentally different from the book I published some years later on Dickens. That book was more Pouletian.

SHENG: *In reading some of your critical works, I could often feel kind of literary elements, even literary passion. In other words, some of your essays themselves are very good literary texts, for example, some passages in Chapter 14 of* Reading Narrative *(1998). I have also noticed that you have very exceptional sensibility and observation to poetry and other literary genres and could always find original perspectives to literary works. Have you ever written any poems or stories? What do you think is the relationship between one's literary criticism and literary production? In addition, you have been interested in science since you were very young, so how has the scientific interest influenced your literary studies?*

MILLER: That's really three questions rolled into one. Like many other people who love literature, but only for a very brief period, when I was quite young, in my teens, I tried to write fiction, but not very successfully. It was not a vocation, not something I really wanted to do, and certainly not something I could do well. I am not afraid to recognize, however, that there is a literary aspect to literary criticism. One has to be very careful in formulating this. Literature is one thing. Literary criticism is another. The relation involves a slight overlapping. In my case, a wistful interest in writing literature was completely transferred to the desire to write literary criticism as best I could. Writing criticism is not, in my case, a substitute for writing poetry and novels, but a complete sublimation of that desire. So that's a tricky question, requiring a careful answer.

In any case, writing literary criticism is great fun for me, more important even than what you call a "passion." I get enormous pleasure from it. I feel in a given case that I have really got hold the poem or novel, that I really understand it, and that I have something to say about it that no one has said before. Getting that down on paper gives pleasure, even though one is never entirely satisfied with a given critical essay. That dissatisfaction is one motivation for more work. Recently, I have been writing a paper on Kafka, for a Kafka conference in Oslo next spring (May 2006). My paper is about

Kafka's novel *The Castle* (1926). That's his last big unfinished novel. It is quite a challenge to understand it and to write something cogent about it. Trying to do this is fun, so it's not so much passion as a certain distinct kind of pleasure.

In answer to your question about the relation between my early interest in science and mathematics and my switch to literary study, I don't really know how to think about this except to say that both value economy and elegance. A good mathematical argument and a good literary critical one might both be described as elegant. Mathematicians admire not only successful pieces of mathematical thinking but also elegance and economy in mathematical proofs. This is something I also admire in literary criticism. Georges Poulet is a marvelously economical critic. He can put a reading of all the multitudinous works of Victor Hugo in twenty pages. That's really something. I have tried, not very successfully, to imitate that admirable sparseness.

There is another feature of my literary study that is transferred from my early study of science. I'm still a kind of, I don't quite say a positivist, but an empiricist. The scientific side of me exists still in the desire to make assertions about literary works that are capable of verification or, on the contrary, disproof. In science, a good hypothesis is what scientists call potentially "falsifiable." Hypotheses in the sciences need to be provable to be either true or false. An example of this would be the situation in the United States now when religious conservatives want to bring back the teaching of what is called "creationism" into our schools. Creationism is teaching that God created the universe, with all its creatures and all fossils, all evidence of evolution, somewhere around 4004 B.C. A new term for this is *intelligent design*. Living things, such religious conservatives argue, are just too complex to have evolved naturally. Some intelligent being must have planned life all the way from bacteria to human beings. The problem is that no way to prove or disprove intelligent design exists. It is not "falsifiable"; that is, it is not a valid scientific hypothesis. Evolution, on the contrary, is testable. You can produce evidence for it that is extremely persuasive for most people. You have fossil evidence in the rocks.

You can make lots of experiments. Modern genetics shows how different living things evolved and how their genomes are related. Someone might say, "the moon is made of green cheese." A scientist would say, "Prove it. Go to the moon and bring back some green cheese." Space missions so far have found nothing but rocks on the moon. "We affirmed," say scientists, "that a scientific hypothesis has to be falsifiable. Our space exploration has proved that the moon, at least not any part of it we have explored, is not made out of cheese, green or any other color." In my view, literary criticism should be like that. How do you prove a given hypothesis about a literary work to be true or false? By citation and by persuasive readings of citations. Literary texts, the words in the page, however problematic they are, are open to deciphering and interpretation. Those words are something concrete we can argue about. They play the role in literary criticism that moon rocks play in science. They provide some empirical evidence, something that might make possible some consensus as to their meaning. I make assertions about Kafka's *The Castle*. I then claim to prove by citations and readings of those citations that what I have said is correct. My evidence, I claim, supports my interpretation. That is the quasi-scientific aspect of literary criticism. My stress on this perhaps distinguishes me somewhat from my Yale School colleagues, though of course not wholly, and indicates the legacy of my early scientific study.

SHENG: *I noticed that you like quoting some phrases or sentences from others before the texts proper. Are these quotations sources of your arguments, or a kind of suggestion, or comparison, or conclusion, or the expanding of your own ideas?*

MILLER: That's a good question. Not so easy to answer. Usually after I have finished reading a given text, I have noted some important passages, at least passages that seem important to me. They tend to be of two kinds. Some are examples of characteristic motifs or themes, passages that support more conventional or traditional readings of the text in question. Some are passages that do not seem to fit the obvious overall pattern. They are interesting because they are anomalous, incongruous. They resist assimilation to a coherent reading. So the choice of citations is not simple. The challenge to me is to fit them all in somehow, even by showing how they do not "fit," to explain why they are there.

    Georges Poulet's technique of citation was somewhat different. He was most interested in passages that supported a coherent, comprehensive, dialectical pattern in a given writer that he had detected or hypothesized. I remember talking to him once years ago when he was writing about the American writer Nathaniel Hawthorne. Poulet was an extremely fast reader, which I am not. He claimed to have read all of Hawthorne's writings in one weekend in order to write a short essay for an addendum on American writers that was added to the English translation of *Etudes sur le temps humain* (1949). He had a hypothesis about the way certain features of Hawthorne's "inner distance," as he called it in the title of one of his books, hung together, but he had not found a citation that matched one stage of that hypothetical trajectory. On that weekend, he found the passage that he had guessed must be there. That made him extremely happy, really elated. It persuaded him his hypothesis had been correct. I am more interested than he was in passages that disconfirm whatever hypotheses I may have at the beginning about a given writer.

SHENG: *The deconstruction criticism and some critical trends based on post-structuralism are often criticized for their nihilism, their indulgence in textual/linguistic play, their evasion of the reality and their indifference to politics and society. But you are generally against this kind of reproach, regarding it as a consequence of misunderstanding and misrepresentation. So speaking from your own critical practice, how has deconstruction affected our reality and society in a constructive way? Do you believe that the deconstruction approach or any critical approach should not lose its artistic independence and become the simplified appendage to reality?*

MILLER: I do think that a lot of people who attack deconstruction have simply misunderstood it. They haven't read our writings carefully, which would seem a minimal obligation before attacking them. They have only read what the newspapers or superficial abstracts say deconstruction is, often in simple repetition of other superficial and incorrect summaries. Nevertheless, I recognize that deconstruction says things that are unsettling to the common sense assumptions many people have about selfhood, about history, about ethics, about literature, and so on. The resistance is not surprising. For example, a basic assumption of the so-called New Criticism was that a good literary work is organically unified. Many teachers and students in the United States fifty years ago accepted that assumption. That meant the goal of criticism was to find and describe the organic unity of a given work. This is very powerful assumption, even heuristically powerful, since it leads students to read carefully. For a deconstructionist such as Derrida, de Man, or me, however, it's not the case, simply not the case, that all good literary works are organically unified. It is perhaps even the case that none of them are. That hypothesis is heuristically powerful too, since it leads readers to look for features, passages that are clearly important but that cannot be incorporated into any organic unity, that don't fit. The presence of such features doesn't necessarily mean the work is bad, incoherent. Quite the contrary. It may indicate that it is a feature of language, however carefully organized, to resist assimilation to the metaphor of an organically unified body. People who make a fetish of "organic unity" are, it may be, not good readers.

To pick up your reference to the claim that so-called deconstructionists are detached from history and politics, it's easy to show that this is simply not the case, especially with Derrida, whose whole life and writings were deeply involved in one or another with political questions and political actions. For example, though he was never a member of the French Communist Party, that refusal was an important political gesture at the time he detached himself from association with the French "Tel Quel" group back in the fifties. Derrida's *Spectres de Marx* (1993) is a thoroughly political taking of position. Much of Derrida's writing, especially the later work, is concerned with such topics as capital punishment, the plight of the homeless, the future of democracy, forgiveness, and state sovereignty. Derrida's seminars on capital punishment did not simply say, "I don't like capital punishment." They proceeded through a careful examination of the history of capital punishment in the west. Membership in the European Union requires the abolition of capital punishment. That has been a problem for the admission of Turkey. When Derrida went to Israel he demanded from his Israeli hosts that a visit be arranged to a Palestinian university, much to the embarrassment of those hosts, though they did what he asked. Something similar about a concern with politics and history can be shown in different ways in my own work, with increasing emphasis in recent years, for example, in *The Ethics of Reading* (1987) and in *Speech Acts in Literature* (2001). The same thing can be said of Paul de Man's work. In the interview with Stefano Rosso de Man gave at the end of his life, in answer to a question about the increasing appearance of the terms *ideology* and *politics* in his work, he says "I don't think I ever was away from these problems, they were always uppermost in my mind."

SHENG: *You have been professor of comparative literature in Yale University and University of California. You have pointed out that the introduction of comparative literature into the college syllabus could be subversive to the authority of departments of English and the study of national literatures is now being replaced by comparative literature and the study of global English literatures. But you have also realized the crises of comparative literature, that is, the language crisis and crisis linked to the development of new media. In your opinion, the lasting crisis of comparative literature does not lie in divergences in theory or methodology but in translation, in the wider sense of the term. But to me, only through the research and development of comparative literature could this linguistic and cultural translation become possible. Hence, the problem of translation is one of the goals of comparative literature studies rather than a crisis.*

You have noticed the relevance between comparative literature and some kind of cultural imperialism and questioned the western centrism in the traditional comparative literature in the west. So what is a global, non-Eurocentric new comparative literature like?

MILLER: The people in the conference I've been attending have given papers and then in discussion have talked a lot about comparative literature in China. There seems to be general consensus. Conference participants for the most part agree that there should be a new comparative literature in the PRC that will be in two ways different from the traditional Eurocentric western one. One way is that it will take as its subject global literature, rather than just European literature. That sounds simple and obvious enough in these days of so-called globalization. Actually it is extremely hard to do. Languages such as Chinese or Japanese or the many African languages belong to such different language families and cultural traditions that it is difficult, well-nigh impossible, to train scholars who have truly global linguistic competence, whereas it was possible to know most of the important languages within a Eurocentric comparative literature. That does not mean we should not try to train students with a new kind of linguistic competence. I believe all students in the United States today should learn one Far Eastern language, preferably Chinese. The other difference in the new comparative literature being developed in the PRC has to do with no longer basing the discipline exclusively on western literary theory. Western literary theory has been developed on the basis of certain literatures, namely, western literatures. It was meant to account for western literature, its features. It would be a mistake to universalize it and try to make it apply to any literature anywhere. It is dangerous to assume that this procedure would work. I think that western literary theory, as well as the traditional European canon of comparative literature, needs to be seen in the light of theories developed in other parts of the world, such as the PRC. What we heard from the papers this afternoon is a new definition of comparative literature as a globalized enterprise. That enterprise would see worldwide literatures simultaneously from the perspective of many different theoretical traditions, many different definitions of what literature is, and of what it is good for, socially and for individual readers. I agree that this is the thing most important to be done at this moment.

The value of theory is to account for particular literary works in the best way possible. I don't have much interest in literary theory as such, in the abstract. The value of literary theory, its usefulness, is to help good reading of literary works and to help account for them. Good literary theory is not an airy abstraction. Literary theory makes statements that look universal but that are actually derived from a particular body of literature at a particular time, written in a particular language, and with a particular function in a particular culture. That's certainly true in western literary theory from Aristotle down to the present. Aristotle gives a definition of tragedy in his Poetics. Tragedy, he says is "a process of imitating an action which has serious implications, is complete, and possesses magnitude; by means of language which has been made sensuously attractive, with each of its varieties found separately in the parts; enacted by the persons themselves and not presented through narrative; through a course of pity and fear completing the purification of tragic acts which have those emotional characteristics." Aristotle doesn't say "some tragedies"; he says "tragedy," implicitly all tragedies. Aristotle's theory, however, which is stated with absolute generality, arises from his specific, narrowly located, even linguistically located goal. He wants to account for Athenian tragedy written in Attic Greek of fifth century B.C. Greece. He wants primarily, one can even say, to account for one tragedy, namely, Sophocles's "Oedipus the King," since he spends most time discussing that one play. It is his paradigmatic tragedy. A disjunction exists between the historical specificity of the works being "theorized" and the absolute generality of Aristotle's theoretical statements. Theoreticians of the Renaissance period in England had great difficulty making what Aristotle says fit Renaissance drama, such as Shakespeare's "Hamlet." Renaissance drama is always to some degree Christian, which Sophocles's plays of course were not.

Theoretical assertions made by present-day theorists, for example, Paul de Man, take the same form. In a famous passage in one of the essays in *Allegories of Reading*, "Allegory (Julie)," de Man says the following: "The paradigm for all texts consists of a figure (or a system of figures) and its deconstruction. But since this model cannot be closed off by a final reading, it engenders, in its turn, a supplementary figural superposition which narrates the unreadability of the prior narration. As distinguished from primary deconstructive narratives centered on figures and ultimately always on metaphor, we can call such narratives to the second (or the third) degree allegories." One of my reactions to this admirably condensed formulation (besides registering how difficult it is to understand) is to say, "Paradigm of all texts? That's a pretty bold statement." If even one text that would not fit that paradigm could be found, de Man's theoretical claim would be disqualified. De Man's assertions arise in a specific essay intended to read and account for just one work by Jean-Jacques Rousseau, *Julie, ou la nouvelle Héloïse*.

The validity of Aristotle's theoretical formulation, or of de Man's, lies not in its universal applicability, but in its ability to account for quite particular works, works located at a particular time in a particular culture. To assume such formulations are valid for all literary work everywhere and at all times is extremely problematic. It becomes particularly problematic if you assume you can apply such theoretical statements to the reading of non-western works.

SHENG: *What do you think of the deconstructive elements and the influences, whether positive or negative, of postcolonialism? You have talked a little bit about Edward Said and Gayatri Spivak and showed your consent to their leftist critical attitude. So what do you think of the trend of postcolonialism in general?*

MILLER: Well, that's something I really know little about. I have read some of Homi Bhabha's work, but not very much of it. I am really not qualified to say much in answer to your question except to say that the current generation of postcolonial critics, a generation that includes Spivak, Bhabha, and Said, has been deeply influenced by so-called deconstruction. At the same time, these critics have reacted against deconstruction in one way or another. Derrida was always annoyed by what Said said about deconstruction because, he claimed, Said had never read him carefully and says things about him (Derrida) and about deconstruction generally that can be shown to be incorrect. Said needed to oppose deconstruction, or thought he did, to establish his own postcolonial theory. He needed his misreading of Derrida as a foil.

Nevertheless, Derrida has had a big, if sometimes somewhat hidden, influence on Spivak, Homi Bhabha, and people like Žižek. Spivak, after all, translated Derrida's *Of Grammatology* into English. Derrida's work is so powerful that it serves as a challenge to the next generation to be different. Postcolonial critics no doubt have some different basic assumptions from Derrida's, but an overlap exists in their common concern for the plight of people in postcolonial societies: children, women, exiles, the homeless, those who continue to be oppressed. Derrida did not mind being disagreed with, but he thought he ought to be understood before being opposed. Said, he said, did not understand him. He wasn't even sure whether or not Said had ever actually read his work. Said was, by the way, a fairly close friend of mine, whereas Derrida did not really know him. I knew Said for many years, during which he patiently tried to educate me, especially about the plight of the occupied Palestinians. I read Said's first book, on Conrad's short fiction, for the Harvard University Press and enthusiastically recommended its publication. I made every effort I could to get Yale to appoint Said as a professor there, without success. I thought he would make a wonderful professor at Yale. He was a legendarily powerful teacher, and of course, his books have had great influence all over the world. I grieved when he died. Nevertheless, I think Derrida was right to say that Said treated deconstruction unjustly.

SHENG: *The ideal university for Derrida is "unconditional," and Said has also warned us of the danger of the accommodation of universities by any organization. You yourself have worried about the donations and aids not only from the government but also from enterprises or multinationals. This invasion or infiltration is now changing the social functions of the humanities in a dramatic way. So how could we scholars of humanities possibly preserve the freedom of speaking and thinking and the independence of research in a commercialized society? If universities should not (solely) be technological and instrumental, then what are the responsibilities of universities?*

MILLER: Ah, good question! Yes, it should be without condition. The most precious thing in our United States universities is what we call "academic freedom." That is the freedom, in principle, to say anything in the classroom, to put anything in question. Literature as a fairly recent institution in the west has in principle the same freedom to say anything and to put anything in question, in a fiction. Like the freedom of speech, and like literary freedom, academic freedom is never totally free. There are always unspoken and tacit restraints on it. Some things you cannot say in the classroom without getting, with justice, into some kind of trouble, for example, so-called hate speech. So academic freedom is never total. Nevertheless, academic freedom is a fundamental right in western universities. It is freedom to value truth-telling and truth-finding over expediency or even practical utility. The first scientists (one was at my university) who reported on the weakening of the ozone layer and its causes were ridiculed and sharply criticized. Few experts believed their findings. Ultimately, they received the Nobel Prize for their work. They had been telling the truth, even though it went against received opinion and against what corporations wanted to hear. Ultimately, they were rewarded for that truth-finding and truth-telling. The danger in our universities now is that professors more and more find sources of money from corporations. This encourages scientists, for example, to do research valuable for its immediate practical use. I think it's wrong to say that knowledge professors discover should be valued for its immediate practical use. The practical utility of a new finding may not be immediately apparent, for example, the discovery of DNA and the human gene. Another example is the development of the original Internet. It was devised as a local means for scientists to communicate rapidly. Few people foresaw that the Internet would become what it is today and that this would happen so rapidly. A scientist doing "pure research" often "accidentally" discovers something that turns out eventually to have a big practical use. That's different from the way pharmaceutical companies give grants to university scientists to do specific research that will help them make new medicines that will make the companies a lot of money.

The university should be the place where people can do research that is free from having any apparent practical use. That facet of academic freedom is difficult to preserve. Even to assert it now, as I've just been doing, sounds utopian. The university's mission is to find out the truth in all fields, for its own sake. That mission is an extremely fragile commitment, particularly nowadays. This is the case, even though the mottoes of many great American universities state that commitment, for example, the four with which I have been most closely associated. "*Veritas vos liberabit,*" "the truth will set you free," is the motto of the Johns Hopkins University, where I taught for many years. "*Lux et veritas,*" "Light and truth," is the motto of Yale University, where I taught after I left Hopkins. Just "*Veritas,*" "Truth," is the motto of Harvard University, where I did my graduate work. The University of California, my present university, has "Let there be light" as its motto. Our research universities are committed to enlightenment, to bringing the truth to light! They are a product of Enlightenment ideals. Nevertheless, it is not without significance that all these mottoes have a Biblical reference. The Johns Hopkins motto is a citation from the Christian New Testament, John 8:31, 32. The University of California motto is from the Book of Genesis. The words *truth* and *light* in the other two mottoes also have a Biblical resonance. United States research universities still carry within their slogans their original Christian heritage, just as the concept of globalization, as Jacques Derrida has argued, depends ultimately on the Christian theological concept of "the world." The French word for globalization is *mondialisation,* which might be translated, literally, as "worldification," that is, making the whole globe one "world."

Another feature of the present-day situation of the university is the globalization of which I have just been speaking. The world is becoming very small, smaller every day. Good universities and good research have an international scope these days. Therefore, universities should be open to researchers and students from all over the world, for example, postdoctoral researchers. Unfortunately, that mission is not always fulfilled. State universities, such as the University of California, feel they have a primary obligation to students from the states that fund them. They feel they have a smaller obligation to educate anybody not from that state, much less students from other countries. That often goes against the primary mission: to find out the truth about everything, to shed light on everything. Global cooperation is necessary to that bringing to light. Why? Because international cooperation is the best way to make progress in getting knowledge. International teams carry on many important scientific investigations. Notice how often Nobel Prizes are given to teams of several people working in different countries, one from Chicago, another from India, another from Germany. They have cooperated over long distances. They work together. That international cooperation depends, in turn, on new teletechnologies: computers, email, the Internet, fiber-optic cables, and so on. The university in our time of globalization must be open to the world. My own work, even though I work in the humanities, is carried on in cooperation with colleagues from all over the world, such as my collaboration in this present interview! It was recorded in China on a small recorder, then transcribed into a computer there, is now being revised by me in the United States, and will be sent back to China by email. Only a few years ago, each of those relays would have been impossible. They depend absolutely on quite new teletechnological devices.

SHENG: *We have an old saying in China, "the spectators see the chess game better than the players," so when interviewing foreign scholars, I often raise the following question: as an "outsider," how do you see the present situation of literary theory circle and literary criticism in China? What should we pay attention to in its future development?*

MILLER: Though as an outsider I understand the Chinese situation only imperfectly, I think perhaps professors here need the courage to develop their own theoretical formulations, rather than depend on the theories of others.

SHENG: *Especially western theories.*

MILLER: Yes, especially western theories. Perhaps we in the west all need to know more about Chinese literary theories. Perhaps no one here recently has worked out a specifically Chinese literary or cultural theory with the power of the theoretical writings of, for example, Frederic Jameson. I gather Jameson has had a large influence in China.

I remember a conference on Marxist literary theory I attended some years ago in, I believe, Guilin. I know a little about Marx, but I read *Capital* to write my paper. I found it interesting, to say the least, a very interesting book. It is also in places a pretty funny book. The footnotes, especially, are wonderfully polemical and ironic. I found also that there is in *Capital* an implicit literary theory of great sophistication. Marx had inherited that post-Hegelian nineteenth-century European tradition of rhetorical knowledge and analysis. He appropriates it to good advantage in order to say what he wants to say, for example, in a famous passage about the table that stands up on its legs and talks. A sophisticated theory of poetic and metaphorical language is present implicitly, or even explicitly, in Marx. He was deeply influenced by Shakespeare and was a superb reader of Shakespeare. I gave my paper (which has been published, such as it is, in Chinese). Then, I asked somebody at the conference, a Chinese colleague, "Why do you need Frederic Jameson and all these western theorists (there were many at that conference) to tell you about Marxist literary theory or about Marx's literary theory? China is supposed to be a communist and Marxist country. Why not have papers on recent Chinese Marxist literary theory?" The person to whom I posed this question answered, "Because we don't have any!" That was amazing to me! Here's a country that is supposed to be committed to Marxism. "We don't have any Marxist literary theory, so we need the westerners to come and tell us what it might be like." I think the Chinese should develop their own Marxist theories of literature. No doubt that is now happening, since the conference I speak of was a good many years ago already.

SHENG: *Even resorting to the Marxist literary theory is still from other country. It's not Chinese.*

MILLER: That's right, it's not Chinese, but China should be developing its own form of indigenous Marxism, including a Chinese-Marxist literary theory. Marx's own writings, I agree, have a specific historical and intellectual context. He derives from a German intellectual tradition. That was also the tradition of George Eliot, the great English Victorian novelist. There is a nineteenth-century German rhetorical theorist named Boeckh. Boeckh is post-Hegelian, like Marx. They speak from the same intellectual heritage. Both Marx and George Eliot have theories of figurative language and theories about literature that are something like Boeckh's. George Eliot had a very sophisticated literary theory, as did Marx, and I would say that the assumptions about literature in George Eliot and Marx are quite similar, but it would take a lot of pages to demonstrate that. It happens, by a happy accident, that George Eliot and Karl Marx are buried within a hundred feet of one another. Years ago, I went to the Highgate Cemetery, north of London, to see the grave of George Eliot. She was, and is, a Victorian novelist important to me in my own work. Her grave, I found, is rather shabby and not well tended. There, less than 100 feet away, is the shining tombstone of Karl Marx, with a bust of Marx on top. When I was there (this was quite a long time ago, still the time of the Soviet Union), there were fresh flowers on Marx's grave. A group of Soviet officials had come to pay their respects to Marx's tomb. You could tell they were from the Soviet Union, because they wore black, bureaucratic, rather shapeless, business suits. That Marx's tomb is within a stone's throw of George Eliot's is for me a contingent expression of the fact that they belong to the same intellectual tradition. They have the same sophistication about rhetorical theory. How that could be appropriated by the Chinese intellectual tradition I do not know, but I say to the Chinese, read Marx! Read George Eliot too! (Laughing)

SHENG: *Reread Marx!*

MILLER: Yes, reread Marx. It may be that in China a kind of line on Marxism exists that is no substitute for returning and returning again to Marx's writings, *The German Ideology*, for example, or the *Grundrisse*, and, of course, *Capital*. This situation may be somewhat parallel to the rather simplified version of Freud used in the first year in psychoanalytical schools in the U.S., where students are trained to be analysts. For the first year, students read Freud, but quite selectively. When they reread Freud later more widely, if they do, they find that he's much more interesting than they thought, more diverse, even less homogeneous.

SHENG: *You have become very well-known throughout the world in the academic sphere, especially in the field of literary studies and literary theory. But for the benefit of young scholars like us and the general readers in the literary field, I want to know, is there any regret in your academic career? If you had an opportunity to start it again, what would you do?*

MILLER: Well one thing I would do, that I wish I had done, is to learn Chinese. I am serious about that. I really wish I had done that, or that I could do it even now.

SHENG: *Yes you have mentioned this on several occasions and Professor Wang Ning likes to quote it to encourage us.*

MILLER: So not having learned Chinese yet is a serious regret. I also somewhat wistfully, now and then, regret the professions I gave up in order to devote myself to literary study. That includes physics, a very specific kind of physics, astrophysics: black holes, the expanding universe, star birth, super novae, and so on. It still fascinates me, cosmology. Astrophysics is an exciting field these days. I read about it in an amateur way in *Science News* and *Scientific American*. That is the other career, the career I never had. I never really wanted to be a biologist. But physics still interests me.

I have another career fantasy: to be an archaeologist. I imagine myself in a pith helmet, digging up ruins or old bones.

So those are slight regrets, not very serious ones. What I really like most is reading literature, teaching it, and writing about it, theorizing about it. That shift from physics to literature was a true vocational decision, the response to what used to be defined as a "calling." OK. Thank you very much. This has been fun. You have asked really good and really provocative questions!

SHENG: *Thank you for your time and for allowing me to talk with you!*

7

On Literature and Ethics

Interview with Constanza del Río Álvaro and
Francisco Collado-Rodríguez

The interview that follows was conducted at the University of Zaragoza,
Spain, on April 29, 2005. Professor J. Hillis Miller had delivered a series
of lectures on ethics and literature as part of the graduate course "Coming
Out of Relativism: The Re-Evaluation of History and Ethics in Recent US
Fiction."

**CONSTANZA DEL RIO ÁLVARO/FRANCISCO COLLADO-
RODRÍGUEZ:** *In your writings, you have repeatedly called attention to
the problematic relationships between individual examples and conceptual
generalizations. In fact, you have been very cautious in advancing that
your selection of examples to illustrate the ethics of reading is arbitrary and
inevitably conveys a certain bias. You have also stated that establishing a
synecdochal link between example and context or example and theory may be
misleading or even wrong. Furthermore, in* The Ethics of Reading *there is the
assumption that each text is unique and demands a unique response. That is,
each reading answers to a singular linguistic imperative. Considering all these
issues, is there still any room left for a general theory of the ethics of reading?*

J. HILLIS MILLER: Yes, of course. It would be a theory based on the problematic you have outlined. What you said in paraphrasing me was theoretical. It did not have any examples. It was a theoretical formulation about singularity and about the problematic relation between example and generalization. It was a theoretical construct. That means you can have a general theory of the difficult relation between general theory and a particular case. You expressed that general theory very well. I do not see any problem with that. It is theory, highly theoretical. It is even general, that is, implicitly applicable, without modification, to innumerable examples. For example, in my lecture yesterday, I was expressing a theory about the specificity of ethical decision *a propos* of Sethe's decision in Toni Morrison's *Beloved*. What I advanced was a theoretical proposition. I do not really see any problem about doing that. There is a problem, however, about how actually to carry out, in a concrete situation where a decision is demanded, what my proposition proposed. I heard at a conference recently in Ghent, in Belgium, a marvelous plenary speech given by a sometime student of mine, Carol Jacobs. She is now a professor of German and comparative literature at Yale. She has been working on Plato's *Republic*. She had a lot to say about the notion of justice, which is what Plato's *Republic* is about. Her lecture was, I would say, very scrupulous. I do not really like the word *deconstruction* anymore, so let me say that Jacob's talk was a putting in question of the traditional assumptions about what Plato was saying by emphasizing the mise-en-scène of the *Republic*. Plato places Socrates in halfway between Athens and Piraeus. He is outside Athens, beyond its borders, but not yet in Piraeus.

Professor Jacobs went on to talk (as people do now, but did not use to do) about the ways Plato's dialogue is a kind of narrative. It tells a story. Then she emphasized the way in which the search in dialogue for justice-dike is not satisfying. That is to say, it turns out to be not easy to define. That is typical of Plato's dialogues: a failure at the end to come to a satisfying conclusion and a promise to go on with investigation at another time. In the question–answer period after Professor Jacob's lecture—this is the point in the story I am telling—somebody in the audience asked her whether she was prepared to generalize on the basis of what she had said about the relations among politics, justice, and individual ethical responsibility. Jacob's is more rigorous than I am. She was firm in her denial. She answered, "No, I have been talking about Plato's *Republic*. I was not saying anything about whether or not what happens in the *Republic* can be universalized. You cannot generalize from what I have said. I was just talking about Plato." That is the correct answer, perhaps even more correct than what I said in my lecture yesterday, in which I succumbed to the desire to generalize. Few people, certainly not I, have Carol Jacobs's rigor.

Here is another example of rigor. The reader encounters a lot of Derrida's own theory in his essay "Force of Law," of the relation between justice and law. This theorizing comes in the preliminary section of that essay, as a preparation for a reading of Walter Benjamin's "Zur Kritik der Gewalt." The first part of congruence between law and justice. Derrida suggests that you could say, "If I follow the law, a pre-existing law, then you could say what I do is lawful, that is, I have obeyed the law." However, you cannot say it is just, since justice for Derrida always involves a free decision. Or, in a quotation he makes from Stanley Fish, "Every judge in applying the law has to make a fresh judgment." You could say that the relationship between the law and any particular case brought before the judge or jury is analogous to the relationship between literary theory or ethical theory and a particular case. Why does the judge have to make a fresh judgment? Because the judge has to decide whether a given law applies to this particular case. That does not go without saying. The lawyer for the defense often tries to defend the accused by saying "This law does not apply to my client. It is inapplicable in this case, because the circumstances of the case are different."

A judge's courtroom decision is a speech act of a peculiar kind. There is also a surprising passage in J. L. Austin's *How to Do Things With Words,* the Bible speech act theory. Austin presents many examples that come from the law and makes many complicated references to lawyers and the law *a propos* of the question of felicitous speech acts—whether a given performative utterance is felicitous speech act has to be uttered in the right circumstances, by the right person, etc. Lawyers, says Austin, have over many years worked out a lot of these problems. They have done this in order to ensure that when the judge says, "I sentence you to six months in jail," the person really goes to jail. Austin faults judges and lawyers for not being aware of the degree to which their speech acts are to a distressing degree arbitrary, rather than prescribed by the law. In the amazing sentence I have already referred to, he says that the judge, in uttering a judgment, "makes law." Probably most judges would be very anxious not to have to accept that responsibility. They would be inclined to say, I imagine, "I am not doing anything but just impartially applying the law." Austin would respond, "You are wrong about that."

Something similar could be said about literary theory. Every reader has theoretical presuppositions. Yale college freshmen and sophomores, whom I used to teach, almost all thought, at least in the '70s and '80s, that they could make a work mean anything they wanted. That is a theoretical presupposition. It was a strange widely shared ideological aberration, part of the culture of those elite students who got into Yale. Nobody reads with an open mind. You can tell students to read without any abstract preconceptions, but of course, they do have preconceptions. You could not make any sense out of any text if you did not have many preconceptions. But when an interpretation of a literary work, which presumably says something about the specific text in question, looks like it ought to be constative, that is to say, a statement of fact, but it always has a performative aspect, any interpretation implies a speech act. "I declare this work means so and so."

That fissure between the constative and the performative matches the disjunction between law and justice. One can imagine a "lawful" reading of a text. We do get those from students. A student takes a given critic or kind of criticism—Judith Butler, feminist criticism, Derrida, Jung, Lacan, or whatever—and simply applies that to the text. Some teachers even like and encourage that deplorable acitivity. You ought to say to such a student, "You haven't really read and worked. You just read into it certain theoretical presuppositions, presuppositions that are not even your own." Everyone, as I have said, has theoretical presuppositions, even if they are tacit and "unconscious." Good reading is defined by the encounter of something in the text that does not fit the theory you have. Good reading contradicts the reader's theoretical preconceptions, his or her expectations about preconceptions, his or her expectations about what will be found in the text read. If a rigid application of a theoretical assumption corresponds to a judgement that just applies the law, a "just" reading is a reading that goes beyond theoretical assumptions to respond to the unique demand the text makes for a "fresh judgment," one analogous to the judgment of the just judge. Accepting this is difficult for students because they think that they are doing just the right thing when they "apply" Freud or whomever. They tell you, "You've been talking about Freud, explaining Freudian criticsm to me, and that is what I thought you wanted me to do." But you must reply, "No, no, no you haven't got the point; you haven't understood. You must read for yourself and are always on your own when you do that." All reading opens on what Derrida calls an "indeterminable future." You never know what is going to happen when you pick up a book and read. So, that would be my answer to your question.

ÁLVARO/COLLADO-RODRÍGUEZ: *When dealing with issues concerning ethics and morals, we have an immediate terminological problem related to these two terms. In your seminar on* Beloved, *you agreed to the opinion that Sethe did the right thing—in the ethical sense—but had no moral right to* *do it. Could we not otherwise think that Morrison's protagonist did the right thing? According to her own personal circumstances that had taught her a private moral law, but she had no ethical right to do so—in the sense that she was killing the other, her children? In other words, coming to a terminological matter, if we cannot get hold of the origin of the ethical, why should we interpret it only in one way?*

MILLER: I remember that Morrison does not use these terms (*ethics* or *morals*). She uses the term *right*, whether it was right to do something. We do not want to foist those distinctions too easily on her. Moreover, what she says is speaking in her own voice on an interview: "It was an impossible decision." An "impossible" decision, that is an interesting way to put it. She means, I take it—though she does not say so—that either way Sethe decided to take—either to let her children be taken back or herself take them back into slavery or to attempt to kill them—she would have done, in a sense, the wrong thing. She would have done something that she had no right to do. However, she had to decide what to do. It means that there is no clear right decision. Her formulation about doing the right thing is not in Morrison's own words either. She says that somebody else analyzing her novel—Morrison does not say who that was—said, "She did the right, but she had no right to do it." I would say that Sethe did the right thing ethically. She acted in a way that is outside the law. Her decision was just, since it was inaugural, initiatory. It came from a spontaneous response to a demand made on her by the situation, by her context, and by her belief that there is another side to send her children to. I think we would have a quite different meaning if she did not have this religious belief. She does not say that her decision was based on a moral law that she had developed as a slave. That is not said anywhere. What she does say is based on her experiences as a slave, but she does not generalize from that to establishing a moral law that is universal in the sense that it says, "it is better to be dead than to be a slave." She does not say that. What she says is that her experiences of slavery have led her to believe that. Nor does she say anywhere that anybody would have done the same thing in the same situation or ought to. She does not say that. That is not in the text. Nor does Morrison—at least in the interviews I have read—say anything like that, that Sethe's is a model for others' behavior. In a sense, you could argue that my imposition on the text is the act of identifying moral with a preexisiting law or habit or whatever. I call that morality, whereas, for me, ethics is always parallel to justice. That is to say, the parallel I would make is between morality and the law, justice and ethics. You could say that what Sethe does is, I would say, ethically right, but she had no moral right to do it. That is the way I would phrase the distinction, clearly reversing the use of moral and ethics that you made. That is perhaps because I am familiar with using it in that way, for example, in the Kantian tradition. The word *moral* is often used in a condescending and in a denigrating way, to tame the unreflective following of a moral rule by someone. Such people behave morally, but they are not really just or ethical, precisely because they do not think of the unique circumstances. You may take as example the way people in my country used to blame the poverty and so-called immorality of black people on racial stereotypes. They would say something like "What do you expect from shiftless black people? They are very immoral. Marriage does not work for them. Black teenagers are always getting pregnant—that is immoral," and so on. "Immoral," however, is the actual circumstance. The life of a particular black person is always complicated, too complicated to fit generalizations about the innate immorality of African Americans. Morrison's *Beloved* attempts to show what life was actually like for black people under slavery. It attemps to justify Sethe's killing of her baby daughter, to persuade us to believe that she was right to do that.

ÁLVARO/COLLADO-RODRÍGUEZ: *So in that sense, the moral is already an interpretation of the ethical. Or is it a misinterpretation of the ethical?*

MILLER: It is an attempt to escape the burden of ethical decision by being able to say, "I do not have to think about this. This is what the Bible tells me: 'Thou shalt not kill.'" That would be a moral law. That is the Old Testament. The story of Abraham and Isaac already raises a question like that Morrison raises about Sethe and *Beloved*. Was Abraham right to be willing to sacrifice his dearly beloved son Isaac? You might say, however, that the New Testament is the place in the Bible where something like the ethical—in Kierkegaard's, Derrida's, or my own sense—is salient. Jesus makes decision difficult, as you know. He says, "I come not to destroy the law but to fulfill it." It seems to me that the change involved in "fulfilling the law" is the reason why it is so difficult to be really a Christian, why there are so few Christians. You have to believe that Jesus is the Messiah; you have to believe you should give all your money to the poor, accept poverty. I do not see too many people doing that. You have to leave your father and mother and follow Him, that is to say, disobey the law that says, "Honor thy father and mother." Jesus is very specific about that. He makes it hard to be a Christian, to say the least.

ÁLVARO/COLLADO-RODRÍGUEZ: *In contemporary theory, the turn to ethics is frequently assiciated with Levinas's reinstallation of the ethical impulse as a presymbolic encounter with the other. Somehow, a religious Logos is recuperated for a contemporary theory in some of his writings, a notion also questioned by Derrida. Ethics, religion, and Logos—what is your opinion about this triad?*

MILLER: Well I do not know as much about Levinas's works as I should. I have read some books by him, but I can speak with only modest authority about Levinas. My position is closer to Derrida's but perhaps not even identical to his because it veers a little more in the direction of scepticism, when I have to deal with formulas like the "wholly other." In Derrida's case, reservations about Levinas always surface. As you probably know, in his essays about Levinas, Derrida is very respectful of him, but he always draws back. Derrida draws back, for example, by saying in effect that Levinas is too much of an orthodox Jew for him. That is to say, there is, for Derrida, too much belief in Levinas in a personified divinity who is male, patriarchal, long-bearded, up there in the sky somewhere, all-powerful, the ultimate appeal. In one of his essays, Derrida comments about Levinas that accuses Levinas—and implicity Judaism in general—of being sexist. Why should Jehovah not be a woman? How does Levinas know that God is a man? What is the point in making this presumption about God's masculinity? Surely, when you read the Old Testament, it is very hard to believe in it without believing in that old man in the sky with a long grey beard. Derrida does not believe in that. I think that is what makes it impossible for him to be identified with any orthodox religion, including Christianity, about which he knew a lot. I remember once, sitting in one of his last seminars, I realized that there I was, in presence of this "deconstructionist" who was supposed to be destroying Western civilization, but he was, on the contrary, giving a long sympathetic seminar about St. Augustine. *The Confessions* was one of his favourite books. Derrida was not critical of Augustine. He was more sympathetic in his treatment of Augustine than in his treatment of Heidegger, or Kant, or Hegel. I thought that seminar on Augustine revealed a lot about Derrida.

Nevertheless, Derrida went to a lot of effort in a long essay to try to distinguish his position from what many people say he is, that is, an example of negative theology. Negative theology is a way, by an adroit use of negation, to generate belief in a traditional monostheistic God. You say, "I do not know what God is. He is not this. He is not that. He is not the other thing, because he is inscrutable and incomprehensible." It is very tempting to say that that is what Derrida is really saying, for example, when he talks about "le tout autre (the wholly other)" in *Donner la mort (The Gift of Death)*. What he says can be interpreted as a kind of negative theology. I find it interesting that Derrida took it upon himself to write an essay in which he says, "No, what I am doing is not negative theology." That is an important move by Derrida.

I guess you would say that in my own case I am more in sympathy with Morrison's Sethe than with Abraham. That is to say, in the ethical decisions that I have to make, I am still waiting to hear the voice from God that tells me what to do, but I have not heard it yet. Abraham hears a command from God to sacrifice Isaac and accepts that command. Sethe hears no such voice. I wish I could see one, as Thomas Hardy once said. In a similar way, I would be very happy to hear a little voice, the little voice of conscience speaking to me, telling me what to do, mediating God's command. So far, thank God, I have not had to make the kind of decision Sethe makes or that Abraham makes. However, my experience is more like hers in finding myself often in a situation where I must decide something important but do not get much help from moral formulas. I feel like I am pretty much on my own in decision-making. That is not too far from Derrida. However, the difference is that Derrida talks about the experience of the demand made on me by the "wholly other," and that sounds to me like some kind of little voice. It is closer to that, in any case, than my sense of having to decide on my own, so Derrida is somehow in between Levinas and me, I would say.

I was brought up a Protestant. My father was a Baptist minister. My brother is a Presbyterian minister. My grandfather taught men's Bible classes in a small Presbyterian church in Virginia for forty years. He read the Bible very well. That is my family heritage. I do not go to church now, but I went to church until I was fourteen or so and attended Sunday School all that time. I am sorry to say that I was often inattentive at church, daydreaming about something or other, and not listening to the sermon. Sometimes I could hear my own father preach, because he was the president of a small Baptist women's college in upstate New York. He was, among his other duties, sometimes at least, the preacher on Sunday for two hundred students at the college. They were all expected to go to church in the college on Sunday. Becoming a Baptist means that you are totally immersed in water at the age of twelve, which is when Jesus was supposed to have been baptized. There is a kind of tank upon a platform. You are dressed in something like a nightgown for the ceremony and bent over backward into the water by the minister. Quite an experience. In other Protestant congregations, babies are baptized at birth. They have no chance to choose. Baptists are given a choice.

You are supposed to reach the age of reason at twelve years of age and to be able to say, "I accept all that is involved." It is like Confirmation for Roman Catholics.

Now, coming back to your question, you asked about the recuperation of the Logos. I do not think that you can avoid recuperating the Logos in one way or another, but that is not an innocent event. As you know, when John in the fourth Gospel says, "At the beginning was the Word, and the Word was with God, and the Word was God," the Greek word for *Word* there is *Logos*. John identifies the Logos with Mediator, the second person of the Trinity: Jesus is the Logos. Obviously, in spite of that association with Christianity, you can have logocentrism without Christianity. It is hard, however, in the aftermath of the appropriation of Greek philosophical thought, either Plato or Aristotle, by Christian theology not to associate logocentrism with Christian theology.

Logocentrism is so intimately woven into our languages—Spanish, English, any European language—that it is very difficult to think against it. You have to use its tools against itself. I will put this another way. Derrida makes many reproaches to "logocentrism," which is, after all, his own invented word. You could say the whole effort of deconstruction as a mode of interrogative thinking is to put logocentrism actively in question. Nevertheless, there is a side of Derrida that is complicit with an ineradicable logocentrism, his reasonable philosophical argumentation, for example, not to mention the traces of religious thinking in his work, whatever his denials. To claim to be free of logocentrism. To say, "I am free of the Logos," is something like saying, "I do not believe in ghosts." Either is a dangerous thing to say. Just saying either is a kind of denegation that obliquely confesses the opposite of what it says.

ÁLVARO/COLLADO-RODRÍGUEZ: *We would like to change the subject now. In a piece that you wrote around 1998, entitled "Literary Study in the Transnational University," you gave a panoramic view of the role and function of the study of literature and literature departments in a university transformed by globalization and new technologies. The university was increasingly run and controlled by multinational corporations, and the study of literature had been replaced by cultural studies. After seven years, have you perceived any changes, for the better or the worse?*

MILLER: That is an interesting question. I have not reflected recently on the way I formulated the question of the university then. That essay was written quite a while ago. I try to be very careful not to succumb, as sometimes older academic people do, to the tendency to say, "Oh, when I was a boy (or girl), things were in good shape in the university. Now things are getting worse and worse." This is the tendency towards idealizing nostalgia. Such people tend to consider that what all these young students and teachers are doing today is pointless evasion, a sell-out. Such people say, "We used really to understand philology and literary history, now young scholar-teachers do not know anything about this great tradition and the ways it was institutionalized." I have to be sure to avoid feeling or saying anything like that. On the contrary, I would say that there is a tremendous amount of intellectual vitality, a touching vitality, in young students and teachers in my country. This is the case with graduate students especially. Many of them have an uncertain future, since there are not enough jobs to go around. They may or may not get a job. Nevertheless, they maintain their integrity. They do dissertations on things that really interest them, even if that might make it even more difficult to get a job. This is a brave acceptance of their vocation even though it may be against their own interest. I find this very touching. It is evidence that humanities study is certainly not going away. I also find very impressive, when I travel here and there around the world, particularly to China—to give one example of a quite different place from the United States or Europe—encountering the same kind of special energy and willingness to think outside the boxes in younger people.

Many young students and teachers in the United States, in Europe, and in East Asia have turned to something called "Cultural Studies." I am not one of those mossbacks who say, "Oh, we must draw the line. We must force students to read *Beowulf* and eighteenth-century English poetry, etc.," texts they may not want to study. They want to work on film, or on television, or even on video games, cultural forms that are of great influence today on what people think, feel, and believe, in short on their ideological convictions and on their consequent actions, for example, the way they vote.

I do think that the role of literature in our culture today is changing and weakening. The evidence for this is clear. So many people spend much more of their time today watching television or using the Internet than they do reading literature. Many people still do read fiction, even though it may be romances, mystery stories, or science fiction, not Chaucer or Dickens. Nevertheless, the actual formation of voters' ideologies in the United States is not determined by reading Shakespeare or George Eliot. Most crucial choices are determined, in good part at least, by television and by other forms of mass media. Since that is the case, it is a good idea to study these media, to find out how they work. To think about new media critically seems to me an urgent necessity. I think this is even truer now that seven years ago, when I wrote the essay to which you refer. We now have generations of young people who have been brought up with computers, mp3, video games, television, and film. The lives of these people have been determined to a great degree by the effects of the new media. It is not unreasonable that they should be interested in analyzing these things. I think it is a mistake to be condescending and say, "Well, the film *The Golden Bowl* is not anything like as good as the novel." The film is different, necessarily different. You can do things with films that Henry James could not do with words on the page, and vice versa. The differences need to be identified, rather than making a judgement.

For example, I think that now it is important to make a serious study of video games, because millions of video games are sold. This study is only beginning. There are many people. Including intelligent college students, who spend a lot of time playing video games. So, I think it would be a reasonable thing to study them. Other issues we should be studying include, for example, the reasons why so many people buy the iPod or these little mp3 players. It is because popular music plays a huge part in their lives. They may be "post-human" when they are walking around plugged into the iPod, but they are plugged into their iPod, and they still look human to me. It follows that it would be a good idea to study the effects on human beings of this situation of being plugged in and also to study the actual content of this music that they listen to.

I discovered recently that there is an important connection of popular music to video games. The audio part of video games used to be just odd sounds, shots when people were killed, etc. Now, apparently, new CDs of pop music are incorporated into the soundtrack of the video games. Often, people would have heard this popular music first in the video game that they play. This means that there is collaboration between the music industry and the makers of video games. The people who make the video games, like the people who make television advertising, are smart and creative people. It would be a mistake to be condescending to them.

My wife and I watch mostly public television (PBS), but we also watch network news and a certain number of network shows, so I see many of these fascinating ads. It is clear that there is an impressive amount of creativity that goes into these ads. I like best the PBS (Public Broadcasting Services) ones, because they are not really ads. There is a series that somebody made for PBS (Alfonso Cuarón's "Fish" ad won an Emmy for Best Commercial). These "ads" are shown over and over, so they really sink into your mind. After they show an episode, they show a caption: "Be creative" or "Be courageous," or something of the sort. There is one that I have seen repeatedly and find absolutely wonderful. It shows a goldfish in a goldfish bowl, watching television. Here is this goldfish, and there is the television set. On the television screen, there is a shot of a salmon leaping up a river falls. Then you see the little goldfish jump out the window. It falls down into somebody's big bottle of water, which a man is just about to put on a truck. He puts it on the truck and drives across a bridge. The little goldfish jumps out of the bottle into the river. In the last shot, you see the little goldfish swimming up the river falls with the salmon. Then the caption says: "Be creative," or "Think big," or something like that. Another episode in the series shows an ordinary looking man, not at all a sophisticated person in appearance. He goes into one of these photobooths where you can take photographs. He takes a whole lot of photographs of himself with various expressions. He puts them in sequence in a book. Then he plays a record of some great tenor singing. He flips through the picture book in time with the record, so it looks like he is singing the aria. Again, there is a little caption that says: "Be courageous," "Think big," "You can do it," "Be creative," or something like that. Oddly enough, I can remember the video part detail, but cannot remember which caption goes with which episode. That proves, I guess, that a picture *is* worth a thousand words!

A lot of creativity also goes into television ads for automobiles. There has been a shift from aiming ads at male buyers of cars to aiming at female buyers. Experts in a market study have discovered that the decision in a family about what car to buy is most often made by the wife. So, they change their tactics somewhat, but they still appeal—they can't resist this—to the idea that you should buy a given car because you can then drive it at 150 km/h on a narrow road. Sometimes the commercial even has a statement at the bottom saying, "This has been done by an expert professional driver. Do not try to do this yourself with your own car." Nevertheless, the appeal is to human fantasy of speed and omnipotence. If I buy this big SUV, then I can imagine myself in possession of all that power and speed. I imagine myself driving off the road, out in the desert somewhere. Many people in California and in other places own these SUVs. Hardly anybody uses them off road in the desert. They just used them to drive the kids to school or to go the supermarket.

ÁLVARO/COLLADO-RODRÍGUEZ: *At the end, the aim of the ad is always to convince you to buy something. All that creativity is only put there for a marketing purpose.*

MILLER: That is right. Nevertheless, one has to recognize the high degree of creativity that goes into commercial advertising. One has to have a double attitude towards them. They have a crass goal, but they are very powerful in their effects on people, and they are often extremely clever. When studying ads, you should compare them with the cultural power of novels in the Victorian period. What to a considerable degree determined the ideology, the beliefs about courtship, marriage, the class structure, and so on of Victorian middle-class people? The answer is novels. They did not have television. They did not have advertising in the same way as we do. They had newspapers with advertising, but the novels had the greatest effect on what people thought and believed, on the way they behaved. If you want to know what the Victorian assumptions were about this or that, read Trollope. I do not think you would say today, "Read Trollope, or read Pynchon, or read Toni Morrison to find out our cultural assumptions." You would say, "Look at video games, look at television ads, look at movies, and look at popular music." There is therefore every reason to study those. I am in favor of doing that. The sad side of this shift is that such study is not quite the same thing as reading Shakespeare, Dickens, Trollope, George Eliot, or Henry James. I am mossback enough to believe that there are cultural losses when so many people do not read or "study" literature anymore.

You were asking about the transnational university. It certainly is the case, that everywhere I go, in the United States and Canada, in Europe, in East Asia, I find traditional literature departments are in jeopardy in one way or another. My colleagues in Irvine—the conservative ones in the English department—are I think naïve in that they do not want to see that what is happening in the German department, the French department, or in any non-English language department, will eventually happen to them. Foreign language departments all over the United States have been amalgamated. The administrator looks at a foreign language department and says, "You have an office; you have three secretaries; you have five full professors and twelve other faculty, and there are only twenty students. It is not economically sustainable." The administrators do not usually ask themselves, "Is it a good thing to have French taught even if there are not many students? Is it good to have people do study and research on French language and literature?" They ask marketing and financial questions instead. If only a few students come to study French, this means for these administrators that they can just put all the foreign language departments together in a single department. They save money by having only one or two secretaries. This means, eventually, that you have Latin, Greek, Chinese, French, German, etc., all in one department. This is just one step from saying, "Do we really need more than one professor of French? Isn't five perhaps too many?" What I find naïve is that some English professors still think English literature is going to survive; therefore, who cares about the others? I would not be so sure, since it is just one more step to ask, "Do we need this many people teaching English literature, *English* literature, in the United States, that is, the literature of a foreign country? Do our students really need to read Chaucer? Do we need someone teaching Old English? Why?" In a university like mine, at Irvine, over half of the students are Asian Americans. Many of them have English as a second language. You can say that we have taught them English so they can be assimilated. We have to do that in order to make them good United States citizens. A number of states, California among them, have passed laws declaring that English is the official language. Therefore, we have to teach our students Shakespeare, to make them good citizens; that is certainly a plausible justification, but I think the reasoning is not clearly thought out by many politicians.

We are now back in a kind of McCarthy period, with the Patriot Act, secret surveillance and wiretapping, etc. The difference between the McCarthy period in the '50s and now is that in those days there was a specific persecution of the universities. There was a lot of interference. There was an attempt to show that university professors were communists, etc. That is not happening now. I think the reason is that they do not care what we humanists teach. They do not think that what goes on in the humanities side of the university really matters. Administrators are able to with a clear conscience say, "Yes, we still have the humanities. They are important here in Irvine." But just what are they good for in relation to the overall mission of the university? I asked this question once of the then president of the nine-campus University of California, President Atkinson, at a reception. He had made a speech a while before about the mission of the University of California. He was defending a huge budget request to the legislature, money from the State, now over three billion dollars. That is about the size of the entire University of California. What he had said was that the central purpose of the University of California is "to make California competitive in the global economy." I think that, if I were in his shoes, I would probably say the same thing. That is the way to get money from the legislature. However, I asked him, "If this is the mission of the University of California, what, in your opinion, is the function of the humanities in relation to that mission? How do the humanities make California competitive in the global economy?" I asked this in the blandest and least hostile way I could think of. He gave me the right answer. It was interesting. Administrators are smart people. "Oh," he said, "I wouldn't presume to tell the humanities what to do." It was an evasion, but a tactful one. If administrators were forced to answer, they probably would say the humanities are there to make good citizens of our people by teaching them how to think critically and how to read the great books of the Western heritage.

It is also interesting that cultural studies has been institutionalized with hardly any resistance from university administrators. Because they might have said, "This is a big change, not teaching Shakespeare anymore and teaching popular music, film, culture generally. You even teach Native American literature. That is not what we thought the English Department was there to do." However, they have not done that. Without protest, they let people who have been hired to teach Flaubert, for example, to change to other things. There was a woman in Irvine's French department who shifted from research on Flaubert to research on black women's fashion magazines. Quite correctly, she saw such magazines as an interesting and symptomatic cultural phenomenon. Nobody tried to stop her from making that radical change in her teaching. It shows the power of academic freedom. In the United States, just because you have been hired to do something, once you have tenure, nobody tries to stop you from teaching whatever you like. I have myself benefited from that in my shift from purely English texts to texts in French and German, along with English. Nobody tried to stop me from becoming a comparatist, though I had no credentials for that.

Since I wrote the essay you mention, the situation has advanced in the direction of further internationalization of the university. For example, since I have been here at Zaragoza on this trip, I have seen in an e-mail that the University of California at Irvine has recently been given a large amount of money to set up a Persian Studies Center. That will make Irvine in Southern California an important place to study Iran, Iraq, and so on. You can see why that has happened. The money apparently came from some very rich Saudi-Arabian donor. The university administration accepted the gift, because the Islamic Middle East is a good thing to study these days, even in a place about as far away from "Persia" as you can get in the United States, though Southern California no doubt has a good many citizens from what used to be called "Persia." That is parallel to the way science has to come to be studied in California, though it was not initially a center for scientific innovation. Anything can and should be studied everywhere, without much reference to local culture. That is a feature of globalization.

On the other hand, I think the main big change that is happening quite rapidly is the emergence of China and India as major capitalist countries with tremendous economic and military power. They are becoming much more powerful economically than Japan because their resources are greater and they have much larger populations. They are also rapidly industrializing. Eighty percent of the goods sold in our mammoth retail store chain, Walmart, are made in China. Why? Because they are cheap and well made, as a result of low labor costs. The United States has lost in recent years one million jobs to China. Nowadays in the United States when you call up to order something from a catalogue, you hear a voice speaking from India. Our retail companies outsource their catalogue answering systems. At the other end of the line, you hear a very polite Indian voice who has the catalogue on the computer screen and from whom you may order this or that article. That is happening more and more. Our government has even outsourced part of the Department of Homeland Security to India. One might object. "This is crazy, this is our homeland security department, and you are now having some of its work done in *India*? What about the security of the Department of Homeland Security?" They answer that it is a matter of saving so many millions of dollars a year. Indians are very good at software. As you know, India has a big Silicon Valley, and they are not doing just routine work. They do high-quality creative software. Technology is a basic component of the so-called posthuman being. Technology skills can be rapidly assimilated anywhere in the world. It does not take generations, as you could argue what humanist study, in a way, does, in spite of the rapid spread of American films and popular music all over the world. I sometimes wonder whether we Americans or United Statesians can ever really understand British literature, in spite of similarity in language. British culture is so different from our own, the class structure, for example. Programming and other technological skills can be rapidly taught to anyone all over the world. Indian workers have become good in this field, as good as or better than our own programmers and computers designers.

ÁLVARO/COLLADO-RODRÍGUEZ: *Finally, why do you not like the use of the word* deconstruction *anymore?*

MILLER: The answer to that is very simple. It is because the word *deconstruction* triggers assumptions in people's minds that are often based on misinformation. That is why. The power of the media is such that they have put in people's minds a distorted conception of what deconstruction is for Derrida, but which, nevertheless, is one widely disseminated concept of deconstruction. That misconception is one of the things deconstruction is. Derrida invented the word. He based it on Heidegger's "Destruktion." Derrida put another syllable in and made it into more complicated term "De-con-struction." Negative and positive together. The word has now become indispensable. My wife shows me uses of the word she finds in home decorating magazines, architectural magazines and so on. She showed me an architect who says, "first we deconstructed the house...."

ÁLVARO/COLLADO-RODRÍGUEZ: *Even here, we have popular uses of the term. The famous chef Ferra Adria also "deconstructs" different dishes. He uses explicitly the term* deconstruction *as in "desconstruir un plato."*

MILLER: That's neat! For the whole world, *deconstruction* has become a necessary word. I am delighted to hear that a great chef deconstructs a dish. However, the term is frequently used in a misleading way in reference to Derrida's work or that of other so-called deconstructionists. Often you hear people saying, "Well, deconstruction, it means destroying everything. Derrida is immoral. He is undermining western civilization. He is a relativist who believes you can make the text mean anything you want, that it has no meaning itself, etc.," so if you say, "I am doing deconstruction," people rush to the conclusion that you are doing what they mistakenly think Derrida was doing. If you try to explain what you are actually doing, it takes a long time, and probably it does not persuade them. They just look puzzled and dubious. They say, "No, no, I know what deconstruction is. It is dangerous. It is the destruction of western civilization. It is the destruction of the recipe and taking apart the fish or the building or the poem or whatever..."

8

For the Reader to Come

Interview with Éamonn Dunne

ÉAMONN DUNNE: *Can I ask you to begin this dialogue from where we left off speaking in Portsmouth?[1] What do you mean when, in your reading of Yeats's "Nineteen Hundred and Nineteen" in* The Linguistic Moment *and in the interview in* Theory Now and Then, *you say "I think my reading of Yeats's poem is right, that all right-thinking people will come, given enough time, to my reading?" Can the act of reading "Nineteen Hundred and Nineteen," when it stumbles helplessly upon those last few enigmatic lines, when it comes face to face with that "it," the linguistic moment as you call it, be polarized into right and wrong? Can we still speak of the proper or improper reading?*

J. HILLIS MILLER: There was a certain degree of irony in what I said. I've found that ironic statements I make are often, understandably, likely to be misunderstood. My statement, however, like most ironies, was a double irony. What I said was in hyperbolic response to the widespread false assumption in those days that we so-called deconstructionists say there is no correct reading of a text, meaning that you can make it mean anything you like. On the one hand, I did mean that what I said about Yeats's poem seemed to me right, correct, a proper and responsible response to the demand the poem makes on me to be read. I gave it my allegiance, and that meant believing, hyperbolically, that "all right-thinking people will come, given enough time, to my reading." Just because I had to say something about that enigmatic "it" doesn't mean what I said was not "right" and "proper," even though what I said was face to face with something wholly other and I had to express that confrontation as best I could. You might even say that it was "just because" I had to express as best I could an encounter with enigma, the "it," the other, that my reading was right and proper. On the other hand, of course I am not so naïve as really to believe that a consensus of right-thinking people as to the right and proper reading of Yeats's poem is likely to happen. That was the other side of the irony. People will always find something more or different to say about the poem, including I myself, but at that moment, I really thought I "had it right," and I wanted to tell my interviewer that. My reading had my full, unreserved, and "excessive" allegiance; otherwise, I would not have written it and published it.

DUNNE: *Staying with Yeats for the moment, your reading of "The Cold Heaven" in* Others *(2001) is an obvious return to this question of the demand or obligation the work makes on you to read it closely, rationalize it, or explain what happens when it is read. You say in several places that you are, and have always been, haunted by this "sense" of a radical otherness in literary works. What strikes me as an overriding concern in this essay is your attention to the urgency of this obligation, the imperative to respond fully to what comes almost as an accident. The word "befalls" in the opening line emphasizes this impromptu event, and your subsequent discussion of the conflicting temporalities of the first word of the poem, "Suddenly," attempts to explicate this surprise even further still, showing that any attempt to still this movement for the sake of hermeneutical closure will ultimately be in vain. Yet there is a sense here, as I find in much of your work, that this sudden incoming or shock encounter with the other, or rather others, is a kind of mixed blessing since this event also destroys that cold comfort of presupposition or expectation. In which case the act of reading, if indeed it is an active reading and an event of discovery and insight, undoes each time the authority of the university to teach "good" reading. Each surprise encounter seems to me to question what has gone before it, the entire edifice that has brought it to that point. It should therefore follow that each act of "good" reading creates a renewed idea of what an active reading should or ought to be. I take it that this is what you mean in your previous answer by "just because"? Could you also perhaps say something more on the subject of this demand from the other and what kind of "justice" we owe to the event of good reading when it happens?*

I hope these questions do not seem overly speculative, but I am interested in the "sense" of what you have been saying in many of your readings. And

*how the joy of reading is also somehow a painful experience. I'm thinking here
also of the ambiguity you have pointed out in the word Derrida often uses:
passion.*

MILLER: Interesting questions. The fact is that I feel elation and intellectual
excitement when being "addressed" by a poem like "The Cold Heaven," not
anxiety, and as I said earlier, I don't worry much about whether or not I'll
reach "hermeneutical closure." I go as far as I can with a given reading, with
the experience of doors opening or insights occurring, going further and
further, in a direction only that poem can take me, as I try to write down
what I think I understand. It's more passion as intellectual excitement than
passion as suffering. Not much suffering in it for me. I don't care much,
either, that each new reading destroys the whole edifice of university
teaching. That edifice can take care of itself. It doesn't really do that anyway,
since one of my obligations, at least in the US, is to see things in a given text
that no one has seen before, so I'm even rewarded for that, if others think
what I claim to have seen is really there. Yes, it is accidental, the poem just
happens to fall under your eye, but it feels like a happy accident, and you
make the best of what befalls you. The obligation is a happy one, to do the
best justice to the poem you can by saying the most you can for it in the hope
that you might transmit something of the poem to others. As you can see,
I'm essentially a cheerful person, like the hero of *Mad Magazine*: "What, me
worry?" I append a piece I wrote for a China conference this past summer
and will use to kick off a seminar in Louvain in a couple of weeks.[2] You might
conceivably find it interesting. As you can see, I really like the Stevens poem.
Like "The Cold Heaven," reading it sends shivers up and down my spine and
makes my hair stand on end. I know there is more in either poem than I shall
ever see or say, and I rejoice in that. It doesn't make me anxious. "Suddenly I
saw the cold and rook-delighting heaven / That seemed as though ice burned
and was but the more ice." "The steeple at Farmington / Stands glistening
and Haddam shines and sways." Wow! What more is there to say?

DUNNE: *I recently came across the following passage from* Opus Posthumous,
*in which Stevens rebukes Plato's arid asceticism for what he refers to himself,
rather enigmatically (maybe oxymoronically), as "poetic truth":*

> *And the wonder and mystery of art, as indeed of religion in the
> last resort, is the revelation of something "wholly other" by which
> the inexpressible loneliness of thinking is broken and enriched.
> To know facts as facts in the ordinary way has, indeed, no*

particular power or worth. But a quickening of our awareness of
the irrevocability by which a thing is what it is, has such power,
and it is, I believe, the very soul of art.

Needless to say, Stevens's expression "wholly other" is more than a little
uncanny, a remarkable augury, perhaps, of what was to come from your own
work and from Derrida's. And yet, of course, the expression seems to be the
only appropriate or justifiable one for that which is utterly unfathomable,
unnameable, secret. It seems that this "wondrous" and "mysterious" a logic
of which Stevens so eloquently speaks inhabits (if that is the correct word)
the language of criticism itself. I think here of Paul de Man's famous phrase
in Allegories of Reading *that the difference between criticism and literature*
is "delusive," that there is a crossing over between what happens in the texts
we read, when we read them, and what happens in the languages we invent
to describe the process. An example from your own work that suggests this to
me is when you are speaking of Stevens in Poets of Reality *you say, "Things as*
they are make up one side of the analogy [between reality and mental fictions],
but the poet's 'sense of the world' is the other, and the life of poetry is the
metamorphosis by which one is swallowed up by the other". Is there a moment
then in what you do in the act of reading and writing (reading/writing) in
which you confront this obligation to respond responsibly by creatively
rereading and rewriting the texts you read? Do you feel, that is, that Stevens's
critics are being called upon to reinvent the "sense" of that world, that they
should know (sense) and not know (sense) this secret simultaneously? Would
you say that the fascination you have with the poetry of Stevens and others is
the very openness of this secret, an impossible possibility?

MILLER: The citation from Stevens's *Opus Posthumous* is really interesting.
I had forgotten that he uses Jacques Derrida's phrase, the "wholly other."
Come to think of it, I suppose some resonance between them on this point
exists, and both, in different ways, have phenomenology as background
and context. In answer to your question, yes, I suppose I try to make my
own words as much in tune with the writer's words as possible, but in
my case at least, this "re-reading and re-writing" also means elucidating,
making clearer, finding out the reasons for a whole repertoire of procedures
designed to bring to light and clarify. The danger, of course, is that the critic
loses what you call the "secret" in the process of knowing or sensing. Stevens
says, "Poetry should resist the intelligence almost successfully," but he may
mean that it loses its status as poetry when it fails to resist the intelligence.
De Man was of course right (he is always right) to say there is no difference

between literature and criticism, but still, I don't ever feel that I am writing poetry. If I could, I would. Nevertheless, the critic is like Stevens in feeling that he or she has never quite "got it right," and therefore I go on trying, just as he went on writing poetry. To "get it right" would be to bring the secret out into the open completely, and that is, happily, impossible, as you say. Always more to write about any given work.

DUNNE: *Your response to this subject of the secret, a bit like the Reverend Hooper's (if he has one?), brings us nicely, I think, on to my next question. I was wondering if you could say a few words concerning free indirect discourse and irony? This is a topic that I have found to be a commanding presence throughout your work. From* The Form of Victorian Fiction *to your most recent essays—and perhaps even from your own Ph.D. thesis, where a singular attention to the language of* Oliver Twist *brings you to an awareness of surprising linguistic and thematic discrepancies—you have been interested in the relationship between the two. You have also spoken of the relationship between FID and irony at some length in* Reading Narrative, *where you refer to irony as "the pervasive trope of narrative" and of citation being a form of incitation. Could you perhaps say something about the importance of developing an awareness of irony in literary study? I'm also conscious of the overlap here between the mode of indirect discourse in my own citations of your work and the nature of the interview. Perhaps there is something to be said about this too?*

MILLER: I don't have much of anything to say about indirect discourse and irony beyond what I have already said in various places.[3] Both interest me, though in different ways. I've always been, from the beginning of my literary study, fascinated by places where straightforward univocal meaning, paraphrasable thematic meaning, is complicated by formal or linguistic complications in literary texts, for example, figures of speech. Indirect discourse is a good example, since it is so conspicuous a feature of novelistic conventions and is so powerful in its ability to present two, not necessarily compatible, points of view at once: that of the character (mimed by the narrator in the third person past tense, whereas it would have been first-person present tense when it happened for the character), and that of the narrator, whose miming ironically undercuts the character's language just by repeating it in another register, as a student mocks his or her professor by repeating exactly, with hardly a curl of the lip, what the professor has said. Indirect discourse both gives the reader wonderful access to what the character was saying or thinking, perhaps something that expresses a prevailing gender, class, race, or social ideology, and at the same time gives the reader a critical distance from that ideological feeling or conviction. Since indirect discourse is "undecidable," like irony itself, in the sense that you cannot be sure whether it is the character's language or the narrator's language (though you can guess), indirect discourse shares the suspension characteristic of irony. Is the narrator really making fun of the character or repeating what he or she said with full approval and allegiance? You can never be sure. An awareness of irony is therefore necessary for good reading, in order to avoid premature and unjustified certainty in a univocal reading, but a gift for irony is not evenly distributed in the population, even in the population of literature students. Some otherwise smart people have a deaf ear for irony. I'm not sure how you can cure that. It may be incurable, the incurable itself, but as Friedrich Schlegel observed, those who think they have mastered irony are the most likely to be caught by it. So watch out!

You are right to say that your citations of my work are an example of this possible irony. How can I, or anyone, know whether you wholeheartedly approve of what I say or are curling your lip as you write down my exact words?

DUNNE: *In your discussion of Heinrich von Kleist in* Versions of Pygmalion *(1990), you say that acts of reading and teaching are elements in a series of acts of violence. Following Kleist's essay "On the Gradual Fabrication of Thoughts While Speaking" and Paul de Man's reference to it in* The Rhetoric of Romanticism, *you say, "The text read by the teacher was itself originally an act of violent linguistic imposition, a case of the fabrication of thoughts while speaking or writing. This must be forgotten by the teacher, who reads the text as a discourse of achieved semantic and referential meaning." You say thereafter that acts of teaching are "political" in the full, radical sense of that word. That there is a blindness in the performative act of relaying this reading in a class to a group of students who may or may not be influenced in a benign manner. As you recall de Man saying at a Yale seminar in your* Speech Acts in Literature *(2001), "You aim at a bear and some innocent bird falls out of the sky" (144). Could you say a little more about this "violence" in reading and teaching—perhaps in your own experience of it? Also, how can a teacher be responsible and/or responsive (or) "just" with the foreknowledge of this necessary predicament?*

MILLER: I suppose I meant "violence" in the Benjaminian sense of "Gewalt," not the same thing as knocking a man down, but an exercise of free sovereignty. That is, neither writer nor teacher can really justify what

they say by reference to some achieved truth, so what they write or say is
at least metaphorically sovereign in the sense of being outside the law or
received opinion, or whatever. Another way to put this is to say that writing
or teaching has a performative as well as constative dimension. It is a feature
of performatives that they make something happen, but something that can
never be exactly predicted beforehand. You aim at a bear and an innocent
bird falls out of the sky. As a teacher, I have an obligation or responsibility
to tell it like I think it is, that is, to read whatever text I am teaching as best
I can and not hide anything. Sometimes, however, a few times in my own
experience, the teacher has the feeling that perhaps it would have been just
as well for this or that student, for one reason or another, not to have read a
given work nor to have heard me say my say about it. I remember an adult
woman in an evening college class of mine years ago who was, so it seemed
to me, unreasonably upset by *Mrs Dalloway*. For most undergraduates, that
novel is a piece of cake, but she was really troubled by it, and I guess also
by what I was saying about it, though that seemed to me tame enough, not
intended to be "violent." I suppose that makes teaching "political" in the
sense that it has unforeseen political effects, even on the way people vote,
even though the teacher hasn't said anything overtly about politics.

DUNNE: *For the past few weeks, I have been thinking about and reading
Hawthorne's tales and notebooks alongside your work* Hawthorne and
History *(1991). I have also been reading up on your debate with D.A. Miller
in the pages of* ADE Bulletin *and your comments in* PMLA *(vol. 103, 1988)
regarding what you say in your "Presidential Address 1986: The Triumph of
Theory, the Resistance to Reading, and the Question of the Material Base"
concerning history, reading, example, and the material base. At all points, you
refer to Paul de Man's writings in one way or another as a crucial point of origin
for your ideas in these areas. You also suggest that the topic of the material
base will need to be rethought, reexamined, and reworked time and again in
the future—a suggestion I take to mean that the thinking of the material base
will be a way of opening questions about lived experience and the inaugural
performance of acts of reading as they occur in time. So, at the risk of quoting
out of context, I cite a few lines from your "Presidential Address" in the hope
that you might say a little more about what you mean by the material base
and how it has influenced your thinking of history: "The uncriticized notion
of the material base is ideological through and through. It is part of Western
metaphysics or of logocentrism. It is the specular reflection of idealism, not
something outside it"; "We know the material only through names or other
signs". I have also noticed that you compare and contrast Derrida's* le tout

autre with de Man's "rhetoricity" in your recent article "Derrida's Remains,"
where you say that Derrida's thought has always been focused on what is
"beyond language." In Literature as Conduct, *you say something similar*
of the later de Man: that his thought of the "nonphenomenal materiality of
language" is perhaps another name for what Derrida calls "the wholly other."
Could you say something about how your own thinking of the performative
inaugurality of the act of reading has been influenced by both writers? What
is different about it? And what do you mean when you say in Hawthorne
and History *that in reading history "the 'I' becomes a linguistic function in*
a process that occurs of its own accord and is authorized by no independent
witnessing 'I'"?

MILLER: It's not easy to answer these questions in a few lines. I hold, with de Man and Derrida, that the commonsense idea of the material is ideological through and through. What that means is suggested in answers Derrida gave in the question-and-answer session after his lecture at the famous Hopkins conference of 1966. A certain now forgotten phenomenological critic, from New York (I believe), one Serge Doubrovsky, reproached him for not recognizing the authority of intentionality and perception (terms important for Merleau-Ponty and Husserl). Derrida replied, "Now I don't know what perception is and I don't believe that anything like perception exists. Perception is precisely a concept, the concept of an intuition or of a given originating from the thing itself, present itself in its meaning, independently from language, from the system of reference…I don't believe that there is any perception."[4] I still remember thinking that was an amazing claim. No such thing as perception! Wow! How could that be? I think Derrida meant by this two things: (1) that so-called perception of material things is always contaminated by language, not something prelinguistic—it's a "concept"; hence, (2) since perception is a concept, it is part of the whole ideological system of assumptions or concepts that makes up what we call logocentrism or Western metaphysics. If you buy perception, you are buying into the whole shebang.

I have said my say about de Man's "materialism without matter" in my essay in *Material Events*.[5] You can say that I agree with de Man and Derrida on materiality, have learned to think about it as a problem not a predetermined solution from them, and from Marx.

Yes, Derrida and de Man converge without quite converging in that both have notions of something "beyond language," for Derrida the "wholly other," for de Man those three curious notions of materiality I discuss in the essay mentioned above. They are by no means saying quite the same thing, however. In certain areas, one cannot have both de Man and Derrida at once. *Il faut choisir.* Certainly what I say about the performative singularity of reading is influenced by both writers, but perhaps I put what they say about singularity and about performatives together in my own way. What I say is simple enough. Every reading is singular in the sense of being carried out by a single person in unique circumstances. Who could deny that? Though you (I) should be respectful and cognizant of the whole tradition of readings of a given poem, novel, or philosophical text, nevertheless you (I) have the feeling of being on your (my) own when trying to figure out what to say about a given text in an essay or a class. I also have characteristically the experience of finding that a given poem, novel, philosophical treatise is surprising in the sense of not seeming to mean what the tradition says it means. My reading (anybody's reading) is performative in the strict sense that it is a way of doing something with words, for example, affecting my students or readers in one way or another by what I say or write, often in unexpected and even dismaying ways, as is the nature or performatives. If you could predict exactly the effect, it would not be a performative. Speech acts exceed cognition. I want of course to say just what the text means, with exact accuracy, but in the course of trying to do this, I necessarily go beyond the text. Empson's pastoral book is a good example.[6] No one had said just that about *Alice in Wonderland*, but it seems right when you read it. Austin says the judge's ruling makes the law, in the sense of deciding how to read the text of the law and in the sense of deciding, never with preordained certainty, that a particular law (necessarily general) fits this particular case in a certain way. In a somewhat similar fashion, the critic's reading makes the meaning of the given text.

DUNNE: *I've just been reading your latest essay in* Critical Inquiry, *"Derrida Enisled," in which you tackle the questions of community and alterity in the writings of Heidegger, Levinas, and Derrida, among others. In this essay, you make a distinction between a Levinasian face-to-face encounter and what Derrida would refer to as the demand made on him by the "wholly other." Indeed, you stress that one way of thinking of the difference between the two thinkers would be to see that the demand goes in an "opposite direction" for each—"I invoke the other" for Levinas and "the other demands that I respond" for Derrida.*

In a recent interview with Constanza del Rio Álvaro and Francisco Collado-Rodríguez in The European English Messenger, *you say that you are somewhat at odds with Derrida's notion of the demand from the wholly other because it implies that there is some "little voice" making that demand. You say that you have the feeling that you are "on your own" in decision making and therefore distance yourself from Levinas and Derrida on this point—no God, no voice. Could you say a little more about this experience of singularity in decision making which differentiates or "enisles" your own work?*

MILLER: No great mystery about this. I have great sympathy for the Derridean idea that the "wholly other" makes a demand on me. In that interview, I confessed that I don't ever experience that call from the "wholly other," to my shame. I don't hear the "still small voice." My receiver must be on the wrong frequency. That doesn't mean that the call (from God or some other form of "the wholly other") is not being made, just that I don't hear it. Maybe someday the call will get through. I'm waiting. I'm aware that my deafness may be just stubborn obduracy. You will note that my language is Protestant. The result of my deafness is that I feel pretty much on my own in making decisions, though I make them as "responsibly" as I can, but I agree with Derrida that a true decision is not preprogramed, or else it would be automatic, not a decision at all. I also agree with him that a decision is a break in the continuity of time and history.

DUNNE: *You have said quite a bit about your decision to study literature in your interview with Julian Wolfreys in* The J. Hillis Miller Reader, *and you have also spoken quite a bit about how you came to study Burke and Poulet in other places. As my own decision to study your work was a direct result of finding a literary critic willing (and able) to discuss Nietzsche as a literary critic, could you perhaps say a little regarding the influence Nietzsche has had over your thinking?*

MILLER: I started reading Nietzsche more or less by accident when I was an undergraduate at Oberlin College; either *Zarathustra* or *Birth of Tragedy*, I can't remember which. I read him initially, I guess, because he was there to be read, probably without much comprehension. I've been reading him off and on ever since. *The Will to Power* and *On the Genealogy of Morals* were a big influence, but I've read most of the other writings too, including of course "Truth and Lie in an Extramoral Sense." His rhetorical theory and practice are of most importance to me, his theory of tropes, his sense of the role of language in ethical judgment (*Genealogy*), politics, and history, so de Man and Derrida on Nietzsche were helpful to me in getting at his work.

DUNNE: *In his* Ethical Criticism, *Robert Eaglestone makes the following criticisms of your ethics of reading:*

> *Miller's own text, then, has offered a deconstruction of the "ethics"*

in The Ethics of Reading *on two grounds. First, from "within" Miller's own text, the repression of history served only to highlight and so to "return" the historically grounded nature of language. This has revealed how Miller has chosen the limits of the field of his argument to draw out his own conclusions. Second, Miller has implicitly denied his own leitmotif in* The Ethics of Reading *by always assuming that "ethics" exists in a certain relation to language which may not be the case—as a result he offers a weak and seemingly insubstantial understanding of "ethics." This "weak" understanding of ethics is highlighted in Critchley, as pedagogic and specifically American, and by Harpham and Norris as simply unethical, turning ethical concerns into simply a way of reading.*[7]

What would be your response to those critics who speak of your ethics of reading as on the one hand anti- or ahistorical and, on the other, as a kind of New New Criticism that disengages from ontological questions in favor of linguistic ones?

MILLER: Any theory of ethics is likely to be controversial, especially if it is of the sort I have proposed. It is likely to bring out unethical self-righteousness, condescension, and distortion. People feel threatened. My critics seem to forget that I was in *The Ethics of Reading* talking about what the title named, namely, the question of whether any sort of ethical obligation is involved in the act of reading, a specific and limited topic. That's not the same thing as the question of my ethical responsibility to my neighbor, though I think it is just denegation to try to deny that language is involved in both cases, but in a different way in each. Language is involved in everything human beings do. I should have thought that was a truism by now; I don't quite understand what Eaglestone (whoever he may be) means by the repression of history. Does he mean I should have seen moral codes as historically determined, that is, as relative, ungrounded except in the ideological assumptions of a certain time, place, class, gender, race, or that I needed to say that Kant's ethical theory came somewhat before the Battle of Waterloo, or what? I believe, on the contrary, that each genuine ethical decision and act is historical. It enters the surrounding historical context to change it, in however small a way. It leaves things different from what they were. It is a historical event, but it is by no means fully determined by that surrounding historical context. My ethical theory is historical through and through. An example would be Sethe's spontaneous decision to try to kill all her children so they won't be taken back into slavery, in Toni Morrison's *Beloved*. I certainly do not turn "ethical concerns into simply a way of reading." That is an unethical distortion of what I have said, if I may dare to say so. The opposition, in my view, is between a view of ethical decision as the mechanical application of a rule ("You shouldn't covet your neighbor's wife, or his ox, or his ass, therefore I had better avoid doing that in this case") and, on the other hand, true ethical decision, which is always a unique response to a unique demand made on me by a unique, singular person (or, in a different way, a unique book). J.L. Austin says the judge's decision makes the law, meaning that it is never possible to make a mechanical application of the law, since the judge, at the very least, has to make an autonomous, in a sense forever unjustified, decision that this particular case fits a given law. My response to the ethical demand another makes on me is like that.

DUNNE: *I find your readings of Nietzsche's use of aphorism to be particularly helpful for my reading of your recent work.[8] I say "recent work" here in terms of the issues presented in* Zero Plus One *and "Z" in Julian Wolfreys's* Glossalalia, *but the question of the zero or zero point brings back to me "instances" in* The Linguistic Moment *and* Ariadne's Thread, *where you speak of performative catachresis and anastomosis: I think, that is, of Ottilie in Goethe's* Die Walverwandtschaften *undoing the ground of Aristotle's metaphorical ratio (AT, 213) or of Wallace Stevens's* Abgrund *in "The Rock." Would you say that in some sense both of these terms (*catachresis *and* anastomosis*) figure in different ways in your earlier work in what you are more recently calling the relationship between zero and one?*

In terms of tempo, you speak of Nietzsche's writings as a musical gesture, a strange crossover between a combination of signs and physical states, an odd combination, if I read you rightly, that undoes the oppositions between literal and metaphorical language by calling the reader's attention to "Bild" (image) and "Gleichnis" (likeness, parable). How important, in light of your reading of Nietzsche's stylistic virtuosity, is the literary critic's sense of rhythm? And can this be learned, or is it innate or instinctual?

MILLER: I hadn't thought of the connection, but I guess you are right that the zero/one relation is another version of catachresis and anastomosis. I've always been obsessed with the various ways you can figure the unfigurable and unnamable, so I keep coming back to different versions of that, I would hope with increasing wisdom and insight, though I'm not at all confident that is the case. It would be a mistake, however, to see all these motifs as different versions of the "same thing." Each terminology has its own structure and laws, things you can say only using those terms. I do think rhythm and tempo are important, though hard to talk about intelligibly, but one feels it, as for example the difference between Nancy's elliptical terseness and obsessive repetition with slight variation of the same phrases, on the one hand, and Derrida's expansive inexhaustibly inventive developments—a wonderful two-hour seminar I once heard on the phrase "je t'aime," for example—on the other.[9] Yes, you are right that something strange happens to the literal/metaphorical distinction by way of the double meanings of "Geichnis" and "Bild" in German. Also a good example of difficulties in translation, since neither English nor French have quite an equivalent word play, just as "Körper" and "Leib" don't mean quite the same things as "corps" and "chair" or as "body" and "corpse," as Derrida himself points out in *Le toucher*, a book I find wonderful but exceedingly difficult.

DUNNE: *Though you say that it is difficult to speak intelligibly about the topic of rhythm and tempo, I would like, if I could, to try to push this question in two slightly different directions, which may end up being similar after all.*

First, in your discussion of Kleist in Versions of Pygmalion, *you speak of "an encrypted anacoluthon," indicating the residual traces of fissures, caesuras, and "antithythmical" inventions that have led to the completed "period" or grammatical construct. The paradox is, as you point out, that the rhythmic interludes, intonations, punctuations have at once everything to do with the semantic content and nothing to do with it. Could you perhaps say a little more about what you mean by this?*

Secondly, I had the privilege of hearing your paper on "touching" at Leeds University last week, in which you play provocatively with the notion of "hand" as "style." You say here, if I have transcribed you rightly, that "style is meaning" and the various meanings of Derrida's work on Nancy are a kind of "ceaseless walk from metonymy to metonymy," exemplified in his lists of "quasi-synonymous" terms for touching. Derrida's book is therefore marked by "perpetual, frustrated, incompleteness." What interests me here is this tactful term quasi-synonymous *and the attention to style as inseparable from meaning. What is the connection, for you, between touching and catachresis?*

MILLER: Gosh, did I really speak of an "encrypted anacoluthon"? I don't have the essay at hand in this house, so I must guess what I meant. An anacoluthon is "a failure in following," such as a subject that doesn't agree with its verb. I suppose I meant that the invention of thoughts while speaking may look like it's perfectly coherent, but since you didn't know what you were going to say when you started speaking and make it up as you go along, what looks like a coherent and grammatical sentence is actually the result of a discontinuous series of "inventions" that only hang together after the fact, in appearance. Something like that.

I meant by "ceaseless walk from metonymy to metonymy" that each of the terms is only adjacent to that vacant, unnamable center. I might better have said "from catachresis to catachresis," but Derrida does not use the word *catachresis*, whereas he does say *metonymy*. Well, style is meaning in the obvious sense that Derrida means it when he says Nancy may appear to be saying the same thing conceptually as Husserl or Merleau-Ponty but is actually saying something quite different from them because he has his own inimitable philosophical style. Like Derrida and unlike Husserl and Merleau-Ponty (at least to the same degree), Nancy is acutely aware of the limitations of language and of the roots within words, so he is constantly playing with these, as in the double meaning of *partage*. No two words in those lists say the same thing. Each has a different root and different semantic associations, so they look like synonyms but are not really synonyms. *Style*, in the sense of the choice of one word rather than another that looks like it says the same thing, therefore determines meaning.

Since there is no "the" touch, since you can never touch touch, no word for touch is adequate to it. It ain't namable. It is a vacant center, so any name for it is necessarily a catachresis.

DUNNE: *In* Literature as Conduct, *you speak of "a desire for infinite freedom and disponibility." "Once you have committed yourself," you say, to a certain action, "there is no returning to your disponibility, your unused freedom and what was, in a sense, your irresponsibility." I find this word* disponibility *intriguing. What do you mean precisely by disponibility? Can anyone really ever be said to be or have been disponible?*

MILLER: *Disponibility* is a somewhat ironic reference to the use of this word by the existentialists, especially Sartre. He had a radical theory of freedom, believing, as I do not, that nothing could alienate a radical "disponibilité," so that if I join the communist party (his example) I have to commit myself again to it every time I wake up in the morning. I agree with you that one is born committed, for example, to a certain race and sex, certain parents, etc., so one is never really disponible, pace Sartre. Nevertheless, I have some measure of freedom, for example, to make promises, to commit myself to a marriage, for example. These commitments are speech acts (unknown as such to Sartre, so far as I remember). They put me where I was not before, however, namely, in a position of needing to be true or false to the commitments I have now made. Sartre is no longer disponible. He cannot renege on his commitment to the Party without betrayal, whereas before he was free to join or not. For me, Meredith's figure of crossing the Rubicon, in *The Ordeal of Richard Feverel*, is the paradigmatic expression of this loss of freedom.[10] I suppose I meant that we all might desire infinite freedom and disponibility but can never ever have it. Derrida's notion of irresponsibility (that we cannot be true to all the responsibilities we have, that we cannot feed all the cats) complicates what I have just said about ethical life quite a bit.

DUNNE: *"The Aspern Papers" seems to me to be an especially suitable allusion to the kind of reading I am currently engaged in with your work and, of course, this interview. I think here of a statement in the Preface to the New York Edition that strikes me as particularly correct: "The historian, essentially, wants more documents than he can really use; the dramatist only wants more liberties than he can really take." James as you know refers here to the "odd law" that the "suggestion" serves the artist better than the "maxim" and is relieved that he did not have to make the decision of whether or not to make contact with Jane Clairmont: "I had luckily not had to deal with the difficult option." The consequences of his not having to make the decision are accordingly inspirational, compelling, provocative. But the gesture here, it seems to me at least, is not toward the relief of not having to deal with an excess of historical information so much as an acknowledgment that the artist is forced to be irresponsible with these "bare facts," that whether or not he is in possession of them the reader/writer must be willing to accept the consequences for having "turned" the "matter" or for having "done things" with it.*

Something similar is striking in Derrida's response to your work in Without Alibi, *where he says that in order to do justice to your work he must propose to you "the most demanding interpretation"; he must put the figure of the anacoluthon (like an acolyte who gives the slip) to work. Would you say that "The Aspern Papers" can be read as an amplified expression of the necessary irresponsibility or injustice of the active reader's response to another's work? Is a just reading in some sense (perhaps this is even too macabre?) a violation of a tomb?*

I suppose, in a way, I'm thinking here of a responsibility to the archive by way of a writing (perhaps re-vision) of another's work and a bearing testimony to it. Would I be right in saying that in the recent papers on Derrida's work, "Derrida's Remains," "Derrida Enisled," etc., you are constantly aware of your responsibility to a memory of a person as well as an obligation to the future of that person's work? How does one deal with this conflict?

MILLER: Yes, reading is the violation of a tomb, all right. Like what John says at the very end of the Bible: Cursed be the one who adds one bit or takes away one bit (John says it more dramatically), but of course active reading is bound to do both of those things.[11] My essays on Jacques Derrida more or less self-consciously add and take away. They are my way of trying to "work through" my mourning at his death, by way of some irreverent serious frivolity, no doubt an unsuccessful attempt, since I think Derrida is right to say mourning and melancholy cannot be wholly distinguished. My Derrida essays are oriented toward the future of his work by way of their implicit and explicit claim that the way to read him is page by page, sentence by sentence, word by word, and with close attention to words, like "reste," that recur. That is the way of reading he advises (and practices) in *Le toucher*: "micrological reading."

DUNNE: *You'll be aware that my questions thus far have steered clear of the biographical. I've noticed that I've been able to get quite a lot of background from the interviews with Moynihan, Olson, and Wolfreys.[12] But seeing as I'm researching a book on your work, I would very much like to know a little more about your own research experience. You've said quite a bit about it already in the Wolfreys interview, but I should like to revisit that point here in the event that other researchers might read this book in future years.*

Here's a quotation from your doctoral thesis: "relating an author's life and his work should be, in my opinion, subsidiary to understanding his work as a series of individual works of art. A good novel should have life and meaning of its own independent of its author."[13] I therefore ask with some trepidation how your early interest in Kenneth Burke and Georges Poulet influenced your work at this stage?

MILLER: Yes, the biographical is boring, certainly so in the case of my quite pedestrian life. My dissertation was written when I was greatly influenced by Burke's writings. It was an attempt to use Burke's idea of "symbolic action" in readings of some Dickens novels, though I was also influenced by work by other scholars on recurrent metaphors, for example, in Shakespeare. This took some courage or, actually, some innocence, since the director of my dissertation, Douglas Bush, more or less detested Burke (because he uses the editorial "we" and other stylistic infelicities, according to Bush, but it was really because he was a "theorist," a Freudian, a Marxist, etc., etc.). Bush read my huge two-volume dissertation in one weekend and had one comment: I think you should use "that" sometimes instead of "which." He must have somehow liked it, since he recommended me for the job at Hopkins, but I certainly never learned that from anything he said. At the time I wrote my dissertation, I did not know Poulet's work at all. That came later, at Hopkins, by an accidental encounter with the first of his essays translated into English, when I was rewriting the dissertation as a book (really starting all over from the beginning; the dissertation and the book are radically different in theme and procedure). I taught myself to be able to read French seriously in order to read Poulet, Sartre, and Valéry. The Dickens book is much influenced by my reading of Poulet in the early 1950s and by my close friendship with him when he was a colleague at Hopkins, before he left around 1958 or so for Zürich. I especially admired and tried to emulate Poulet's succinctness and his "dialectical" movement, in an essay, from stage to stage toward some neat conclusion. My reading of Poulet sort of put Burke in the shade for the moment, though my turn to Derrida in the late 1960s was in a way a return to Burke. I still think Poulet is a terrific critic, though I am no longer a "critic of consciousness," as you have probably noticed. Poulet and I and another colleague, a deep-dyed New Critic named Earl Wasserman, used to have lunch together at the Hopkins Faculty Club at least once a week and argue endlessly about literature and how to write about it. Those lunches were my real education. Ah, those were the days! Bliss was it in that dawn to be alive![14]

DUNNE: *You have remained throughout your career remarkably prolific; do you have a working routine?*

MILLER: Complex and somewhat tedious story, since my writing practice has been different at different times. My dissertation (two big volumes never published) was written, with invaluable stylistic help from my wife of three years, and with a new baby in the apartment, in about six months, I have no idea how. Then at Hopkins it took me five or six years to write my first book, entirely different from the dissertation. I remember wondering, in some despair, if it would ever get finished. The next two books were written in Europe with the leisure provided by a Guggenheim, and another Guggenheim, and a National Endowment for the Humanities Fellowship later on helped with later books. When I got to Yale, I was so busy with various small administrative duties (chair of English, director of the Literature Major, director of Graduate Studies in Comparative Literature) that I set up a regimen of getting up at 5 and working until 8, keeping a notebook even when I wasn't actively writing an essay or book. Sometimes sort of like playing scales for a pianist. After that my day was given to chairing and teaching. My deliberate model was Anthony Trollope, who wrote his 47 novels that way, while a post office employee (not all that different from chairing a big fractious department). I still recommend that practice of writing something every day to my graduate students as the way to get a dissertation done. Write something every day, even if it is just a line or two. Writing is a form of thinking, a way to discover or articulate ideas you did not know you had. Your fingers on the keyboard or grasping the pen seem almost to think for you. Inarticulate, wordless, ideas are just that, airy nothings. I still have the 15 or 20 notebooks, with entries written all over the world, in airports, on planes, in Australia on a lecture tour, early in the morning at home in Bethany, Connecticut, etc. While still at Yale, I shifted straight from handwriting to the computer and still keep, though not so compulsively, a digital notebook with dated entries. At Irvine, I had more time and managed to write and publish a lot of books, though they all came out of graduate teaching there. Other books from that Irvine teaching still remain in draft form. Now in more or less retirement in Maine I have been able to continue being productive, with less distraction, still writing mostly in the morning. I still try out my ideas in an annual "mini-seminar" at Irvine and of course at all those conferences and in those lectures. I've done all this writing because I really enjoy doing it. It is my vocation, along with teaching. I should stress that most of my books and essays, almost from the beginning, have come out of teaching, both undergraduate and graduate teaching, as well as a series of summer seminars for college teachers through the National Endowment for the Humanities (NEH) and the School of Criticism and Theory. My hapless students have been guinea pigs over the years for work I've been doing. No better way to see whether or not a reading of some work or other, or a theoretical trajectory, will fly or should sink without a trace.

DUNNE: *Do you have any advice for critics of your work? In other words, do you have an image of a reader-to-come?*

MILLER: I have no confidence that my work will go on being read, though of course I hope it will. Who knows? I have been lucky in having lots of readers of many different sorts over the years all over the world, mostly generous and good readers. I am immensely touched by an experience I have had fairly often. Young persons (or perhaps not so young nowadays) come up to me after a lecture or at a conference, or send me emails, to say that they want me to know they read some essay or book of mine when they were undergraduates or graduate students or young teachers and that this has strongly influenced their own thinking about literature ever since. What could be nicer! Especially nice is the accidental quality of these events. They just happened on my work or some teacher assigned some essay or book.

My own discoveries of Burke, or Poulet, or Derrida happened that way, fortuitously. That serendipitous reader is the reader-to-come I hope I go on having. My advice to critics of my work is to pretend they know nothing about received opinion concerning my work but to read it as if they were that undergraduate who just happened to come upon it.

Notes

1   Begin here by returning to a question I first put to Miller at the "Counter-Movements: Institutions of Difference" conference at the University of Portsmouth on July 24, 2006.

2   I am grateful to J. Hillis Miller for sending on an essay entitled "A Defense of Literary Study in a Time of Globalization and the New Tele-Technologies." Here Miller argues, via a subtle reading of virtuality and secrecy in Wallace Stevens's poem "The River of Rivers in Connecticut," that literature's performative force often reveals something "other" which cannot be so effortlessly achieved in other media. "I conclude," he says here, "that what we call written literature has an almost unique and irreplaceable performative function in human culture, even in a time of globalisation and the increasing dominance of new teletechnologicoprestidigitizing media."

3   See especially "Friedrich Schlegel: Catachresis for Chaos" in *Others* (Princeton, NJ: Princeton University Press, 2001), pp. 5–42; "Friedrich Schlegel and the Anti-Ekphrastic Tradition" in *Revenge of the Aesthetic: The Place of Literature in Theory Today*, ed. Michael P. Clark (Berkley, CA: University of California Press, 2000), pp. 58–75; and "Indirect Discourse and Irony" in *Reading Narrative* (Norman, OK: University of Oklahoma Press, 1998), pp. 158–177.

4   See Jacques Derrida's response to Serge Doubrovsky's criticism of his "Structure, Sign and Play in the Discourse of the Human Sciences" in *The Structuralist Controversy: The Languages of Criticism and the Sciences of Man*, ed. Richard Macksey and Eugenio Donato (Baltimore, MD: The Johns Hopkins University Press, 1970), p. 272.

5   J. Hillis Miller, "Paul de Man as Allergen" in *Material Events: Paul de Man and the Afterlife of Theory*, ed. Tom Cohen, Barbara Cohen, J. Hillis Miller, and Andrzej Warminski (Minneapolis, MN: University of Minnesota Press, 2000), pp. 183–204.

6   See William Empson's *Some Versions of Pastoral* (London: Penguin, 1995), pp. 203–233.

7   Robert Eaglestone, *Ethical Criticism: Reading After Levinas* (Edinburgh: Edinburgh University Press, 1998), p. 82.

8   See J. Hillis Miller's "Aphorism as Instrument of Political Action in Nietzsche" in *Parallax*, vol. 10.3 (2004), pp. 70–82.

9   Miller has discussed this example at some length in *Speech Acts in Literature* (Stanford, CA: Stanford University Press, 2001), pp. 134–139. See also his

meditative responses to the question posed in Trollope's *Ayala's Angel* "How can I know when I am in love?" in *Black Holes* (Stanford, CA: Stanford University Press, 1999), pp. 279–311 (alternately).

[10] The remarkable passage from George Meredith's *The Ordeal of Richard Feverel* (Westminster: Archibold Constable, 1902) is as follows: "Although it blew hard when Caesar crossed the Rubicon, the passage of that river is commonly calm; calm as Acheron. So long as he gets his fare, the ferryman does not need to be told whom he carries: he pulls with a will, and heroes may be over in half-an-hour. Only when they stand on the opposite bank, do they see what a leap they have taken. The shores they have relinquished shrink to an infinite remoteness. There they have dreamed: here they must act. There lie youth and irresolution: here manhood and purpose. They are veritably in another land: a moral Acheron divides their life. Their memories scarce seem their own! The Philosophical Geography (about to be published) observes that each man has, one time or other, a little Rubicon—a clear or a foul water to cross. It is asked him: 'Wilt thou wed this Fate, and give up all behind thee?' And 'I will,' firmly pronounced, speeds him over. The above-named manuscript authority informs us, that by far the greater number of caresses rolled by this heroic flood to its sister stream below, are those of fellows who have repented their pledge, and have tried to swim back to the bank they have blotted out. For though every man of us may be a hero for one fatal minute, very few remain so after a day's march even: and who wonders that Madam Fate is indignant, and wears the features of the terrible Universal Fate to him? Fail before her, either in heart or in act, and lo, how the alluring loves in her visage wither and sicken to what it is modelled on! Be your Rubicon big or small, clear or foul, it is the same: you shall not return. On—or to Acheron!—I subscribe to that saying of The Pilgrim's Scrip: 'The danger of a little knowledge of things is disputable: but beware the little knowledge of one's self!'" (p. 232).

[11] See St. John of Patmos's account of this dangerous supplement in the closing remarks of the Bible, Rev. 22.17–21. "And the Spirit and the bride say, Come. And let him that is athirst come. And whosoever will, let him take the water of life freely. For I testify unto every man that heareth the words of the prophecy of this book, If any man shall add unto these things, God shall add unto him the plagues that are written in this book: And if any man shall take away from the words of the book of this prophecy, God shall take away his part out of the book of life, and out of the holy city, and from the things which are written in this book. He which testifieth these things saith, Surely I come quickly. Amen. Even so, come, Lord Jesus. The grace of our Lord Jesus Christ be with you all. Amen." I am here using *The King James Version* for my quotation.

[12] For interviews with Miller covering this ground, see especially Robert Moynihan's *A Recent Imagining: Interviews With Harold Bloom, Geoffrey*

Hartman, J. Hillis Miller, Paul de Man (Hamden, CT: Archon Books, 1986), pp. 99–131; Imre Salusinszky, Criticism in Society: Interviews With Jacques Derrida, Northrop Frye, Harold Bloom, Geoffrey Hartman, Frank Kermode, Edward Said, Barbara Johnson, Frank Lentricchia, and J. Hillis Miller (London: Methuen, 1987), pp. 209–240; Julian Wolfreys, ed., The J. Hillis Miller Reader (Edinburgh: Edinburgh University Press, 2005), pp. 405–422; and Gary Olson's "Rhetoric, Cultural Studies, and the Future of Critical Theory: A Conversation With J. Hillis Miller" in JAC 14.2 (1992), pp. 317–345.

[13] Miller's thesis, Dickens' Symbolic Imagery: A Study of Six Novels, was presented to the English Department at Harvard University on March 31, 1952. My copy, obtained from the British Library, is in three volumes and is 580 pages long.

[14] The allusion here is to Wordsworth's The Prelude, Book xi. l. 108 (1850 version): "Bliss was it in that dawn to be alive, / But to be young was very Heaven."

9

"You See You Ask an Innocent Question and You've Got a Long Answer"

Interview with Éamonn Dunne, Michael O'Rourke, Martin McQuillan, Graham Allen, Dragan Kujundžić, and Nicholas Royle

J. HILLIS MILLER: You want me to read the questions?

ÉAMONN DUNNE: *What are you reading now?*

MILLER: I have a truthful answer to that question. I am reading one of the volumes of Henry James's New York Edition. The one that collects the stories that he says are on the international theme written essentially in the 1880s, so they are all quite early. The volume begins with a quite extraordinary preface about the international theme. Why am I reading that? Because I promised to go to what I consider to be a very strange conference at Oxford in about three weeks (the end of June 2012) on "Henry James at Oxford." Henry James received an honorary degree from Oxford, but that isn't even mentioned in Kaplan's biography so it's not a big deal, and Henry James's connection with Oxford is pretty marginal.[1] He went there for the first time rather early in his life. My Oxford inviters admit this: it's just an excuse to have a party at Oxford. I go all the way there, and then I go to Munich and

Augsburg. I go all the way to Oxford to talk for twenty minutes. But I chose these stories partly because one of them was commissioned by an Oxford graduate from Merton College who lived in Paris and ran a transatlantic magazine, but I was also searching for something to talk about, and those stories involve international encounters, as you know if you've read them: "Lady Barbarina," which is the most famous one, but there's also one called "A Bundle of Letters." These stories tend to be epistolary, which is interesting. I was especially attracted by one of them, the one that involves Americans going to Europe and the question of intermarriage between Americans and Europeans. I was interested in that one because the woman is from Bangor, Maine, which is just sixty miles from where I live. James imitates her accent. You see you ask an innocent question and you've got a long answer.

But my Oxford friends asked me to bring in certain things. They prescribe; people are always telling me what I should write. They wanted me somehow to bring J.L. Austin in. He was certainly from Oxford. I'm happy to do that. James of course had no way of knowing *How to Do Things with Words*, but I've written a book on speech acts in Henry James [*Literature as Conduct: Speech Acts in Henry James*], which uses speech act theory and that was the connection that interests my Oxford inviters. So I have asked myself, "Are there any performatives in this volume of James stories?" Of course, there are lots of performatives in the stories, but the one that really interests me is in the preface. It is quite extraordinary. The preface makes a sociological hypothesis: in 1908 during that period when he's writing the prefaces, says James, the international theme no longer exists because there's been, according to him, a fusion, whereas in the 1880s there was a real difference between Americans and English, or sometimes French, people. The question of intermarriage between them could in the 1880s be a legitimate subject for writing. James even excludes *Portrait of a Lady* from that. The fact that the characters are Americans or French or English is not, he says, important in *The Wings of the Dove* and *The Golden Bowl* or even in *Portrait of a Lady*. That's interesting as a sociological hypothesis and very problematic. In that short quarter of a century or a little more, national distinctions had disappeared, says James. No more international theme. So maybe claiming that is a performative. How do you prove his claim? Is it not valid just on his say-so? There's also an extraordinarily condescending passage in the preface where he says, in effect, "now [1908] when I go to a great hotel or when I look in the bank at the people who sign their names on checks or when I see the people on a transatlantic boat, I haven't the slightest idea who they are. They have these long names that are not Anglo-Saxon names. I have no idea what they are thinking and feeling, whereas I used to believe I knew that about people in hotels, etc. They were my sort." That is a very condescending and racist passage. Its innocent blatantness surprised me a little bit. But there is one genuine performative and this will be my subject in my Oxford talk—I only have twenty minutes, six pages —and I've already talked six pages here. I'm talking fast so I won't have to answer the very hard questions at the end.

Here's the performative: he's talking about "Lady Barbarina." It's the longest and the first in this volume of stories. It's about an American doctor who courts and marries an English noblewoman and brings her to New York. She finds it horrible! But then she has a chance finally to go back home. He promises to take her back in the summer to visit her home and visit England, and he knows after a while that if he takes her she'll never come back to New York because she finds Americans uncultured, even in New York among the rich. He's a rich doctor, and there are parties and so on. The performative is in the preface where James says that generally speaking, both historically and in the other stories in his volume, it's the young American woman who goes to Europe and marries there. "Lady Barbarina" reverses that because it's an Englishwoman who marries an American. By the way, James doesn't comment on a fact that strikes me as crucial. Not a single one of these stories leads to a happy marriage. It never does in James. He was incapable of imagining a happy heterosexual marriage. Well there is one. The sister of Lady Barbarina marries a cowboy from the west. She's a bad girl. She goes out to parties at night. Lady Barbarina brings her sister with her to New York and she elopes. So the doctor (his name is Doctor Lemon) goes all the way to the horrible (to James) west coast, to California, to try to rescue the sister-in-law, but he discovers it's too late. They really are legitimately married. The performative is the statement he makes in the preface in which he admits that this is not historical, that he didn't have historical experience of a marriage of an English noblewoman and an American doctor. So he says I forged the documents. And that would be a speech act. So it's based on a forged historical nontruth, but he says he was so satisfied with these forged documents that he was able to write this story. It is a wonderful story. Now I've given my little talk so I don't have to go to Oxford.

NICHOLAS ROYLE: *If you were sailing to a desert island and could only take six poems with you, what would they be? If you were sailing to a desert island and could only take six novels with you, what would they be? Is there any single author whose work you have not yet read and would like to take along on the same trip?*

MILLER: I have thought a bit about this. As usual, Nick's questions are sly and difficult. I can tell you which books of poetry I would bring…but not quite "it would maybe be a poem by…" Well I can say I'd take *The Prelude*. I'm going to be stuck for a long time on that desert island! Not *The Excursion* but *The Prelude*. That's a single poem. I don't think I'd take Tennyson's *The Princess*, although I might. One thing we haven't talked about at all (and there would be a lot to say about this) and that is the placement of "Tears Idle Tears" in *The Princess*.[2] The lyric has a context. It's sung by a man pretending to be a woman who's invaded this women's collective, so he's dressed in drag, something you don't really expect to find in Tennyson. And I've never really quite worked out the function of the context, so I might bring *The Princess*. I would want to bring poems that I haven't satisfied myself by writing about. You can always go back to great poems. I think since I haven't already written on "The Owl and the Sarcophagus," I would certainly take a [Wallace] Stevens poem. And I would like to have some Hardy to read but Nick has said one poem and it wouldn't be *The Dynasts*. I would have to take something like the poems 1912–1913. You see, I don't really come up much beyond modernists. I stop with Stevens in the poems that come to my mind. I don't know if that is six, but you get the general idea.

The novels: again I would want to take very long ones that I haven't satisfied myself that I know. One of them answers the next question—I stand here to confess, it's a speech act: I confess—I have never read Richardson, ever. I have had no particular occasion to. I would take Richardson's *Clarissa* along. On this desert island, I would probably take a Jane Austen novel because I haven't really worked on Jane Austen. I've read them. I don't know quite which one, *Emma* maybe, maybe *Mansfield Park*. I mean they are all wonderful. I've been talking recently in lectures about the gothic side of *Atonement*. The epigraph from Ian McEwan's *Atonement* is from *Northanger Abbey*, so there's a literal reference. I might re-read *Northanger Abbey*, which I haven't done for a while. But I certainly would take a George Eliot novel that I don't know as well as I know *Middlemarch*, so it wouldn't be *Middlemarch*. It might be *Daniel Deronda*, which I have taught but I don't feel that I have mastered. It's a wonderful novel that I find more interesting than other George Eliot novels that I have taken seriously. I would certainly take Proust because though I've written on Proust, I have never really read all those 3000 pages. When I started teaching Proust, I said to myself if I start with *Swann's Way* I'll never get out of *Swann's Way*. What people normally teach is *Swann's Way* and then *Le Temps Retrouvé* at the end. So I decided I won't do that. I'll read the parts about Marcel's long affair with *Albertine*. In English, one part is called *The Sweet Cheat Gone*, or *Albertine Disparue* in

French. I'd take the French because that would slow me down. I remember I was reading it in French. I came upon a sentence that was syntactically odd. I could read it; I knew what all the words meant, but syntactically it didn't make sense. Proust's syntax is sometimes very complicated. So I said I'll look at the translation. I looked at the standard translation and found that the translator had just left the sentence out! He obviously didn't know what it meant either. So you have to read the French. My earlier work on Proust has been published now.

I am reading for the first time some so-called Postmodern Fiction. I don't really feel I would know what to say about *Gravity's Rainbow*; to some degree it troubles me, bothers me. I tried to read it but I think it might be good for me to read the whole of *Gravity's Rainbow*, hence my answer about another author I haven't read that I'd like to read. It's not something you would do overnight, reading Richardson or Pynchon either, which is maybe why I haven't done it.

MARTIN MCQUILLAN: *Have you ever thought about writing a novel?*

MILLER: The answer is, sure, who hasn't? But I know I couldn't do it. This reminds me of a story I told at Lancaster.[3] There's a question about my mother later on here. My mother at some point called me Hillis Junior because I'm a junior. She was a Southerner, and I hated that. "Hillis Junior! Come here Hillis Junior!" She said at some point when I was in graduate school or maybe already teaching, "Hillis Junior, why don't you write a romance?" "Housewives in Wisconsin write romances," said my mother. She figured I was wasting my talents writing literary criticism. My answer was quite truthful. I said, "Mother if I could I would," but I knew that I couldn't. Also I've resisted a version of that question: "Have you written your memoirs?" I've told stories all the time about de Man or Derrida, about my mother, but I have a resistance to doing a memoir or autobiography partly because though I'm not all that modest a person, I still ask myself, "Are people really going to interest themselves in my life?" I'd rather write some more criticism, so I doubt if I will do an autobiography. It's now very popular. Lots of academic people write their memoirs sooner or later, partly justifying it, as I might mine, by the fact that it has lots of true stories about people whose work is known. Edward Said was a close friend of mine. I would have stories to tell about him. But my memoirs are not going to be a bestseller.

New Media and Telepathic Technologies

DRAGAN KUJUNDŽIĆ: *How can understanding contemporary media help us reread literary tradition? I am specifically thinking about reading the mediatic in the literary. Was it always there, and if so, how?*

MILLER: We have talked quite a bit about this, you and I, at one time or another. This is obviously a big topic that almost anybody these days is interested in. Nick Royle talked about it. Two answers: one would be that I have a theory that I call "anachronistic reading." Which means that I think reading these old works (say Richardson, or Jane Austen, or whoever) trying to make yourself as though you were an eighteenth-century person, which is what I was taught to do, you learn all about the culture, etc., etc. I'm very dubious about that. I want to know what *Clarissa* would mean for me today, what use it would be today. And I think that's a rather different question from asking what its role was in its original historical context. There's a part of me that says "so I'm supposed to read the *Elizabethan World Picture* by Tillyard in order to think like an Elizabethan." I don't want to think like an Elizabethan. I don't really think I can. I don't think you can suspend your present-day picture. You read those old works today with an awareness of the change in media. That means I am quite different from readers of *Middlemarch* when it first came out. They had no way of imagining the changes in media to come. Knowing the new media gives us a special perspective on *Middlemarch* because it's easier for us to see ways in which the fact that it's a printed novel published in parts and so on limits its possibilities of meaning. So that would be one answer.

The other answer would be to say that the transformation of these old printed books into Kindle editions and other e-texts gives us a new perspective on literature. I'm not at all against e-books. Having them gives us an opportunity to reflect on the effects of new media. What's the difference between reading *Middlemarch* in a printed book and reading it on Kindle? There are a lot of differences. I think it's a useful way of thinking about new media to have works that exist in both. That's what I mean by "the medium is the maker": that the medium has a decisive effect on what you can say in the medium.[4] And nineteenth-century novelists exploited the medium of the printed book in different ways. Trollope uses the medium of the published, printed book in a way different from the way George Eliot does. That's a challenging topic for research and reflection.

MCQUILLAN: *What does a deconstructive film look like?*

MILLER: We've just seen that [a deconstructive film]! We've heard that question before today. It's a trap. Martin has already put down all these brilliant people that he was interrogating and has given his own answer, which is meant to be decisive. I accept his answer.[5] The only thing that I can add to it—and this seems willfully, trivially paradoxical but I think it does mean something—is there is no such thing as a nondeconstructive film. That is to say even the most banal Hollywood film that follows the conventions (for example, of film noir) nevertheless has some element of one feature of deconstruction, namely, self-reflection about the medium itself and in that sense a kind of undoing of the medium. Given time, I could show that every Victorian novel, even the most subservient to the conventions of the Victorian novel, has some place or other in it where there is a reflection on the medium. So I think that's a general thing. You can call that self-deconstruction if you like. It certainly is one feature of deconstruction. Then you would have to say (the reason I say it is kind of trivial) it might not be very interesting to observe that with some films or novels. There are obviously some that are more interesting than others. Nevertheless, I think it is a kind of nonquestion because there is no absolute distinction between the so-called deconstructive film and the completely conventional one. I noticed, by the way, in some of the examples that Martin showed, I was having trouble trying to watch the film. You intended this. Listening to you talking about me and Walter Benjamin at the same time as showing film clips distracted me. I missed some parts of that, but the examples you gave were all I guess deconstructive.

But I did notice something quite often in the cinematic examples: that is—I talked about this at Lancaster—the question of stage play. What do actors and actresses in films do with their hands? There's been a kind of transformation. It used to be in the great days of Humphrey Bogart and in some of these film clips that Martin showed that what you do is light a cigarette, as the very beautiful actress in the film about the philosopher you showed did. She is shown lighting a cigarette. It has no obvious symbolic meaning. It is hard to say that it does anything other than to give her something to do with her hands and mouth. It's vaguely erotic, perhaps. So if you look at old films you find that a huge amount of time is spent lighting cigarettes and smoking. This is true of the film of *Atonement*, as a period touch. In the novel of *Atonement*, there is a lot of smoking, but there's even more smoking in the film. Cecilia is going swimming and lights a cigarette, which is very improbable. So to get up on the diving board, she has to throw the cigarette away.

Nowadays with things I watch on television it's the cell phone. You have to fill in space with something, and the actor's or actress's cell phone rings, and the character takes the phone out. It's a substitute for smoking partly because we know about smoking now. It's not always a good thing. And part of my reaction to the *Atonement* film when everybody is smoking is to say, "Stop it at once! You're killing yourselves!" Humphrey Bogart died of lung cancer. He smoked not only in his films but in real life. So one can imagine a cinematic performance of Hamlet in which Hamlet would light up and say "to be or not to be—PUFF—that is the question—PUFF PUFF!!!" And that Shakespeare might have written that in. You can see how conventional it is and really weird. Most people don't smoke that much.

MCQUILLAN: *Literature is an invention of the eighteenth century, film is an invention of the twentieth century; how can we think that difference beyond the epochal?*

MILLER: Well, I'm thinking, I'm not quite sure about my answer to the question, but novels and films are powerful media that each has its own mediatic effects. No doubt they belong to their centuries. But I think it is important always to remember that each is a technological means of reproduction. The print epoch, what you can do with printed texts, is to some degree subservient to historical changes in technology. Books used to be typeset by hand; then came the linotype. Now more recently it's the computer that sets books. So when you say literature is an invention of the eighteenth century, that means Derrida was right when he said that literature belongs to the age of the rise of the middle class and of bourgeois finance capitalism. It would have been impossible earlier according to him, during the middle ages or in the Renaissance. Literature also depends, says Derrida, on freedom of speech, which of course people don't have in the same way under different regimes, however democratic they in principle are. In a democracy, there is at least pro forma permission to say anything and to not be put in prison for it, but that freedom is always limited nevertheless. There are limits to free speech, as we all know from our teaching. Teaching in Britain and in the United States is wonderfully free. There's nobody in the classroom reporting what I say, deciding whether it's politically acceptable or not. I can choose to a considerable degree what texts I teach, and so on. It's a marvelous kind of freedom. Nevertheless, there is a limit. There is a point beyond which some of the students would complain about what Professor Miller is teaching and how he's teaching it. Things might happen to me as a result. Nevertheless, I think Derrida is right to connect literature and free speech. Why is that? Because you can always say of the narrator, the telepathic narrator, and of all of the characters, "That's not me or any real person; that's fiction!" In *Crime and Punishment*, Dostoyevsky could always say, "I'm not an axe murderer; I'm just writing a novel about somebody who is an axe murderer; don't blame me." Dostoyevsky did suffer exile for speaking out, but in general I think Derrida is right to connect literature and free speech.

One other question I've been asked has to do with the visual and literary. I think I can say two things about that, so I'm coming on now to Graham Allen's question. Let's hear it, and I'll try to speak to both Martin's and Graham's questions.

GRAHAM ALLEN: *You have written frequently about the new digital media that is shaping our society. Do you think, as many have asserted, that our culture has become an essentially visual rather than literary one? And if the answer is yes, what are the consequences for us?*

MILLER: So we think of those together: film as an invention of the twentieth century. That is certainly true, but I think we need to define carefully the difference between novel and film—which I've said is a technological one. The technological goes beyond the epochal. Again, I think Derrida is right when he says that the new regime of telecommunications, which he only in part foresaw, but he means things like the Internet and email and so on, will put an end to so-called literature, psychoanalysis, philosophy, and love letters. That is in *The Postcard*. He says that from this perspective, the political regime is secondary, meaning that the technological media that are dominant in a given period have the same power, let's say in Russia or China, than they do in the United States or Ireland or England. That's an interesting claim: that media are more powerful than political forms. And he uses the word *regime*, which implies national sovereignty. I think he is probably right in that counter-intuitive claim. Look at the Arab Spring and how much that has depended on the cellphone. It's as though the possession of the cellphone by these young people in these North African countries was necessary to the almost inevitable result: the toppling of these regimes. The political regime was secondary to a particular kind of postdemocratic democracy that's built into the cellphone. (What has happened since this interview in Egypt is not all that reassuring. The ubiquity of the mobile phone by no means guarantees democracy. Terrorists make strategic use of the cellphone. All cellphone conversations more or less worldwide, but including those of United States citizens, are nowadays being recorded by the National Security Agency in the United States. That is not exactly a big advance in democracy with its guaranteed right to privacy.)

That leads me to the opposition between the visual and literature. I'm asked, "Do you think as many have asserted that our culture has become an essentially visual rather than a literary one?" And I think my answer would be to say that in general that's true, but I think the distinction between the visual and the literary can be exaggerated. I would also agree with what Paul de Man says in "The Resistance to Theory." Rather than developing an entirely new interpretative technique for strongly visual media like film, television, or video games, we must, de Man said, learn how to "read pictures" rather than "to imagine meaning." He meant, I think, that visual media use versions of tropological identifications and displacements—metaphors, metonymies, and the like—as in the metonymic juxtapositions of montage, going back to the comparison, in Eisenstein's *Battleship Potemkin*, of the rioting crowd to swarming maggots, and leading up to those present-day television ads that try to persuade you that buying a certain automobile will give you possession of the beautiful actress or the handsome actor who presents the car. Moreover, a film is full of language. It's not purely visual. A lot of people have been studying this recently in a serious way, for example, Tom Cohen's brilliant work on Hitchcock's films. Moreover, there's an important visual aspect to works in the print epoch, for example, printed novels: the format, the binding, the advertising that's put inside, the size of the typeface, all sorts of things that make a printed novel a visual artefact. They were also all illustrated (or tended to be illustrated). It's only recently, partly because of the impact of this shift in interest to the visual and to the techniques that are needed to read the visual (these are not quite the same as those necessary for reading texts), that people have noticed that Eliot's, or Trollope's, or Dickens's novels originally had illustrations. The versions of those novels I first read, modern paperback editions, had no pictures at all. The original illustrations were not assumed to be important to their meaning. I was talking to somebody today about the great Blake archive at the University of Virginia, which reproduces what Blake's pages really looked like. The earlier authoritative David V. Erdman and Harold Bloom edition of Blake doesn't have any pictures at all.[6] It simply, very scrupulously, with all the powers of textual scholarship, gives you the words that were on those pages. And now we would look upon that as a falsification of Blake's mixed media productions. So I think I would say that all these media, printed novels, films, etc., are both visual and textual in different proportions, though I wouldn't deny the importance of the difference in proportion.

I know this best from the comparison of films to novels. There are things you can do in a novel, for example, the way the original printed version of *Atonement* uses free indirect discourse. In that form of language, the narrator speaks for the character in the third-person past tense, for something that was, for the character, in the first-person present tense. This creates a double language that makes that kind of discourse always ironic. It's like the student who simply repeats what the teacher has said, but the repetition is very cheeky, ironic, and defiant. The thing I have learned from Nick Royle is to substitute the term *telepathic narrator* [for *omniscient narrator*]. That's a marvelous insight. The narrators of Victorian novels generally are usually called omniscient. That brings in a whole host of perhaps inadvertent theological implications. Such narrators are better described as telepathic in the sense that they are granted insight into what the characters are thinking and feeling. Reporting that insight is a powerful convention in the novel, even though I myself do not believe we can ever know for sure what another person is thinking or feeling.

I think all of these media (novels, films, television, video games) are already mixed. A film is never purely visual, despite the fact, to go back to *Atonement* for a moment, that you can't do free indirect discourse in the film version, or at any rate it is quite awkward. You must have a voiceover, and so on. So what's the substitute for that in film? Film conventions make much use of something that you can't easily do in the novel. That is the prolonged shots of the characters' faces. If you just watch carefully a film instead of taking it for granted, you will notice that a huge amount of cinematic time whether in a film or in a television program is just shots of one or another character's face. A face that is not necessarily saying anything. For example, in *Atonement*, there is a prolonged shot of Robbie Turner's face just before he makes love to Cecilia in the library. We just see his face. It doesn't look particularly sexually aroused; it's just his face. And that's supposed to give you insight. Faces—I don't think they actually do this—are supposed to tell you what the characters are like and what they are thinking and feeling. This is a substitute for free indirect discourse. You can't easily do this in a novel; you can't easily do this with words. Imre Kertész's *Fatelessness* would be another example. Most of that novel is in first person. He's talking about his memories of himself. The film spends a large amount of time just looking at the actor's face.

I would add one final thing to my answer to your question: I think from my experience, let's say with my grandchildren, that film as such, in the sense of movies that you go to watch in a theater, is actually playing a lesser role in young people's lives. They don't go to the movies so much.

There is sociological evidence for this. Movie theaters are closing all over the place. A huge number of people see movies; they make a lot of money. But there are many people who don't watch them or watch them only on a computer screen. My grandson Jeremy would be an example of this. His life is visual all right; he plays a lot of video games. It's also auditory; he listens to mp3 music. It's not that he doesn't use the new media. But he doesn't go to the movies much, and he doesn't watch Internet movies very much. He is a creature, you might say, of a slightly later generation for whom film is much less central than it has been. So I think just to say that there is an opposition between visual film and printed book is an oversimplification of what the new media are actually doing to people's experience of imaginary narratives.

My bottom line is that all media are in various combinations mixed media.

DUNNE: *You've been speaking recently about the New Humanities.[7] Could you elaborate a little on what you think they might be and if they can be achieved in what you call "these bad days"?*

MILLER: "These bad days" is a citation from a Matthew Arnold poem. Well that's both an easy question and an impossible question. How do I know what the new humanities are going to be? It's up to the young people to fight it out with the deans and try to save the humanities in whatever way they like. But I think it would behoove people who are in the humanities, especially those in literary studies and languages, to think about this and not simply to assume that they can go on with the current department structure and all the other present-day aspects. I think they are in jeopardy. The English departments feel that they are invulnerable. The French departments and the German departments used to think, "they won't touch us." Now many of them are gone. Will there always be an English department? I'm not so sure of that. The number of English majors in the United States has gone down from 8% of all undergraduates to 4%. Only half as many people, as a percentage, now major in English. The number of people who major in languages has gone from 2% to 1%, so you can see why it comes to the mind of a dean "Gee, do we really need the French department? They don't have any majors. We've got eight professors over there. Why not just abolish that department?" A spectacular example of this sort of thing is the state university at Albany where an administrator closed Jewish, French, German, and Russian studies. He just closed them arbitrarily because he had the power to do that and wanted to use the money otherwise. My advice to Albany—not to any of you, it's your own business what you do—would have been to tell the English department at Albany to take this as an opportunity to sit around together and concoct a new program that would not be called the English department but something like "Teaching How to Read Media" or "Understanding Media." This new department would include film studies and also include all those other language programs, so students could read literature and theory in the original. You've got to know German to read Heidegger or Adorno properly, French to read Derrida or Baudrillard. So rescue the languages as part of this program! I don't know whether it would work. You could at least try. You could say, "We're teaching students essential skills in how to live in this world of new media. We're teaching them how to read television ads and political ads and not to be so bamboozled so easily by the lies they tell." Television ads have a complex rhetoric, which I have begun to study. At Lancaster, I gave one example. In the United States, NBC Television News shows every night over and over again from night to night an ad sponsored by the American Petroleum Institute. The speaker on the screen is not an oil tycoon, the people who are making billions. It's a very charming young woman. She comes out on the screen, accompanied by brilliant graphics, and says, "I have good news for you. We have enough oil and gas, especially if we accelerate fracking (which is the extraction of gas from shale), to last for another 100 years. We'll produce millions of jobs. This is the solution." What she doesn't say of course is that fracking will accelerate climate change and pollute the ground water where fracking is done. There soon won't be any New York City left, not to speak of my house in Deer Isle Maine, or most of Florida. So, it's a lie; the ad is a lie, a gross lie. But it's very persuasive. The speaker is a woman, an attractive woman, persuasive, a very good actress. The argument is not made by the actual people who are doing this fracking. Sometimes such ads show bearded intellectual-looking engineers doing some of the talking. They too are part of our ideology of the good guys.

I think it would be a good thing to incorporate in the teaching of *Middlemarch* the teaching of how to read these ads. You could defend the teaching of *Middlemarch* by saying that the topic of misreading, of misinterpretation is a central feature of literature. You want to find out how to interpret lies or mistakes? Read *Middlemarch*, in which Dorothea is a spectacular misreader of Casaubon, or read Jane Austen, read *Pride and Prejudice* and learn from Elizabeth Bennett's misinterpretations how not to do it. Misreading is a constant theme in novels, not only women misreading but also men. Think of Conrad's Lord Jim. It's not just courtship and marriage either. It's often gross errors in reading other people in other situations, so reading novels would be a lesson in the rhetoric of bad reading generally. I can imagine a whole program that wouldn't be called

the Department of English but called "The Department of Rhetoric" or
something like that. The University of California at Berkeley has such a
department. I don't know what you would call it in a given university that
you could get away with, but you see what I mean. That might be a way of
saving not only the English department but also the study of languages. Part
of the reason the latter disappears is that people ask, "Why do I need to
learn French? What possible use is it? English is the dominant language all
over the world. Anything important will almost immediately be translated
without loss into English." Such a department might persuade people that
you need to read important texts in the original languages.

Influences

MICHAEL O'ROURKE: *As you are introduced in the film* The First
Sail, *Pamela Gilbert lists queer theory among your many interests. Even
in your most recent book on George Eliot, we can find a concerted critique
of phallogocentrism, but there is a sense that this turn to queer modes of
thinking only happens in your "later" work.[8] Are you ambivalent about your
commitments to this field? Maybe you could say a little about the belated (if
it is) interest in a domain of inquiry that your own writing actually helped to
foster (I'm thinking particularly here of the work of Eve Sedgwick and Judith
Butler)?*

MILLER: Eve Sedgwick was my student. I directed her dissertation, which
was on gothic novels. It wasn't yet the topic she became famous for. I didn't
anticipate that in anything she said to me or in papers that she had written.
Direct is a strong word for any help I gave her. She would bring me a chapter,
and I would say, "Thank you Eve, I look forward to seeing the next one."
But we had a cordial relation. I saw her the last time near the end of her life,
and we had a constructive talk. Butler was a graduate student at Yale. I also
have known her a long time, but not quite in the same way. Queer theory as
such didn't exist in those days. I've always been interested in some writers
(without worrying very much about it) who in fact were pretty certainly
gay, like Walter Pater, Wilde (I greatly admire Wilde, no doubt about his
queerness), Proust, and Henry James. That hasn't kept me from reading
work by these people, far from it, but I've been led by recent queer theory
writing on James, for example, the outing of Henry James, to ask myself
what difference it makes if you know that about James to your reading of the
novels? So for me queer theory is really useful as a way of asking that kind
of question. I think in James's case I've already mentioned in passing the

interesting fact that no happy heterosexual marriages are presented in these stories he wrote at the end of the 1880s. There's also an amazing passage that Kaplan quotes from James's first visit to Oxford as a quite young man in 1879. He writes a letter to his brother William about that visit. He does talk about the beautiful college buildings and so on, but what he really emphasizes is those strong and healthy and muscular and fair-haired undergraduates rowing their boats and so on. I think it is probably a totally unconscious passage, in the sense that at that stage of his life he perhaps didn't really know why he found these young men so attractive. It is helpful to have that information as a way of reading James's fiction. Kaplan's biography tries in a very balanced way to talk about James's unfulfilled homosexuality. So it's because other people have done this that I began to think about this topic.

My recent essay in the area of queer theory, which Pamela Gilbert may be referring to—I don't remember whether I'd written this essay then—is an article on Derrida's *Le Droit de Regard*.[9] Derrida gave me a copy of this at some point, and I always remember what he said as he handed it to me— he gave me copies of all of his books; it wasn't particularly that one—he said, "Don't just look at the pictures, read my essay." And I didn't in fact at that time follow his advice. I looked at the pictures. Quite extraordinary photographs done by a friend of his, Marie-Françoise Plissart. They are certainly an invitation to queer theorizing. Eventually I read the Derrida essay, which is amazing. Every new essay by Derrida I read, I say this is his masterpiece because they are all so good. But I did feel that once again with the Droit de Regard essay when I finally got around to not just looking at the pictures. If you don't know this book, the photos show very beautiful women in lesbian intercourse. They're quite explicit. Benoît Peeters, who is a Belgian, was one of the collaborators in the making of this book. He tells the complex story of how Derrida was persuaded to write an essay for this book. Peeters has now published a huge book on Derrida, a very good book.[10] So I chose, on Michael O'Rourke's invitation, to write an essay for a collection of writings about that aspect of Derrida without thinking too much about what that commitment might mean. I asked myself what do I really make of Derrida's essay? It is a serious investigation of narrative connection and how you can tell a story without any captions in just a series of pictures. Show me some pictures and I'll make a story out of them. It is also about a kind of circularity in storytelling, at least in the series of photographs in Droit de Regard. The last photo ties back to the first.

I want to say a word about Graham Allen's wonderful paper, which may or may not be helpful, about the structure of repetition and déjà vu.[11] I thought of those topics in relation to the fact that *The Triumph of Life* is unfinished. Scholars have said that well had he not drowned he would have finished it. And there are two ways of taking that. My esteemed Shelleyean colleague at Hopkins never wrote about the *Triumph of Life* because he was an organic unity person. He said, "it's not finished; I don't know how it would have come out, so I can't write about it."[12] Mike Abrams, on the other hand, finishes it for you and claims it would have had a happy ending. This strikes me on the whole as unlikely. It shows how cheerful Mike Abrams is. For him, everything has a happy ending. My question would be "Could he have ever finished it?" However, for better or worse what we have is a text that is not finished. I think it is a little too easy to assume that it would have had an unequivocal ending, happy or unhappy. That is for me somehow related to its structure. That would be a different way of talking about the structure of déjà vu, or the structure of repetition, or of the uncanny. This would be, to invoke a Derridean word, a structure of invagination. That word names an organ that is put inside another organ. It's a medical term. Derrida uses it in the "Law of Genre" to talk about Blanchot.[13] It would also work to interpret *Atonement*, which also has that structure of invagination. You're reading something that is inside but also at the same time outside. Things in *Triumph of Life* have happened more than once, always as déjà vu, so which is the original and which is the copy? There's a kind of oscillation. Derrida's example of invagination is a glove. You take a glove and you put the finger of the glove inside so the outside of the glove has now become the inside and the inside has become the outside in a disquieting oscillation. Blanchot's *La Folie du Jour* (*The Madness of the Day*) is an example. That's the example that Derrida uses. He uses the term rather casually, but I find it very valuable as a way of dealing with such textual structures.

In the case of *Atonement*, you read something that you think is controlled by a telepathic male narrator. It must be McEwan imagining himself telling a story. So you read it all the way through that way and then come to the last part, which is in first-person present tense by the aging Briony.[14] At that point, you discover that what you have been reading is not the primary text. It's a text inside the frame narrative written by Briony, so it's invaginated. It's both inside and outside at the same time. And it is helpful as a notion that probably would help us think about the *Triumph of Life*. That structural feature would have something to do with its unfinishable quality. It is a feature of invagination that it sets up an endless oscillation as Derrida says. I could go on and on and on and you could go on and on and on saying it first this way and then that way and then this way again and that way. It's uncomfortable making, as the *Triumph of Life* is. It's not just that it's gloomy. It's the way that the language is put together that's unsettling, uncanny, as Graham says.

ALLEN: *Have you any words on the legacy of the work of Barbara Johnson, who passed away a few years ago?*

MILLER: I haven't been able to bring myself to read Barbara Johnson's latest work, to my shame. I read little bits of it when it came out. I think she's terrific. It's a great sadness that she died so young. She died of central nervous system lymphoma. What was so good about her? Well for one thing she was a terrific translator. The translation of Derrida's *Dissemination*. Derrida was very lucky in his translations: Kamuf is a superb translator; Alan Bass is a superb translator. But maybe Barbara Johnson is the best of all. Her command of both French and English is such that she can think of puns in English that correspond to untranslatable puns in French. There is no way you can translate the play on words in Derrida's French, but Johnson is clever enough to think of something that carries the pun over with a quite different play on words. I remember meeting her at the end of this [the translation of *Dissemination*[15]]—she did it in one summer—in New Haven, meeting her outside the college where my office was. She said, "I've worked all summer on this translation, and it was horribly difficult work. It took a whole summer." She was the first person—at a conference somewhere in Tennessee I think, where we both were and she gave a paper—to make me reflect a little bit about the possible or perhaps inevitable sexism built into the terminology of deconstruction and of the Yale School. She had firsthand experience of Yale, and she made me worry about that issue. It was a polite paper but a very intransigent one. She accused all those men (we were all men in the "Yale Mafia") of being sexist. Her brand of deconstruction strikes me as having a salutary feminist slant to it. I was talking about not writing memoirs, but if I were to do so, I'd have some stories about Barbara Johnson. We both went to Oberlin College. Oberlin puts a mark on you. It makes you earnest, moral, responsible. But also politically and socially progressive. Both Barbara and I were products of Oberlin. It was originally a Congregationalist-affiliated school. Oberlin has a Protestant earnestness that remains in some church schools even when they have become quite secular. We all still had to go to "chapel" once a week, but the talks there were not religious, no hymn singing. Oberlin was the first coeducational undergraduate college in the United States. It was a station on the Underground Railway, used during the Civil War to help slaves escape to Canada. Several of the Chicago Seven in the anti–Vietnam War protest demonstrations at a Chicago Democratic National Convention in 1968 were from Oberlin.

I was sitting innocently in my office one day at Yale and there came a knock at the door. This tall, awkward young woman came in and said, "You are to examine me in Wallace Stevens," and I said, "What?!" It turns out the French department at that time at Yale had the requirement that graduate students had to pass an examination in something outside of French. So she had decided—I had never taught her or met her up to that point—that she wanted to do Wallace Stevens. I said "okay," and we agreed that she would read the poems. She came in a couple of months later, and what happened was sort of spooky, not the usual exam situation—there was no witness for this, it was entirely solitary, for one thing. We had a little chat about Wallace Stevens, and I said "You pass; I pass you." Another performative! I declare that you pass. And much later on, as you know, she left Yale for Harvard—after she had made tenure at Yale, which was unusual for an assistant professor in those days. She did not leave for Harvard because she didn't have a permanent job at Yale. She was appreciated there. And when she went, I remember Paul de Man saying, "That is very bad news for Yale." He saw Barbara Johnson as the future of the Yale French department. We taught together in the lit major. She was a brilliant teacher in that famous Yale undergraduate program. When she got to Harvard, she shifted, with Marj Garber's help, to the English department from the French department. The reason she gave is kind of ironic. She said, "I got tired teaching Harvard undergraduates how to say 'please pass me the butter' ['passez-moi la buerre, s'il vous plaît']" so they could know what to say when they went to Paris in the summer. She thought the English department would be a happier place for her, a place where she could teach more usefully. That move always seemed to me somewhat ironic, because as far as I know, the only institutional authorization whatsoever that she had to be a professor of English at Harvard was that examination I gave her on Wallace Stevens. It was a great sadness to me when she died so young. She was brilliant, really gifted.

O'ROURKE: *In their movie* Derrida, *Kofman and Dick ask him, "If you had a choice what philosopher would you like to have been your mother?" He responds by saying this would be impossible because the figure of the philosopher is always a "masculine figure" for him.*[16] *I want to put the same question to you slightly reframed: firstly, if it were possible for you, what philosopher would you like to have been your mother? And, since we know so much about your relationship with your father, can you tell us a little about your mother and whether she in any way influenced the shape of your thinking?*

MILLER: I see what Derrida meant. It's true, the figure of the philosopher is masculine. When I read this question, I asked myself what in the world would I say? Which philosopher would I choose to be my mother? And I had two answers. It's a question of the mother–son relation. For me, it wouldn't be Derrida or de Man or Kant or Hegel, but Nietzsche or Austin. I think I would have liked to have had J.L. Austin, the author of *How to Do Things With Words*, as my mother because I never met him.[17] I don't think of him as particularly motherly, but nevertheless it's a nice fantasy. He was a very quirky and very funny man who died young, like Barbara Johnson. But his personal life is a mystery, to me at least. If you just read the books (*How to Do Things With Words*, plus a book of collected essays, there isn't very much), you don't find out much about his personal life. All I know is that he was a professor of moral philosophy at Oxford. That boggles the mind. The man who invented that subversive thing, the speech act, and who was so funny and witty, being in charge of "moral philosophy"! As you know, Austin gave *How to Do Things With Words* as lectures at Harvard for an annual lecture series in the philosophy department. There was a confluence, a convergence not of the twain, as in Hardy's poem about the Titanic and the iceberg, but of three or four people, a convergence that never really happened. The year that Austin's lectures were given was a year or two after Derrida was at Harvard for a year. (I'm thinking of the way in which speech act theory is so important for me and for Derrida and de Man). I graduated from Harvard in 1952, two or three years before Austin came. He gave these lectures in 1953 or 1954 or something. Paul de Man was a junior fellow at Harvard at the same time, but I think this was the year that he decided to go to Ireland. He was here [Dublin] for a year studying Yeats because Yeats was part of his dissertation. So he just missed him. Derrida was there on the exchange with the École Normale, but I think not in the same year as Austin's lectures. John Hollander was also a junior fellow at the same time. One of the people who did hear the lectures on *How to Do Things With Words* and whose professional life was transformed by it was Stanley Cavell. Cavell talks eloquently about having heard these lectures and thinking they were wonderful. What I remember de Man saying is that Austin was known as this crazy Englishman who was giving a set of lectures that nobody understood, just as Derrida was known as a crazy Frenchman who had come all the way to Harvard to study phenomenology. Harvard is not exactly the place you would think to do that. In fact, he [Derrida] was living with his wife-to-be. They were married in Cambridge. They were living surreptitiously in a graduate dorm. He had to sneak Marguerite into his apartment at night.

I think of Austin's speech act theory as being incredibly problematic, complicated, and contradictory. Austin had a brilliant gift for choosing examples that go against what he is trying to say. It is hard to tell whether that is deliberate or not. For example, the theory of speech acts, as you know, posits that an ideal speech act uses a first-person pronoun with a verb in the present tense: "I promise," "I confess," "I warn," etc. One of his examples is this: you are standing in a field and there's this enormous bull about to charge. You don't say "may I respectfully warn you that there is an enormous bull in the field about to charge." There isn't time for that. You just say "BULL!" No first-person pronoun, no present-tense verb, but it is a felicitous performative. Two other examples, one of which recurs in one of his philosophical essays: there's a great British war ship and someone goes down with a bottle of champagne, cracks it on the prow, and says "I christen thee the Joseph Stalin." This would have been during the cold war. Austin asks, "What would you say about that?" Two things, he says first that it's a damn shame and secondly that the ship is not really christened the Joseph Stalin. Because it's the wrong person, without authority, at the wrong time and so on. But then you say to yourself, "Gee, I don't know, can you really be sure that this was not going to be effective, a 'felicitous' speech act?" What constitutes a felicitous christening? It's not so easy to decide about that. The other example is even more problematic. He says that for a felicitous performative, I must not be acting on the stage, or writing a poem (as he says elsewhere), or making a joke. These would be make-believe speech acts. The example is of a marriage performed on the stage. The couple of actors are surely not really married. That seems sensible; otherwise the actor and actress in the play would be married in the make-believe ceremony. But when you begin to think about it, you realize that a wedding ceremony is also a kind of play. It is a text that is performed over and over, an example of iterability. It is a performance. Therefore you are in a way an actor in a play even at your own wedding. Nobody doubts that they aren't exactly the same thing, but nevertheless the similarity leads you to begin to think about it. For anybody that's been married—and I have been married for over sixty years—there are still moments where you ask yourself, "When the minister said 'I pronounce you man and wife' were we really married? Maybe we've been living in sin for all these years." "How do we know the minister was authorized to perform a marriage?"

Another of Austin's examples is the purser on a boat. The captain can marry people, but nobody else on a ship can do so. So if you were married by the purser it wouldn't be a valid marriage. This leads you to think about what constitutes a valid marriage. There have to be witnesses and so on.

The apparently straightforward example now begins to appear problematic and leads you to think about marriages in general. I don't know how it is here in Dublin, but in the States—I know about the customs of Protestant weddings—there is a practice wedding beforehand. The minister instructs the couple, "And then I say 'now you say I do' and you say 'I do' and then I say 'I now pronounce you man and wife.'" There's a superstition about this against the bride playing her own role in the practice wedding. The maid of honor plays the bride's role. Why are they then not married at the practice wedding? The minister has said the right words. He has the power to do this. The couple have given the right responses. The obvious question is "Why is the bridegroom not married to the maid of honor?"

Austin is wonderful. He never authorized the publication of his lectures, claiming they were provisional and needed more work. The very end of *How to Do Things With Words* recalls Socrates in one of the Platonic dialogues, the *Protagoras*. Austin ends his lectures by saying it is clear that we haven't really straightened this out. We need to go back and work on it some more. This is like Socrates saying to Protagoras, "We really don't yet know what virtue is; we need to go back and start over again. Are you ready?" And Protagoras says, "No Socrates, I suggest that we come back to this at some future time." And that's the end of the dialogue. And *How to Do Things With Words* ends somewhat in the same way. It's high praise to say that the rhetoric of Austin's book overall is structured somewhat like this Platonic dialogue, with Austin playing all the roles, and with a similar conclusion in uncertainty.

I was going to explain why I wish I had had Nietzsche as my mother, my mother philosopher, but there isn't time to explore this. We need to come back to it at some future time. You can see why I also have a filial relation to Austin. About my mother: Whenever I am asked about my relation to my mother, I think of that Freudian joke: "Oedipus schmoedipus, so long as you love your mother!" My father was a very competitive person, a college and then university president. We used to play tennis together until I was about 13. I then beat him one time. He never played with me again. He was a very competitive player of—I'm not so competitive at that—the card game "bridge." He used to play with my brother and me and my mother. He always won. My mother would be my partner usually, since my brother was younger. That was supposed to give my mother some slight advantage, but she was as expert a player as my father. My father always won because he had the courage to bid competitively and daringly, whereas my mother and I would look at our cards and say "three spades." He would bid on the same hand a grand slam. He made good on those extravagant bids just often enough to end up with the top score.

My mother was a farm girl as my father was a farm boy. When my father was courting her she was still at home on the family farm in Virginia. She was the oldest of a farm family of five children. She had beautiful chestnut-colored hair. Pictures of her as a young woman are really striking. I can see why my father fell in love with her. He was a marathon runner. He would come to court Nell (Critzer) at her home, but he would also be practicing for his next marathon run at the University of Richmond in Virginia. He was known as Nell's crazy boyfriend who runs the roads around rural Virginia in his underwear. You can see that I have trouble talking about my relation to my mother rather than my relation to my father. I think it was because she had very high hopes for me as they both did, but mother was more inclined to think that she knew how these hopes should be fulfilled: I should become a doctor, or I should write romances rather than getting a Ph.D. in English. I had somehow to resist her power much more than my brother did (I have a brother three years younger). I didn't have the feeling that his life had been planned for him by her. When I used to go off to Oberlin by train I would get on the train, and I would immediately light a cigarette. At the age of 16 smoking was an act of defiance, of filial defiance, because I knew my mother—not my father, my mother—would greatly disapprove of this. Going off to college was a form of freedom. It is very hard thinking back on it to see how my mother's force of personality was experienced by me as a threat. Because it was entirely loving, benign, and so on. My father died at the age of 53 of a rheumatic heart, which now would be operable, including at the hospital at Gainesville, Florida, part of which is named for him. This is because the last thing he did as president of the University of Florida before his final illness was to get money appropriated to establish a medical school there. He had to persuade the Florida legislature to do that. My mother lived for another 30 years working in that hospital as a patient counsellor. If somebody was a patient there who was going to be in hospital for a while for a serious operation, mother would find the family a place to stay, talk to them, and so on. She did that for a long, long time for a not very big salary. She lived in a small apartment in Gainesville. She died in 1983 in the hospital named for her long-dead husband. My brother and I when we knew that she wasn't going to live much longer would go down on alternate weekends to visit her. I used to feel that it was really weird to be walking into a hospital called the J. Hillis Miller Health Centre, passing the portrait of my father, which hung in the hallway, and then going up to see my mother on her deathbed. I've always thought that I have a great opportunity since I have the same name as my father. If I'm ever ill I will present myself at the J. Hillis Miller Health Centre and say, "I am J. Hillis Miller! Take care of me!"

As you can see, it's difficult for me to reflect clearly about my relation to my mother, so it was a sharp question and one I've never been asked before. Bottom line: Oedipus Schmoedipus.

Notes

1 Fred Kaplan, *Henry James: The Imagination of a Genius, A Biography* (Baltimore: Johns Hopkins University Press, 2009).

2 "Tears Idle Tears" is a poem by Alfred, Lord Tennyson, which Miller has written about—"Tennyson's Tears" in *Topographies* (Stanford: Stanford University Press, 1995)—and also discusses in the film *The First Sail*. Dunne and O'Rourke's presentation "Miller's Idle Tears" (you can read it at https://www.academia.edu/2007623/Millers_Idle_Tears) and Nicholas Royle's talk "Up" both meditated on this poem and Miller's readings of it.

3 Just before the event in Dublin, Miller participated in another event at Lancaster University entitled "J. Hillis Miller: The Theory to Come—An International Symposium." At the airport in Manchester, security asked Hillis where he was coming from. He replied, "a conference." "What was the conference about?" the guard asked. Hillis responded "It was about me." The next question was "What are you going to Dublin for?" "A conference" was the same response. Again they asked, "What is the conference about?" Hillis replied, "At the risk of sounding immodest, it is also about me."

4 J. Hillis Miller, *The Medium Is the Maker: Browning, Freud, Derrida and the New Telepathic Ecotechnologies* (Brighton: Sussex Academic Press, 2009).

5 Miller is referring to Martin McQuillan's paper "Celluloid Philosophy," which interrogated the question of what is and is not a deconstructive film.

6 See William Blake: *The Complete Poetry and Prose*, ed. David Erdman with a commentary by Harold Bloom, newly revised edition (New York: Anchor Books, 1988).

7 See, for instance, J. Hillis Miller's "Sovereignty Death Literature Unconditionality Democracy University," in *Deconstructing Derrida: Tasks for the New Humanities*, ed. Peter Pericles Trifonas and Michael A. Peters (New York: Palgrave, 2005).

8 J. Hillis Miller, *Reading for Our Time* (Edinburgh: Edinburgh University Press, 2012).

9 Miller had not yet written this essay at the time Gilbert was introducing him in the film. It is the "Preposterous Preface" to *Derrida and Queer Theory*, ed. Michael O'Rourke.

10 Benoît Peeters, *Derrida: A Biography* (Cambridge: Polity Press, 2012).

11 Miller is referring to the paper presented by Graham Allen, "*The Triumph of Life* and the Reversibility of Art."

12 Miller is referring here to Earl Wasserman.

[13] Jacques Derrida, "The Law of Genre," trans. Avital Ronell, *Critical Inquiry* 7.1 (1980): 55–81.

[14] Ian McEwan, *Atonement* (New York: Anchor: 2003).

[15] Jacques Derrida, *Dissemination*, trans. Barbara Johnson (Chicago: University of Chicago Press, 1983).

[16] Kirby Dick and Amy Ziering Kofman (Dir.) (2002), *Derrida* (Jane Doe Films, 2002). See also Dick and Kofman, Derrida: *Screenplay and Essays on the Film* (Manchester: Manchester University Press, 2005).

[17] J.L. Austin, *How to Do Things With Words* (Cambridge, MA: Harvard University Press, 1975).

10

Isn't It a Beautiful Day?

Interview with Bradley J. Fest

BRADLEY J. FEST: *Much has already been made of your "turn" from phenomenological criticism toward deconstruction in the late 1960s and early 1970s. I have been quite interested, however, to note how this turn took place in certain ways around the poetry of William Carlos Williams. In 1966, Williams largely functioned as the hero of your third book,* Poets of Reality, *a book I find to be quite powerful still. The book of critical essays you edited concerning him the same year remains a remarkable volume, not least for being the first place that made readily available the fascinating prose sections of* Spring and All *(1923). (I have found the passages in* Spring and All *where Williams has the imagination to annihilate all human life to be continually striking, particularly considering the various ways disaster has been represented since Williams was writing.) By 1970, however, you were writing about Williams quite differently in "Williams's* Spring and All *and the Progress of Poetry." You use that essay to address broader concerns about "progress" and "decline" in the humanities. The end of that essay also shows you citing the work of, among others, Jacques Derrida, Michel Foucault, and Gilles Deleuze. You returned to this essay and your earlier introduction to the book of essays on Williams with significant revisions quite a few years later in* The Linguistic Moment *(1985) and then returned to Williams again to begin your 1986 presidential address to the Modern Language Association.*[1]

Over this twenty-year period, what role do you think Williams played in your thinking? Has he continued to be a presence in your thought?

J. HILLIS MILLER: Well, yes. It's true that he was important at the moment when I started writing about him in *Poets of Reality*, but I would like to stress two features of that. One of them answers two questions: why did I write about Williams? Why did I include him in that book? Because I immensely admired his poetry, not particularly the prose. I found Williams's poetry extraordinarily beautiful, both rhythmically and in all kinds of other ways, thematically and so on. I thought "By the Road to the Contagious Hospital" (1923) was a terrific poem. I delighted, and still delight, in Williams's poetry of small insignificant things. There are lots and lots of such poems that are superb, right on down to the end. "Asphodel, That Greeny Flower" (1955) is a wonderful poem. But Williams was a challenge to the methodology of reading that at that point I thought I was using. He just doesn't give much of a handle to so-called phenomenological criticism, or criticism of consciousness. I found that very interesting. Here was a poet that I immensely admired who didn't give me a handle to talk about the *cogito*. What's the *cogito* of William Carlos Williams? And he didn't seem to allow much for dialectical procedures such as Poulet uses in his essays, or for Pouletian abstractions about consciousness. So I was really trying to figure out how to say something sensible about Williams when I started working on him and reading him. In those days, I was very much a Pouletian, a critic reading everything Williams had written in the attempt to make a total coherent interpretation of his work. Now I would feel less compelled to do that. This, as you know, in Williams's case means a lot of prose: *The Autobiography* (1951), the *Selected Letters* (1957), and so on. So, yes. Williams has played a special role in my development, but it's also true that I've returned to him partly because I was more than once asked to write something new about him. There were not all that many people who had taken Williams seriously enough to write in detail about him. So when somebody wanted to do a book or a journal issue about Williams, they would sometimes turn to me. But I also continued to find him worth thinking about and writing about.

In some ways, Wallace Stevens has been more important for me over the years than Williams. Stevens is an earlier interest, going back to graduate school. And he's a different kind of challenge. What do you do with a poet who is conspicuously philosophical, who knew continental philosophy? I don't see Williams sitting down in the evening to read Edmund Husserl or Martin Heidegger.

The theme that is so important for you, of the annihilation of all human life, in my opinion has a specific origin: Rimbaud. I am sure Williams had read Rimbaud, whose work would have been available at that time, either in translation or in the original. Williams of course read French. And as you know, he was Hispanic, or partly Hispanic. So he's a minority poet. He was more aware of that than many of his readers have been. After all his middle name was Carlos. *Kora in Hell* (1920) and the prose in *Spring and All* I think are directly indebted to Rimbaud's *A Season in Hell* (1873) and to Rimbaud's poetry, where that theme appears, the theme of a total annihilation, followed by an instantaneous recreation, everything exactly as it was...This is also a theme in Mallarmé in a famous pronouncement that I paraphrase from memory and truncate: "I say: a flower! And musically there arises the absence of all bouquets."[2] The word *flower* annihilates flowers and replaces them with another existence, a poetic existence. So Williams's notion of annihilation has a history. It's pretty powerfully repeated in Williams in a way that I've always found slightly paradoxical because he was a very nice man, which I would not say about Wallace Stevens or about Rimbaud either. Stevens was apparently cordially disliked by all his colleagues in the insurance company where he was a vice president, the Hartford Accident and Indemnity Company. Apparently, as a businessman he was not a likable person. But Williams comes through to me as a likable person.

By the way, I heard both of these people read their poems when I was a graduate student at Harvard. This experience confirmed my feelings about Williams and also about Stevens. At Stevens's reading, he was very austere. He was "tall and of a port in air,"[3] like his jar in Tennessee in "Anecdote of the Jar" (1923). He stood up there as if alone. He read poems like the late poem "Large Red Man Reading" (1950) and the wonderful poem "Credences of Summer" (1947): "Now is midsummer come and all fools slaughtered."[4] It was a pretty big room, and I happened to be near the front. As time went on, he began to read more and more softly, you might say inwardly, for himself. I could hear him, but the people in the back of the room couldn't hear him any longer and started getting up and leaving. He paid no attention whatsoever. He went right on as if the audience was not there. And in a way it was a kind of defiant thing to do. He could have raised his voice.

The reading of Williams I remember as being a joyful occasion. There was a series of poetry readings at Harvard with people like Robert Lowell, E. E. Cummings, and other poets who were famous at the time, and the Williams reading was one of them. The poem that I especially remember hearing him read, which he read with great gusto, was "The Sea Elephant" (1930). I remember the wonderful way he read the B-L-O-U-A-U-G-H in the poem, and the wonderful way in which he said that. This is the sound of the sea-elephant, this "Blouaugh!"[5] It was great. And then I remember after the reading happening to be out on one of the streets adjacent to the

Harvard Yard and seeing this great poet getting into a very shabby car, all alone, nobody there with him. I have no idea whether they were going to give him a meal or not, but it looked to me like he was getting in his car to drive back to Rutherford, New Jersey. There was a sort of poignant isolation in this. Whereas Stevens was a Harvard man and felt at home there, Williams was in a strange place.

So yeah, Williams, he's a presence in my thought, as has been Thomas Hardy. Williams is somebody that I come back to repeatedly and from different angles. He came to my mind when I was asked by the *Dædalus* people—the journal of the American Academy of Arts and Sciences—to participate in a conference at Bellagio in Italy that was followed by a publication in *Dædalus* on the question of progress in the humanities. They didn't impose Williams on me; I chose to go back to Williams. This is evidence that yes, he has been important to me. He is still important. So that's my answer to that. Do you have any questions about him I haven't answered? I think often of that image of this somewhat shabby, tall, angular man getting into this quite old, worn-out car to drive all the way back from Cambridge, Massachusetts, to Rutherford, New Jersey, which is a pretty good distance, in the late afternoon...I may have this all wrong. He may have been going back to get his coat and tie to go out to dinner.

FEST: *I appreciate in your answer, as so often in your work, you emphasize the text, that it was something specific about Williams, about* Spring and All, *about* Kora in Hell. *In your MLA address, you talk about* In the American Grain *(1925), that it was about the specific moments in the text rather than some larger project that you were trying to impose upon the text.*

MILLER: Everybody knew the red wheelbarrow poem,[6] and I greatly admired it. Since my *métier* is teaching and writing about works of literature, I asked myself, "Why would I teach this?" What would I expect from the class? How could it go beyond simply reading the poem and saying, "Isn't that beautiful?" That's about five minutes. What do I do with the other forty-five minutes of the fifty-minute hour? Those were real questions for me.

I do have a story about *Spring and All.* The stories I am telling, by the way, are meant to be emblematic or parabolic, a way of saying much in little, though perhaps enigmatically. When I started working on Williams, the prose in *Spring and All* had never been republished. It didn't exist for most readers. I had at Hopkins, and still have as a friend, a professor named Richard Macksey. Dick Macksey is one of the great book buyers and collectors in the world. When he needed some money for something, he just sold his row of Yeats first editions to make a hundred thousand dollars or so. He bought a big house in Baltimore, complete with a ping pong table. In two weeks, the ping pong table was covered with books. He has a great collection of little magazines up on the third floor of this house. He had eventually to build an addition for his books, which has a projector and some other equipment. So whenever a book was not in the Hopkins library, I would go to Macksey and see if he had it.

Here is my story about Macksey and books. I used to read the French phenomenological critic Jean-Pierre Richard. One of his later books is a big book on Mallarmé, after the ones on French fiction and then poetry that were so important for me. I ordered the Mallarmé book from a French bookseller. It came one day and was on my desk, just opened. Macksey happened to come in my office. "Oh," he said, "you have the Richard book on Mallarmé?" I said, "Yeah, I'm not going to have time to read it over the weekend; would you like to borrow it?" So away he went with the book. He'd been so generous with me, in a way I'll tell you about in a minute, that I didn't think it would be polite or courteous later on to say, "Dick, by the way, where's my copy of Richard's *Mallarmé*?" Some months went by, and I was in his house—living room full of books, there were bookshelves everywhere, in this big Roland Park house in Baltimore—and there on a shelf was my book. So I took it down. There were a lot of people there, so Macksey wasn't watching me. I opened it up, and it said "Richard A. Macksey" and a date, in his handwriting. He had apparently forgotten it was not a book he had ordered for himself. I just put it back on the shelf and ordered myself another copy.

Here's an example of his generosity. He owned the first edition—Dijon, 1923—of *Spring and All* at a time when none of the prose was available in any other way. And I at some point said, "Dick, you don't happen to have the first edition of *Spring and All?*" He said, "I've got that." It's a very valuable book. It has got a little blue cover. And it has the poems interspersed with the prose. It's important, by the way, always to remember that the prose and the poetry in the original book are interspersed. You're reading the prose, and then suddenly there's one of these great poems, which were later abstracted and put in *The Collected Early Poetry* (1951), but not in the way they were originally published, mixed with the prose. Williams said, "I had a lot of fun doing it; it had no circulation."[7] How could it? Dijon? I remember I learned once from James Loughlin when I was quoting from the complete version in the New Directions volume *Imaginations* that there's no copyright; he couldn't copyright it, I guess maybe because he was not a French citizen. So if you happen to have now the New Directions book that has the prose, you don't have to get permission to cite it, though it would still be a courtesy to do so. Williams didn't own a copyright.

So Macksey loaned me this precious little paperbound book. Our youngest daughter, Sarah, was at that point about four years old, just learning to walk, just at that stage where you can reach up on a bookshelf and pull yourself up. I made the mistake of putting this book on a lower shelf in my study in our house in Baltimore. I came in and there was Sally sitting on the floor with the book. She had torn the cover. So I went to Macksey and said, "Dick, I'm very sorry to report that your copy of *Spring and All* is not so pristinely beautiful any longer." And he said, "It doesn't matter." He was very nice about that. That was my way of being able to read the prose with the poems. *Kora in Hell* was available, the whole thing. But the prose in *Spring and All* is, I think, a wonderful clue to what Williams thought he was doing, at least at that stage. So that's another parabolic anecdote. It's emblematic both of Richard Macksey's extraordinary generosity and of the fortuitous way scholarship gets done, at least mine, not to speak of the role of our three children in my life. Sally was already proleptically a book-reading intellectual at four, as she has certainly become for real, as have our other two older children.

FEST: *It has been highly educational to read the various conversations and debates surrounding deconstruction that stemmed from review essays you wrote during the early and mid-1970s. One of these reviews addressed Joseph N. Riddel's deconstructive reading of Williams, to which Riddel wrote a response.[8] Your review essays of M. H. Abrams's* Natural Supernaturalism *(1971) and Edward Said's* Beginnings *(1975) also occasioned considerable further discussion. Your exchange with Abrams and Wayne C. Booth has been particularly enlightening for me to read, and it appears to have continued far past "The Critic as Host" (1977). Abrams, who will turn 101 this month, continued to comment upon deconstruction during the 1980s. And a young Donald E. Pease largely used this exchange to write a commentary on your work in 1983, which he has since significantly reconsidered.[9] How important do you think the conversation with Abrams was? Do you feel like that conversation continues to resonate to this day?*

MILLER: There would be two things to say about that. One, concerning my quarrel with Joe Riddel, who was a friend of mine. I offended him by my criticism. He said to me in a letter in response, "Well, it's clear that I should go spend all my time playing golf." Well, this was somebody that I considered to be a friend of mine. That he was hurt was painful to me. My quarrel with him was that he wasn't deconstructive enough, that there was too much undigested Heidegger taken without interrogation. I was really saying, "Joe, you're not really reading. What you're saying—the theoretical, philosophical stuff doesn't quite fit the text that you're talking about." And that offended him. I think I was right, but I think probably humanly I was wrong because he was a sensitive person. He taught in California, and I saw him occasionally out there after I moved to Irvine. I was deeply saddened by his early death.

Abrams, on the other hand, is important enough, big enough, and generous enough to take care of himself. I've only written about three or four negative reviews in my life. There's one of Paul Ricoeur, the big book on narrative.[10] I've always been surprised by the responses.

FEST: Time and Narrative *(1983–1985), the three-volume one?*

MILLER: Yeah, the big three-volume one. I read it in French, then in English. And now I've discovered, to my amazement, that people I criticize feel hurt. I don't quite understand it, because other people do this and the recipients take it for granted. I think it's because I'm assumed to be "Mr. Nice Guy." It happened to me when I was hired at Yale. It took them quite a while to figure out that I'm not really, on the intellectual side, all that much of a nice guy. That really distressed them because they discovered that they had misunderstood me as a person. They didn't like this. When I decided to move from Hopkins to Yale, I grew a beard here in Maine. So I showed up at Yale in the fall with a beard. The beard was supposed to signify my incapacity for ever being an administrator of any kind. Two things happened. One, all my colleagues, three or four of them at least—Geoffrey Hartman, Bart Giamatti, and such—grew beards themselves. To me, that seemed my effect on these people. And within two years, I was chair of the English department. So it didn't work in any kind of way, either to distinguish me from my colleagues or to get me out of administrative work.

In the case of the review of Abrams's *Natural Supernaturalism*, he too was offended. I wrote this review in the most honest kind of way, trying to express my disagreement, not so much with the historical assumptions of his book as with the readings that he had made of romantic philosophers: Kant, Hegel, the sort of basic presuppositions he makes. And that really bothered him. There was an MLA encounter where he sort of turned away and refused to talk to me. We made peace later on, but I learned a lesson. Which is if you're considered to be Mr. Nice Guy, don't write negative reviews, just write reviews that say how wonderful the book is. *Natural Supernaturalism* really *is* a wonderful book, but I took issue with some of its premises.

There's quite a lot at stake in the issues between me and Abrams, not only in ways of reading Kant, Hegel, Wordsworth, the German romantics, and the whole intellectual sequence that Abrams is trying to recover. Abrams was right to be upset, and he has his own sharp polemical side. "The Critic as Host" was a response on my part to something he said that struck me as pretty sharp. I paraphrase and extrapolate: "Deconstructive reading is parasitical on the ordinary reading, the commonsensical reading, the reading everybody would make, the correct reading, the reading that I, Meyer Abrams, would make."[11] That's just the issue. It's possible that the commonsense, received reading is wrong. Abrams was unwilling to entertain the possibility that this might be the case. I found his reaction surprising. I guess it makes sense, since I put his whole enterprise in question.

My presentation of "The Critic as Host" was an occasion, a panel in which I appeared with these people on the stage at the MLA. I presented a paper and encountered Wayne Booth again there—there would be a lot to say about my relationship to Wayne Booth over the years. Again, that was less of a quarrel, just disagreements between us, and a very touching effort on Wayne Booth's part to convert me to the commonsense, Wayne Boothian way of reading. (After all, he wasn't a Mormon for nothing.) I remember at one point Wayne Booth saying to me, "You're not like those other people," meaning Derrida, de Man, Hartman, and Bloom. He meant that I was traveling in bad company, that the real me would be a very different sort of person. But that was rather different from my relation to Abrams, which became cordial again later on. I sent a message to him on his hundredth birthday and would have gone to Cornell if I could have done so—was invited to go to Cornell. Who could be unhappy that such a learned and nice man has lived so long and remained active and mentally vigorous? But Mike Abrams is a little too cheerful for me.

And again, I have a story. These are parables or allegories. They have a point. This is Mike Abrams in essence for me: when Harold Bloom was visiting Cornell. Harold was an undergraduate at Cornell and, so I gather, actually was in undergraduate courses taught by Mike Abrams. Imagine, even if you're Mike Abrams, having Harold Bloom in your freshman/sophomore course! (Bloom apparently corrected Abrams now and then: "Professor that was 1801, not 1802.") At any rate, it's a typical day in Ithaca in the winter. Bloom is there as a visitor for a year. This is after Bloom is well-established as a professor at Yale. It's snowing. This is in the sixties, the late sixties. The African-American students have occupied the administration building. For Bloom, this was the end of the world. He's very conservative politically, in spite of always voting for Democratic candidates. He was full of anxiety about the future, not only of Cornell but also of everything else. So they meet. Bloom meets Abrams. Snow. Catastrophe on the campus. Riots and so on. Abrams turns to Bloom and says, "Harold, isn't it a beautiful day?" That's Abrams. That's Abrams in a nutshell, and I immensely admire that.

Pease is a little different. We've made peace long since. I've lectured at Dartmouth at his invitation, and he was, as you know, invited to participate in that conference about my work and did a very good paper on it. He had the feeling, mistakenly, that I had been brooding over his early essay about me, which I hadn't. It's okay. It's a free country. But he did change, as you said, and I think what's at stake there is rather different. Pease is a very distinguished Americanist. He is one of the founders of the new kind of American studies that's going on now, somebody that has done wonderfully good work over the years in changing American studies from a relatively conservative "America is best" kind of attitude to the sort of thing it is now. Pease has been really important in doing that. So my relation to Pease is really quite different from my relation to Booth or Abrams. I have had nothing but admiration for Pease and his work all along. I can also see why he would have found what he understood as deconstruction to be troubling the agenda that he had.

I've been surprised that "The Critic as Host" took hold the way it did, genuinely surprised. Because I didn't think of it when I wrote it as a kind of position piece that would be anthologized and read all over the world. Often that's what people have read of my work and really little else. That's fine with me, but it was a genuine surprise. It shows the domination of theoretical discourse over readings during the last twenty or thirty years. If somebody asked me, "Which of your essays do you think everybody ought to read?" my answer would likely be some essay that was actually a reading of a work of literature. The fact that has not happened—what everybody reads by me is a polemical, theoretical piece that belongs to a specific moment in American academic history—has surprised me, but I've learned something from that. I'm happy to have people read "The Critic as Host." I don't disown it, but it does need to be put back in context, which was a very overdetermined moment.

FEST: *It's interesting because reading through even just a small body of your work, "The Critic as Host" stands out as unlike a lot of the rest of your writing. Most of your work reads specific works of literature, specific texts. I appreciate "The Critic as Host," but I've been much more captivated by your other work, to be honest.*

MILLER: Good. And remember, "The Critic as Host" is not about a particular literary text, but it *is* about the word *parasite*; it's about the word *host*—a multiplicity—it's really about language. And it does have a literary background, which is Wallace Stevens. I think—I haven't read this essay for a long time—I think I refer to Stevens, to the last set of poems by Stevens. My essay is literary through and through, or linguistic through and through. What I did was to pick up on that word *parasite* and worry the word *parasite*, and that's the basis. But I think also it may be partly why the essay is read. It's sort of interesting to know that the word *host* has these multiple meanings and that the word *parasite* also does. I got the parasite stuff from Derrida, as I've got so much, because there's a text that I had read prior to my essay where he talks about the word *parasite*.[12] And so I looked it up in my *American Heritage Dictionary* and the *OED*. It means somebody who, at the table, is put beside the bread, *para sitos* (παράσιτος), down the table, because he's a hanger-on in the court. It has a very specific source, an interesting etymology. A parasite is somebody who is fed when he doesn't really deserve to be fed, and I read all that into what Abrams was saying about me and about deconstruction as being parasitical. There's a great poem by Thomas Hardy about the parasitical ivy that kills the great oak tree.[13] It may have been in Abrams's mind.

FEST: *I ask about Abrams not only because of the historical importance of the exchange between the two of you but also to address your take on romanticism. In the collection on Williams, you included brief essays by Yvor Winters and Wallace Stevens that call Williams "romantic" fairly bluntly. Winters wrote that Williams "is an uncompromising romantic."[14] Stevens said that "there are so many things to say about him. The first is that he is a romantic poet."[15] You were clear then, and became clearer in the subsequent things you wrote, that you did not feel Williams was romantic at all (with the exception of his very earliest poetry). This was largely before the appearance of* Natural Supernaturalism. *Was Williams an important foil to Abrams for you? Did your thinking about the lack of romanticism in Williams resonate with your criticism of Abrams at the time?*

MILLER: I don't remember that it did, but it may well have, there may well have been a connection. What I would say now would be slightly different about Williams and romanticism. On the one hand, both Winters and Stevens wanted to put Williams down. They were competitive, particularly Winters.

FEST: *Yeah, that little essay is very strange.*

MILLER: I actually had a chance to speak to Winters about that essay. I had to get his permission to republish it in the collection I made. He must have been pretty much in his old age. He came to Hopkins to give a talk. I had to drive him to the faculty club or something, so we had a slight chance to talk. I mentioned his take on Williams, and he was absolutely intransigent. In effect, in order to defend his particular kind of moral poetry, Winters's kind, he had to say bad things about Williams. Stevens's case is a little different, since they were more or less friends, collaborators. On the one hand, these fellows play hardball; they're very competitive, and it was a nasty thing to say on Stevens's part: that he's a romantic poet, that he's like Wordsworth or Shelley or something like that. So, there's a context for these remarks. On the other hand, my old *Dædalus* essay in effect is arguing that there is a sort of perennial group of theories of poetry—the imitative one, that is, the *mimesis* one; the revelation one; and an independent-creation one. Those are indeed present everywhere in romanticism, as well as everywhere else in Western poetry. So yeah, it's true that you can plausibly make Williams a romantic poet. I think maybe what Stevens meant, and even Winters, was that it's a little too cheerful, Williams's poetry. It's romantic in the sense of hiding the anxious kind of sensibility. Williams is not so threatened as both Stevens and Winters were, in their different ways, in their poetry. Stevens had to build up a big philosophical apparatus in order to defend himself. He talks about that: the line as a defense against the world. Williams, on the other hand, cheerfully said, "The world is me, I am the world," and so on. It was always a beautiful day for Williams. What I really love about Williams—because I'm that way myself—are the poems about little insignificant things, as I have already said, his celebration of that little piece of green bottle glass, or the bit of parsley by the sink, or the great poem about the plums in the refrigerator that he had eaten, and the poems about wildflowers, not about beautiful flowers in the garden, but about chicory and daisies, Queen Ann's Lace.[16] "No ideas but in things,"[17] but what common, disregarded things! That's wonderful. There's no other poet I know that quite does that: celebrates insignificant things in that way. There are poems by Stevens about things, little things, but they're always surrounded by a huge apparatus, whereas Williams just says, "A bit of green bottle glass," and that's wonderful, I think. All of my work on Williams was a celebration of that feature of his poetry.

FEST: *Thank you very much for indulging me and talking about Williams specifically and those early review essays. The rest of my questions are a bit*

*broader and more about your work in general and your thinking about the
current state of things.*

*Though I read a few of your essays when I was an undergraduate, I
arrived at a serious reading of your work more recently through the slightly
circuitous path of your early writing on Williams. I imagine others have found
many diverse entrances into your criticism as well, especially considering the
breadth and volume of your writing, and that these entrances have changed
the further we get away from the height of deconstruction. In the last decade
there has been considerable attention paid to your long career, with at least
three issues of journals devoted to your work, two collections of essays, a
monograph by Éamonn Dunne, a reader, and even a film.[18] I know many
writers forswear reading or engaging with their reviews or commentary, but
it appears that you have been closely and generously involved in most of
these projects, participating in conferences and colloquia, contributing essays
yourself, or agreeing to be interviewed frequently. I know this is probably a
difficult question, but what sense do you have about how people approach
your work? Are there aspects of your work that you feel have been overlooked?
Engagements you are surprised by or things you did not foresee?*

MILLER: You didn't mention the book by my Spanish colleague, Manuel
Asensi.[19] And you didn't mention, because there's no reason why you
should know, but two or three books have been published in China, not only
collections of my essays translated into Chinese, with introductions, but at
least two or three Chinese Ph.D. dissertations on my work. I'm very proud
of those even though I can't read them.[20] I corresponded with the author
of one of them in particular; a graduate student who had lots of questions
would send me emails: "What did you mean on page so and so of such and
such a book? Could you explain this further?" and so on, and I cooperated.
So I have been very well treated around the world. I'm especially honored
when I have an email out of the blue, by somebody either in this country or
somewhere, anywhere around the world, saying, "I read such and such an
essay"—not always "The Critic as Host," often something else—"when I was
a sophomore in college, and it's always been very important for me." It's
often an essay about somebody they were reading, somebody was teaching
Tennyson or some other author about whom I've written. That is very
moving for me because it is unpredictable which of these essays of mine they
have read, and it's a delight to know they have had influence.

Oh, by the way, that film by Dragan Kujundžić will be followed now by
a book that transcribes the text of the film, as well as including other essays.
I have the manuscript of this. It is an example where I collaborated because

it was an interview. The interview records what I actually said when asked the kinds of questions that you're asking me now. So that will be coming out. And there are lots of interviews that go on all the time, some of which are published, some of them are podcasts, which I never quite get around to looking at.

My sense is that my work has been approached with generosity and, on the whole, accuracy. I have no complaint. I can't say, "I've been consistently misunderstood." I don't think that's the case. Éamonn Dunne's book—that was a dissertation written for the University College Dublin—that's a very interesting book, so is the long essay by Manuel Asensi in *Black Holes* (1999), a book of which I did half. And I intended in that book to make my part so different from my earlier work that Manuel Asensi's part on my work would be all wrong. It didn't work. He found something that I hadn't reflected upon as a kind unifying theme that goes through all my work. So I've learned from what people have said about my work. I certainly have been surprised by the diversity of people who have been engaged in my work and for whom it's been important in multiple ways. But what I really care most about is when it helps them do their own work.

The only aspect of my work that I feel has been overlooked…I have been trying to think of one and have come up with the following: my work has been perhaps taken a little too solemnly. That is, I consider irony important in my own work, including "The Critic as Host." There's a kind of irony in saying, "Abrams, you use this word parasite, were you at all aware what lies behind that word? I don't think so…" So the essay is an ironic attack on Abrams. He casually used this everyday idiom, borrowed from Booth, but it has more implications than he thought. And that's irony. It goes along with something that I have talked about often: the immense joy I have had doing literary study. I wouldn't do this if it weren't fun. But the fun part leads to a certain degree of irony in my style. Sometimes I say things which were intended to be an ironic miming of a mistake. I thought the context would make that clear. People will nevertheless quote that as if it was me solemnly, without irony, saying, "I believe so and so."

What I've discovered about this is several things about irony. One is that a sense of irony, an ability to understand irony, is crucial to literary studies because literature is full of ironies of one sort or another. And second, a sense for irony, a gift for recognizing irony, is unevenly distributed in the population, including the population of students of literature. A sense for irony is not the same thing as high intelligence. There are some who don't have that sense and therefore miss ironies. Irony is dangerous because it's very annoying if you discover somebody has meant to be ironic and you've missed it. Because it shows that you're an idiot, and you don't really like that.

One of my disagreements with Wayne Booth—though I don't know that I ever explicitly quarreled with him about that—was his theory that ironies are easy to understand and are controllable. He wrote a whole book about irony. Give Wayne Booth credit. He was smart enough to see that irony was a challenge to his own way of reading literature and to take up irony, to try to reduce it, in the sense of saying, "Come on, there's no problem about irony. If it's pouring rain outside or snowing, and I say, 'Isn't it a beautiful day?' You know that this is meant ironically, that I am saying one thing and meaning another." I don't think, by the way, that Abrams meant what he said to Bloom ironically. For him, well, snow is beautiful. It was a beautiful day. But you see the difference. It's interesting that Wayne Booth has two or three sentences in which he more or less dismisses the German romanticists, especially Friedrich Schlegel. As a result of hearing Paul de Man give a whole seminar on Friedrich Schlegel and irony, Friedrich Schlegel is for me the great theorist of irony. It's not something Mike Abrams makes a whole lot of either. So it's not just that my own ironies are missed, but I think the role of irony in literature is to some degree missed more than it ought to be.

For some reason, I've been going back to read and write about Paul de Man recently, something I have resisted doing. He was my colleague, so why should I write about de Man? People can read him for themselves. But I've been rereading some of his work. I think the essay called "The Concept of Irony" (1996) is a wonderful essay because it encapsulates what was a whole semester's admirable graduate seminar at Yale on irony.[21] De Man, much more than I am, was consistently ironical in his teaching. People talk about the solemn, dark deconstructionists, etc. De Man was not like that. His seminars were very funny much of the time and the irony one particularly. He was such a wonderful teacher that the room was full of students on the first day, many of whom were just there as auditors. Also there were lots of faculty members there, as was usual when he gave a graduate seminar. So he was beginning his course on irony and Friedrich Schlegel. The room was full of people. De Man, with his big Belgian nose, sort of looked up under his eyebrows and said, "I should perhaps begin by saying that this course will not help you at all to pass your graduate oral examinations. In fact," he said, "it might actively inhibit the passing of those examinations. So I suggest that any of you who were planning to use this course for that purpose should perhaps leave right now." And of course nobody left. If *I* said this, people would leave. They would take me seriously. Everybody sat right there. It was a marvelous ironic beginning to a seminar on irony. Another emblem there!

"The Concept of Irony" essay is an amazing distillation of a thirteen-week, two-hours-a-week graduate seminar into a one-hour lecture, including even a little section on Johann Gottlieb Fichte. There was a marvelous presentation on Fichte that took him two hours to do as part of the Yale seminar. It was really, however, a seminar on Friedrich Schlegel and Schlegel's theory of irony. One of the things Schlegel says about irony is double: if you don't have it, you won't get it. De Man quotes this at the beginning of the lecture, "The Concept of Irony," to which he adds, "so we can stop right here, and all go home."[22] Schlegel also says irony is unevenly divided in the populace, but then he goes on to say something much more troubling. That is, it's just the people who think they understand irony and therefore think they can use it as a way of fooling other people, who are going to be most its victims. In other words, it's not something you can master, according to Friedrich Schlegel. Irony is the unmasterable, par excellence.

FEST: *I'm glad to hear that your answer is irony. That's an important part of your work. I really appreciated the end of* Reading Narrative *(1998) where you trace this long genealogy from the* Poetics *and* Oedipus the King, *and end by discussing irony. And I have to mention one of my favorite moments in "The Rhetoric of Temporality" (1969), de Man's other essay on irony: what "may start out as a casual bit of play...soon reaches the dimensions of the absolute."*[23] *Even the smallest irony can explode to the greatest limits.*

MILLER: Schlegel says, "One little irony produces a million other little ironies. What Gods are going to save us from all these ironies?"[24] So there was a big influence of Friedrich Schlegel on de Man. If you go to the normal scholarship on Friedrich Schlegel, of which there's a lot, from René Wellek on down to Ernst Behler, there's a big critical *Ausgabe*, a huge edition of Friedrich Schlegel's writings, and so on—I think people tend to assimilate him to his brother August Wilhelm Schlegel and say they are all part of a theory of romanticism, etc. He's very different from August Wilhelm. He changed over the years. He converted to Catholicism, so his later work is much more conventional and conservative than the early work. The work around 1798–1800 in the critical fragments, these are, like fragments generally, not all that easy to understand. I think there's been a resistance to understanding them, so that de Man had some work to do in that seminar. Wayne Booth thought he could just write two sentences about Schlegel and irony, whereas for de Man, Friedrich Schlegel is the great theorist of irony. His theory was seen as threatening in his lifetime and thereafter by many important thinkers. It had to be put down, both by Hegel in what he says about irony and, more importantly, by Kierkegaard in *The Concept of Irony* (1841), his dissertation. De Man observes that the title of his lecture, "The Concept of Irony," is ironical in the sense that it is a reference to Kierkegaard's book. If de Man had lived a little longer, he would have written in more detail about Kierkegaard and then about Adorno and the Frankfurt School. But he did talk a bit about Kierkegaard's *Concept of Irony* in that seminar. Kierkegaard's view is that in order to see irony as a stage in a spiritual development that will lead to a happy, religious conclusion, one must oppose Friedrich Schlegel's assertion that once you are trapped by irony you can't get out. Kierkegaard resists Schlegel by attacking Schlegel's novel *Lucinde* (1799), as had already been done by Hegel.

If you want to put Friedrich Schlegel down, you talk about his obscene novel *Lucinde*. How could somebody who wrote this dirty book be taken seriously? There's a big polemic in Kierkegaard's *Concept of Irony* against the *Lucinde*. That polemic is a little bit hard for us today to contextualize. The United States is still to a considerable degree puritanical, and many of its citizens take for granted that an obscene book should be censored. Nevertheless, we are exposed by the media to obscene words and acts all the time. Think of *American Psycho* (1991). Think of Lady Gaga. One of the great erotic books of German romanticism is Goethe's *Die Wahlverwandtschaften* (1809), *Elective Affinities*. It is not obscene in the way *Lucinde* is, which has all sorts of references to private parts and so on— but *Die Wahlverwandtschaften* really would be banned by many today. It would be considered an obscene book. The *Elective Affinities* has a powerful aura of eroticism about it, but it is at the same time an absolutely wonderful book. I didn't read it in college or graduate school because it was not part of the curriculum. Why was it not part of the curriculum? Because it was considered, as opposed to *Wilhelm Meister* (1795–1796) and *Faust* (1832), to be slightly suspect. George Eliot and her partner, George Henry Lewes, read *Die Wahlverwandtschaften* in German to one another at night. They were, if I remember correctly, living in Germany at the time. It had a big influence on George Eliot's *Daniel Deronda* (1876). So it has had a kind of underground history within literature in English. There is an appreciative essay by Auden about *Die Wahlverwandtschaften*, and there was a translation into English in the mid-nineteenth century. Though I studied German in college and had every reason to have encountered this book, I had never read it until de Man and I taught it in Lit Z, a lower level undergraduate course in Yale's Literature Major. There were three Lit Major beginning courses at Yale. One year, I taught Lit Z with de Man, who usually taught it with Hartman or with Andrzej Warminski—they were team-taught courses—but one year de Man and I taught it together. Lit Z was essentially a course in tropological reading or rhetorical reading. The texts changed every year. De Man chose to have

Elective Affinities as one of the texts that year. So that's when I read it for the first time, when I was full professor at Yale. It is a wonderful book that everybody should read.

FEST: *In your 1986 presidential address to the MLA, you responded to the fear that "there is a crisis in English studies or in the humanities generally, that theory is destroying literary studies and that something urgently needs to be done to eliminate the theorists." You stated, quite emphatically, that "there is no crisis in the humanities." You went on to say that the situation is "quite the opposite. There is, rather, a tremendous vitality, a multiform intellectual energy and healthy diversity in all the fields and modes of our discipline."*[25]

The perception of the situation seems quite a bit different today. In the past month David Brooks's op-ed piece in The New York Times, *"The Humanist Vocation," has sparked a flurry of rather familiar debates. In the article, he declares that the humanities are in decline and that this decline is largely the fault of humanists themselves. Brooks appears to be revisiting similar ground to what you were responding to in 1986. As someone who has been educated well after the wake of theory, and even after the heyday of cultural studies, Brooks's points seem relatively anachronistic to me. I find it difficult to believe that someone in Brooks's position in this day and age can still believe, after all the vital, multiform, and diverse work in the humanities over the past decades, that at one point "the job of the humanities was to cultivate the human core, the part of a person we might call the spirit, the soul, or, in D.H. Lawrence's phrase, 'the dark vast forest,'" but now the humanities are "less about the old notions of truth, beauty and goodness and more about political and social categories like race, class and gender."*[26] *How does one even respond to such a statement except by advising Brooks to enroll in a few humanities courses? Was not one of the goals of your 1970 essay on Williams to combat just this kind of hyperbole and oversimplification?*

One of the most notable respondents to Brooks has been the past president of the MLA, Michael Bérubé. In his recent article in The Chronicle of Higher Education, *"The Humanities Declining? Not According to the Numbers," he points out that Brooks's argument about declining undergraduate enrollment is just flat out wrong. Despite this, Bérubé and most others would grant that "there is indeed a crisis in the humanities…It is a crisis in graduate education, in prestige, in funds, and most broadly, in legitimation."*[27] *This current crisis is something you seem deeply aware of in the piece you sent me, "Cold Heaven, Cold Comfort: Should We Read or Teach Literature Now?"*[28] *It is also a crisis any newly minted Ph.D. on the job market feels acutely. How do you compare the sense of crisis today with that attending the reaction to theory from both the left and the right during the 1980s? Do you think it is possible that the humanities (or indeed, anything) can ever escape a sense of perpetual crisis? It seems very difficult to say that "there is no crisis in the humanities" today, but for very different reasons. What are your thoughts on this?*

MILLER: That is a question it would take me quite a while to talk about in detail, but I'll be brief. First, maybe I should begin from the Brooks/Bérubé issue. I agree with you that Brooks doesn't exactly know what he's talking about, but he does express a very widespread conviction that if the humanities would just cultivate the human core—meaning teach "American values," the part of the person we might call the "spirit" or the "soul"—then money would be forthcoming and all would be well. It's because humanists do other things that the humanities are supposedly in decline. A while ago, the villain was theory. Deconstructive theory was a special target of this hostility. Now it's teaching about categories like race, class, and gender. That's why the humanities are in such bad shape.

So what's wrong with Brooks's idea about what humanists should do, which a lot of people would buy and which is to some degree inscribed into the new and widely accepted idea of the "common core"? The Common Core is a complicated project, but the concept is accepted by many state legislatures and state governors, as something they are prepared to institutionalize in education in their states. It goes from K-12, on through college, with things to be learned at each grade level. The idea for the humanities part—it sounds perfectly plausible—is that everybody ought to learn how to read and write and that they ought to have some introduction to reading literature. The document allows for considerable flexibility in the choice of texts. And how could anybody say they are against the idea that there ought to be some kind of standards all across the country? What's wrong with it is obvious, and that is that an enormous diversity exists in the country of the sorts of people that you find in a given grade school, high school, or undergraduate classroom. And it's not only race, class, and gender that cause this diversity, but all sorts of other economic factors, etc.

FEST: *And increasingly international students as well.*

MILLER: Yeah. For example, over half of the undergraduate students at Irvine have English as a second language. And I often find myself on the campus there surrounded by people, young people, students, none of whom are speaking English. They are speaking Cambodian, Vietnamese, Korean, Chinese, you name it, mostly East Asian languages. There are twenty-two different languages, they discovered, spoken at home by kindergarten students in Orange County. Orange County is a very affluent part of the world, generally speaking. That was surprising. You would have to be down to Ukrainian and various African languages to get twenty-two different languages when they ask these kids what language is spoken at home. I'm not saying everybody shouldn't read Shakespeare, but it's going to be read differently depending upon what sort of people are doing the reading and teaching.

The other thing that I find troubling about the common core—which, in a way, is echoed in Brooks's "cultivate the human core" in that word *core*—is the assumption that we're all really alike and that emphasis on race, class, and gender obscures this idea. Probably Brooks would be in favor of the common core. And I wouldn't try to stop it, as some right-wingers are doing, presumably because it stresses critical thinking, talking, and writing—having factual support for your positions; I'm just worried about it. I think the best teaching is done—anywhere, at any time—by people who are relatively free, both to teach to the students who happen to be in their classes, starting from where the students are, and also to teach things that they are themselves interested in. So that to be told, "this is your curriculum for today," I would find this very inhibiting, if not paralyzing.

I'll give you another anecdote about this, another emblem. I taught the first year after I got out of graduate school at Williams College. I had the illusion—it was a mistake—that I really wanted to teach at an undergraduate college like Oberlin, where I went as an undergraduate. During the course of that year, I discovered that my real vocation was for teaching at a graduate university. Happily, in the middle of that year, I got the job at Hopkins, which was the turning point of my career. I undoubtedly would have been fired at Williams since almost all nontenured faculty were "rotated out," as they were at Yale in my time there. Everybody taught at Williams—it was a small English faculty—in the obligatory freshman/sophomore literature courses. Maybe they were all freshman, I can't remember. The course was divided into sections. Some sections were taught by the senior people in this small department of eight or so, as well as by the two or three junior people. I was not an assistant professor, just a lecturer. Every week there was a meeting in which, essentially, the senior people told us, the younger people, how to teach Swift's *A Tale of a Tub* (1704) or whatever the book was for that week. Then we were supposed to go off and do that. I found that obnoxious. Who were they to tell me how to teach or how to read *A Tale of a Tub*? If I'm going to be any good at this at all (teaching), I need to read it for myself and decide what is important about it for me. Most of all, I have to take account of who happens to be in my class. (Williams was all men still at that point). So I spent my time figuring out ways to undermine the party line. The only difficulty was that the students all knew what the party line was and that this was going to be the basis of the final examination. So it was a hard way to start my teaching career, particularly because of course they gave the most junior people the eight o'clock classes. I would meet students in a dark classroom at eight o'clock in the morning in January, students who had just come back from a house-party weekend at Smith College or wherever and were still sometimes intoxicated, wearing their formal clothes—they'd been at a formal dance. This is a parable of how dangerous it is to prescribe the curriculum and how to teach it. The Common Core, by the way, makes a point of not prescribing *how* a given topic should be taught, just the topics that must be covered in a given year. So that's a big plus for the Common Core. And who could reasonably be against one main goal of the Common Core, which is to improve what students actually know about language and literature and can do responsibly with language (for example, make a persuasive argument based on facts) by the time they graduate from high school or college?

Here is an answer to a later question you ask about my supposed pessimism concerning the current situation: I don't think the whole situation for humanities teachers is terrible these days, though big problems exist. Much of humanities teaching is done by part-timers. We talked earlier yesterday a little bit about their plight: underpaid, little job security, few or no benefits. Nevertheless, an enormous amount of the really good, heroic teaching is done by people at the bottom end of the hierarchy all over the country. They're my unsung heroes. I know some of them. They are good teachers in part because they are often in a situation in which there is relatively little constraint. There's probably more of a constraint in courses on composition (you have to teach the comma splice). But in the area of literature there's still quite a lot of freedom. I know that from evidence I have from students of mine at Irvine and at Yale too, who are still teaching in these underdog situations at little places all around the country. Most of them are wonderfully devoted and creative teachers. I'm full of admiration for the good work they are doing in difficult situations. I also much admire the many nontenured faculty and tenured faculty who are faithfully doing their best to teach literature in difficult situations. It should always be remembered, however, that over 70% of the teaching in all fields in higher education in the United States is now done by those ill-paid underdog adjuncts. That is where most of the teaching action is. One more important factor: an immense amount of really impressive, diverse, and innovative work in the humanities is being published all over the world, in books, essays, journal issues, more and more as e-texts, or available as e-texts. Conferences abound. That ebullience hardly indicates a "crisis in the humanities"; rather, the reverse.

Now, the question about numbers and the actual situation, the Bérubé article: since I am a past president of the Modern Language Association, I am part of a valuable little listserv group that consists of all the people still extant who were presidents of the Modern Language Association. The group is run by Rosemary Feal, the current executive director of the MLA. Various issues come up for this listserv, and statements are circulated online. For example, we've exchanged some strong opinions about the American Academy of Arts and Sciences' recent report about the humanities and social sciences.[29] It is a noble and high-minded report. We should be grateful for the support of these distinguished people. The AAAS commission consists of fifty people, many of whom are university presidents or public figures like David Brooks, who is on that commission. A few distinguished professors from elite institutions. Not one single adjunct teacher is on the commission, not one. Little input from community colleges, which play an increasingly essential role in higher education, as most people know. Only one out of the twelve college and university presidents or chancellors of systems on the commission (presidents of Duke, Harvard, Penn, Stanford, Notre Dame, George Washington, NYU, University of Miami, Cornell; chancellors of the University of Texas, the University of California) is from a community college (Miami Dade College). There is little evidence given from the people who are actually doing the work of teaching and scholarship about the state of the humanities or suggestions for what ought to be done. Most of the commission members probably have little idea what it's like to be an adjunct teacher in a less than elite place or in a community college and facing a class in such a place. I read recently in a blog about somebody who teaches literature at a university that is not far from Walden Pond in Massachusetts. When he met his first-year students in the beginning class, he found that not one of them had ever heard of Thoreau. Not one. Here they were fourteen miles away from Walden Pond, and nobody had ever heard of Thoreau.

On the other hand, these students are probably terrific users of iPhones and iPads, of Twitter and Facebook. They have a tremendous verbal ability. It may be a slightly different kind of language. I know this from our grandson, a computer science expert. What he wants to say in an email he can say very succinctly, very correctly, very forcefully. He's a good writer.

I think Bérubé's evidence is somewhat misleading. He's got statistics that show that there's no decline in humanities enrollments. On the other hand, there's contrary evidence, for example, the great reduction in numbers of English majors at Yale. Discussing this discrepancy has been part of the give and take on this past-presidents' listserv. Yale is a great place to do humanities, partly because if your papa is the CEO of a large company and you're going to go into his company when you get out of Yale, you can major in anything; it doesn't matter all that much. Or the English major is a perfectly good preparation for going to law school, if that's what your goal is, as is true for many Yale undergraduates. Moreover, the humanities at Yale are extremely strong—brilliant teachers like Dick Brodhead, now president of Duke and the head of that AAAS commission. He was a teacher in the English department or American Studies program at Yale when I taught there. I evaluated his dissertation when I first went to teach at Yale. He was a terrific undergraduate lecturer at Yale, one of the best, and Yale has wonderful teaching. The number of English majors there, however, has gone down in a very short time—since I forget whether it was '91, '96, something like that—from 160 to 69. In other words, it's roughly a third as many. And this is a big, very distinguished department, but fewer are majoring in English. More and more English majors at Stanford are concentrating on creative writing. I think Bérubé, by focusing on the total numbers, makes the situation look better than it is. Many of the courses in his statistics are probably required beginning courses that people have to take for "distribution." And relatively fewer of such courses are in literature. More of them would be in film studies, popular culture, etc. I'm not against that. It's simply that it's not the same thing as talking about the fate of the teaching of literature and identifying how many people take that seriously. So I think there is at least that kind of crisis. The evidence is that English majors across the country—this is the statistical evidence—have gone down from eight percent to four percent. The high number was not all that long ago, ten, twenty years ago. The foreign language majors have gone down from four percent to one percent. Nevertheless, David Brooks's judgment much oversimplifies a complex situation. All those teachers who are still earnestly teaching old-fashioned print literature as a way to learn how to live should not be forgotten.

FEST: *There has been considerable fuss in recent years over the so-called digital humanities, to the point that I believe my institution is now even offering an introductory undergraduate course with that title. You have commented on the changes that technology has wrought in your own scholarship in a number of places, most recently in* The Medium is the Maker *(2009). About that book, you write that its composition "is possible only because it is being written on* *a computer connected to the Internet. This is so because I am exploiting all the prestidigitizing powers of the word processor—ease of virtually limitless revision and interpolation, spell and grammar checks, possibility of multiple backups, ability to send the file anywhere in the world as an attachment to an email, ability to 'google' and 'wiki' almost anything, and so on."[30] I would add to this list the conversation that we are currently having. There are many who would celebrate this prestidigitization, but I often feel that this celebration is concomitant with certain strains of neoliberalism and the corporatization of the university. And clearly there are people who are critical or skeptical of the digital humanities. What do you think the impact on humanistic study these "bio-techno-prosthetic apparatus[es]"[31] have had and will have? How do you think all those myriad devices will impact reading and literature? Contrary to my students' perception of themselves as people who do not "read" all that much, I like to point out to them that they are reading all the time, perhaps more than ever—text messages, emails, tweets, status updates, etc.—but they tend not to think of this as "reading" in the same way. And surely you mean something quite different by "reading" in your work than the distracted reading produced by texts and tweets. Why do you think that there is a perceived gap between digital reading and good old analog book reading? What is at stake for the humanities and the digital humanities? Where do you think we are being led by the digital? Is it in any way toward what you call, in* The Ethics of Reading *(1991), a "millennium of readers"?*

MILLER: Did I speak of such a "millennium"? Hmmm. I've looked it up and find that my sentence is from the de Man chapter and was meant to be distinctly ironic: "I would even dare to promise that the millennium [defined just before as 'universal justice and peace among men'] would come if all men and women became good readers in de Man's sense, though that promise is exceedingly unlikely to have a chance to be tested in practice."[32] In other words, I add today, "Fat chance!"

I have various things to say about the questions you have just raised. I think the change from printed books to digital technologies is a millennial change, a total change in the way we live now. I think it is irresistible. It is not anything that is going to stop or that can be stopped. That doesn't mean that there won't be lots of printed books, old and new, for a long time yet. But it means that their role in people's lives is going to be diminished and is already being diminished. It's not the end of the world. There can be a shift to other forms of what we thought of as literature. The print epoch replaced the manuscript one, as we know, and it's had a good run. The period of the novel has gone from the late-seventeenth century to today.

Thousands and thousands of printed novels are still being published all over the world. That's not going to stop overnight. But I think, just looking at it candidly, that novels have less effect on most people's lives than they used to. In the nineteenth century, young people learned about courtship and marriage, how to behave in the world, how to get ahead, and so on, from reading novels. Now I think they more and more learn that sort of thing from television, from the internet, from video games, from Netflix, and from the interchanges with their friends on Facebook and Twitter.

Though I would have some things to say about the difference between reading a printed book and reading the same text online in an e-text, nevertheless, it's still a form of reading literature. The difference is pretty obvious. It's a difference of context. The printed book belongs to the print epoch. So you think of libraries, holding the book in your hands, and so on. A printed book belongs to a whole different technology and way of living from using the Internet. Reading an e-text of the same book is different, even though it's the same book, the same words. An e-text has certain advantages. It's searchable. It's likely to cost nothing or practically nothing. Project Guttenberg, for example, has free downloadable e-texts of seventy books by Joseph Conrad. You can get an immense number of books in the traditional literary canon online for free. You can carry a given e-text around and read it with an iPad—I use a MacBook Air—or read it in bed. So it's not the case that you can't use the new technologies in the same way you do a printed book. Nevertheless, the context is different. Now the book belongs to the expanse of the enormous, disorderly cyberspace. The Internet gives access to a huge collection of texts, graphics, and music, of which printed canonical literature in e-form is only a tiny, tiny part. I've just written a new piece about "Why read literature?" I've recently revised this for an issue of *Dædalus* (again, *Dædalus*!) about what humanists do and what I say they should do. I could send you that, by the way.

FEST: *I would love to see it.*

MILLER: What I say in that essay would answer some of these questions you've asked toward the end of your last set of questions. I agree with you that people are reading all the time, they're very adept readers. I've mentioned my grandson, who has an ability not just to read but to do all sorts of things with a computer I can't do—with video games, which he's very good at, which involve certain eye–hand coordination, with downloading and listening to music, and so on. So I agree with you that a huge amount of reading is happening that is simply different from reading a printed book.

My parabolic anecdote about this is I was on an airplane, coming back from California after my last mini-seminar there last May. I walked down the aisle of the airplane. There were ten people with iPads or e-readers or some such gadget, reading. They all looked to me as if they were reading works of fiction, not playing a video game or solving crossword puzzles. They were definitely reading texts of some sort. It wouldn't have been polite to stop and ask them just what they were reading. But they weren't playing computer games. They were reading some text or other. Eight of them were doing it on an e-reader, and only two, with printed books. Now it's more likely people would carry an iPad on the airplane than a bunch of books, so it may not be a fair evaluation, but I think my airplane experience nevertheless tells you something about the rapid replacement of printed books by digital books.

Another story: I was the other day in my doctor's office waiting for some routine test or other. There were five other people: a mother and daughter, an older man, a younger woman, I forget the fifth—there were five other people. Every single one of them was using an iPhone. Not just some of them, but all of them, every one of them. That's a big change.

You'll see in my paper for *Dædalus* that I believe the rapid development of MOOCs—massive open online courses—shows that the new technology is irresistible, even in the area of teaching. It isn't that people don't think about whether MOOCs are a good idea or not, but it seems impossible to stop it whatever you think. Once you can do it, you do it. Once somebody discovered that you could develop with the new technology courses that could be taken by a million people all over the world at once, it began to be done. Now many elite universities, Harvard, MIT, Stanford, and many distinguished teachers, have got on that bandwagon. They are now predictably trying to figure out how to make money from MOOCs. MOOCs are transforming higher education in the same radical way as digitization is transforming the culture of the printed book. As MOOCs come to prevail, a lot of college teachers will be put out of work, just as email has caused big financial problems for the snail mail postal system. Why should I pay way over a hundred thousand dollars to get an education in situ at a less well-known university when I can get a Harvard or Stanford education almost for free online? The answer of course is that the "in situ" gives you a lot more than just information, however "interactive" MOOCs are: meeting other students, including sorts of people you have never met before; learning how to socialize; learning about courtship; etc. MOOCs are without a doubt a force for democracy by giving students all over the world access to elite lecture courses. Nevertheless, any course in any field, but especially in the humanities and social sciences, will have ideological biases, often subtle ones. I worry about a million people worldwide being subject to the same often covert ideological bias in the way a given topic is taught, even though I might agree with that bias. Part of the glory of the present college and university system is the great variety of attitudes and approaches in teaching. The AAAS Commission, by the way, gives MOOCs and other online teaching resources a thumbs up.

Who would have predicted that the iPad or the iPhone or similar devices would so rapidly become almost universally "necessary"? Not at all that easy to foresee. I have and use an iPhone, though without command over many of its wonderful "features." It keeps doing things I am not aware of having asked it to do.

FEST: *In your recent work, you have increasingly commented upon contemporary events: the disastrous wars in Iraq and Afghanistan, the dire ecological condition the species faces in the present and future, the various other catastrophes and disasters that seem to be happening with increased frequency, the national security state, etc. Do you have any thoughts about PRISM? About the inhuman or nonhuman forces of contemporaneity that, though they emerge from the human, appear to be unassailable to older humanistic modes of thought? How these new technologies of control are "reading" the world in ways that are increasingly unrecognizable?*

MILLER: A long history of concern in the West for surveillance and privacy exists, in literature and philosophy, for example, in Bentham and Foucault. A brilliant book by David Rosen and Aaron Santesso, *The Watchman in Pieces: Surveillance, Literature, and Liberal Personhood*, traces this complex history. Nevertheless, the new technological forms of surveillance have put us in a new world for universal spying, by corporations as well as by the government. I think PRISM is an example of technological irresistibility. They find you can do it with the new gadgets, so they cannot resist doing it. The National Security Agency has a job to do. Our government and military have persuaded themselves ideologically that there is a terrible threat from terrorists, etc., and they're hired to protect us from terrorist attack. I think PRISM is a bit of overkill, to say the least. There are two enormous buildings in the United States full of servers and storage facilities, one in the West, one in the East. Billions and billions of our tax dollars go into this. Then they discovered—that's the billions and billions of dollars—that you could use this new technology to surveil everything. And they found that irresistible. Though there is—I've read carefully a lot about this—a court appointed by the president (by the way, appointed originally by George W. Bush, so this court is, or was until recently, all six Republicans, not surprisingly). In theory, the NSA has to go to them and say, "Can we look at so-and-so's emails?" The court has never turned a request down yet, so we are told. It's apparently a complete rubber stamp. The authorities evidently haven't been telling the truth about much of this. They say, "Well, we just have a list; we're not looking at actual emails or listening to recorded phone calls." Apparently that's not true, as we learned from Edward Snowden's revelations. Apparently there's much actual reading of emails, of listening to phone calls, and of watching things like Skype, which they have access to by way of Microsoft. Much more than we have been told. So we have to take for granted, as I have for a long time, that our emails and all the rest of our digital texts are totally public. Actually, my emails belong to Irvine. I use their server and their email address. That means it's in their server. Not only is it in their server, but if you look at the fine print, if they happen to want to read it, they can—good luck to them on that. It's not all that interesting. This potentially total surveillance is a recent transformation of the human situation that goes along with being plugged in as you and I are now. We wouldn't be able to do this Skype interview without this new technology. It gives us this marvelous opportunity to talk to one another face to face at a distance. But the NSA can call it up and watch it and listen to it. That is a big change in the way we live now. And I guess you could define it by saying: no more privacy.

I learned the other day—it's an interesting bit of information—that the Russians are considering having no more highly secret documents that are digitized. They are going to have them all on pieces of paper.

FEST: *I haven't looked at the entirety of the American Academy of Arts and Sciences Report yet, but immediately after the title page, one of the things that they say the humanities is good for is to help national security experts plan for the complex global conflicts of the future.[33] This is rather chilling to me and is one of the reasons I asked about the digital humanities. Your sense about how technology is changing potentially changes how we define the human, what we mean by human, and thus what we mean by the humanities, what we study and what we do. You seem to be concerned with our contemporary situation quite a bit in your recent work, but as I said, your "Cold Heaven, Cold Comfort" essay says that, well, maybe all we have left is the ability to debunk aesthetic ideology, to debunk lies, to see through the veils that are put in front of us. I'm skeptical that that's the "use" for the humanities. I would like to think that maybe if the challenge to the human itself is so palpable* *and obvious to all of us, that maybe remembering all those good things that the humanities did do for so many years—and print culture—should be reemphasized.*

MILLER: I agree. I would say that there are three reasons now why we should read or teach literature. Perhaps the primary one is pleasure, the pleasure of the text, and the pleasure of dwelling in an imaginary world. I've said in recent essays a lot about what that means and what there is about human nature that makes us able to read a novel and think of its characters almost as real people.[34] That's clearly the major reason for reading or teaching literature. That's why I read, teach, and write about novels and poems.

The second reason is that you do learn something about the real world and about cultural history from literature. Even from a lyric poem like Yeats's "The Cold Heaven" (1914), you learn something about William Butler Yeats; you learn something about what rooks are like, what the weather is like in Ireland, and so on. From a big novel like *Middlemarch* (1874), you learn a lot about social relations in Victorian England. From a David Foster Wallace novel, you learn a lot about things in the United States. That learning is valuable. So literature is a way of learning about social relations and social rules, about landscapes, cityscapes, house interiors, food at different times and places, and so on. It is also a way of learning about the history of the various concepts and ideas that are important at a given time. An example is the brilliant account, in the book I've mentioned by Rosen and Santesso, of the tangled development in the West since the Renaissance of ideas about privacy, surveillance, and personhood. These ideas are once again at the forefront as we respond to revelations about massive surveillance by our National Security Agency. It is extremely useful to know that these ideas have a history.

The third reason to read and teach literature is also of great importance. An instinctive anxiety about this third reason probably lies behind Brooks's resistance to what the humanities are doing today. This third reason could be given the shorthand name of "training in critical thinking." In Texas, forbidding the teaching of critical thinking was a plank in the Republican platform of 2012. I found that interesting. The Texas GOP sees critical thinking as enough of a threat to propose a law prohibiting students in Texas from learning how to do it. How does reading and teaching literature train people in critical thinking? A long answer would be necessary, but a short answer would be that many famous novels—*Northanger Abbey, Pride and Prejudice, Madame Bovary, Middlemarch, Lord Jim*, and many others—show protagonists making disastrous choices based on false thinking governed by mistaken figurative displacements.

If we had more time, I would say more about that, but we are running out of time. Maybe I'll send you one of my recent essays about Paul de Man and "The Resistance to Theory" (1982). For him, the resistance to theory is a resistance to what you learn by way of theory about ideology. And learning this strikes me as a social good. How can we understand the mechanism whereby huge numbers of people in the United States think Barack Obama is a Muslim and not a citizen of the United States? Or who think climate change predictions are a hoax perpetrated by power-mad scientists? Or who think Obamacare is doomed to fail and will cost billions? How did that happen? Learning about literature and literary theory can be a big help in teaching students how these and other politicians' lies come to be believed. There is a big resistance to letting that be taught. The resistance to Paul de Man capitalized on the revelation of his wartime writings, which I condemn completely, to dismiss all his work.[35] De Man's later work is written against the ideology that the young Paul de Man had: the belief in certain ideas about nationalism, race, etc., that underlie those early writings, for example, the notorious anti-Semitic one. Racism and nationalism are things he was vehemently opposed to later on, for example, in his antipathy to Heidegger. I remember the first time I met him (yet another anecdote) I said I was reading later Heidegger with much interest, and he said, with great urgency, "That's very dangerous. If you must read Heidegger, read *Sein und Zeit* (*Being and Time*)" (1927). It was only later on that I realized the source of the urgency in his warning. He saw, much more than I did then in my naïveté, what is dangerous about later Heidegger. This danger lies not just in Heidegger's sympathy with Nazism, but in the German nationalist ideas that permeate his work. I think there is no excuse for not reading (critically) de Man's mature writing and his teaching about how to read critically. If you want to reduce it to a sentence, critical thinking means learning how to understand the effects, both cognitive and performative, of tropological displacements. De Man says just this in "The Resistance to Theory": "What we call ideology is precisely the confusion of linguistic with natural reality, of reference with phenomenalism. It follows that, more than any other mode of inquiry, including economics, the linguistics of literariness is a powerful and indispensable tool in the unmasking of ideological aberrations, as well as a determining factor in accounting for their occurrence."[36]

Literature is a good place to learn how ideology is based on false tropological equivalents. Such displacements are the basis of politicians' lies. Clearheaded experts like Paul Krugman in his *New York Times* op-ed pieces use critical thinking to make you realize, for example, that the equation by conservative politicians of family finances—you should balance the family budget—and national finances is a mistake. It's a false tropological analogy. The United States is not like a family, partly because the government prints the money. They control the money supply, etc. A nation is on an entirely different scale and operates with a different mechanism and context from a family. It is a false analogy but a very powerful one. It is used by conservative politicians to say, "We should go for austerity. We should cut Medicare, cut Social Security because we don't have enough money for these, just as a family should not spend more than it makes." That argument is based on a false comparison. I think teaching literature or teaching literary theory would help students learn the critical thinking that would allow them to expose such lies and mistakes. Though learning critical thinking is only the third reason to read and teach literature, it is an important third. If the Texas Republican Party wants to keep Texas citizens bamboozled by false beliefs about Obamacare, climate change, the need for deregulation, reduced taxes on the rich, etc., they are certainly right to want to forbid the teaching of critical thinking.

The astute reader will have noted that in transferring critical thinking from literature to life I am using an analogy. The difference, however, is between taking a figurative transference literally and using that mode of critical thinking called the linguistics of literariness, or knowledge of tropes, to account, with appropriate modifications, for ideological aberrations in two different realms: in literary works, on the one hand, and in the real world, on the other.

Notes

1. See J. Hillis Miller, *Poets of Reality: Six Twentieth-Century Writers* (Cambridge, MA: The Belknap Press of Harvard University Press, 1966); "Williams's *Spring and All* and the Progress of Poetry," *Dædalus* 99, no. 2, Theory in Humanistic Study (1970): 405–34; "Williams," in *The Linguistic Moment: From Wordsworth to Stevens* (Princeton: Princeton University Press, 1985), 349–89; "Presidential Address 1986: The Triumph of Theory, the Resistance to Reading, and the Question of the Material Base" *PMLA* 102, no. 3 (1987): 281–91; and J. Hillis Miller, ed., *William Carlos Williams: A Collection of Critical Essays* (Englewood Cliffs, NJ: Prentice-Hall, Inc., 1966).

2. "*Je dis: une fleur! et, hors de l'oubli où ma voix relègue aucun contour, en tant que quelque chose d'autre que les calices sus, musicalement se lève, idée rieuse ou altière, l'absente de tous bouquets*" (Stéphane Mallarmé, "Avant-dire au René Ghil 'Traité du verbe,'" in Œuvres *complètes*, vol. 2, ed. Bertrand Marchal [Paris: Gallimard, 2003], 678).

3 Wallace Stevens, "Anecdote of the Jar," in *Wallace Stevens: Collected Poetry and Prose*, eds. Frank Kermode and Joan Richardson (New York: The Library of America, 1997), 61, l. 7.

4 Stevens, *Wallace Stevens*, 322, l. 1.

5 William Carlos Williams, "The Sea-Elephant," in *The Collected Poems of William Carlos Williams: 1909-1939*, vol. 1, eds. A. Walton Litz and Christopher MacGowan (New York: New Directions, 1991), 341–43, ll. 24, 56, 65.

6 See Williams, "The Red Wheelbarrow," in *Collected Poems*, vol. 1, 224.

7 "Nobody ever saw it—it had no circulation at all—but I had a lot of fun with it" (William Carlos Williams, *I Wanted to Write a Poem: The Autobiography of the Works of a Poet*, ed. Edith Heal [Boston: Beacon Press, 1967], 38).

8 See J. Hillis Miller, "Deconstructing the Deconstructers," *Diacritics* 5, no. 2 (1975): 24–31. This is a review of Joseph N. Riddel, *The Inverted Bell: Modernism and the Counterpoetics of William Carlos Williams* (Baton Rouge: Louisiana State University Press, 1974). Riddel responded in "Response: A Miller's Tale," *Diacritics* 5, no. 3 (1975): 56–65.

9 See M. H. Abrams, *Doing Things With Texts: Essays in Criticism and Critical Theory*, ed. Michael Fischer (New York: W. W. Norton and Co., 1989), especially 113–34 and 237–363; Donald E. Pease, "J. Hillis Miller: The Other Victorian at Yale," in *The Yale Critics: Deconstruction in America*, eds. Jonathan Arac, Wlad Godzich, Wallace Martin (Minneapolis: University of Minnesota Press, 1983), 90–108; and "American Literary Studies and American Cultural Studies in the Times of the National Emergency: J's Paradoxes," in *Provocations to Reading: J. Hillis Miller and the Democracy to Come*, eds. Barbara Cohen and Dragan Kujundžić (New York: Fordham University Press, 2005), 159–96.

10 See J. Hillis Miller, "But Are Things as We Think They Are?" *TLS* 4410 (1987): 1104–5.

11 Abrams's use of the word *parasitical* was actually a quotation of Wayne C. Booth, which Miller notes at the beginning of "The Critic as Host": "At one point in 'Rationality and Imagination in Cultural History' M. H. Abrams cites Wayne Booth's assertion that the 'deconstructionist' reading of a given work 'is plainly and simply parasitical' on 'the obvious or univocal reading'" (J. Hillis Miller, "The Critic as Host," *Critical Inquiry* 3, no. 3 [1977]: 439). See Abrams, 126; and Wayne C. Booth, "M. H. Abrams: Historian as Critic, Critic as Pluralist," *Critical Inquiry* 2, no. 3 (1976): 441. Miller's "Critic as Host" was later considerably revised and expanded and collected in Harold Bloom et al., *Deconstruction and Criticism* (New York: Continuum, 2004), 177–207.

12 See Jacques Derrida, "Signature evenement context," in *Marges de la philosophie* (Paris: Les Editions de Minuit, 1972), 365–93. This has been translated as "Signature, Event, Context," in *Margins of Philosophy*, trans. Alan Bass (Chicago: University of Chicago Press, 1982), 307–30. See also

Limited Inc, trans. Samuel Weber and Jeffrey Mehlman (Evanston, IL: The Northwestern University Press), esp. 90–91.

[13] See Thomas Hardy, "The Ivy-Wife," in *The Complete Poetical Works of Thomas Hardy*, vol. 1 (New York: Oxford University Press, 1982), 75.

[14] Yvor Winters, "Poetry of Feeling," in *William Carlos Williams*, 66.

[15] Wallace Stevens, "William Carlos Williams," in *William Carlos Williams*, 62.

[16] See Williams, "Between Walls," "Good Night," "This is Just to Say," and "Daisy," in *Collected Poems*, vol. 1, 453, 85–6, 372, and 160–1, and "Asphodel, That Greeny Flower," in *Collected Poems: 1939–1962*, vol. 2, ed. Christopher MacGowan (New York: New Directions, 2001), 310–37.

[17] See Williams, "Paterson," in *Collected Poems*, vol. 1, 263; "A Sort of Song," *Collected Poems*, vol. 2, 55; and *Paterson*, revised ed., ed. Christopher MacGowan (New York: New Directions, 1992), 9.

[18] See the *Journal for Cultural Research* 8, no. 2 (2004): 99–215; *Critical Inquiry* 31, no. 2 (2005): 684–736; *Comparative Literature Studies* 50, no. 2 (2013): 342–63; Carol Jacobs and Henry Sussman eds., *Acts of Narrative* (Stanford: Stanford University Press, 2003); Barbara Cohen and Dragan Kujundžić, eds., *Provocations to Reading: J. Hillis Miller and the Democracy to Come* (New York: Fordham University Press, 2005), which also collects some of the essays from the special issues of the *Journal for Cultural Research* and *Critical Inquiry*; Éamonn Dunne, *J. Hillis Miller and the Possibilities of Reading: Literature After Deconstruction* (New York: Continuum, 2010); J. Hillis Miller, *The J. Hillis Miller Reader*, ed. Julian Wolfreys (Stanford: Stanford University Press, 2005); and *The First Sail: J. Hillis Miller* (dir. Dragan Kujundžić, 2011).

[19] See Manuel Asensi, *J. Hillis Miller; or, Boustrophedonic Reading*, trans. Mabel Richart (Stanford: Stanford University Press, 1999). This volume also contains J. Hillis Miller's *Black Holes*.

[20] For a selection of some of the work being done on Miller in China, see Fengzhen Wang, "One of the Yale Four," *Foreign Literature* 11 (Published in People's Republic of China, 1987): 80–4; "J. Hillis Miller," from *Dictionary of Literary Biography*, Chinese trans. by Yang Ming-Chen, *Chung-Wai Literary Monthly* 20, no. 4 (1991): 11–6; also in this issue of the *Chung-Wai Literary Monthly* see "J. Hillis Miller: Another Kind of Victorian," Chinese trans. by Chang Chin-Chang and Yu Hui-Chin, 53–74; Ying-Hui Cheng, "Miller on Hardy," 76–85; Yu-Cheng Lee, "The Politics of the Ethics of Reading," 86–94; Te-hsing Shan, "A Form of Parabasis: An Interview With J. Hillis Miler," 95–115; Shen Dan, "On Certain Limitations of Stylistics as Seen in Contrast with the Analytical Models of David Lodge and J. Hillis Miller," *Journal of Peking University* (1992): 91–7; Te-hsing Shan, "On J. Hillis Miller's Concept of Cultural Criticism," *Chung Wai Literary Monthly* 22, no. 3 (1993): 5–26; "Illustrating *Illustration*: An Interview with J. Hillis Miller," *Con-Temporary* (1993): 49–71; and *Dialogues and Interchanges: Interviews with Contemporary Writers and Critics*, ed. David D. W. Wang (Taipei: Rye Field Publications,

a division of Cité Publishing Ltd., 2001), 267–89, 291–310; Ning Yizhong, "Miller's Theory on Literary Theory Translation," *Foreign Languages and Their Teaching* 5 (1999): 37–9; Lian Duan, *A Cross-Cultural Approach to Art Criticism* (Xinan Shifan Daxue Chubanshe, 2004), 12–4, 17; and Yuan Gao, dissertation in Chinese about J. Hillis Miller, Beijing Language and Cultural University, 2009.

21 See Paul de Man, "The Concept of Irony," in *Aesthetic Ideology*, ed. Andrzej Warminski (Minneapolis: University of Minnesota Press, 1996), 163–84. This essay was transcribed and edited from a lecture originally given at Ohio State University, Columbus, Ohio, April 4, 1977.

22 De Man, "The Concept of Irony," 164.

23 Paul de Man, "The Rhetoric of Temporality," in *Blindness and Insight: Essays in the Rhetoric of Contemporary Criticism*, revised 2nd ed. (Minneapolis: University of Minnesota Press, 1983), 215.

24 "*Welche Götter werden uns von allen diesen Ironien erretten können? [. . .] Ich fürchte, wenn ich anders, was das Schicksal in Winken zu sagen scheint, richtig verstehe, es würde bald eine neue Generation von kleinen Ironien entstehn: denn warhlich die Gestirne deuten auf fantastisch*" (Friedrich von Schlegel, "Über die Unverstandlichkeit," in *Kritische Friedrich-Schlegel-Ausgabe: Charakteristiken und Kritiken I [1796–1801]*, vol. 2, eds. Ernst Behler, Jean-Jacques Anstett, and Hans Eichner [Munich: Verlag Ferdinand Schöning, 1967], 369–70).

25 Miller, "Presidential Address 1986," 290.

26 David Brooks, "The Humanist Vocation," *The New York Times*, June 20, 2013, http://www.nytimes.com/2013/06/21/opinion/brooks-the-humanist-vocation.html?hpand_r=2and.

27 Michael Bérubé, "The Humanities Declining? Not According to the Numbers," *The Chronicle of Higher Education*, July 1, 2013, http://chronicle.com/article/The-Humanities-Declining-Not/140093/. For Bérubé's own presidential address see "How We Got Here," *PMLA* 128, no. 3 (2013), 530–41.

28 This has been published as J. Hillis Miller, "Should We Read or Teach Literature Now?" *Literature and/as Ethics*, ed. Martin Middeke et al., special issue of *Anglia*, 129, nos. 1–2 (2011): 1–11.

29 See American Academy of Arts and Sciences, *The Heart of the Matter: The Humanities and Social Sciences for a Vibrant, Competitive, and Secure Nation* (Cambridge, MA: American Academy of Arts and Sciences, 2013), http://www.humanitiescommission.org/_pdf/HSS_Report.pdf.

30 J. Hillis Miller, *The Medium Is the Maker: Browning, Freud, Derrida and the New Telepathic Ecotechnologies* (Portland, OR: Sussex Academic Press, 2009), 10.

31 Miller, *The Medium is the Maker*, 12.

32 J. Hillis Miller, *The Ethics of Reading: Kant, de Man, Eliot, Trollope, James, and Benjamin* (New York: Columbia University Press, 1987), 58.

33 The actual language is as follows: "Who will lead America into a bright future? [...] Experts in national security, equipped with the cultural understanding, knowledge of social dynamics, and language proficiency to lead our foreign service and military through complex global conflicts" (American Academy of Arts and Sciences, i).

34 See, for instance, J. Hillis Miller, *On Literature* (New York: Routledge, 2002).

35 For Miller's reflection on the de Man affair, see "Paul de Man's Wartime Writings" and "An Open Letter to Professor Jon Wiener," in *Theory Now and Then* (Durham: Duke University Press, 1991), 359–68 and 369–84.

36 Paul de Man, "The Resistance to Theory," in *The Resistance to Theory* (Minneapolis: University of Minnesota Press, 1986), 11.

11

A Critical Story So Far

Interview with Christopher D. Morris

CHRISTOPHER D. MORRIS: *Michael Asensi compares your prose with that of Borges—apparently straightforward and lucid but also double. I see an example of this in your recent figure of theory as the "handmaiden" of criticism. The figure echoes the longstanding medieval and renaissance trope whereby the term* handmaiden *was given to philosophy in its relation to theology, as in the writings of Boethius or the tradition of the academic trivium. Does this backstory of your figure affirm that today the study of literature has taken the place of theology, as in Matthew Arnold's hope? Does your phrase point to an unavoidable theological dimension in criticism? Is what Burke called a "God-term" or what de Man called a "theotrope" just as ineradicable from literary studies as it is from any other? We can't shake this handmaiden, even if we might want to?*

Does this figure have anything to do with what you've written about hands, *in your work on Nancy and Derrida? That is, as a beguiling figure for a seemingly authentic sign? Would you comment on the relation between theory and criticism in the context of the "handmaiden" metaphor?*

MILLER: I don't know where the word *handmaiden* came to me from. Probably as a way of calling attention to the figure behind the perfectly idiomatic phrase "Theory is ancillary to reading literature." I think my primary motive when I said that was to put down theory and to challenge the idea that theory is a separate enterprise—as many people think it is, with courses in theory, etc. No, theory is only interesting if it leads to good readings. But I was aware that to say that is a polemical argument. Many people see theory as a separate enterprise that doesn't necessarily have to do with anything except defining the postmodern or whatever. But *handmaiden* is a loaded word; you're right. It was also intended to imply that theory is really kind of feminine, feminine in the sexist, "masculinist" sense of subordinated to the man, as the Virgin is subordinated to God.

But there's another thing that you didn't mention. Not only was philosophy the handmaiden to theology, but the word is used for the Virgin Mary, as the handmaiden of the Lord. *Ancilla.* It's in Luke 1:38: Mary's answer to the Angel at the Annunciation: "And Mary said, Behold the handmaid of the Lord" ("Ecce Ancilla Domini"). I'm not a Catholic, so I don't know all the terminology, but the word *ancilla* is a key term in defining the role of the Virgin. That would connect easily to Dante's *Divine Comedy,* where Beatrice is a handmaiden for the Pilgrim's access to God, though in the end the Pilgrim's more direct access to God is by way of the Virgin Mary, as for Catholics generally. The last Canto of Dante's *Paradise* begins with an invocation of the Virgin: "O virgin mother, daughter of thy Son..." This slippage is of course a frequent feature of medieval and Renaissance love poetry in Europe.

On the other hand, I don't think and never have thought that literature and theology can't be separated. Works of literature are *not* sacred. They are secular, including *The Divine Comedy,* whatever Dante said about it. So I'm an old-fashioned, trained-as-a-Protestant person. There's the Bible, and that's sacred scripture, and there's Trollope and Pynchon, and Virginia Woolf and Conrad. They make a different use of language. To take them as somehow giving you access to something like God or heaven or whatever is idolatry. There's only one sacred book in Christianity, and that's the Bible. So there's an irony on my part in borrowing a term that I was aware on some level is essentially a theological term to define something that I see as resolutely secular. That doesn't mean that there are not religious works of literature that are written by people with religious belief. My model here might be Gerard Manley Hopkins. Hopkins worried all his life about the status of his poetry, which often deals with theological subjects—he was a Jesuit priest—and the danger that it might become a substitute in some way for scripture, but he never made that confusion. That was the problem: his poetry, he was convinced, was of no use to salvation for him. It was just literature. That's why he felt so guilty about writing those poems. It was only when his Rector, his spiritual advisor, said, "Father Hopkins, it's OK. You can write a poem," that he wrote "The Wreck of the Deutschland." There's no doubt that "The Wreck of the Deutschland" is a religious poem, but that would never have led Hopkins to say, "I'm a prophet. I'm writing another piece of sacred text that ought to be added to the Bible."

MORRIS: *In* The Medium Is the Maker, *you define deconstructive reading as ironic miming, using the example of Derrida's reading of Freud. Derrida, you say, does no more than string together apparently extraneous metaphors in Freud's discourse, with an effect that is "devastating for any project of conceptual unification about 'what Freud said' and also very funny." You also accept that your own paraphrase of Derrida's "Telepathy" effects an irony similar to the one produced by his miming of Freud.*

Two questions. First, would it follow that your reading of "Telepathy" is devastating for any conceptual unification about "what Derrida said" in his essay? Second, is there a prospect of infinite regress here? You argue that reading as ironic miming disrupts what Derrida calls "hypnopoetics" or writing's capacity to lull the reader to accept a kind of dream state. If so, doesn't ironic miming provide only the illusion of true awakening from hypnosis, since it must simultaneously induce, elsewhere, a new one?

MILLER: Yes on the second question. Irony is only to a certain degree powerful or effective. It certainly re-establishes something nonironical somewhere. You're right about that. On the other hand, I've always thought—I'm now back to question one—that irony is a fundamental trope not only of literature but also of criticism, at least my criticism, and it's often misunderstood by people. So why do I use irony? For several reasons. Apparently it's intrinsic in my attitude towards things to be ironic. And I think it's related to one of the primary reactions I had to literature as a child, which was really a reaction to ironies in *Alice in Wonderland* or in the Pooh books or whatever. There's obviously a relation between irony and wordplay. I didn't think of those books as teaching me how to behave, nor did I think that I was reading great literature. I just thought it was wonderfully enjoyable to enter into their imaginary worlds. I was aware, nevertheless, that it was not like the real world. I had a feeling that world must exist somewhere on the other side of the mirror. For some reason, I found those children's books also hilariously funny. I can still remember when I was reading the chapter in one of the Winnie the Pooh books—by this time I was able to read books for myself; I don't know how old I was, eight or so—reading the chapter in which Piglet meets the heffalump. "Heffalump" is the closest they could come to saying "elephant." Pooh has given up one of his jars of honey as bait. He puts the jar in a pit they have dug to trap heffalumps, but he wants to find out whether it's really honey all the way down, and so he has to taste it. He says, "Well, there might be cheese on the bottom, so I need to do a little more testing." So Pooh the bear puts his head further and further down, eats more and more of the honey, and eventually gets his head stuck in the honeypot in the pit. Then Piglet comes along and peers over the side to see whether they have caught a heffalump. And at that very moment, Pooh, with his head in the honeypot, lifts up his head, pot and all, and makes a load roaring noise of sadness and despair. Piglet is terrified. "Help! Help! A horrible heffalump, a heffable horrilump," etc. The wordplay calls attention to those words and to the alliteration, in case you hadn't noticed it. I literally fell out of my chair. I thought this was so hilariously funny. That is still one of my main sources of pleasure in literature. It's a pleasure in wordplay and irony. The Pooh books were surely written for children but also for adults. Adults would know the "heffalump" was a child's word for elephant, and so on. We adults are supposed to notice all that, but that doesn't get around the fact that I enjoyed two things: irony or wordplay and the creation through words (not through any visual images) of a totally wacky imaginary world, which you can enter only by reading that book.

That's why I like literature. Though I recognize the power of film and visual images, nevertheless, my problem with films made of novels—however good they are—is that there are all sorts of things in printed books that you can't transfer easily. There are things you can do in film that you can't as easily do in books—for example, facial expressions—but if you look at a film that's made from a novel and set one beside the other, you may say to yourself, "That's interesting. The novel is made up of a lot of words, many of which have to do with the interiority—subjectivity, consciousness—of one or another of the characters." You can't do that easily in a film. It's very awkward to say in a film what the characters think. And films, to a large degree, are made up of shots of people's faces, with not even much in the way of expressions. There's only so much you can do with film. Aspects of film are like figures of speech—montage, for example, we all know about this. Hitchcock used a lot of language and printed signs and so on that would have an ironic reference. So there are things you can do. But they go against the grain of the medium, which is to show pictures. The video game *World of Warcraft*, is also primarily—not exclusively—the exploitation of a visual medium. It shows people acting and doing things, so it has the limitations of film, however fantastic technically these new video games are. They are amazing. They are triumphs of using the medium to create landscapes and all sorts of virtual realities. So I wouldn't knock them, but I am interested in the difference.

I'm interested also in the question of why I don't find them very compelling. I don't think it's just a reaction against the violence, although that does trouble me, just as does the amount of violence shown on the evening news. We watch in my home the *NBC Evening News*. I'd have two observations about this daily half hour. One of them is be that almost half of it is made up of advertisements for poisonous nostrums. I say "poisonous" because they mostly have similar terrifying warnings: "Some people have come down with cancer, heart attack, stroke; if you have an erection lasting more than four hours, see your doctor immediately." The rhetoric of these ads is amazing, because by law they have to give these warnings. If you only listen to the warnings you'd say, "Boy, I'd die before I'd take that medicine. There are things that can happen if you take this that are lethal!" Meanwhile, what's shown in the video part of it is these happy people whose lives have been transformed for the better because they took that medicine. Such ads take up fifteen minutes out of the half hour. In the other fifteen minutes (of "news"), there are often shots of horrible violence, which are shown over and over again. How people can stand this without reacting to it beats me. People starving in South Sudan. People who've been blown up. They show the blood on the sidewalk and the mutilated corpses. So that's the other half of it. PBS, which we also watch, follows the NBC news on a different channel and isn't all that much better. *NBC Evening News* gives a distressing report about conditions in the United States today, if you read between the lines a bit: "We've got big problems in the United States these days: a very high level of poverty. A huge number of children don't get enough to eat. An unacceptably high level of unemployment. People's pensions are being reduced or eliminated. The discrepancy between rich and poor is enormous. Global warming is causing fires, floods, tornadoes." I don't have to repeat all of these things. *NBC Evening News* has a solution, however. In their "Making a Difference" segment at the end of each day's news, they suggest that doing good to your neighbor will solve everything. They do this by showing touching examples of such good doing.

MORRIS: *In* The Medium is the Maker, *you discuss telepathy as an analogy for reading—for the activities of narrators inhabiting the minds of their characters and of readers inhabiting the minds of both characters and narrators. In* The Conflagration of Community, *you write about Kafka: "Nevertheless, it almost seems as though Kafka must have had some occult telepathic premonition of what the genocide could be like, though he got the details a little garbled." This sentence extends the telepathy analogy from reading to prophecy: the author is given knowledge of future events knowable only to a later reader. Doesn't* *this procedure, which you've also called "anachronistic" reading, flaunt the fallacy Gadamer referred to as the hermeneutic circle—that readers discover or invent in texts only what they've already brought to them?*

MILLER: That remark was ironic. It was a reference to a feature of something that involves telepathy, and that is spirit mediums. You go to a medium, and the medium is supposed not only to bring your dead grandmother back to talk to you, but also to foresee the future. Fortune telling. So there's a relationship where you break through to another world. I don't happen to believe this, so that's what's ironic about it for me. It almost seems as if— said I, ironically—that Kafka had a premonition about what Auschwitz was going to be like, but of course he didn't really foresee the future.

He had some basis for guesswork about that, because of the extreme anti-Semitism in his native city and in Austria and Czechoslovakia and Germany generally. Anti-Semitism was strong at that point and was always part of that culture. So you wouldn't have had to be too prophetic in order to have foreseen something like the Shoah might happen, but I don't think anyone was likely to have foreseen the true horrors of the camps and the gas chambers. I go on to talk in my book about the facts concerning this in relation to Kafka. Kafka would almost surely have died in the camps if he hadn't died before the Nazis took over. Three of his sisters died in the Holocaust, as did other members of his family. So it's not a joke to refer to what happened to Kafka and his family and to what it was like to be a Jew in Prague at the time Kafka lived there. It's an irony to say it seems he had foreknowledge, but it's a serious irony in the sense of saying that Kafka's works reflect not only the bureaucracy in Prague—as everybody knows in *The Castle* and *The Trial*—but also indirectly, without making too much of a point about it, the situation of being a Jew in that bureaucracy, which he had experienced. So he didn't have to be a supernatural prophet to see that this was a very unstable situation and that bad things could happen. I don't think Kafka foresaw the camps, however, because at that point—1920 or so—they would have seemed so unlikely to most people and still seem so unlikely to me. (The German people were and are so civilized—Goethe, Mozart in Austria, the German Romantics, etc. Theirs is a high point of western civilization. But they became murderers big time, in a highly scientific and technological way.) The only way in which you could have had any guess that this could happen—*a* way—would have been to suffer anti-Semitism at that time and to foresee what might occur, to guess what endemic anti-Semitism might lead to.

That's all I meant, and I don't think there's a hermeneutic circle there. I stress the fact that I didn't say he *did* foresee; I said, "It almost seems as if…"

MORRIS: *Together with your self-described "political turn" since about the year 2000, there's been an accompanying "personal turn," an increasing number of autobiographical references—for example, to your ancestry (which includes supporters of the Confederacy), to your wife (whom you cited as a reference for a detective story that bore out a point you were making), to your residence in Deer Isle, Maine (and to the question whether you can be considered part of a valid "community" there). What is strange about this "personal turn" is that it coexists in texts that make clear that personal attestation must always be challenged, that identity can only be partially (and always perhaps mistakenly) known, and that identity is multiple and complex. Given this context of deep suspicion of the autobiographical, what value do you assign to its recent appearance in your writing? Is it simply an instance of de Man's observation that we can't help recommitting the errors we denounce?*

MILLER: Yes, that would be de Man's theory; it would be a good one: I can't resist doing something I say is bad. It might also be the garrulousness of old age creeping in. People tend to talk about and be interested in their pasts as they get older.

I have an enormous notebook, a folder, made by a cousin of mine with genealogies and so on, going back both to the English side and to the German side of my mother's family—she hasn't learned as much about the German side. I was brought up to believe that my real ancestry was Scots-Irish and English, with names like Rodes—without the "h"—and Hopkins. That again was a falsification. My maternal grandmother's name was Minnie Schultz, and that's not a Scots-Irish or English name. My mother's maiden name was Critzer, which is another Pennsylvania-Dutch name, so what I really am is Pennsylvania-Dutch, with all the complexities of that, with an admixture of Scots-Irish and English. And I find that interesting in my old age. But I wouldn't use this as a means of understanding or predicting what I've written as a literary critic, any more than I sympathize with so much of the work now done in cultural studies, which explains literature away by explaining the cultural position of the author. This strikes me as reductive, partly because it doesn't require any reading of the work, because you've explained it already. The author was so and so. George Eliot's *Middlemarch* is explained by the fact that she was a daughter of an estate agent, so she knew about rural class relations from somebody, her father, who was neither in the working class nor in the aristocratic class. This gave her unexampled insight into social relations in middle England. Therefore, *Middlemarch*.

It's an explanation that doesn't explain. The same reservation should be applied to me. My interest in my own ancestry is frivolous and not really related to any of the work I have written. It doesn't predict the work I've done any more than Kafka's life experience can predict *The Castle* or *The Trial* or *Amerika*, which are literary miracles. They're not explainable by any kind of autobiographical causes and are the result of amazing verbal and narrative gifts, somewhat like those of A. A. Milne, though of course in a quite different tonality. We know where Milne came from: he was a more or less ordinary highly educated Englishman and novel writer who happened to have a son. Put all of those things together and they don't explain *Winnie-the-Pooh*.

MORRIS: *So the autobiographical references in your writing could be stripped out without damage?*

MILLER: Yes. One of the things that's happened is that—more and more to my shame that I've fallen for it—people want me to talk about that sort of thing, just as you have here today. "Tell me about this change from Poulet to Burke. Is it really of major importance to you?" You didn't choose to ask me, for example, whether I still think I was right about Gerard Manley Hopkins in *The Disappearance of God*. That was less interesting to you than essentially inviting me to speak autobiographically. That happens to me all the time. Or interviewers want me to talk about theory, as in a way you have.

There are six books I'm working on now. One of them is for the "Communities in Fiction" series I mentioned, with Fordham. The second is one that I've been invited to do for a long time. I've sort of put it off. It's a collection of some of the lectures I've given in China over the years, at many different Chinese universities. I'm putting it together now; it's an enormous amount of work. Fifteen out of thirty or more lectures given in different places in China from 1988, the date of my first visit there, up until 2012. I find it interesting that most of them are on things like the future of literary studies, because that's what a given conference has tended to be about. That's what they wanted me to talk about. I've had great difficulty getting them to let me talk about anything else when I'm invited over there. I really have to push them. "Well, I really don't want to walk about theory or the future of comparative literature; I would like to do a reading of a literary work." And they say, "Well…" So I have to sneak the readings in by the back door, so to speak. One of them, for example, is an essay that I originally gave over there apropos of the question of "Literature Reading and Research," I'm dubious about World Literature for various reasons. My question was,

"What would you have to tell a Chinese audience of student-readers about a given work in the English or American literature section of an anthology of world literature?" What would they need to know, for example, in order to understand Yeats's wonderful poem "The Cold Heaven"? That gave me an opportunity to talk about that poem, to read it out loud, and to suggest a reading, but it had to have an excuse. The excuse was that I can show that such a poem wouldn't be all that easy to explain, and you'd have to explain a whole lot of things, not just one or two. But that would be equally true for an American undergraduate who has expert facility with *World of Warcraft*, or *Call of Duty*, but who knows little or nothing about English and American literature, even though she or he has been forced to read some of it.

MORRIS: *So you feel responsible for your readings of specific works and authors but not for the larger implications of your work?*

MILLER: Oh, no. I'm as happy to talk about the larger implications, and I take full responsibility for them. I prefer to do that, however, as in the case of a conference on world literature I attended in Shanghai, as a way of raising some questions about the larger context. World literature is a big thing nowadays. Think of David Damrosch. I said that it is a problem that these textbooks tend to be all in English. That is a form of imperialism. Such textbooks are used all over the world, in India and in China itself, although China more resists American intellectual imperialism than some other places do. I'm not saying that it isn't a good idea for me or for my students to have read some Chinese poems in translation or some African stories in translation. That's better than nothing. But it's not really an equivalent for reading such works in the original and from inside the culture. Most textbooks in world literature represent a tiny sample from each country. The segments are like representing English literature by a scene from *Hamlet*, a poem by Wordsworth, maybe a poem by Tennyson along the way, and a poem by Yeats. That's almost as close as you get by representing Chinese literature with a few poems from the *Classic of Poetry* and a chapter from *The Dream of the Red Chamber*. People spend their whole lives studying Chinese literary works! So there's the problem of translation and representation. The choices that you make are crucial and inevitably beg a lot of questions. I'm not saying World Literature as a discipline shouldn't happen, but that people should be self-conscious about what is problematic about it.

I believed in what I was saying in my lecture called "Cold Heaven, Cold Comfort: Should We Read or Teach Literature Now?" It was given in September 2010 at a conference about "Literature Reading and Research" in

Guanzhou, PRC. I was very earnest in the generalizations I made. But it did also give me an opportunity to do what I really most like to do, which is to talk about works of literature, in this case Yeats's "The Cold Heaven":

> Suddenly I saw the cold and rook-delighting heaven
> That seemed as though ice burned and was but the more ice...

It's a marvelous and very moving poem. What I hoped to do was transmit some of my enthusiasm to my listeners in the Guangzhou University of Foreign Studies. (Guangzhou is the current name of what used to be called Canton by Westerners; it's no longer called Canton).

So, that's my response to that.

MORRIS: *Your work has often made use of the concept of nothingness. In* Poets of Reality, *we read of a "nothingness" behind the signs of Stevens's poems. In* Black Holes, *zero becomes a name for what Derrida calls the* tout autre. *In* Zero Plus One, *the zero of mathematics is discussed in the work of Blanchot, Iser, and de Man. Amalgamating de Man and Derrida, you hold that zero has two referents: first, as a placeholder in a mathematical series; second, as an unnamable emptiness. You claim that the second sense of zero may function in the same way de Man's definition of irony does, as the element heterogeneous to the system that gives rise to it.*

In the history of philosophy, the second sense of nothingness may have been derived in part from the contemplation of empty space—as in the source of Pascal's fear of those "infinite empty spaces"; however, in concepts such as vacuum fluctuations or the Higgs boson, physics has recently asked us to rethink that concept of nothingness as not an absolute emptiness, after all, but as a place of instability and invisible matter. If physics succeeds in destroying the second referent of zero, would there be any longer an element heterogeneous to the system of numeric signs that gives rise to it? Would the literature, philosophy, and literary criticism that invoke it become untenable?

MILLER: That's an interesting and complicated question. At bottom, it's a question of the relevance of scientific references in the humanities. Scientists are quite reasonably suspicious of that—as, for example, the famous Sokal hoax. What he wanted to show was that people in the humanities don't have the slightest idea of rational cogency or of science.

I would make a distinction—a distinction with some permeable borders—between the zero in mathematics, on the one hand, and, on the other hand, information that physicists give us as to whether space is empty or not. Whether there's nothing out there. The zero in mathematics is to a considerable degree an artifact of a system of numbers which may or may not have any relation whatsoever to the real world.

A friend of mine in England, Julian Wolfreys, said he was doing a glossary of critical terms, and he'd lost his "zero person." Would I quickly write something about it? So I got into it. What did I know about zero? I found its history and the concept itself fascinating. It comes from the Arabs, apparently, perhaps by way of Spain. We didn't have zero in European mathematics until the Renaissance. (There are different stories about how it got into our mathematics. And that's interesting in itself; there's a history.) We wouldn't have computers unless we had zero. Computers depend on the binary, zero-and-one opposition. I was interested in all that. Whether it has anything at all to do with emptiness in literature or not or is purely figurative is another question. There's plenty of talk about solitude and emptiness in literature, but that doesn't necessarily have anything to do with zero in mathematics. It might or might not, depending a little bit on who was using the term. What might be more interesting would be the question of why people who write poems and plays and novels need the concept of emptiness or zero. You don't really need mathematics to study that question, though it might help. It depends a little on whether the author in question knew anything about mathematics. De Man did. So your question is a complicated one, but I don't think we can take for granted the transferability of the meaning of this word from one context to another without remembering that it's a figurative transference.

So, I'm going to stay on the side of the scientists who are very suspicious of the loose use by humanists of terms that they borrow in a freehand way from science, without remembering that there's a difference.

MORRIS: *Wouldn't you agree that a constant throughout your career has been valorization of figures of ungroundedness like oscillation, hovering, or equipoise? Haven't you consistently admired writing that expressed a simultaneity of antithetical statements or seemed to defy the law of noncontradiction and invoke these figures as a means of capturing it? For example, in* Poets of Reality, *you write that Stevens's late poetry "is full of things which are neither quite one thing nor quite another, but are poised halfway in an unlikely equilibrium." In* Fiction and Repetition, *you write that Virginia Woolf's* Between the Acts *affirms three contradictory possibilities and that the reader cannot master this "oscillation" in the text. Fast forward. Your later work invokes Derrida's notion that the words of literature "hang in the air and keep an impenetrable secret or secrets". In* The Conflagration of Community, *you praise Nancy's thesis/antithesis without sublation, which produces "a suspended or hovering self-cancelation."*

First, does your frequent use of this figure across your career amount to what Paul de Man called "aesthetic ideology"? Is oscillation "sublime"? Second, the mention of de Man brings up a variant of this figure that may reflect your fraught, arms-length relationship with his writing. As an example of de Man's "allergenic" element, you cite his penchant for "climactic, mind-twisting, generalizing affirmation," which you say "hangs in the air alone, validated primarily by de Man's own say-so." But why should a figure of hovering be praiseworthy in the case of Stevens, Woolf, and Derrida but suspicious in the case of de Man?

MILLER: My praise of oscillation might be an ideology, an unwarranted presupposition or giving high marks to indecisiveness. But aesthetic ideology as I understand it—let's say Warminski's definition on the basis of reading so much de Man—is precisely the opposite: it's associated very firmly with things like organic unity. A good work is going to be organically unified. Everything is going to fit. That doesn't exonerate my high marks for suspension perhaps from being an ideological presupposition, but I don't think you can tar what I say about de Man with that particular feather, since I meant to be praising him not to be expressing a suspicion of him.

Why am I interested in that sort of suspension between irreconcilable opposites? It doesn't mean that I'm necessarily right to find this everywhere, but my target is organic unity. It's been the suspicion that I've had ever since my Hopkins days when I used to argue with Earl Wasserman, my close colleague at Hopkins. For him, a work of literature was not good unless he could show that every part of it hangs together as a coherent "organic unity"—that was his term. That was the term people at Yale also used in the heyday of the New Criticism. I had an instinctive suspicion about that, I think because my empirical experience was that there are works of literature— seemingly good works, powerful and persuasive in allowing me, *Wuthering Heights,* for example, access to an imaginary world that's distinctive and interesting—that have passages that seem important but which can't be fitted in to any organic unity scheme that I can imagine. And that struck me as interesting. Wasserman's response in effect was to say, "Well, I can make it fit." So we had endless arguments about that. I certainly would admit that the organic unity presupposition is heuristically very powerful. It drives the reader to try to make everything fit and to recognize things that are important. I also question, however, whether logic—for example, in the sense of the excluded middle or in the sense of a progressive dialectic— necessarily works for literature. Our minds are trained by philosophy and by a general tradition of rationality to think in terms of patterns like dialectical synthesis, so we assume that a good work of literature is likely to dramatize some antitheses that are eventually reconciled. Why should that be the case? Literature is not philosophy; it's not necessarily logical. So, I resisted these presuppositions in order to defend what I saw as the multitudinousness of given works of literature, in all kinds of ways—multiple plots that can't really be synthesized, characters that can't really be judged as simply good or bad but are somewhere in between, systems of figurative language in which you can show the same figures are related and recur but that they can't be put together in a pattern that makes logical sense. To some degree, my target was my own earlier work—for example, the Ph.D. dissertation on Dickens, where I wanted to show that everything hangs together in a Dickens novel. I demonstrated that with citations. A lot of your questions remind me, for better or for worse, of my skepticism about the relationship between theoretical formulations and what you actually find in a work of literature. So I take pleasure in finding those things that are important but don't fit.

Your second question?

MORRIS: *It seemed that you were blaming de Man for what you in other contexts valorized.*

MILLER: No, I don't think I was blaming him. I was trying to define what one finds when one reads de Man, or when I read de Man, at any rate. That is, that these formulations—like, "One sees from this that the impossibility of reading should not be taken too lightly"—are funny and ironic but that they don't seem to follow logically, at least not on a superficial look, from what has come before. They're surprising. And they're meant to be some form of summary of what he's been saying, or they're meant to be earned by the argumentation of the early part of the essay. But even with the whole essay read carefully, they're not transparent or predictable conclusions. Why shouldn't the impossibility of reading be taken lightly? I can go on reading and can make sense of what I read. I don't think I was criticizing de Man. I was just characterizing him. In fact, I think these formulations are an important part of the brilliant rhetorical strategies of de Man's essays.

The simplest response might be that recently—I didn't use to do this much at all—I've found myself rereading Paul de Man and following his advice about taking the impossibility of reading seriously. For example, the rhetorical strategy of his essays differs a lot from Derrida's. Derrida tends to start an essay or a seminar by making some kind of apodictic and puzzling statement (like the short first paragraph of "White Mythology"), which then the whole seminar gradually explains, whereas de Man's tends to begin beguilingly by summarizing previous criticism, which is what you're taught to do, by a tradition of graduate school term papers and so on, and then showing through actual readings—who could object to this as a procedure?—in effect (and explicitly, at least in one case that's famous for me) what it actually says. I'm thinking of his essay on Benjamin's "The Task of the Translator." De Man recapitulates what other people have said about that essay and then asks, "What does Benjamin say? What does he say, in the most immediate sense possible?" And that seems innocent. He persuades you that he has no presuppositions; he's just looking at the text, and who could object to doing that? Then of course he finds that the essay says something entirely different from what the critics have made it say. That, heuristically, is extremely powerful. De Man shows how previous critics are wrong by looking at specific passages and making readings of them that you can try to challenge, but only with difficulty. De Man was very difficult to challenge. I know this from having watched people in his seminars try to do that, without much success. For better or for worse, he was very powerful in arguments. Then the essays tend to culminate in one of those general formulations. That's the rhetorical strategy, and I think he gets away with it.

So I found myself saying, "Well, let's turn the tables on de Man. Let's look at one of his famous essays and see if we can decide what Paul de Man actually says." The essay that has interested me recently—it's a somewhat arbitrary choice—is the one called "The Resistance to Theory." It's an interesting de Man essay because it makes a lot of turns and twists and ends up by saying, "Theory is the resistance to theory," an extremely counterintuitive formulation. De Man's strategy was to go through a process of reading that made counterintuitive formulations plausible. Like the one about the materiality of language. They tend to come at the end, not at the beginning. If you attended his seminars, as I did for quite a while, you knew that the whole two hours (or more than two hours, because he tended to run over) was going to be for the sake of something said quietly at the very end, not at the beginning. It was something worked toward very slowly and scrupulously.

So I don't think I was criticizing de Man. I have discovered that in "The Resistance to Theory" if you set out to figure out what he actually says, you find it ain't all that easy. And again, most of the generalizations about that essay, as about de Man generally, aren't really quite on the mark. Few people read de Man at all anymore in any case. The discovery of his wartime writings has worked as an excuse for not reading him. He tends these days not to appear in any of the essays I evaluate for journals. Derrida is beginning to disappear, too. Reading de Man is hard work. I heard the "The Resistance to Theory" lecture when he presented it at Yale. The one that was transcribed from a tape and then published was the version that he gave at Cornell. Interesting questions were asked afterward by Meyer Abrams, Dominick La Capra, Neil Hertz, and others. They are included in the published transcription, with de Man's answers. The version I heard at Yale, the same lecture, wasn't written down either. One of the extraordinary things about de Man was he could produce as a splendid public lecture something that he had been too lazy or dilatory to write down, something that was extremely complicated and exigent in its connections from one place to another. The people at Yale were smart enough to be driven up the wall by that lecture. There were people in the room—Peter Demetz, for example, and others—who were Benjamin specialists. They were smart enough to see that if de Man was right, their work on Benjamin was wrong. It happens that it *was* wrong. Criticism of Benjamin generally tends to oversimplify and to make him more positive than he really was. He's a very complicated, tricky kind of writer, so that to try to get something positive for cultural studies or for a theory of translation out of Benjamin, you've got to do some distortion, and de Man was in effect pointing that out. I don't think literature and theory or criticism are the same thing by any means because criticism is a reading of some text, in this case a work of theory by Walter Benjamin, whereas when writing a work of literature you are much more on your own.

All I was saying was that these enigmatic statements de Man makes don't appear to follow logically from what he said up to that point, and in that sense, they hang in the air. By the way, "The Resistance to Theory" essay interests me partly because it was rejected by the Modern Language Association. That's a wonderful story. Here they had this masterwork of modern theory that they could have published, but I can see why they didn't. They were smart enough to see that it was very uneasy-making. So they were able to say, "It doesn't do what we want." And what they got in the essay by another scholar that was finally published was an objective survey of different critical movements. What de Man wrote for them was a serious essay about literary theory. That essay has what for me is an absolutely crucial de Man passage, which I've quoted quite frequently and worry about. In a way, "The Resistance to Theory" is an attempt to explain this passage that comes quite early in the essay, the definition of ideology: "what we call ideology is precisely the confusion of linguistic with natural reality, of reference with phenomenalism," and so on to the end of the paragraph. That passage strikes me as very helpful. It explains something that to me is a big puzzle. How can politicians—for me, as a progressive, much more often Republicans than Democrats, though both of them do this—get people to believe lies, contrary-to-fact statements. And the answer is that's what ideology *is*: its belief in something that is not true. And politicians do this by the manipulation of figures of speech, the aboriginal error of getting people to take figurative statements literally. Often they are taken in by their own errors.

A good example is an argument that seems so plausible—that it's wrong for the United States government to run up big deficits because the situation would be just like in a family, where you wouldn't want to go in debt. So people think, "Gee, you're right. You get into big trouble if you can't pay your bills, and then you must borrow more money, and then you go bankrupt." But the two are not analogous. The federal government is not like a family. For one thing, it can print money, which you and I can't do in our households. Except for your friend Stephen Burroughs; he didn't have any trouble. Counterfeiting is a good example: a figure of speech that's like real currency that you try to get people to take literally. And de Man's writing has been a tremendous help in getting me to understand that process. The formulation I've cited is quite compacted and enigmatic. The rest of the essay helps you to understand it. I've recently written a long essay trying to figure out what de Man really says in "The Resistance to Theory."

A final comment on this. People are annoyed by the difficulty of Derrida and de Man. "Oh, I tried to read Derrida, and it just didn't seem to be worth it." That's their business, and the same thing, even more, could be said about de Man. He's *not* easy to understand. And it's not because it's not understandable; it's just that it takes a lot of effort. So people say, "It must be gobbledygook, because I don't understand it." That's a mistake. There are two areas I can name in a minute where difficulty reigns and where people in general don't assume that this means it must not make sense.

One is science, where it's not at all intuitively understandable that the bitter cold weather and deep snow we've been having recently is a concomitant of global warming. Why is that vortex coming down from Canada? It's because there used to be a barrier in the form of the arctic ice. Now that the arctic ice is vanishing, that arctic cold air can come down into Canada, and then the jet stream carries it down into the United States. So people who deny climate change would say, "That doesn't make sense. It's three degrees below zero. Come on, don't tell me anything about global warming." Nevertheless it's a perfectly routine, logical, scientific argument, which is hard to understand. It entails a lot of physics, a lot of stuff having to do with the air, air temperatures, and reflections from polar ice. (The whiteness is gone so the water now absorbs polar sunshine.) It's a complicated scientific argument, which some people would have trouble understanding, but most people would not say that means it can't be true. (Still, the other day Rush Limbaugh did claim that all this stuff about the polar vortex is a hoax, a plot on the part of the left wing.)

The other place where difficulty reigns is literature itself. Anybody who says Shakespeare is easy to understand and assumes that if it's literature I must be able to understand it easily talking through their hat. It's not. You could spend your whole life trying to figure out what's going on in *Hamlet*. Or in *As You Like It*, as far as that goes. Literature—including all generally prized canonical literature and also newer uncanonical literature—is difficult, at *least* as difficult as Paul de Man, and probably more so. Just try to explain T. S. Eliot's "Gerontion" to someone who doesn't catch its multitudinous allusions and its other challenging linguistic features.

MORRIS: *I have two questions about a passage in* Speech Acts in Literature *where you've been describing Derrida's writing as a "doing what he talks about." You then put a question to yourself that you don't answer, in this book or others: just how, I ask, do marks turn into forces?…This process seems to me extremely mysterious and problematic…Names* can *hurt you. But just how does that happen? How do little marks on paper or trivial modulations of air, ripples that would not even cause a leaf to tremble, come to have earthshaking physical effects, as when the right person in the right circumstances says, "I declare war," or when I say "I love you" and am believed?…This mystery is the secret transference from meaningful marks to physical force that makes it possible to do things with words. Is this transference after all no more than a metaphor…? First, if future researchers wanted to get an answer to this question, what discipline should they be working in? Psychology? Linguistics? Philosophy? Genetics? Second, you stake your readings, of James, Kafka, and others, on the operation of language as performative; however, you are unable to explain how this operation takes place. What distinguishes your work from a negative theology that would ask readers to accept the performative "on faith" or as just another theotrope? What gives the performative an ontological status superior to that of the ego, the class struggle, gender, God, etc.?*

MILLER: I don't think there's a lot of deep mystery about the performative effectiveness of speech acts. It's not a matter of taking something on faith; it's a matter of empirical evidence that in fact reading and exposure to other signs does have effects in the real world. I don't see that anybody could deny that, partly because of the people who claim plausibly that this is the case. An example would be Paul Ryan reading Ayn Rand's *Atlas Shrugged* in high school or early college. Somebody told him to read this, and according to him—I see no reason to doubt this—it changed his life. What's the evidence for this? The positions he holds as a politician come straight out of Ayn Rand. He's attempting to institute her ideas of the struggle for survival, etcetera, and he says so. I don't see that there's any reason to doubt that he has been deeply influenced by reading a book and that it has determined his whole career.

MORRIS: *But you can't say* how *it happens.*

MILLER: Ah, now the "how." Well, I might call on our friend Henry Staten, who has a theory called "physio-psychology." And the argument is that the human body is essentially energy, an energy with desires to survive like animals do, and so on. And that psychology and physiology are closely related. Alexander Bain said so. Nietzsche said so. You don't need cognitive science to tell you that. Plenty of theoretical and even measurable evidence exists for the way words work, on the body and on bodily energy, and then actually doing things, including saying other things, like Paul Ryan does. That makes an I-don't-think-particularly-mysterious linkage between reading and its absorption into the individual's psychology which is related to physiology, which then drives a kind of life force or energy.

So that's really quite old-fashioned. That instigates me to say that I find the current vogue of cognitive science among people who do cultural studies and so on suspicious, because a lot of this depends on supposed scientific evidence that doesn't seem to me to prove anything very much. For example, there are a lot of people who want to find out what happens to the body and the brain when you read. And this consists, as far as I can tell, primarily of connecting electrodes to people's heads and saying, "Oh, look. He's reading page 350 of *Middlemarch* and these parts of his brain light up." I have no doubt that is true, but so what? I cannot see that that proves anything except that that segment of your brain lights up. In other words, part of my response to your question is to say that the search for scientific evidence for this—in a lot of senses of "scientific"—may be barking up the wrong tree, at least so far. It's much easier to believe that I read Ayn Rand's *Atlas Shrugged* and then seriously the ideas I've encountered there in my mind, which is connected to my body, and this leads me to spend a huge amount of energy trying to bring into existence Ayn Rand's ideas. I don't see that that's mysterious, and it doesn't go by way of which parts of my brain light up when I read *Atlas Shrugged.* It doesn't need that.

MORRIS: *If you hold that—whatever the shortcomings of cognitive science now—ultimately there will be an explanation in science for answering the question you asked but didn't answer in* Speech Acts, *then it would be correct to say that you're an empiricist.*

MILLER: Yes, in this case, though I don't like being pigeon-holed. I'm arguing from the fact that it manifestly happens, this connection that means speech acts—some of them—make things happen in the real world. That's a little different from the purely Austinian conventionality of speech acts, like "I now pronounce you man and wife," where the performative efficacy depends on the context. Like that little problem in Utah: are those same sex couples married or not? Utah says no, the federal government says yes, and these sayings would or would not be felicitous speech acts depending on whether or not they were recognized as having legal authority. In that sense, they're a fiction. All that's happened is that somebody in the right situation has uttered the words. Whether they are married depends on a complicated context. That's also true of reading Ayn Rand. It's not quite so simple; it's reinforced by a lot of other things for Paul Ryan that may have turned him into an Ayn Randian. That it actually has political felicity depends on his getting elected and there being other Ayn Randians—the whole context of the Tea Party.

MORRIS: *Then the language of science can refer accurately to the process of assimilation, to the converting of marks into behavior, and at some point science will be able to answer this question as to how marks become forces?*

MILLER: Yes, I suppose so, though I'm not holding my breath. And I've done my best to answer your questions without appeal to cognitive science and neuroscience and so on, partly because neuroscience at this point is so primitive. Making such an appeal would be a good example of people outside the field appropriating things from inside the field in a way that's dubious. An example of this would be the so-called mirror neurons, which are supposed to give us sympathetic understanding of what the other person is thinking. Now, I tried this out on my granddaughter, who has a Ph.D. from Brandeis in neuroscience, and her response was interesting. She said, "Yes, that was a while ago. It's a disproved theory." Still, there's been a huge amount of literature—because it's consoling—that tells me that I really have a kind of understanding of what the other person is thinking because the theory of mirror neurons tells me so. Meanwhile, neuroscience is doing some more empirical investigation and discovering that this was a false lead. So, you want to be careful about basing a whole social or psychological theory on evidence from science, because science tends to develop and to show that previous ideas were wrong. Suppose we still believed that the sun goes around the earth—it does, in a sense, if you look at it from the right perspective.

MORRIS: *In other interviews, you've spoken of de Man nearing death saying ruefully that he hadn't changed Yale "one iota" or of Leo Spitzer after retirement saying that, despite his long list of publications, "I'm nothing." Your replies to them protested against their gloomy self-assessments; still, they raise larger issues about academic writing today. Bill Readings's* The University in Ruins *argues that the modern university is no longer able to name the objects of its inquiry. If his diagnosis is at all plausible (and setting aside for a moment his Lyotardian prescriptions), aren't there even more grounds today for the pessimism of de Man and Spitzer as they reflected on their lifelong work?*

MILLER: Two or three things to say about that, and I'll try to do it as briefly as possible. One would be to say that the humanities side of universities and colleges these days is in some difficulty, because there are many fewer jobs than candidates. Moreover, a rapid shift is taking place toward cultural studies away from literary studies. Even people who are called professors of English often don't really study English literature; they study cultural studies, of which literature is a minor part. One of my theories about why the change from old-fashioned literary studies to cultural studies was so prompt and uncontroversial is that by that time, nobody cared. The people in charge of universities, usually scientists, viewed the humanities over there with the attitude "They can do whatever they want. It has no serious import." I've often quoted some high administrator at Harvard—I think it was Larry Summers when he was president of Harvard, at any rate somebody there— as saying, "The humanities are a lost cause." I think what he meant was, "We've got a big research university here, gigantic amounts of resources, endowments, and money coming in like anything, and what's going on over in the humanities doesn't really matter. They can do whatever they like." And that's an argument for giving them less and less money.

So I'm glad that I'm not in charge of a humanities division, as my friend Georges van den Abbeele is. (He's now the Dean of Humanities at Irvine.) He's got a real problem. To some degree, it's the professors with the best will in the world who are changing the orientation of research. A lot of disagreement exists from one university to another about what cultural studies really mean and what people ought to be hired. There's a laudable need now to hire people who do minority studies and world literature, even though it's outside the narrow bounds of English literature. However, the situation hasn't settled back down again yet to any widespread consensus. That may be all to the good. There was a time, at Hopkins, when I could have told you exactly what you need to learn in order to become a professor of Victorian literature—which courses you need to take, what things you need to read, and so on. That's no longer the case. I could also have told you what social and personal good it was to study English literature. It taught you the ethos of your country, which you learned by studying the literature of a foreign country, so reading English literature taught you how to be a good American. A clear contradiction there! I don't think anybody believes any longer that reading *Middlemarch* is going to make you a good American. (It was English literature in those days; American literature didn't really count for much.) But it all made sense, even if it reflected many prejudices. During the nineteen years I was at Hopkins, the English department didn't have a single tenured woman. Not one. So I think the revolution that's brought women in has been long overdue. Now there are lots of women in English departments, including the Hopkins one, but there are other problems at this point that can't entirely be blamed on the fact that public universities, supported by states, are generally in bad shape financially. States certainly have less money to invest in education, or have until recently. And the fact that the money had dried up gives administrators an excuse to rearrange things the way they want. All the talk is of the need for more and better science, math, and engineering. The humanities haven't been faring very well in that atmosphere. So that's the gloomy side of it.

The opposite side of it, I think, needs to be equally stressed. I read lots of manuscripts—book manuscripts and journal manuscripts that presses, editors, and authors send me from all over the world—and I continue to be absolutely amazed by the high quality of these essays. I don't necessarily always agree with them, either methodologically or in their conclusions. Still, the amount of intellectual energy and commitment, both to teaching and to scholarship, that continues to exist in the humanities is to me amazing, because much of this work is done by adjuncts, who have no security, no pensions, few if any benefits, and so on. Over seventy percent of teaching across the disciplines in American colleges and universities is done by adjuncts these days. The adjuncts in the humanities, overworked and ill-paid, go on writing brilliant essays and books. That fact should never be forgotten. An example is a really wonderful book written by a longtime adjunct at Chapman College in Orange County, Cristina Vischer Bruns. Bruns's book *Why Literature? The Value of Literary Reading and What It*

Means for Teaching is about teaching literature in the current situation. It is based on her experience doing this year after year at Chapman. It's a book as good as Mark Edmundson's books about teaching the humanities. Mark Edmundson is a distinguished professor at the University of Virginia who's written very good books about the humanities—what ought to be taught and so forth—but *her* book is equally good and persuasive. She's been down there in the trenches for ten or fifteen years—actually *teaching* in—today's circumstances and in a less elite place than Virginia. Bruns's book is well-written; it's very smart; it's very balanced—it's a wonderful book. And I mentioned an essay on Walter Pater that I've just been reading. It's a great essay. The author knows all of the Pater secondary literature. She knows Pater very well. Who cares at this point about Pater, except as a part of queer studies? The essay grows out of queer studies, so it has that energy behind it, but goes well beyond that context.

So, talk about suspended contradictions! Conditions today make it extremely difficult for good work to be done: books in the humanities sell practically no copies; they're very expensive. Henry Staten's book (*Spirit Becomes Matter: The Brontës, George Eliot, Nietzsche*, Edinburgh University Press) will probably sell in hard cover for $200. Who's going to have that much money? It's another wonderful book. There will be, I hope, a paperback and an e-text, because a couple of years ago Amazon announced that they were selling more e-texts than printed books. That's a big transformation. So e-texts really matter. But I don't expect my new book for Fordham (*Communities in Fiction*) will sell a lot of copies. It will be read by some people, but if I had to live on my royalties I would be much thinner—thinner than I am. On the other hand, that's what I love to do, and I go on doing it, but so do a lot of people who are in much worse purely human circumstances than I am, who have to face year after year first-year students who are ill-prepared and who are in the writing course because they have to be, not because they want to learn to write well—that is a *very* hard teaching situation, and many, many young people (and some older people) go on heroically doing such teaching. They are my heroes, these people. It would be nice if their situation were better.

These wonderful essays that people now are writing—often adjuncts in a bad situation in every way—*are* published. A tremendous proliferation of journals is occurring, all over the world. I happen to be involved with some of them in places like Australia. *Derrida Today* comes from Australia. And in England, new journals are appearing in great numbers. That's interesting, because you'd think that the economic situation would make it impossible to start a new journal. They seem, however, to carry prestige in universities and colleges; money for them is available. A big proliferation of online journals is also taking place. My good Australian friend Sigi Jöttkandt is running the Open Humanities Press. OHP is a big operation that gives its imprimatur to online journals of all sorts. They have to be vetted by a committee to be sure they are using peer review, etc. OHP also publishes books now. These are available online as well as in on-demand hard copies from the University of Michigan Press. The new book that Tom Cohen, Claire Colebrook, and I are doing, which is to some degree on de Man and theory, will be the third book I've been involved in that will be published online by the Open Humanities Press. The other is a small collection of my essays over recent years being translated into German by a gifted professor at the University of Konstanz, Monika Reif Hülser. The Open Humanities Press was anxious to spread out and do some works in languages other than English. This book is part of the internationalization or globalization of what's going on in the humanities.

So, one can exaggerate the degree to which the humanities are in terrible difficulty. They're flourishing in a sense, and they're in a rapid period of transition, not necessarily a bad thing. It's reassuring that not only are there a lot of bright people teaching and even writing things, but what they write gets circulated. People have an opportunity to read it.

So my response is double, to your question. The university is in ruins, as Bill Readings said, but it goes on flourishing in the ruins.

MORRIS: *The origin of your career in Victorianism reminds me of a story you told at the School of Criticism and Theory at Dartmouth about Matthew Arnold's visit to your alma mater, Oberlin, to deliver a lecture. Apparently, Oberlin was a dry campus at the time. Nevertheless, Arnold requested whisky, and when it arrived, it came with a teaspoon. That story frames you as a kind of inheritor of Arnold and him as a man for whom balances between restraint and intoxication, scholar and gypsy, were always in play but subordinated to the mission of writing criticism as a moral enterprise. More than Derrida, more than de Man, Poulet, or Kenneth Burke, could it be said that your true godfather is Arnold, the man who urged more "sweetness and light," the man of disbelief who nevertheless wrote literary and cultural criticism as a means of temporizing, of stalling for time, in hopes of keeping the door open for future generations who might someday be able to solve these insoluble problems?*

MILLER: Oberlin was, by the way, still dry when I was a student there from 1944 to 1948. Well, I would be greatly honored if people thought that I could write at all like Matthew Arnold. By the way, here's the rest of that story. He didn't ask for the whisky at the lecture. He was staying at the president's house at Oberlin. The maid asked him if there was anything he needed before he went to bed, and he said he'd like some whisky. That's when she brought the bottle of whisky with the teaspoon. She thought of it as medicinal. So that's a good metaphor for the disjunct at the time between Arnold and Oberlin.

That reminds me of the fact that the first humanities course I took at Oberlin when I entered in 1944—I don't suppose such courses are given in many places any more—was a required freshman course essentially in Victorian prose. Everybody had to take it. You read Huxley, Arnold, Newman. The notion was that these Victorian prose worthies would teach you something about what a college or university education was good for. That was the emphasis. That's why we read Newman (not Newman's sermons, but Newman's *The Idea of a University*). That's interesting. The people in charge at Oberlin thought that it was good for everybody to read not only Arnold but also Huxley and Newman. (I don't remember if Ruskin was included; Ruskin would have been included at Yale in a similar course.) So all around in American colleges and universities in the period before the New Criticism, the required freshman course was often a course in Victorian prose. That would be almost unthinkable now. It was ostensibly a course in writing as well as in the idea of what a university is, so these writers were presented as models of prose to imitate. Just try it. Try to write like Newman or Arnold! They're so suave and clever, so masterful in style, and so different from one another in manner of writing.

So for you to compare anything I write to Arnold's writing is high praise indeed, even though there sure is a lot of nonsense in Arnold, as I would see it now. This nonsense is especially connected to the idea that he, Matthew Arnold, can tell you what is the best which has been thought and said in the world. Come on, Matthew, how do you know what that is? For Arnold, it was Greek, especially Greek more than Latin, but also Latin literature as a kind of basis for becoming educated. But as I asked in one of my early essays on Arnold, how do you tell whether something is the genuine best, the best that has been thought and said in the world? Look at Arnold's "touchstone" essay, "The Study of Poetry" (1880). "I, Matthew Arnold, will now give you some examples." He calls these as touchstones. A touchstone, as you know, was a way of telling whether a given lump was a genuine piece of gold, because it would make a mark on the touchstone. All of Arnold's examples are of suffering and loss. That's interesting. It betrays something about Arnold that you would not necessarily think until you looked at his touchstone passages. One is Helen's speech in the *Iliad* about her brothers Castor and Polydeuces. She assumes they are both still alive, but they are both dead: "they ere now were fast holden of the life-giving earth there in Lacedaemon." Or Hamlet's dying words: "Absent thee from felicity awhile…" And so on with the other touchstones. If you just go through Arnold's citations, you can see that his examples are not innocent. Arnold doesn't admit that, but he inadvertently betrays his assumption about what is really powerful in poetry, what would be a touchstone. If it's like Dante or like Shakespeare or like Homer in the passages he cites, then it really counts. And I would find that argument dubious. Why should all good poetry be about suffering and loss?

On the other hand—and this will be my final remark about this—I have always from the beginning attempted to write my essays with a likely audience in mind, an audience primarily of students and younger faculty, because I think it's maybe too late to change many older faculty. I know it's too late for anybody to try to help me, at any rate. What I want is to be read by younger people. I want to write as clearly and persuasively and powerfully as I can for them, to convey to them primarily the joy I have in reading literature. One unintended result of this is that—as opposed to whatever one says about Derrida and de Man, who *are* hard to understand—people can understand what I say and are likely to notice things that they wouldn't have noticed in Derrida because they wouldn't understand what he was saying as well. They do understand what I'm saying, and they say, "What? You can't really mean this!" So the unintended consequence is that some of these ideas, like some of the ones you've asked me about, like the idea of suspended contradictions— you didn't even utter the word *undecidability*, that was piece of reticence on your part—people know what I'm talking about when I say that, whereas with Derrida they might miss it. And de Man's work, for better or for worse, contains relatively few passages about actual works of literature. There are some, for example, on Baudelaire. There's an essay about Hölderlin's poems, but it is called "Heidegger's Exegeses of Hölderlin." Its goal is through close reading of passages in Hölderlin's poems to show that "*it is the fact that Hölderlin says exactly the opposite of what Heidegger makes him say*" (de Man's emphasis). De Man's remarks on literature tend to come along with theoretical discussions rather than being upfront readings of literary works.

So, yes, that's what I most want to do. I think that it's partly a matter of growing older—you lose touch with younger people or feel that you do—but it's partly because the younger people really are different now. It's much harder to persuade them that they ought to rush home and read Trollope's *The Last Chronicle of Barset*. It was easier earlier to assume that doing that was going to make some difference. I think that's less the case now, for reasons I tried earlier to give, having to do with video games and the rest of it. So that's a double answer to that.

I was reading some Matthew Arnold just the other day, because I needed to find the phrase "the best which has been thought and said in the world," and I couldn't quite remember where it was. I thought it was in *Culture and Anarchy*, so I got the book down, but I couldn't find it. So I went online, and of course *Culture and Anarchy* is available in two or three different e-text versions. I googled and found it in a minute. One of the places where the phrase is used is in the "Preface" to the 1869 edition. So I acquired almost instantly what you might call "spurious learning." The Internet is good at giving you that. I could then refer back to the page number in the standard R. H. Super edition of *Culture and Anarchy*. I've become more and more conscientious about putting URLs in. I put down the URL in this case because I knew that readers these days, such as I, are much more likely to go to an Internet e-text of *Culture and Anarchy* than they are to have it on their shelves or to be willing to go to the library and take it out. I give the URL, and then they can check on the citation if they want. I think most people these days know how to do this even better than I do.

MORRIS: *Our interview in Sedgwick ended with that response. Later I sent you a supplementary question: "Do you think your reading of Gerard Manley Hopkins in* The Disappearance of God *is correct? When I re-read your response on page nine of the interview, I thought you cited this question as an example the kind you wished an interviewer would ask—as opposed to questions, say, about the turns in your career, the future of the profession, your personal life, theory, etc. Personally, I like the idea of your reaffirming your early work, which I continue to admire even after the turns that followed."*

MILLER: You have called my bluff. The answer is yes and no. (Another suspended contradiction!) Yes, on the one hand, I think I understood Hopkins well at that time and could show the hanging together of his ideas in his prose and in his poetic practice as well as the evolution of these through his life as a writer. I think I was right about inscape, instress, *haecceitas*, pitch, selving, and the rest of his key ideas, along with their systematic interconnection. It's a theological system, of course, and has the usual fissures and inconsistencies of such systems, but it is extremely impressive nevertheless in its attempt to balance Scotus and Loyola. I had for some years read Hopkins with great intellectual as well as emotional exhilaration, initially the poems, for example, "The Windhover": "I caught this morning morning's minion, king- / dom of daylight's dauphin, dapple-dawn-drawn Falcon, in his riding…" Or the opening two lines of "Spelt from Sibyl's Leaves": "Earnest, earthless, equal, attuneable, ' vaulty, voluminous…

stupendous / Evening strains to be tímes vást, ' womb-of-all, home-of-all, hearse-of-all night." Wow! So I wanted to understand the poems that moved me so much, and I think I succeeded in explaining them in their context of Hopkins's other writing.

On the other hand, I certainly would not write an essay on Hopkins in the same way now, as a progression from one stage to another illustrated by citations taken out of context. I'd be more likely to see those "stages" as unresolved conflicts, "undecidabilities." Just understanding Hopkins's "system," moreover, did not and does not make me a Catholic, much as I admire Catholic thought. Nor do that book and all those essays I have written about Thomas Hardy's works mean that I "agree" with Hardy's worldview. My criticism is a complex kind of role-playing, but without the total uncritical adherence Georges Poulet calls for in his "criticism of consciousness." I retain, always, a degree of critical distance. Hopkins says in his *Commentary on the Spiritual Exercises of St. Ignatius Loyola* that each self, each "self-taste," is unique, "more distinctive than ale or alum, more distinctive than the smell of walnutleaf or camphor, and is incommunicable by any means to another man (as when I was a child I used to ask myself: What must it be to be someone else?). Nothing else in nature comes near this unspeakable stress of pitch, distinctiveness, and selving, this selfbeing of my own. Nothing explains it or resembles it." The figure of self-tasting strikingly makes the sense of selfhood a bodily sensation, not an abstract purely spiritual concept, as do also the figures of smell. Reading literature critically is a way of experiencing over and over with works by different authors, in a way as intimate as those most intimate of senses, taste and smell, what it would be like to be someone else, while at the same time keeping a distance from those experiences. Literature speaks the unspeakable and finds resemblances for what resembles nothing else.

The critical distance expresses itself in the ever-present irony of miming what those others say. Citation is ironic holding at arm's length. A given passage is detached from its context and held up as if with tweezers for analytical inspection or, since we are talking about pieces of language, detaches them for rhetorical reading. Hopkins's metaphor of self-taste, if you think about it, is incoherent. Ale or alum come in from the outside and produce an effect on the taste buds. Surely Hopkins does not mean that my self-taste comes from the outside, but rather that it is intrinsic. Unless he means, as might well be the case, though he does not say so here, that my self-taste comes from God as His gift of my unique selfhood. Sure enough, in one of the late so-called terrible sonnets, "I wake and feel the fell of dark, not day," Hopkins says just that: "I am gall. I am heartburn. God's most deep decree / Bitter would have me taste: my taste was me." If you want to emphasize what is problematic about a metaphor, just bind the two halves with a ligature made of some form of the verb to be: "my taste *was* me." The word *gall* here alludes to the wine [or vinegar] mixed with gall [used in this case to name bitters of any kind] that Jesus was offered to drink as He hung on the cross (Matthew 27–34). Jesus "tastes" but does not drink. Hopkins covertly compares his suffering with that of Christ, a standard Christian figure.

I'm also extremely dubious now about the rather loosely used encompassing generalization behind *The Disappearance of God*. It seems to me extremely unlikely, pace Heidegger on the "occultation of Being," that whatever God there is would choose to withdraw Himself from the world on January 1, 1750, or when Queen Victoria took the throne on June 20, 1837. More likely "the disappearance of God" has to do with the loss of Christian faith that so many Victorians experienced as a result of new scientific discoveries like the actual age of the earth and our evolution from monkeys. These are still sticking points for those who want to be Christians. The Bible is pretty definite about the age of the earth and about human beings' origin. Geology and evolution challenged those.

I'd also be more likely now to take a single poem and try to do a detailed reading of that. I did something of the sort in a later essay on "The Wreck of the Deutschland" (See "The Linguistic Moment in 'The Wreck of the Deutschland,'" *The New Criticism and After*, ed. T. D. Young [Charlottesville: University Press of Virginia, 1976], 47–60). I by no means, however, repudiate my essay on Hopkins in *The Disappearance of God*. I encourage everyone to read it. It still seems to me a good essay.

Bibliography

J. HILLIS MILLER

Authored Books

Charles Dickens: The World of His Novels. Cambridge: Harvard University Press, 1958. Also in Midland Book paperback (Indiana University Press, 1969).

With George Ford, Edgar Johnson, Sylvere Monod, and Noel Peyrouton. *Dickens Criticism: Past, Present, and Future Directions*. The Charles Dickens Research Center, 1962.

The Disappearance of God: Five Nineteenth-Century Writers. Cambridge: Harvard University Press, 1963. Also in Schocken Books paperback, 1965. Reprint. Urbana and Chicago: University of Illinois Press, 2000.

Poets of Reality: Six Twentieth-Century Writers. Harvard University Press, 1965. Also in Athenaeum paperback, 1969.

The Form of Victorian Fiction. The Ward-Phillips Lectures for 1967. University of Notre Dame Press, 1968. 2nd ed., with a new preface. Cleveland: Arete Press of Case Western Reserve University, 1979.

Thomas Hardy: Distance and Desire. Harvard University Press, 1970.

Fiction and Repetition: Seven English Novels. Harvard University Press, 1982. Chinese translation by Wang Hongtu. Tianjin People's Publishing House, 2007.

The Linguistic Moment. Princeton University Press, 1985. Paperback edition, 1987.

The Ethics of Reading. Columbia University Press, 1986. Paperback edition, 1989. *L'etica della lettura*. Italian translation by Vita Fortunati and Giovanna Franci. Modena: Mucchi editore, 1989. Japanese translation by Chikai Ito and Yukio Ohshima. Hosei University Press, 2000. Romanian translation by Dinu Luca. Preface by Mircea Martin. Bucharest Grupul Editorial ART, 2007.

Versions of Pygmalion. Harvard University Press, 1990.

Victorian Subjects. Hertfordshire: Harvester Wheatsheaf, 1991.

Tropes, Parables, Performatives. Hertfordshire: Harvester Wheatsheaf, 1991.

Theory Now and Then. Hertfordshire: Harvester Wheatsheaf, 1991.

Hawthorne and History. Oxford: Basil Blackwell, 1991.

Fiction and Repetition. Japanese translation (Japanese translation rights arranged with Harvard University Press). Tuttle-Mori Agency, 1991.

Ariadne's Thread. New Haven: Yale University Press, 1992. Japanese translation. Tokyo: Eiho Sha, 2003. Serbo-Croatian translation of parts of the chapter on "Character" by Aleksandar Stevic. *txt.* Belgrade, 2005. 61–85.

Illustration. London: Reaktion Books, 1992. Harvard University Press, 1992. German translation by Monika Reif-Hülser. Konstanz: Konstanzer Bibliotek, 1993. Japanese translation by Ozaki Akihiro and Kato Masayuki. Hosei University, 1996.

A Ética da Leitura: Ensaios 1979–1989. Rio de Janeiro: Imago, 1995. Portuguese translation of selected essays 1979–89 JHM by Eliane Fittipaldi and Katia Orberg.

New Starts: Performative Topographies in Literature and Criticism. Taipei: The Institute of European and American Studies, Academia Sinica, 1993.

Topographies. Stanford University Press, 1994.

New Starts. Chinese translation.

Topographies. Stanford: Stanford University Press, 1995.

Deconstruction Revisited. Trans. Ying-Jian Giuo et al. Beijing: Chinese Social Science Press, 1998.

Reading Narrative. Oklahoma University Press, 1998. Chinese translation by Shen Dan. Weiming Translation Library, 2002. Japanese translation.

With Manuel Asensi. *Black Holes/J. Hillis Miller or, Boustrophedonic Reading.* Stanford University Press, 1999.

Speech Acts in Literature. Stanford: Stanford University Press, 2001.

Others. Princeton: Princeton University Press, 2001.

On Literature. London: Routledge, 2002. Farsi translation by Ali Taghizadeh. Qoqnoos Press, 2005. Korean translation. Seoul: Dongmoonsun Publishing Co via KCC Agency, 2005. Japanese translation. Iwanami Shoten via Japan Uni Agency, 2008. Chinese translation. *O literaturze.* Polish translation by Krzysztof Hoffmann. Posnan: Biblioteka przestrzeni teorii, 2014.

The Indigene and the Cybersurfer. Changchun: Jilin People's Press. 2004.

Zero Plus One. Universitat de València: Biblioteca Javier Coy d'estudis nord-americans, 2003.

Literature as Conduct: Speech Acts in Henry James. New York: Fordham University Press, 2005.

The J. Hillis Miller Reader. ed. Julian Wolfreys. Edinburgh: Edinburgh University Press and Stanford: Stanford University Press, 2005.

Etica lecturii. Romanian translation of *The Ethics of Reading.* Trans. Dinu Luca. Preface by Mircea Martin. Bucharest: Grupul Editorial ART, 2007.

For Derrida. New York: Fordham University Press, 2009.

The Medium Is the Maker: Browning, Freud, Derrida and the New Telepathic Ecotechnologies. Brighton; Portland: Sussex Academic Press, 2009.

The Conflagration of Community: Fiction Before and After Auschwitz. Chicago: University of Chicago Press, 2011.

With Claire Colebrook and Tom Cohen. *Theory and the Disappearing Future: On de Man, on Benjamin.* London and New York: Routledge, 2012.

Reading for Our Time: Adam Bede and Middlemarch Revisited. Edinburgh: Edinburgh University Press, 2012. Reviewed by Rachel Bowlby. "Waiting for the Dawn to Come." *London Review of Books* 35.7 (April 11, 2013): 32–34.

Communities in Fiction. New York: Fordham University Press, 2015.

An Innocent Abroad: Lectures in China. Evanston: Northwestern University Press, 2015. Chinese translation. Nanjing University Press, 2016. Translation of review of *An Innocent Abroad* by Ming Dong Gu, with photos of JHM lecturing in China: http://mp.weixin.qq.com/s/_QLsUN7NMl4AhFha6B-sEQ.

*With Tom Cohen and Claire Colebrook. *Twilight of the Anthropocene Idols*. London: Open Humanities Press, 2016.

*With Ranjan Ghosh. *Thinking Literature Across Continents*. Durham, North Carolina: Duke University Press, 2016.

Selected Writings of J. Hillis Miller [Chinese]. Ed. Wang Fengzhen. Beijing: China Social Sciences Press, 2016.

Lektüren—Interventionen: Literature und dei Zeichen der Zeit. Ausgewählte Studien. Gathered, introduced, and translated by Monika Reif-Hülser. London: Open Humanities Press, 2016.

Literature Matters. Ed. Monika Reif-Hülser. London: Open Humanities Press, 2016. English version of *Lektüren—Interventionen*.

First Sail. Dir. Dragan Kujundzic. 2016. Christopher Morris. Review of *First Sail*. "'Everything Has Been Put Together Wrong': Dragan Kujindzic's *The First Sail* and the 'Remains' of Deconstruction." *intèrkùltùràlnòst*. Novi Sad, Serbia (October 2016): 121–31.

Edited Books

Charles Dickens. *Oliver Twist*. With Introduction. Holt, Rinehart, and Winston, 1962.

Charles Dickens. *Our Mutual Friend*. With afterword. New American Library, 1964.

With Roy Harvey Pearce. *The Act of the Mind: Essays on the Poetry of Wallace Stevens*. Johns Hopkins Press, 1965.

William Carlos Williams: A Collection of Critical Essays. With introduction. Twentieth Century Views series. Prentice-Hall, 1966.

Charles Dickens. *Bleak House*. Ed. Norman Page. With introduction. Penguin Books, 1971.

Aspects of Narrative. Selected papers from the English Institute with a foreword. Columbia University Press, 1971.

With Edward Mendelson and Thomas Hardy. *The Well-Beloved.* The New Wessex Edition. London: Macmillan, 1975.

With Tom Cohen, Barbara Cohen, and Andrzej Warminski. *Material Events: The Afterlife of Paul de Man.* Minneapolis: University of Minnesota Press, 2001.

Articles

"D. H. Lawrence: The Fox and the Perspective Glass." *The Harvard Advocate* 137 (December 1952): 14–16, 26–28.

"The Creation of the Self in Gerard Manley Hopkins." *ELH* 22 (1955): 293–319.

"Franz Kafka and the Metaphysics of Alienation." *The Tragic Vision and the Christian Faith.* Ed. N.A. Scott, Jr. Association Press, 1957. 281–305.

"The Anonymous Walkers." *The Nation* 190 (1960): 351–354.

"'Orion' in the 'Wreck of the Deutschland.'" *Modern Language Notes* 76 (1961): 509–514.

"The Theme of the Disappearance of God in Victorian Poetry." *Victorian Studies* (March 1963): 207–227.

"The Literary Criticism of Georges Poulet." *Modern Language Notes* 78 (December 1963): 471–488. Also in *The Quest for Imagination.* Ed. O. B. Hardison, Jr. The Press of Case Western Reserve University, 1971. 191–205.

"Wallace Stevens' Poetry of Being." *ELH* 31 (March 1964): 86–105.

"Some Implications of Form in Victorian Fiction." *Comparative Literature Studies* 3.2 (1966): 109–118. Also in *Mansions of the Spirit; Essays in Religion and Literature.* Ed. G. A. Panichas. NY: Hawthorn Books, 1964. 200–212.

"The Antitheses of Criticism: Reflections on the Yale Colloquium." *Modern Language Notes* 81.5 (1966): 557–571.

"The Geneva School: The Criticism of Marcel Raymond, Albert Beguin, Georges Poulet, Jean Rousset, Jean-Pierre Richard, and Jean Starobinski." *The Critical Quarterly* 8.4 (Winter 1966): 302–321; also in The Virginia Quarterly Review,

XLIII, 3 (Summer 1967), 465–488. Spanish translation. *Asomante* 24 (Abril–Junio 1968): 7–23; and *Modern French Criticism*. Ed. J. K. Simon. Chicago: University of Chicago Press, 1972. 277–310.

"Charles Dickens." *New Catholic Encyclopedia* 4. McGraw-Hill, 1967. 856–57.

"Literature and Religion." *Relations of Literary Study: Essays on Interdisciplinary Contributions*. Ed. James Thorpe. New York: MLA, 1967. 111–126. German translation in *Interdisziplinare Pespektiven der Literature*. Stuttgart: Ferdinand Enke, 1977. 132–150. Also in *Religion and Modern Literature: Essays in Theory and Criticism*. Ed. G. B. Tennyson and Edward E. Ericson, Jr. William B. Eardmans Publishing Company, 1975. 31–45.

"Thomas Hardy: A Sketch for a Portrait." *De Ronsard à Breton: Hommages à Marcel Raymond*. Paris: Corti, 1967. 195–206.

"Three Problems of Fictional Form: First Person Narration in *David Copperfield* and *Huckleberry Finn*." *Experience in the Novel*. Ed. R.H. Pearce. English Institute Essays for 1967. New York: Columbia University Press, 1968. 21–48.

"William Carlos Williams: The Doctor as Poet." *Plexus* 3.4 (June 1968): 19–20.

"'Wessex Heights': The Persistance of the Past in Hardy's Poetry." *The Critical Quarterly* 10.4 (Winter 1968): 338–339. Also in an expanded version as "History as Repetition in Thomas Hardy's Poetry: The Example of 'Wessex Heights.'" *Victorian Poetry*. Stratford-upon-Avon Studies. Ed. M. Bradbury and D. Palmer. Edward Arnold, 1972. 222–253.

"I'd Have My Life Unbe: la ricerca dell'oblio nell'opera di Thomas Hardy." Italian Translation. *Strumenti Critici* 9 (1969): 263–285.

"Williams' *Spring and All* and the Progress of Poetry." *Daedalus* 99 (1970): 405–434.

"Geneva or Paris? The Recent Work of Georges Poulet." *University of Toronto Quarterly* 39 (1970): 212–228.

"Virginia Woolf's All Souls' Day: The Omniscient Narrator in *Mrs. Dalloway*." *The Shaken Realist: Essays in Modern Literature in Honor of Frederick J. Hoffman*. Ed. Melvin J. Friedman and John B. Vickery. Louisiana State University Press, 1970. 100–127. Korean translation. 2012.

"The Sources of Dickens's Comic Art: From *American Notes* to *Martin Chuzzlewit.*" *Nineteenth-Century Fiction* 24.4 (March 1970): 467–476.

"The Interpretation of *Lord Jim.*" *The Interpretation of Narrative: Theory and Practice.* Ed. M.W. Bloomfield. Harvard English Studies 1. Cambridge: Harvard University Press, 1970. 211–228.

"Georges Poulet's 'Criticism of Identification.'" *The Quest for Imagination.* Ed. O.B. Hardison, Jr. The Press of Case Western Reserve University, 1971. 191–224.

"The Fiction of Realism: *Sketches by Boz, Oliver Twist,* and Cruikshank's Illustrations." *Charles Dickens and George Cruikshank.* William Andrews Clark Memorial Library, University of California, 1971. 1–69. Also in *Dickens' Centennial Essays.* Ed. Ada Nisbet and Blake Nevius. Berkeley, Los Angeles, and London: University of California Press, 1971. 85–153.

"The Still Heart: Poetic Form in Wordsworth." *New Literary History* 2 (Winter 1971): 297–310.

"Tradition and Difference." *diacritics* 2.4 (Winter 1972): 6–13.

"The Stone and the Shell: Wordsworth's Dream of the Arab." *Moments premiers.* Paris: Corti, 1973.

"Narrative and History." *ELH* 41.3 (Fall 1974): 455–473.

"Deconstructing the Deconstructers." *diacritics* (Summer 1975): 24–31.

"Optic and Semiotic in *Middlemarch.*" *The Worlds of Victorian Fiction.* Ed. Jerome H. Buckley. Harvard English Studies 6. Cambridge, MA, and London, England: Harvard University Press, 1975. 125–145.

"Fiction and Repetition: *Tess of the d'Urbervilles.*" *Forms of Modern British Fiction.* Ed. Allen Warren Friedman. Austin and London: University Press, 1975. 43–71.

"Myth as 'Hieroglyph' in Ruskin." *Studies in the Literary Imagination* 8.2 (Fall 1975): 15–18.

"The Year's Books: Literary Criticism." *The New Republic* (November 29, 1975): 30–33.

"Stevens' Rock and Criticism as Cure." *Georgia Review* 30 (1976): 5–31. Also in *Wallace Stevens*. Modern Critical Views. Ed. Harold Bloom. New York: Chelsea House Publishers, 1985. 75–95.

"Ariadne's Thread: Repetition and the Narrative Line." *Critical Inquiry* 3.1 (Autumn 1976): 57–77. Also in *Interpretation of Narrative*. Ed. Mario J. Valdes and Owen J. Miller. Toronto, Buffalo, London: University of Toronto Press, 1978. 148–166.

"Beginning With a Text." Review of E. W. Said's *Beginnings. diacritics* 6.3 (Fall 1976), 2–7.

"Walter Pater: A Partial Portrait." *Daedalus* 105.1 (Winter 1976): 97–113.

"The Linguistic Moment in 'The Wreck of the Deutschland.'" *The New Criticism and After*. Ed. T. D. Young. Charlottesville: University Press of Virginia, 1976. 47–60.

"Ariachne's Broken Woof." *The Georgia Review* 31.1 (Spring 1977): 44–60.

"The Critic as Host." *Critical Inquiry* 3.3 (Spring 1977): 439–447. Also in *Deconstruction and Criticism*. New York: The Seabury Press, 1979. 217–253. Reprinted in *Theories: A Reader*. Ed. Sean Matthews and Aura Taras Sibisan. Bucharest: Oaralela 45, 2003. 92–101.

"Nature and the Linguistic Moment." *Nature and the Victorian Imagination*. Ed. U.C. Knoepflmacher and G.B. Tennyson. Berkeley, Los Angeles, London: University of California Press, 1977. 440–451.

"The Problematic of Ending in Narrative." *Nineteenth Century Fiction* 33.1 (June 1978): 3–7.

"Narrative Middles: A Preliminary Outline." *Genre* 11 (Fall 1978): 375–387.

"On Edge: The Crossways of Contemporary Criticism." *Bulletin of the American Academy of Arts and Sciences* 32.4 (January 1979): 13–32. Also in *Romanticism and Contemporary Criticism*. Ed. Morris Eaves and Michael Fischer. Cornell University Press, 1986. 96–126.

"Theology and Logology in Victorian Literature." *Journal of the American Academy of Religion* 47.2 Supplement (June 1979): 345–361. Also in *American Critics at Work: Examinations of Contemporary Literary Theories*. Ed. Victor A. Kamer. Whitson Publishing Co., 1984. 193–209.

"The Function of Rhetorical Study at the Present Time." *The State of the Discipline: 1970s–1980s*. Special issue of *ADE Bulletin* 62 (September–November 1979: 10–18. Also in *Teaching Literature, What Is Needed Now*. Ed. James Engell and David Perkins. Harvard English Studies 15. Cambridge: Harvard University Press, 1988. 87–109.

"Beguin, Balzac, Trollope et la Double Analogie Rédoublée." French translation by Georges Poulet. *Albert Beguin et Marcel Raymond*. Colloque de Cartigny. Paris: Corti, 1979. 135–154.

"A 'Buchstabliches' Reading of *The Elective Affinities*." *Glyph* 6 (1979): 1–23.

"Kenneth Burke." *International Encyclopedia of the Social Sciences: Biographical Supplement* 18. Ed. David L. Sills. New York: The Free Press; London: Collier Macmillan, 1979. 78–81.

"Theoretical and Atheoretical in Stevens." *Wallace Stevens: A Celebration*. Ed. Frank Doggett and Robert Buttel. Princeton: Princeton University Press, 1980. 274–285.

"The Figure in the Carpet." *Poetics Today* 1.3 (Spring 1980): 107–118.

"*Wuthering Heights* and the Ellipses of Interpretation." *Notre Dame English Journal* 12.2 (April 1980): 85–100.

Review of *Conrad in the Nineteenth Century*, by Ian Watt. *Book World. The Washington Post* (April 6, 1980): 1, 8.

"Theory and Practice: Response to Vincent Leitch." *Critical Inquiry* 6.4 (Summer 1980): 609–614.

"The Rewording Shell: Natural Image and Symbolic Emblem in Yeats's Early Poetry." *Poetic Knowledge: Circumference and Center*. Ed. Roland Hagenbuchle and Joseph T. Swann. Bonn: Bouvier Verlag Herbert Grundmann, 1980. 75–86.

"*Middlemarch*, Chapter 85." *Nineteenth-Century Fiction* 35.3 (December 1980): 441–448. Reprinted in *George Eliot: Modern Critical Views*. Ed. Harold Bloom. New York: Chelsea, 1986. 175–81.

"A Guest in the House: Reply to Shlomith Rimmon-Kenan's Reply." *Poetics Today* 2.1B (Winter 1980/81): 189–91.

"The Disarticulation of the Self in Nietzsche." *The Monist* 64.2 (April 1981): 247–261.

"Character in the Novel: A Real Illusion." *From Smollett to James: Studies in the Novel and Other Essays Presented to Edgar Johnson.* Ed. Samuel I. Mintz, Alice Chandler, and Christopher Mulvey. Charlottesville: University Press of Virginia, 1981. 277–285.

"Topography in *The Return of the Native.*" *Essays in Literature* 8.2 (Fall 1981): 119–134.

"The Ethics of Reading: Vast Gaps and Parting Hours." *American Criticism in the Poststructuralist Age.* Ed. Ira Konigsberg. *Michigan Studies in the Humanities* (1981): 19–41.

"The Two Allegories." *Allegory, Myth, and Symbol.* Ed. Morton W. Bloomfield. Harvard English Studies 9. Cambridge: Harvard University Press, 1981. 355–370.

Introduction. *Cousin Henry* 1. By Anthony Trollope. New York: Arno Press, 1981. v–xiii.

Introduction. *Lady Anna* 1. By Anthony Trollope. New York: Arno Press, 1981. v–xiv.

"Dismembering and Disremembering in Nietzsche's 'On Truth and Lies in a Normal Sense.'" *Boundary 2* 9.3 and 10.1 (Spring/Fall 1981): 41–54.

Review of *Celestial Pantomime*, by Justus George Lawler. *Commonweal* (October 23, 1981): 601–604.

"Trollope's Thackeray." *Nineteenth-Century Fiction.* University of California Press, 1982. 350–357.

Review of *The Interpretation of Otherness*, by Giles Gunn. *The Journal of Religion* 62.3 (July 1982): 299–304.

"From Narrative Theory to Joyce; From Joyce to Narrative Theory." *The Seventh of Joyce.* Ed. Bernard Benstock. Bloomington, IN: Indiana University Press; Sussex: The Harvester Press, 1982. 3–4.

"Parable and Performative in the Gospels and in Modern Literature." *Humanizing America's Iconic Book.* Ed. Gene M. Tucker and Douglas A. Knight. Chico: Scholar's Press, 1982. 57–71.

"Composition and Decomposition: Deconstruction and the Teaching of Writing." *Composition and Literature*. Ed. Winifred B. Horner. University of Chicago Press, 1983. 38–56.

"'Herself Against Herself': The Clarification of Clara Middleton." *The Representation of Women in Fiction*. Ed. Carolyn G. Heibrun and Margaret R. Hogonnet. Baltimore: The Johns Hopkins University Press, 1983. 98–123.

"The Two Relativisms: Point of View and Indeterminacy in the Novel *Absalom, Absalom!*" *Relativism in the Arts*. Ed. Betty Jean Craige. Athens: University of Georgia Press, 1983. 148–170.

"Mr. Carmichael and Lily Briscoe: The Rhythm of Creativity in *To the Lighthouse*." *Modernism Reconsidered*. Ed. Robert Kiely. Cambridge: Harvard University Press, 1983. 167–189.

"Stevens' Rock and Criticism as Cure." Chinese translation by William K. Wimsatt. *Chung-wai Literary Monthly* 13.6 (November 1984): 68–93.

"The Search for Grounds in Literary Study." *Genre* (Spring/Summer 1984): 75–97. Also in *Rhetoric and Form: Deconstruction at Yale*. Ed. Robert Con Davis and Ronald Schleifer. Norman: University of Oklahoma Press, 1985. 19–36.

Introduction. "Interview With Paul de Man." By Robert Moynihan. *The Yale Review* (Summer 1984): 576–602.

"Constructions in Criticism." *Boundary 2* 12.3/13.1 (Spring/Fall 1984): 157–172.

"Thomas Hardy, Jacques Derrida, and the 'Dislocation of Souls.'" *Taking Chances: Derrida, Psychoanalysis and Literature*. Ed. Joseph H. Smith and William Kerrigan. Baltimore & London: The Johns Hopkins University Press, 1984. 135–145. "Thomas Hardy, Jacques Derrida, et la dislocation des âmes" (French translation). *Confrontation, Cahiers* 19 (Printemps 1988): 155–166.

"*Heart of Darkness* Revisited." *Conrad Revisited: Essays for the Eighties*. Ed. Ross C. Murfin. University of Alabama Press, 1985. 31–50. Also in *Joseph Conrad, Heart of Darkness, A Case Study in Contemporary Criticism*. Ed. Ross C. Murfin. New York: Bedford Books, 1989. 209–224.

"Topography and Tropography in Thomas Hardy's *In Front of the Landscape*." *Identity of the Literary Text*. Ed. Mario J. Valdés and Owen Miller. Toronto, Buffalo, London: University of Toronto Press, 1985. 73–91.

"Impossible Metaphor: Stevens's 'The Red Fern' as Example." *The Lesson of Paul de Man*. Ed. Peter Brooks, Shoshana Felman, and J. Hillis Miller. *Yale French Studies* 69 (1985): 150–162.

"The Two Rhetorics: George Eliot's Bestiary." *Writing and Reading Differently: Deconstruction and the Teaching of Composition and Literature*. Ed. G. Douglas Atkins and Michael L. Johnson. Lawrence: University Press of Kansas, 1985. 101–114.

"La Señora Dalloway: La repetición como resurrección de los muertos" (translation into Spanish). *La Desconstruccion: Los criticos de Yale*. Montevideo, Uruguay: Comision Fulbright, Diciembre 1985. 13–21. From *Fiction and Repetition*, 176–202.

"Dismembering and disremembering in Nietzsche's 'On Truth and Lies in a Nonmoral Sense.'" *Why Nietzsche Now?* Ed. Daniel O'Hara. Bloomington: Indiana University Press, 1985. 41–54.

"Walter Pater: A Partial Portrait." *Walter Pater*. Modern Critical Views. Ed. Harold Bloom. New York: Chelsea House Publishers, 1985. 75–95.

"Gleichnis in Nietzsche's *Also Sprach Zarathustra*." *International Studies in Philosophy* 17.2 (1985): 3–15.

"The Critic as Host." *Critical Theory Since 1965*. Ed. Hazard Adams and Leroy Searle. Florida: Florida State University Press, 1986. 452–468.

"Kriticar kao domacin" [Critic as Host]. *Letopis Matice srpske*. Novi Sad, Februar [February] 1985. 226–233.

"When Is a Primitive Like an Orb?" *Textual Analysis: Some Readers Reading*. Ed. Mary Ann Caws. New York: MLA, 1986. 167–181.

"How Deconstruction Works." *The New York Times Magazine* 9 Feb. 1986: 25.

"President's Column." *MLA Newsletter*.

> "Responsibility and the Joy of Reading." (Spring 1986): 2.

> "Responsibility and the Joy (?) of Teaching." (Summer 1986): 2.

> "The Obligation to Write." (Fall 1986): 4–5.

"The Future for the Study of Languages and Literatures." (Winter 1986): 3–4.

"Is There an Ethics of Reading?" *Proceedings of the 58th general meeting of the English Literary Society of Japan*. Tokyo, Japan: English Literary Society, 1986. 2–25. Also in *Reading Narrative*. Ed. James Phelan. Columbus: Ohio State University Press, 1989. 79–102.

"Catachresis, Prosopopoeia, and the Pathetic Fallacy: The Rhetoric of Ruskin." *Poetry and Epistemology*. Eds. Roland Hagenbüchle and Laura Skandera. Regensburg: Verlag Friedrich Pustet, 1986. 398–407.

"La Figure en 'La Muerte y la Brújula' de Borges: Red Scharlach como Hermeneuta." Spanish translation by María Inés Segundo. *La Descontruccion*. Coordinated by Lisa Block de Behar. *Diseminario*. Montevideo, Uruguay: XYZ Editores, 1987. 163–173.

"Lectura de Escritura: George Eliot." Spanish translation by Laura Flores. *La Descontruccion*. 175–196.

"¿Existe una Etica de la Lectura?" Spanish translation by Raquel García de Sanjurjo. *La Descontruccion*. 197–226.

"Figure in Borges's 'Death and the Compass': Red Scharlach as Hermeneut." *Dieciocho* 10.1 (Spring 1987): 53–61.

"The Imperative to Teach." *Qui Parle* 1.2 (Spring 1987): 1–7.

"Presidential Address 1986. The Triumph of Theory, the Resistance to Reading, and the Question of the Material Base." *PMLA* (May 1987): 281–291.
"The Ethics of Reading." *Style* 21.2 (Summer 1987): 181–191.

"Deconstruction in Japan? A Letter to Professor Taketoshi Furomoto." Japanese translation in Kobe, Japan newspaper (February 1987).

"Topography and Tropography in Thomas Hardy's 'In Front of the Landscape.'" *Post-Structuralist Readings of English Poetry*. Ed. Richard Machin and Christopher Norris. Cambridge: Cambridge University Press, 1987. 332–348.

"El Crítico como huésped, J. Hillis Miller." Spanish translation by Bárbara Trotsko and Manuel Alcides Jofré. *Para leer al lector*. Ed. Manuel Alcides Jofré and Monica Blanco. Santiago: Universidad Metropolitana de Ciencias de la Educación. 223–255.

With D. A. Miller. "The Profession of English: An Exchange." *ADE Bulletin* (Winter 1987): 41–58.

"L'Apocalisse Non è Mai Ora." Italian translation by Liliana Cioppettini. *In Forma Di Parole* (Ottobre, Novembre, Dicembre 1987): 25–36.

"El kritikus mint házigazda." Hungarian translation by Zsélyi Ferenc. *Filozófiai Figyelö* 9.3–4 (1987): 101–127

"Wallace Stevens." *Critical Essays on Wallace Stevens.* Ed. Steven Gould Axelrod and Helen Deese. Boston, MA: G.K. Hall & Co., 1988. 77–83.

"William Carlos Williams and Wallace Stevens." *Columbia Literary History of the United States.* Ed. Emory Elliott. New York: Columbia University Press, 1988. 972–992.

"Humanistic Research." *ACLS Occasional Paper* 6 (April 15, 1988): 25–30.

"Paul de Man's Wartime Writings." *TLS* (June 17–23, 1988): 676, 685.

"Reply to Eugene Goodheart." *PMLA* (October, 1988): 820–821.

*"Do Things Fit What We Imagine." Trans. Ho Bai Hua. *Reports on Foreign Literature* 2 (1988): 33–37.

"Literature and History: The Example of Hawthorne's 'The Minister's Black Veil.'" *The Bulletin of the American Academy of Arts and Sciences* 41 (February 1988): 15–31.

"Hieroglyphical Truth' in *Sartor Resartus*: Carlyle and the Language of Parable." *Victorian Perspectives.* Ed. John Clubbe and Jerome Meckier. London: Macmillan Press, 1989. 1–20.

"'Reading' Part of a Paragraph of *Allegories of Reading." Reading de Man Reading.* Ed. Lindsay Waters and Wlad Godzich. Minneapolis: University of Minnesota Press, 1989. 155–170.

*"The Function of Literary Theory at the Present Time." *The Future of Literary Theory.* Ed. Ralph Cohen. New York & London: Routledge, 1989. 102–111. *Chinese translation in *Dong-fang-cong-kan* (Oriental Series). Guillin: Guangxi Normal University: 2006. 15–29.

"Prosopopeia and *Praeterita." Nineteenth-Century Lives.* Ed. Laurence Lockridge, John Maynard, and Donald Stone. Cambridge: Cambridge University Press, 1989. 125–139.

"An Open Letter to Professor Jon Wiener." *Responses on Paul de Man's Wartime Journalism*. Lincoln and London: University of Nebraska Press, 1989. 334–342.

"Prosopopoeia in Hardy and Stevens." *Alternative Hardy*. Ed. Lance St. John Butler. London: Macmillan Press, 1989. 110–127.

"*Praeterita* and the Pathetic Fallacy." *Victorian Connections*. Ed. Jerome McGann. Charlottesville: University Press of Virginia, 1989. 172–178.

"Face to Face: Plato's *Protagoras* as a Model for Collective Research in the Humanities." *The States of "Theory."* Ed. David Carroll. New York: Columbia University Press, 1990. Republished by Stanford University Press, 1994. 281–295.

"Narrative." *Critical Terms for Literary Study*. Ed. Frank Lentricchia and Thomas McLaughlin. Chicago: The University of Chicago Press, 1990. 66–79. 2nd ed., 1995.

"Defending Deconstruction." *Wilson Quarterly* (Summer 1990): 143.

"Literatur und Illustration." German translation by Martin Heusser. *Neue Zürcher Zeitung* (August 1990): 66.

"Translating the Untranslatable." *Goethe Yearbook*. Vol. 5. Ed. Thomas Saine. Columbia (South Carolina): Camden House, 1990. 269–278.

"Laying Down the Law in Literature: The Example of Kleist." *Deconstruction and the Possibility of Justice*. Spec. issue of *Cardozo Law Review* 11.5–6 (July/ August 1990): 1491–1514.

"Quando Un Privitivo E Como Un Orbe" (Spanish trans.). *Trends in Contemporary American Criticism, Ilha Do Desterro* 22 (2nd Semester, 1989): 72–99.

"Teaching Middlemarch: Close Reading and Theory." *Approaches to Teaching Eliot's Middlemarch*. Ed. Kathleen Blake. New York: Modern Language Association, 1990. 51–63.

"Ottica e semiotica in *Middlemarch* di G. Eliot." Italian translation by Marta Garulli. *Il Lettore di provincia* 22.78 (settembre 1990): 41–52.

"Naming and Doing: Speech Acts in Hopkins's Poems." *Religion & Literature* 22.2–3 (Summer–Autumn 1990): 173–191.

"Wuthering Heights" (excerpt from *Fiction and Repetition*). Chinese translation by Wang Hong-to. *Shanghai Literary Theory* (1990): 73–80.

"El crítico como anfitrión." Spanish translation by Maria José Gimeno and Manuel Asensi. *Teoría literaria y deconstrucción*. Ed. Manuel Asensi. Madrid: Arco/Libros, 1990. 157–170.

"Stevens, from *The Linguistic Moment*." *Criticism*. Ed. Charles Kaplan and William Anderson. New York: St. Martin's Press, 1991. 738–762.

*"The Role of Theory in the Development of Literary Studies in the United States." *Divided Knowledge*. Ed. David Easton and Corinne Schelling. Newbury Park: 1991. 118–137.

"Preserving the Literary Heritage." *Commission on Preservation & Access Report* (July 1991): 1–7.

*"Foreword: Border Crossings." Chinese translation by Shan Te-Hsing. *Chung-Wai Literary Monthly* 20.4 (Sept. 1991): 4–9.

"Two Forms of Repetition." Trans. Wang Hong-Tu. 28–51.

"Border Crossings: Translating Theory" (Chinese translation). *EurAmerica* 21.4 (December 1991): 27–51.

"Deconstruction and Cultural Criticism." *Cardozo Law Review* 13:4 (December 1991): 1255–1261.

"Literary Theory, Telecommunications, and the Making of History." *Scholarship and Technology in the Humanities*. Ed. May Katzen. London: British Library, 1991. 11–20.

"The Mirror's Secret: Dante Gabriel Rossetti's Double Work of Art." *Victorian Poetry* 29.4 (Winter 1991): 333–349. Reprinted in *Victoriam Poets: A Critical Reader*. Ed. Valentine Cunningham. Chichester, West Sussex: Wiley Blackwell, 2014. 27–45.

"Cultural Criticism in the Age of Digital Reproduction." *Genre* 24.4 (Winter, 1991): 435–459.

"*Wuthering Heights*: Repetition and the Uncanny." *Wuthering Heights*. Ed. Linda Peterson. Boston: Bedford Books of St. Martin's Press, 1992. 371–384.

"Translation as the Double Production of Texts." *Text and Context: Cross-Disciplinary Perspectives on Language Study.* Ed. Claire Kramsch and Sally McConnell-Ginet. Lexington, MA: D. C. Heath and Company, 1992. 124–134.

"Deconstruction Now? The States of Deconstruction or Thinking Without Synecdoche." *Afterwords.* Ed. Nicholas Royle. Tampere, Finland: Outside Books, 1992. 7–18.

"Interlude as Anastomosis in *Die Wahlverwandtschaften*." *Goethe Yearbook.* Vol. 6. Ed. Thomas Saine. Columbia (South Carolina): Camden House, 1992. 115–122.

"Theory and Translation in Comparative Literature." *Bologna: La Cultura Italiana e Le Letterature Straniere Moderne.* Vol. 2. Ed. Vita Fortunati. Bologna, Italy: Longo Editore Ravenna, 1992. 31–41.

"Literature and Value: American and Soviet Views." *Profession* 92 (MLA, 1992): 21–27.

"Temporal Topographies: Tennyson's Tears." *Victorian Poetry* 30.3–4 (Autumn–Winter 1992): 277–289.

"Responses." *The Yale Journal of Criticism* 5.2 (Spring 1992): 182–187.

"Border Crossings: Translating Theory." Chinese translation by Shan Te-hsing. *Con-Temporary Monthly* 75 (July 1992): 28–47.

"Performative Realism: Faulkner's *Absalom, Absalom!*" *EurAmerica* 22.3 (September 1992): 1–21.

"Thinking Like Other People." *Wild Orchids and Trotsky.* Ed. Mark Edmundson. New York, NY: Penguin Books, 1993. 289–305.

"Nietzsche in Basel: Writing Reading." *Journal of Advanced Composition* 13.2 (Fall 1993): 311–328.

Introduction. *Jude the Obscure.* By Thomas Hardy. New York: Alfred A. Knopf, 1992. vii–xxi.

"Is Literary Theory a Science?" *Realism and Representation.* Ed. George Levine. Madison, WI: University of Wisconsin Press, 1993. 155–168

"Cruce de Fronteras: Traduciendo Teoría." Spanish translation by Mabel Richart. *Cuadernos Teóricos* 4 (May 1993): 7–67.

"Image and Word in Turner." *Word & Image Interactions.* Ed. Martin Heusser. Basel, Switzerland: Wiese Verlag, 1993. 173–189.

*"Temporal Topographies: Tennyson's Tears." Chinese translation by Chen Tung-jung. *ChungWai Literary Monthly* 22.1 (Sept. 1993): 122–138.

"*Mrs. Dalloway*: Repetition as Raising of the Dead." *New Casebooks, Mrs. Dalloway, and To the Lighthouse.* Ed. Sue Reid. London: Macmillan Press, 1993. 45–56.

"Is Deconstruction an Aestheticism?" *Nineteenth-Century Prose* 20.2 (Fall 1993): 23–41.

"A Response to Jonathan Loesberg." *Victorian Studies* 37.1 (Autumn 1993): 123–128.

"The Genres of *A Christmas Carol*." *The Dickensian* 89.431 (Winter 1993): 193–206.

"Yale Si Irvine: Momente Ale Deconstructiei Americane" [from *Versions of Pygmalion*]. Romanian translation by Florin Berindeanu. *Viata Romaneasca* 88.6–7 (June–July 1993). 118–127.

"The Search for Grounds in Literary Study." *Contemporary Literary Criticism* Ed. Robert Con Davis and Ronald Schleifer. New York: Longman Publishing, 1993. 109–121.

"Border Crossings: Translating Theory." *Haritham* 1.2 (1993): 105–125.

*"Border Crossings: Translating Theory." *Selected Essays of the Third Conference on American Literature and Thought: The Literary Section.* Ed. Shan Te-hsing. Taipei: Institute of European and American Studies, Academia Sinica, 1993. 1–27.

"Shelley's 'The Triumph of Life.'" *Shelley.* Ed. Michael O'Neill. Longman Critical Readers. London: Longman Group UK Limited, 1993. 218–240.

"Derrida's Topographies." *South Atlantic Review* 59.1 (January 1994): 1–25.

*"The Role of Theory in the Development of Literary Studies in the United States." Trans. Fengzhen Wang. *Divided Knowledge*. Beijing: Social Sciences Document Press, 1994. 85–107.

"Beginning From the Ground Up." *Critical Architecture and Contemporary Culture*. Ed. William J. Lillyman, Marilyn F. Moriarty, and David J. Neuman. New York & Oxford: Oxford University Press, 1994. 13–19.

"Pater, Walter." *The Johns Hopkins Guide to Literary Theory & Criticism*. Ed. Michael Groden and Martin Kreiswirth. Baltimore, MD: The Johns Hopkins University Press, 1994. 556–558. Revised version: *The Johns Hopkins Guide to Literary Theory & Criticism*. 2nd ed. Ed. Michael Groden, Martin Kreiswirth, and Imre Szeman. Baltimore, MD: The Johns Hopkins University Press, 2005. 720–22.

"The Ethics of Topography: Wallace Stevens's 'The Idea of Order at Key West.'" Trans. Su-ying Lin. *Chung Wai Literary Monthly* 22.8 (January 1994): 74–105.

"Nietzsche in Basel: Writing Reading." *Composition Theory for the Postmodern Classroom*. Ed. Gary A. Olson and Sidney I. Dobrin. Albany: State University of New York Press, 1994. 277–294.

"Return, Dissenter." *TLS* (July 15, 1994): 10.

"Les topographies de Derrida." French translation by Marie-Pierre Baggett. *Le passage des frontières. Colloque de Cerisy*. Paris: Galilée, 1994. 193–201.

"A dekonstruktorok dekonstruálása." Hungarian translation by Szarka Attila. *Helikon* 1–2 (1994): 77–90.

"Border Crossings." Korean translation by Gyung-ryul Jang. *Contemporary Criticism and Theory* 8 (1994): 252–279.

"Literary Study in the University Without Idea." *Proceedings of the 1994 ELLAK International Symposium, English Studies in Korea: Retrospect and Prospect*. The English Language and Literature Association of Korea, 1994. 283–302.

Foreword. *The Critical Double: Figurative Meaning in Aesthetic Discourse*. By Paul Gordon. Tuscaloosa and London: University of Alabama Press, 1995. ix–xx.

"William Carlos Williams." *Critical Essays on William Carlos Williams*. Ed. Steven Gould Axelrod and Helen Deese. New York: G. K. Hall & Co., 1995. 92–102.

"The Disputed Ground: Deconstruction and Literary Studies." *Deconstruction is/in America*. Ed. Anselm Haverkamp. New York: New York University Press, 1995. 79–86.

"Sam Weller's Valentine." *Literature in the Marketplace: Nineteenth-Century British Publishing and Reading Practices*. Ed. John O. Jordan and Robert Patten. Cambridge: Cambridge University Press, 1995. 93–122.

"Discorso presidenziale 1986. Il trionfo della teoria, la resistenza alla lettura e la questione della base materiale." Italian translation by Simonetta Mustari. *Decostruzione e/è America*. Ed. Andrea Carosso. Torino: Editrice Tirrenia Stampatori, 1995. 199–212.

"Border Crossings, Translating Theory: Ruth." *EST XI: Grunnlagsproblemer I Estetisk Forskning*. Ed. Karin Gundersen and Ståle Wikshåland. Oslo: Norges forskningsråd, 1995. 25–39.

"Ideology and Topography in Faulkner's *Absalom, Absalom!*" *Faulkner & Ideology*. Ed. Donald M. Kartiganer and Ann J. Abadie. Jackson: University of Mississippi Press, 1995. 253–276.

"Parabolic Exemplarity: The Example of Nietzsche's *Thus Spoke Zarathustra*." *Unruly Examples: On the Rhetoric of Exemplarity*. Ed. Alexander Gelley. Stanford: Stanford University Press, 1995. 162–174.

*"Black Holes in the Internet Galaxy: New Trends in Literary Study in the United States." Chinese translation by Tung-jung Chen. *Chung-wai Literary Monthly* 24.1 (June 1995): 72–89.

"History, Narrative, and Responsibility: Speech Acts in Henry James's 'The Aspern Papers.'" *Textual Practice* 9.2 (Summer 1995): 243–267.

"The University of Dissensus." *The Oxford Literary Review, The University in Ruins* 17.1–2 (1995): 121–143.

*"Recent Developments in the Study of English and American Literature in the U.S." Chinese translation. *Foreign Literature* 3 (1995): 3–9.

"The Roar on the Other Side of Silence." *Edda* 3 (1995): 237–245.

"The 'Grafted' Image: James on Illustration." *Henry James's New York Edition: The Construction of Authorship*. Ed. David McWhirter. Stanford: Stanford University Press, 1995. 138–141.

"What is the Future of the Print Record?" *Profession 95*: 33.

"Hypertekstens etik." Danish translation by Karen-Margrethe Simonsen. *Passage* 20/21 (1995): 241–263.

"Il trionfo della teoria, la resistenza alla lettura et la questione della base materiale." Trans. Paolo Prezzavente. *Il neostoricismo*. Ed. V. Fortunati and G. Franci. Mucchi Editore, 1995. 251–288.

"Reply to Hans Hauge." *Edda* 4 (1995): 355–357.

"The Ethics of Hypertext." *Diacritics* 25.3 (Fall 1995): 27–39.

"The Other's Other: Jealousy and Art in Proust." *Qui Parle* 9.1 (Fall/Winter 1995): 119–140.

"Picture This: J. Hillis Miller on W. J. T. Mitchell's *Picture Theory*." *Artforum* (January 1996): 18, 99.

"The Other's Other: Jealousy and Art in Proust." *Skrift* 16.1 (1996): 52–67.

"Narrative." *Critical Terms for Literary Study*. 2nd ed. Chicago: University of Chicago Press, 1995. 66–79.

"*Heart of Darkness* Revisited." *Heart of Darkness*. By Joseph Conrad. Boston, NY: Bedford Books, 1996. 206–220.

"Governing the Ungovernable: Literary Study in the Transnational University." *Between the Lines* 2.2 (Winter 1995): 2–3.

"The Topography of Jealousy in *Our Mutual Friend*," *Dickens Refigured: Bodies, Desires and Other Histories*. Ed. John Schad. Manchester and New York: Manchester Press, 1996. 218–235.

"Border Crossings, Translating Theory: Ruth." *The Translatability of Cultures*. Ed. Sanford Budick and Wolfgang Iser. Stanford: Stanford University Press, 1996. 207–223.

"Literary Study in the University Without Idea." *ADE Bulletin* 113 (Spring 1996): 30–33.

*"Black Holes in the Internet Galaxy: New Trends in Literary Study in the United States." *Modern Literature and Literary Theory Revisited*. Ed. Francid

K. H. So and Hsiao-yu Sun. Kaohsiung: Department of Foreign Languages and Literature, National Sun Yat-sen University, 1996. 17–41.

"Literary Study in the Age of Reproduction." *Why Literature Matters: Theories and Functions of Literature.* Ed. Rüdiger Ahrens and Laurenz Volkmann. Heidelberg: Universitätsverlag C. Winter, 1996. 297–310.

"'Le Mensonge, le Mensonge Parfait': Théories du mensonge chez Proust et Derrida." Trans. Yasmine Van den Wijngaert, revue par Changal Zabus et Cécile Hayez. *Passions de la littérature.* Ed. Michel Lisse. Paris: Galilée, 1996. 405–420.

"Just Reading *Howard's End.*" *Howard's End.* Ed. Alistair M. Duckworth. Boston, NY: St. Martin's Press, 1996. 467–482.

"Dickens's *Bleak House.*" *Charles Dickens.* Ed. Steven Connor. London and New York: Longman, 1996. 59–75.

"Miller contro Miller: una polemica." Trans. Paolo Prezzavento. *Studi de Estetica* 13.1 (1996): 191–236.

"Literary Study in the Transnational University." *Profession 1996* (1996): 6–14.

"Derrida's Others." *Applying to Derrida.* Ed. John Brannigan, Ruth Robbins, and Julian Wolfreys. New York: St. Martin's Press, 1996. 153–170.

"Ideology in Trollope's *Ayala's Angel.*" *Journal of Literary Criticism* 8.1 (June 1996): 1–6.

"The Roar on the Other Side of Silence: Otherness in *Middlemarch.*" *Rereading Texts/Rethinking Critical Presuppositions.* Ed. Shlomith Rimmon-Kenan, Leona Toker, and Shuli Barzilai. Frankfurt am Maim: Peter Lang, 1997. 137–148.

"Los estudios literarios en la universidad transnacional." Trans. Mabel Richart. *Eutopías, 2° Epoca* 142 (1996): 1–23.

Introduction. *Marion Fay.* By Anthony Trollope. London: The Folio Society, 1997. xi–xvix.

"Sharing Secrets." *The Secret Sharer.* By Joseph Conrad. Ed. Daniel R. Schwarz. Boston and New York: Bedford Books, 1997. 232–252.

Foreword. *Publishing in Rhetoric and Composition*. Ed. Gary A. Olson and Todd W. Taylor. Albany: State University of New York Press, 1997. xi–xv.

"English Literature in the United States Today." *Fissions and Fusions. Vol. 3. Proceedings of the First Conference of the Cape American Studies Association.* Ed. Loesley Marx, Loes Nas, and Lara Dunwell. Bellville: University of the Western Cape, January 1997. 4–20.

"Forum." *PMLA* (October 1997): 1137–1138.

"L'etica dell'ipertesto." *Cultura, Scienza Ipertesto.* Ed. and trans. Daniela Carpi. Ravenna: Longo Editore, 1997. 63–77.

"Cultural Studies and Reading." *ADE Bulletin* (Fall 1997): 15–18.

Reply to letter on "The Changing Academy." *Profession 97* (New York: MLA, 1997): 233–235.

"'O Sole Mio!': The Sun in Proust's 'Séjour à Venise.'" *Miscelánea Journal of English and American Studies* (1997): 231–240.

*"Effects of Globalization on Literary Study." *Arbejdspapirer.* 16–98. Pamphlet published by the Department of Comparative Literature, University of Aarhus.

"Should We Read *Heart of Darkness*?" *Arbejdspapirer.* 17–98. Pamphlet published by the Department of Comparative Literature, University of Aarhus. Reprinted in *Heart of Darkness.* By Joseph Conrad. Norton Critical Edition. 5th ed. Ed. Paul B. Armstrong. New York and London: W. W. Norton & Company, 2017. 369–380.

*"Effects of Globalization on Literary Study." *Arbejdspapir.* 56. Pamphlet published by the Institut for Litteraturvidenskab, University of Copenhagen.

"Ibid." *Foreign Literatures* 4 (1998): 3–8.

"Interpretation in *Bleak House*." *New Casebooks, Bleak House.* Ed. Jeremy Tambling. Houndmills and London: Macmillan Press, 1998. 29–53.

"The Double Wisdom of the Serpent." Chinese translation by Ning Yizhong. *Foreign Literatures* 4 (1998): 3–8.

"From 'On Edge: The Crossways of Contemporary Criticism.'" *Literary Criticism.* Ed. Charles E. Bressler. New Jersey: Prentice-Hall, 1999, 138–146.

"Reference in *The Wings of the Dove*: Literature as Speech Act." *Graat No. 20, Ré-Inventer le Réel*. Tours: Université de Tours, 1999. 165–177.

"Lying Against Death: Out of the Loop." *Arbejdspapir*. 26–99. Pamphlet published by the Department of Comparative Literature, University of Aarhus.

"Friedrich Schlegel and the Anti-Ekphrastic Tradition." *Litteraturkritik & Romantikstudier* 24. Series out of the University of Aarhus.

*"Will Comparative Literature Survive the Globalization of the University and the New Regime of Telecommunications?" *Tamkang Review* 31.1 (Autumn 2000): 1–21.

*"Will Comparative Literature Survive the Globalization of the University and the New Regime of Telecommunications?" (different version). *Comparative Literature Worldwide: Issues and Methods*. Vol. 2. Ed. Lisa Block de Behar. Montevideo: Fundación Fontaina Minelli, 2000. 245–266.

"Swinburne/Whistler: 'Before the Mirror.'" *The Journal of Pre-Raphaelite Studies* 9 (Spring 2000): 12–24.

"'World Literature' in the Age of Telecommunications." *World Literature Today* 74.3 (Summer 2000): 559–562.

"*The Mayor of Casterbridge*, the Persistence of the Past, and the Dance of Desire." *New Casebooks, The Mayor of Casterbridge*. Ed. Julian Wolfreys. Houndsmill and London: Palgrave, 2000. 21–30.

"Passions, Performatives, Proust." *REAL* 16 (2000): 32–42.

"Passions, Performatives, Proust." *Arbejdspapir*. 28–00. Pamphlet published by the Department of Comparative Literature, University of Aarhus.

"Deconstruction and a Poem." *Deconstructions: A User's Guide*. Ed. Nicholas Royle. Houndmills, Basingstoke, Hampshire: Palgrave, 2000. 171–186.

With Tom Cohen and Barbara Cohen. "A 'Materiality Without Matter'?" *Material Events: Paul de Man and the Afterlife of Theory*. Minneapolis: Univeristy of Minnesota Press, 2001. vii–xxv.

"Paul de Man as Allergen." *Material Events: Paul de Man and the Afterlife of Theory*. Ed. Tom Cohen, Barbara Cohen, J. Hillis Miller, and Andrzej Warminski. Minneapolis: University of Minnesota Press, 2001. 183–204.

*"On the Authority of Literature." Lecture on Modern Literature. April 17, 2001, Baylor University. Published as a pamphlet for local circulation by the Department of Literature, Baylor University, 16 pp. Reprinted in English in *Lectures by Famous Teachers*. Tianjin: Tianjin People's Publishing House, 2003. 28–62. Chinese translation in *Cultural Studies* 4. Central Compilation and Translation Press. 65–83.

*"Promises, Promises: Speech Act Theory, Literary Theory, and Politico-Economic Theory in Marx and de Man" (in Chinese). *Research on Marxist Aesthetics* 4. Guilin: Guangxi Normal University Press, 2001. 24–34. Also in *New Literary History* 33.1 (Winter 2002): 1–20.

"Moments of Decision in *Bleak House*." *The Cambridge Companion to Charles Dickens*. Ed. John O. Jordan. Cambridge: Cambridge University Press, 2001. 49–63.

"Derrida and Literature." *Jacques Derrida and the Humanities*. Ed. Tom Cohen. Cambridge: Cambridge University Press, 2001. 58–81.

"La saggezza doppia del serpente." *Il perché della letteratura*. Trans. Alessandro Bertani. Ed. Giovanna Franci and Marco Malaspina. *Studi di estetica*. Bologna: CLUEB, 2001. 113–122.

"Literary Study Among the Ruins." *Diacritics* 31.3 (Fall 2001): 57–66.

"The Aftermath of Victorian Humanism: Oscar in *The Tragic Muse*." *Renaissance Humanism—Modern Humanisms(s): Festszchrift for Claus Uhlig*. Ed. Walter Göbel and Bianca Ross. Heidelberg: C. Winter, 2001. 231–239.

"Will Literary Study Survive the Globalization of the University and the New Regime of Telecommunications?" *Real: Yearbook of Research in English and American Literature*. Ed. Winfried Fluckes, Herbert Grabes, Jürgen Schlaeger, and Brook Thomas. No. 17: *Literary History/Cultural History: Force-Fields and Tensions*. Ed. Herbert Grabes. Tübingen: Gunter Narr Verlag, 2001. 373–386.

"How to Be 'in Tune with the Right' in *The Golden Bowl*." *Mapping the Ethical Turn: A Reader in Ethics, Culture, and Literary Theory*. Ed. Todd F. Davis and Kenneth Womack. Charlottesville and London: University Press of Virginia, 2001. 271–285.

"Questionaire" (on globalization and travel). *Sites: The Journal of 20th-Century Contemporary French Studies/Revue d'études françaises* 5.1 (Spring 2001): 221.

*"The Story of a Kiss: Isabel's Decisions in *The Portrait of a Lady*." *American Vistas and Beyond: A Festschrift for Roland Hagenbüchle*. Ed. Marietta Messmer and Josef Raab. Trier: Wissenschaftlicher Verlag, 2002. 95–108.

"Lo studio della letteratura sopravviverà alla globalizzazione dell'univversità ed al nuovo regime delle telecommunicazioni?" Trans. M. Giovanna Onorati. *Estetica e Differenza*. Ed. Paola Zaccaria. Bari: Palomar Edizioni di Alternative s.r.l., 2002. 71–81.

"Geglückte und mißlungene Sprechakte in Kafkas *Der Proceß*." German translation by Charlotte Oldani and Beatrice Sandberg. *Franz Kafka: Zur ethischen und ästhetischen Rechtfertigung*. Ed. Beatrice Sandberg and Jakob Lothe. Freiberg im Breisgau: Rombach, 2002.

"Lying Against Death: Out of the Loop." *Acts of Narrative*. Ed. Carol Jacobs. Stanford: Stanford University Press, 2003. 15–30. Volume in honor of J. Hillis Miller.

"Die Festlegung des Gesetzes in der Literatur—am Beispiel Kleists" (translation of "Laying Down the Law in Literature: The Example of Kleist"). Trans. Nikolaus Müller-Schöll. *Kleist lessen*. Ed. Nikolaus Müller-Schöll and Marianne Schuller. Bielefeld: transcript Verlag, 2003. 181–208.

"The 'Quasi-Turn-of-Screw Effect': How To Raise a Ghost with Words." *The Oxford Literary Review* 25 (2003): 121–137.

"Oscar in *The Tragic Muse*." *The Importance of Being Misunderstood*. Ed. Giovanna Franci and Giovanna Silvani. Bologna: Pàtron Editore, 2003. 49–61.

"Zero." *Glossalalia—An Alphabet of Keywords*. Ed. Julian Wolfreys. Edinburgh: Edinburgh University Press, 2003. 369–390.

"Time in Literature." *Daedalus* 132.2 (Spring 2003): 86–97.

"Indigene and Cybersurfer." *Ariel* 34.1 (January 2003): 31–52.

Introduction. *The Swiss Family Robinson*. By J. D. Wyss. New York: Signet, 2004. 1–9.

*"Will Literature Survive the Globalization of the University and the New Regime of Telecommunications?" *Critical Zone 1: A Forum of Chinese and Western Knowledge*. Hong Kong: Hong Kong University Press; Nanjing: Nanjing University Press, 2004. 153–164.

"The History of 0." *Zero and Literature.* Ed. Rolland Munro. Spec. issue of *Journal for Cultural Research* 8.2. (April 2004): 123–139.

"Zero Among the Literary Theorists." *Zero and Literature.* Ed. Rolland Munro Spec. issue of *Journal for Cultural Research* 8.2 (April 2004): 165–181.

"Moving *Critical Inquiry* on." *Critical Inquiry* 30 (Winter 2004): 414–420. Chinese translation in *Frontiers of Literary Theory.* Beijing: Peking University Press, 2005. 26–31.

"Reading *The Swiss Family Robinson* as Virtual Reality." *Children's Literature: New Approaches.* Ed. Karín Lesnik-Oberstein. London: Palgrave/Macmillan, 2004. 78–92.

Introduction. *The Swiss Family Robinson.* By J. D. Wyss. New York: Signet Classics, 2004. 1–9.

*"Speech Acts, Decisions, and Community in *The Mayor of Casterbridge.*" *Thomas Hardy and Contemporary Literary Studies.* Ed. Tim Dolin and Peter Widdowson. Houndmills, Basingstoke, Hampshire: Palgrave Macmillan, 2004. 36–53.

"Aphorism as Instrument of Poilitical Action in Nietzsche." *Parallax* 10.3 (July– September 2004): 70–82.

"'Taking up a Task': Moments of Decision in Ernesto Laclau's Thought." *Laclau: A Critical Reader.* London and New York: Routledge, 2004. 217–225.

"Fate (*Schicksal*) in Walter Benjamin's *Zur Kritik der Gewalt.*" *Law, Justice, and Power: Between Reason and Will.* Ed. Sinkwan Cheng. Stanford: Stanford University Press, 2004. 231–239.

*"Material Interests: Modernist English Literature as Critique of Global Capitalism." Chinese translation by Yifan Zhang and Yingjian Guo. *Journal of Zhengzhou University.* 5 (2004): 127–130.

Contribution to the Forum on "The Legacy of Jacques Derrida." *PMLA* 120.2 (2004): 482–484.

"Une profession de foi." *Jacques Derrida.* Ed. Marie-Louise Mallet and Ginette Michaud. Spec. issue of *L'Herne* 83 (2004): 307–311.

*"What Is a Kiss? Isabel's Moments of Decision." *Critical Inquiry* 31.3 (Spring 2005): 722–746.

*"The (Language) Crisis of Comparative Literature" (Chinese translation). Beijing: Peking University Press, 200?. 1–15

*"Analyzing Jacques Derrida's 'Wholly Other' from Sovereignty and Unconditionality." *Journal of Tsinghua University (Philosophy and Social Sciences)* 20.2 (2005): 29–32.

"Henry James and 'Focalization,' or Why James Loves Gyp." *A Companion to Narrative Theory.* Ed. James Phelan and Peter J. Rabinowitz. London: Blackwell, 2005. 124–135. Chinese translation of the whole volume in Weimeng Translation Library. Beijing: Peking University Press, 2007.

*"Thomas Pynchon's 'The Secret Integration' as Postmodern Narrative." *Foreign Languages and Culture Teaching and Research* 18.1 (June 2005): 1–9. *Chinese translation in *Dongfang Congkan* (Oriental Series). Guillin: Guangxi Normal University Press, 2006. 15–29.

Foreword. *Conrad in the Twenty-First Century: Contemporary Approaches and Perspectives.* Ed. Carola M. Kaplan, Peter Mallios, and Andrea White. New York and London: Routledge, 2005. 1–14.

"Three Literary Theorists in Search of 0." *Provocations to Reading: J. Hillis Miller and the Democracy to Come.* Ed. Barbara Cohen and Dragan Kujundzic. New York: Fordham University Press, 2005. 210–227.

"The Ghost Effect: Intertextuality in Realist Fiction." *Symbolism: An International Annual of Critical Aesthetics.* Vol. 5. New York: AMS Press, 2005. 125–149.

"A Conclusion in Which Almost Nothing Is Concluded: *Middlemarch*'s 'Finale.'" *Middlemarch in the Twenty-First Century.* Ed. Karen Chase. Oxford: Oxford University Press, 2006. 133–156.

"Digital Blake." *The Seeming and the Seen: Essays in Modern Visual and Literary Culture.* Ed. Beverly Maeder, Jürg Schwyter, Ilona Sigrist, and Boris Vejdovsky. Bern: Peter Lang AG, International Academic Publishers, 2006. 29–49.

"Forum." *Public Intellectuals: An Endangered Species?* Ed. Amitai Etzioni and Alyssa Bowditch. Lanham, Maryland: Rowman & Littlefield Publishers, Inc., 2006. 195–197. Reprinted from the Modern Language Association of America from *PMLA* 112.5 (1997): 1137–1138.

"Lina" (translation of "Line"). *Ariadne's Thread: Story Lines.* Trans. Krzystofa Hoffmanna. *Przestrzenie TEORII* 6 (2006): 299–325.

*"Individual and Community in *The Return of the Native*: A Reappraisal." *Thomas Hardy Reappraised: Essays in Honour of Michael Millgate*. Ed. Keith Wilson. Toronto: University of Toronto Press, 2006. 154–173.

"Derrida's *Destinerrance*." *Modern Language Notes* 121 (2006): 893–910.

*"Derrida's Remains." *After Derrida*. Spec. issue of *Mosaic* 39.3 (September 2006): 97–211.

"The Late Derrida." *Adieu Derrida*. Ed. Costas Douzinas. London: Palgrave-Macmillan, 2007. 134–152.

"Derrida Enisled." *The Late Derrida*. Ed. W. J. T. Mitchell and Arnold I. Davidson. Spec. issue of *Critical Inquiry* 33.2 (Winter 2007): 248–276.

"'Don't Count Me In': Derrida's Refraining." *Thinking Institutions*. Ed. Simon Morgan Wortham. Spec. issue of *Textual Practice* 21.2 (2007): 279–294. Also in *Encountering Derrida: Legacies and Futures of Deconstruction*. Ed. Allison Weiner and Simon Morgan Wortham. London: Continuum, 2007. 45–57.

"Performativity as Performance/Performativity as Speech Act: Derrida's Special Theory of Performativity." *Late Derrida*. Ed. Ian Balfour. Spec. issue of *The South Atlantic Quarterly* 106.2 (2007): 219–235.

"Performativitás mint performansz/performativitás mint beszédaktus: Derrida sajátos performativitás-elmélete." Trans. Éva Antal. *Performa* 3 (2016). 1–38. http://performativitas.hu/cikk/index.php?mid=sRiqzRG8CE1CQy&per=#epub cfi(/6/2[miller]!4[miller]/2/2/4/1:0

"Boundaries in Beloved." *Cinema Without Borders*. Ed. Jeffrey R. Di Leo. *symplokē* 15.1–2 (2007): 24–39.

"The Poetics of Cyberspace: Two Ways to Get a Life." *Contemporary Poetics*. Ed. Louis Armand. Evanston, IL: Northwestern University Press, 2007. 256–278.

*"A Defense of Literature and Literary Study in a Time of Globalization and the New Tele-Technologies." *Neohelicon* 34.2 (2007): 13–22.

"What Do Stories About Pictures Want?" *For W.J.T. Mitchell*. Ed. Lauren Berlant, Bill Brown, Dipesh Chakrabarty, Arnold I. Davidson, Elizabeth Helsinger, Francoise Meltzer, Ricahrd Neer, and Joel Synder. Spec. issue of *Critical Inquiry* 34.5 (2008): 59–97.

"Touching Derrida Touching Nancy: The Main Traits of Derrida's Hand."
Derrida Today 1.2 (May 2008): 145–166.

"Priča o poljupcu: Izabeline odluke u Portretu Jedne ledi" (translation of
"The Story of a Kiss: Isabel's Decisions in The Portrait of a Lady"). *Literature
as Conduct: Speech Acts in Henry James.* Trans. Nebojša Marić. *txt: časopis za
književnost i teoriju književnosti* 15–16 (June 2008): 3–36.

"El Coloquio de los Perros como Narrativa Postmoderna." Trans. María Jesús
López Sánchez-Vizcaíno. *La Tropelía. Hacia el Coloquio de los Perros.* Ed. Julián
Jiménez Heffernan. Tenerife; Madrid: Artemisaediciones, 2008. 33–98.

"Reading (about) Modern Chinese Literature in a Time of Globalization." *China
in the Twentieth Century.* Ed. Wang Ning. Spec. issue of *Modern Language
Quarterly* 69.1 (March 2008): 187–194.

*"A Defense of Literary Study in a Time of Globalization and the New
Teletechnologies." *Translating Global Cultures: Toward Interdisciplinary
(Re)Constructions.* Ed. Wang Ning. Beijing: Foreign Language Teaching and
Research Press, 2008. 29–46.

"Derrida's Politics of Autoimmunity." *"Who?"or "What?"—Jacques Derrida.* Ed.
Dragan Kujundžić. Spec. issue of *Discourse: Journal for Theoretical Staudies in
Media and Culture* 30.1–2 (Winter & Spring 2008): 208–225.

*"Will Literary Study Survive the Globalization of the University and the New
Regime of Telecommunications?" *Deconstruction Reading Politics.* Ed. Martin
McQuillan. Houndmills, Basingstoke: Palgrave Macmillan, 2008. 80–96.

"'Material Interests': Conrad's Nostromo as a Critique of Global Capitalism."
Joseph Conrad: Voice, Sequence, History, Genre. Ed. Jakob Lothe, Jeremy
Hawthorn, and James Phelan. Columbus, OH: The Ohio State University
Press, 2008. 160–177. Partially translated into Chinese as "Material Interests:
Modernist English Literature as Critique of Global Capitalism." Trans. Yifan
Zhang and Yingjian Guo. *Journal of Zhengzhou University* 5 (2004): 127–130.
A somewhat longer version was given in English as a lecture at an International
Conference on Globalization and Local Culture held June 5–9, 2004, at
Zhengzhou University, and again at an International Conference on *Critical
Inquiry* held June 12–15, 2004, at Tsinghua University in Beijing.

"Derrida's Ethics of Irresponsibilization; or, How to Get Irresponsible, in Two
Easy Lessons." *Literature and Ethics: Questions of Responsibility in Literary
Studies.* Ed. D. Jernigan, N. Murphy, B. Quigley, and T. Wagner. Amherst:
Cambria Press, 2009. 15–35.

"Foreword: A Portrait of the Artist as a Young Post-Modernist." *Flann O'Brien: A Portrait of the Artist as a Young Post-Modernist.* 2nd ed. By Keith Hopper. Cork: Cork University Press, 2009. ix–xi.

"'Mr. Sludge, C'est moi': The Conflict of Media." *The Hopkins Review* 2.2 (Spring 2009): 239–259.

"Modernist Hardy: Hand-Writing in *The Mayor of Casterbridge*." *A Companion to Thomas Hardy.* Ed. Keith Wilson. Chichester, West Sussex: Wiley-Blackwell, 2009. 433–449.

"Literatura i Biblia. Filiacja niemożliwa" (translation of "Literature and Scripture. An Impossible Filiation). *For Derrida.* Trans. Krzysztof Hoffman. *Przestrzenie TEORII* 11 (2009): 255–270.

"Performativivity1, Performativity2." *Studies in Pragmatics 6: Language in Life, and a Life in Language: Jacob Mey—A Festschrift.* Ed. Bruce Fraser and Ken Turner. Bingley, UK: Emerald Group Publishing Limited, 2009. 307–312.

"Babble Before Babel." *Babel: Für Werner Hamacher.* Ed. Ers Engler. Basel: Weil am Rhein, 2009. 296–303.

"Who or What Decides for Derrida: A Catastrophic Theory of Decision." *The Catastrophic Imperative: Subjectivity, Time and Memory in Contemporary Thought.* Ed. Dominiek Hoens, Sigi Jöttkandt, and Gert Buelens. Palgrave Macmillan, 2009. 9–25.

"The Circle and the Straight Line in William Faulkner's *Light in August.*" *Literature and Circularity.*" Ed. Christoph Henke and Martin Middeke. Special focus volume of *Symbolism.* Vol. 9. Ed. Rüdiger Ahrens and Klaus Stierstorfer. New York: AMlS Press, 2009. 141–160.

*"The University, With Conditions." *The Future of Higher Education: Perspectives From America's Academic Leaders.* Ed. Gary A. Olson and Jon. W. Presley, Boulder and London: Paradigm, 2009. 73–82.

Foreword (in Japanese translation). *Society and Culture in the Times of Elizabeth Gaskell: A Bicentennial Commemorative Volume.* Ed. Mitsuharu Matsuoka. Hiroshima: Keisuisha, 2010. vii–xiii.

"A Salute to Harold Bloom." *Harold Bloom 80.* New Haven: Yale University, 2010. 43–44.

"Hands in Hardy." *The Ashgate Research Companion to Thomas Hardy*. Ed. Rosemarie Morgan. Farnham, Surrey: Ashgate Publishing Limited, 2010. 505–516.

Review of *George Eliot's Intellectual Life*, by Avrom Fleishman. *George Eliot-George Henry Lewes Studies* 58–59 (September 2010): 118–122.

"Performativity₁/Performativity." Lars Saetre, Patrizia Lombardo, and Anders M. Gullestad. Ed. *Exploring Textual Action*. Aarhus: Aarhus University Press, 2010. 31–58.

*"Challenges to World Literature." *Comparative Literature in China* 4 (2010): 1–9.

"The Sense of an Un-Ending: The Resistance to Narrative Closure in Kafka's *Das Schloß*." *Franz Kafka: Narration, Rhetoric, and Reading*. Ed. Jakob Lothe, Beatrice Sandberg, and Ronald Spiers. Columbus: The Ohio State University Press, 2011. 108–122.

"Anachronistic Reading." *Derrida Today* 3 (May 2010): 75–91.

"Literature and Scripture: An Impossible Filiation." *Exit: Endings and New Beginnings in Literature and Life*. Ed. Stefan Helgessson. Amsterdam and New York: Rodopi, 2011. 203–218.

"Literatura i Biblia: Filacja niemozliwa." Polish translation by Krzysztof Hoffman. *Przestrzeni Teorii* 11 (2009): 255–270.

"Robert Browning." *The Cambridge Companion to English Poets*. Ed. Claude Rawson. Cambridge: Cambridge University Press, 2011. 392–407.

"Resignifying Excitable Speech." *Women's Studies Quarterly* 39.1 & 2 (Spring/Summer 2011): 223–226.

"The Act of Reading Literature as Disconfirmation of Theory." "Theory Today." *Frame* 24.1 (May 2011): 18–31.

"Exergue," "Brisure," "Jeu," and "Trace." *Reading Derrida's Of Grammatology*. Ed. Sean Gaston and Ian Maclachlan. London and New York: Continuum, 2011. 38–51.

"Should We Read or Teach Literature Now?" *Literature and/as Ethics*. Ed. Martin Middeke et al. Spec. issue of *Anglia* 129.1–2 (2011): 1–11.

*"Globalization and World Literature." *Comparative Literature: Toward a (Re) construction of World Literature.* Ed. Ning Wang. Spec. issue of *Neohelicon* 38.2 (2011): 251–265.

"The Presence to Oneself in Decision-Making." *Le Concept de presence/The Concept of Presence.* Ed. Mircea Martin. Spec. issue of *Euresis* 1–4 (2011): 18–31.

"Imre Kertész's *Fatelessness*: Fiction as Testimony." *After Testimony: The Ethics and Aesthetics of Holocaust Narrative for the Future.* Ed. Jokob Lothe, Susan Rubin Suleiman, and James Phelans. Columbus: The Ohio State University Press, 2012. 23–51. This is a version of a chapter in *The Conflagration of Community.*

"How to (Un)Globe the Earth." *Globing the Earth: The New Eco-logics of Nature.* Ed. Ranjan Ghosh. Spec. issue of *SubStance* 127.41 (2012): 15–29.

"Paul de Man at Work: What Good is an Archive?" *The Political Archive of Paul de Man: Property, Sovereignty, and the Theotropic.* Ed. Martin McQuillan. Edinburgh: Edinburgh University Press, 2012. 149–156.

"Some Versions of Romance Trauma as Generated by Realist Detail in Ian McEwan's *Atonement.*" *Trauma and Romance in Conbtemporary British Literature.* Ed. Jean-Michel Ganteau and Susana Onega. New York: Routledge, 2012. 90–106.
http://jprstudies.org/2014/02/review-trauma-and-romance-in-contemporary-british-literatureedited-by-jean-michel-ganteau-and-susana-onega/

"Prologue: Revisiting '*Heart of Darkness* Revisited' (in the Company of Philippe Lacoue-Labarthe)" and a reprint of "*Heart of Darkness* Revisited." *Conrad's Heart of Darkness and Contemporary Thought: Revisiting the Horror With Lacoue-Labarthe.* Ed. Nidesh Lawtoo. Bloomsbury: Bloomsbury Academic, 2012. 17–35, 39–54.

"Po co czytac literature?" (Polish trans. of "Why Read Literature?" 4th chapter of *On Literature*). *Przestrzenie Teorii* 17 (2012): 219–243.

"Ecotechnics: Ecotechnological Odradek." *Telemorphosis: Theory in the Era of Climate.* Vol. 1. Ed. Tom Cohen. Ann Arbor, MI: Open Humanities Press, 2012. 65–103.

"The Truly Critical Critic." Preface to *Crritic.* Ed. John Schad and Oliver Tearle. Brighton: Sussex Academic Press, 2011. xi.

"Absolute Mourning: It Is Jacques You Mourn For." *Re-Reading Derrida: Perspectives on Mourning and Its Hospitalities.* Ed. Tony Thwaites and Judith

Seaboyer. Lanham, Maryland, Boulder, New York, Toronto, Plymouth, UK: Lexington Books, 2013. 9–21. (Also in *For Derrida*).

"Stray Savages All Around: Performative James or Fiction as Forgery." *Literary Imagination* 15.1 (2013): 52–64.

**"Cold Heaven, Cold Comfort: Should We Read or Teach Literature Now?" *The Edge of the Precipice: Why Read Literature in the Digital Age?* Ed. Paul Socken. Montreal and Kingston: McGill-Queen's University Press, 2013. 140–155.

With Margaret Barrow, Robert Savino Oventile, and Manya Steinkoler. "Literature, Community, and Contestation, an Interview With J. Hillis Miller." *Teaching Literature in Community College Classrooms: Traversing Practices*. Ed. Margaret Barrow and Manya Steinkoler. Boston: McGraw-Hill, 2013. 8–16.

**"Literature Matters Today." *Literature Matters*. Ed. Ranjan Ghosh. Spec. issue of *SubStance* 42.2 (2013): 12–32.

Preface. *Reading Theory Now: An ABC of Good Reading With J. Hillis Miller*. By Éamonn Dunne. New York, London: Bloomsbury, 2013. ix–xiv.

Response. *Forum on J.Hillis Miller*. By Éamonn Dunne, Peggy Kamuf, and Justin Halverson. *Comparative Literature Studies* 50.2 (2013): 358–363.

"Religio-politique de l'auto-immunité chez Jacques Derrida." Trans. Brigitte Weltman-Aron. *Appels de Jacques Derrida*. Ed. Danielle Cohen-Levinas and Ginette Michaud. Paris: Hermann, 2014. 261–276. This essay is drawn in augmented and revised form from Chapter 6 of my *For Derrida*, listed above.

"*Mrs. Dalloway*: Repetition as the Raising of the Dead" (Korean translation; from *Fiction and Repetition*). *Mrs. Dalloway* (Korean translation, with critical essays). Cambridge, MA: Harvard University Press, 1982.

"Literature Matters Today." Chinese translation by Xialin Ding. *Guo Wai Wen Xue (Foreign Literatures)* 2 (2013): 3–8.

**"Should We Read or Teach Literature Now?" *Narrative Ethics*. Ed. Jakob Lothe and Jeremy Hawthorn. Amsterdam and New York: Rodopi, 2013. 13–24. "'Waves' Theory: An Anachronistic Reading" and "La theorie des Vagues: lecture anachronistic." *Virginia Woolf Among the Philosophers*. Ed. Chantal Delourme. Spec. issue of *Le tour critique* 2 (2013): 113–120, 121–129. 26 Jan. 2014. http://letourcritique.u-paris10.fr/index.php/letourcritique/issue/view/3

"Text; Action; Space; Emotion." *Exploring Text and Emotions*. Ed. Lars Saetre, Patrizia Lombardo, and Julien Zanetta. Aarhus: Aarhus University Press, 2014. 91–117.

"Grenzgänge mit Iser und Coetzee: Literature lessen—aber Wie und Wozu?" (translation of the first annual Wolfgang Iser Memorial Lecture, 2011). Trans. Monika Reif-Hülser. Konstanz: UVK Universitätsverlag, 2013.

"The Mirror's Secret: Dante Gabriel Rossetti's Double Work of Art." Reprinted in *Victorian Poets: A Critical Reader*. Ed. Valentine Cunningham. Chichester, West Sussex: Willey/Blackwell, 2014. 27–45.

**"What Ought Humanists to Do?" *Daedalus* 143.1 (Winter 2014): 19–34.

"Derrida and de Man: Two Rhetorics of Deconstruction." *A Companion to Derrida*. Ed. Zeynep Direk and Leonard Lawler. Chichester, West Sussex: Wiley Blackwell, 2014. 345–361.

"Why Literature?" *Criterion: A Journal of Literary Criticism*. Provo, UT: Brigham Young University Press, 2014. 1–3.

"*The Waves* as Exploration of (An)aesthetic of Absence." *(An)aesthetic of Absence/Une asthétique de l'absence*. Spec. issue of *University of Toronto Quarterly* 83.3 (Summer 2014): 659–677.

"How to Read the Derridas: Indexing *moi et moi*." *A Decade after Derrida*. Spec. issue of *Oxford Literary Review* 36.2 (2014): 269–273.

"Tales out of (the Yale) School." *Theoretical Schools and Circles in the Twentieth-Century Humanities: Literary Theory, History, Philosophy*. Ed. Marina Grishakova and Silvi Salupere. New York and London: Routledge, 2015. 115–132. "Sekrety szkoty (z Yale)." Polish translation by Krzysztof Hoffmann. *Przestrzenie Teorii* 26 (2016): 233–253.

"How to Read the Derridas: Indexing *moi et moi, Der und Der, me and me, this one and that one*." *Reading Miller reading Derrida*. Spec. issue of *Derrida Today* 8.1 (2015): 2–17.

With Bradley J. Fest. "'Isn't It a Beautiful Day,' an Interview With J. Hillis Miller." *boundary 2* 41.3 (Fall 2014): 123–158.

On Literature: Thinking in Action (Arabic translation). El Gabalaya St. Opera House, El Gezira, Cairo: National Center for Translation, 2015.

"Au coeur des ténèbres: un récit parabole." French translation by Georges Roiron. *Joseph Conrad*. Ed. Josiane Paccud-Huguet and Claude Maisonnat. Paris: Les Cahiers de l'Herne, 2014. 96–101.

Review of *Spirit Becomes Matter*, by Henry Staten. *Modern Language Quarterly* 77.2 (June 2016): 268–271.

"On First Looking into Derrida's *Glas*." *Paragraph* 39.2 (July 2016): 129–148.

"Comes the Revolution." *Theory Matters: The Place of Theory in Literary and Cultural Studies Today*. Ed. Martin Middeke and Christoph Reinfandt. London: Palgrave; Macmililan, 2016. 17–31.

"A Dialogue Between Zhang Jiang and J. Hillis Miller." *Comparative Literature Studies* 53.3 (2016): 562–610.

"Deconstructive Reading and Rhetoric Reading:A letter to Zhang Jiang" (in Chinese). *Literature and Art Studies (Wen Yi Yan Jiu)* (July 2015): 68–72.

"The Second Letter to Zhang Jiang" (in Chinese). *Literary Review* 4 (2015): 8–12.

"Glossing the Gloss of 'Envois' in *The Post Card*." *Going Postcard: The Letter(s)of Jacques Derrida*. By Vincenty W.J. van Gerven Oei. Columbia, South Carolina: Punctum Books, 2017. 11–41.

"Salt and Pepper to Taste." *Satzzeichen: Scenen der Schrift*. Für Bettine Menke. Ed. Dietmar Schmidt, Helga Lutz, and Nils Plath. Berlin: Kulturverlag Kadmos, 2017. 186–191.

"On First Looking Into Derrida's *Glas*." *New Crirtical Thinking: Criticism to Come*. Ed. Julian Wolfreys. Edinburgh: Edinburgh University Press, 2017. 176–194.

Foreword. Moby Dick *and Melville's Anti-Slavery Allegory*. By Brian R. Pellar. Cham, Switzerland: Springer International Publishing, 2017. v–vi.

Interviewers

Graham Allen is Professor of Literature at University College Cork. His bestselling and widely-translated critical books include *Intertextuality* (2000, 2nd edition in 2011) and *Roland Barthes* (2003).

Francisco Collado-Rodríguez is Professor of English and American Literature at the University of Zaragoza. He is the author of *El orden del Caos: Literatura, Política y Posthumanidad en la Narrativa de Thomas Pynchon* (2004), among other works.

Constanza del Río Álvaro is Senior Lecturer at the Department of English and German Philology of Zaragoza University and is the coeditor of *Memory, Imagination and Desire in Contemporary Anglo-American Literature and Film* (2004).

Dragan Kujundžić is the director of *The First Sail: J. Hillis Miller* (2012) which is the first feature length film to catalogue the life and work of J. Hillis Miller.

Éamonn Dunne currently teaches at Ruamrudee International School, Bangkok, Thailand. He is the author of *J. Hillis Miller and the Possibilities of Reading: Literature after Deconstruction* (2010) and *Reading Theory Now: An ABC of Good Reading with J. Hillis Miller* (2013), and the coauthor of *The Pedagogics of Unlearning* (2016).

Bradley J. Fest is Assistant Professor of English at Hartwick College. His work has appeared in *boundary 2, The b2o Review, Critical Quarterly*, and *Critique*. He is the author of two volumes of poetry, *The Rocking Chair* (2015) and *The Shape of Things* (2017).

Martin McQuillan is Professor of Literary Theory and Cultural Analysis and Dean of the Faculty of Arts and Social Sciences at Kingston University, London, where he is also Co-Director of The London Graduate

School. He is the author of *Roland Barthes: or the Profession of Cultural Studies* (2011).

Christopher D. Morris is Charles A. Dana Professor of English (Emeritus) at Norwich University. His latest book is *The Figure of the Road: Deconstructive Studies in Humanities Disciplines* (2007).

Michael O'Rourke works mostly at the intersections between queer theory and continental philosophy. He is the co-editor of *Love, Sex, Intimacy and Friendship Between Men, 1550–1800* (2003), *Queer Masculinities, 1550–1800: Siting Same-Sex Desire in the Early Modern World* (2006), *The Ashgate Research Companion to Queer Theory* (2009), and *Speculative Medievalisms: Discography* (2013).

Gary A. Olson is President of Daemen College. He is a scholar of rhetoric and culture as well as a literary biographer. His latest book *is A Creature of Our Own Making: Reflections on Contemporary Academic Life* (2013).

Nicholas Royle is Professor of English at the University of Sussex. He is the author of *Veering: A Theory of Literature* (2011) and *In Memory of Jacques Derrida* (2009), and coauthor of *An Introduction to Literature, Criticism and Theory* (2016).

Imre Salusinszky is an Australian journalist and English literature academic. He is the author of *Criticism in Society: Interviews with Jacques Derrida, Northrop Frye, Harold Bloom, Geoffrey Hartman, Frank Kermode, Edward Said, Barbara Johnson, Frank Lentricchia and J. Hillis Miller* (1987) and editor of *Northrop Frye's Writings on the Eighteenth and Nineteenth Centuries* (2005).

Anfeng Sheng is Professor at the Department of Foreign Languages and Literature in Tsinghua University. He is the coeditor of two important anthologies: *An Anthology of the Twentieth Century Chinese Prose* and *An Anthology of the Twentieth Century Chinese Literary Theory and Criticism* (both forthcoming in Springer).

Fengzhen Wang is a scholar of the Chinese Academy of Social Sciences. His works include *Encounters: Views on/of 21 Foreign Critics* (2009), *Selected Works of Fredric Jameson* (14 volumes, 2016, editor and co-translator), and *Dialogues on Cultural Studies: Interviews with Contemporary Critics* (2002, coedited with Shaobo Xie).

Julian Wolfreys is Professor of English Literature at the University of Portsmouth and Director of the Centre for Studies in Literature and the editor of *The J. Hillis Miller Reader* (2005). He has published works on literature of the nineteenth and twentieth centuries, English and European modernism, film studies, and Jacques Derrida. *Silent Music* (2013) is his first novel.

Shaobo Xie teaches literary theory, postcolonial literature and theory, and translation studies in the Department of English, University of Calgary. Among his recent publications are "Cosmopolitanism and Cultural Translation" (*Theoretical Studies in Literature and Art*), "Translation and Transformation: Theory in China and China in Theory" (*ISSJ*), and "Is the World Decentered? A Postcolonial Perspective on Globalization" (Routledge Anthology *Global Literary Theory*).

Index

Page numbers in bold refer to chapters where the indexed authors were also the principal interviewers.

www.ingramcontent.com/pod-product-compliance
Lightning Source LLC
Chambersburg PA
CBHW071531110726
47908CB00007B/1839